BUILDING BRIDGES OVER TROUBLED WATERS:

ENHANCING PASTORAL CARE & GUIDANCE

Editors
David Herl, Ed.D. &
Mark L. Berman, Ph.D.

Building Bridges Over Troubled Waters:
Enhancing Pastoral Care & Guidance

Edited by:
David Herl, Ed.D.
Mark L. Berman, Ph.D.

The Rhodes-Fulbright Library

ISBN: 1-55605-367-3

Library of Congress Control Number: 2004106388

WYNDHAM HALL PRESS
Lima, Ohio 45806
www.wyndhamhallpress.com

Printed in The United States of America

TABLE OF CONTENTS

Spirituality, Religion & Psychology: Core Concepts for Building Bridges for the Troubled Parishioner/Congregant
by David Herl,Ed.D.
Akron Children's Hospital; Mind Matters Group

Caring for the Soul & the Self: Perspectives on Pastoral Helping
Rev. Kevin Gillespie, S.J., Ph.D. - Loyola College in Maryland

Cultural Diversity Perspectives in Pastoral Care & Counseling
K. Elizabeth Oakes, Ph.D. - Loyola College in Maryland

Religion as a Meaning System: Implications for Pastoral Care & Guidance
Israela Silberman, Ph.D.
Department of Psychology ~ Columbia University

Pastoral Care as Practical Theology:
Bridges for Theory & Practice at the New Millennium
Carrie Doehring, M.Div., Ph.D. - Iliff School of Theology

Stormy Weather: Understanding Domestic Violence & Child Sexual Abuse
Stephen A. Dean, Ph.D. - Melymbrosia- Canton, Ohio

DEDICATION

With much gratitude and love to my parents, Harold & Lilla Herl, for your sharing and instilling the value and blessings of faith, trust , and prayer. -DH

ACKNOWLEDGEMENTS

The nascent idea for this book developed throughout the course of the first editor's collaboration with clergy in consulting/providing psychological treatment, and conducting seminars to refine pastoral care skills by incorporating behavioral sciences and contemporary psychological discoveries.

The first editor is grateful for early collaboration and ongoing support of Rev. Daniel Grossoehme, BBC who graciously contributed to this project. Also, deep appreciation to my colleague, friend, and associate with Mind Matters, Dr. Stephen Dean, faculty for clergy seminars.

We would like to express heartfelt gratitude and appreciation to the following clergy who were supportive and willing to allow us to collaborate and provide training with clergy: Rev. Msgr. John Zuraw, Executive Director, Clergy & Religious Services-Roman Catholic Diocese of Youngstown, Ohio; Rev. Mary C. Carson , Assistant to Bishop for Ministry Development, Episcopal Diocese of Ohio; Bishop Gilbert I. Sheldon & Msgr. Kurt H. Kemo, Vicar General, Roman Catholic Diocese of Steubenville, Ohio. Thank you all for the rich opportunity to also learn from your dedicated clergy and lay members as to their unique needs and struggles in their pastoral care journey and mission.

My (DH) many thanks to the staff at the Jackson Township Branch of the Stark County District Library for your kindness and valuable research assistance. Special gratitude and thanks goes to Kathy Bruhn, MLIS, Reference Librarian, for her research expertise, enthusiasm, and interest in the project. You are all appreciated.

Our joint thank you is extended to our publisher, WYNDHAM HALL PRESS, and particularly, the Managing Editor, Mark McCullough, for your guidance, flexibility, and belief in the core value of this project for all faiths and religious communities.

The first editor wishes to express deep appreciation to his co-editor, Mark , who willingly joined this project after it's initial development and who provided the authorship experiences to fine tune and craft the chapter presentations plus more.

Our relationship as colleagues and friends began in the mid-1970's ~ an era particularly exciting in mental health and psychology for many reasons. It has been interesting to reflect upon our career paths, diverse interests, and how we discovered a strong, united interest in the area of bringing psychology to pastoral care, including a domain often overlooked~clergy wellness and self-care.

Most important, we cordially express our deepest thanks , appreciation, and unwavering respect to the contributing authors. Each author's contribution and expertise provided both an important and unique dimension to the project. It is true, in all respects, that the absence of any of the chapters would have resulted in a glaring lacuna. Without each of you, this project would have been below our expectancy for this important mission.

Our very best wishes to you, our colleagues, in your professional and personal lives~ much happiness and many blessings.

PREFACE

The longing and quest for meaningful and stabilizing experiences through organized religions and spiritual events are salient throughout the world. Religion, in America, is particularly widespread with more churches, temples, and mosques than any other country on a per capita basis.

Such interest and prevalence of religion and spirituality have been commensurate with faith community members' requests and pressing needs for pastoral care and guidance.

Congregants seem increasingly eager and motivated to , specifically, seek out clergy and church associates for pastoral care to assist them in resolving life struggles and problems. Often, the problems and issues presented or which emerge are laden with complexities.

The editors embrace the notion that a close collaboration between religion and psychology/behavioral sciences is essential in today's world and, furthermore, that a standard of care for clergy should systemically prevail which fosters both religious/spiritual and emotional/psychological growth and integration.

The purpose of **Building Bridges Over Troubled Waters: Enhancing Pastoral Care & Guidance** is to bring to clergy and faith communities knowledge from the behavioral sciences which can enhance pastoral care skills in meeting parishioner/congregant needs in vital and sustaining ways.

Those in the human social service and mental health/substance abuse professions will also benefit from the authors' insights and knowledge as it pertains to embracing spirituality and religion within the helping relationship alliance.

The book consists of nineteen chapters and three major sections. The first section, *Foundations of Pastoral Care*, focuses on the basic elements of how clergy can and should provide care to their parishioners.

In Chapter One, Dr. David Herl presents an overview of how clergy can provide pastoral care for parishioners as well as how to utilize a collaborative consultation approach to maximize benefits from intervening. His interest in this topic originated over three decades ago when he co-facilitated a seminar aimed at helping clergy deal more effectively with congregants and their personal needs.

In Chapter Two, Reverend Kevin Gillespie offers rich perspectives for pastoral intervention which includes effective contemporary strategies for ministerial caregiving while embracing notions of both the soul and the self.

Professor E. Elizabeth Oakes, in Chapter Three, discusses the importance and value of culture as a contributant to psychosocial , religious, and physical dimensions that define people as individuals. She points out specific important reasons for understanding diversity and multiculturalism and offers the pastoral caregiver valuable guidance in how to acquire such training and understanding.

Chapter Four, authored by Dr. Israela Silberman , clearly establishes the importance of the rich diversity and uniqueness of meanings of religion for pastoral care in aiding and assisting faith community members to cope with adversity and promote peace in the world order. This chapter integrates important understandings of both religious and psychological-motivational meaning systems which encompasses beliefs, goals, and need satisfaction of troubled congregants.

Chapter Five, prepared by Professor Carrie Doehring, illustrates well articulated, diverse options and models for integrating pastoral theology with effective pastoral care and counseling/psychotherapy. Doehring points out that providing pastoral care to congregants can involve major challenges, but often results in major benefits to recipients.

Section Two , *Caring for Parishioners* , targets a wide range of specific needs of parishioners based upon various human conditions, problem presentations, and "trials and tribulations".

Chapter Six, by Dr. Stephen A. Dean, identifies domestic violence is one of society's most serious problems. He suggests crucial ways that clergy can help congregants who are victims of such violence. Dr. Dean also makes important suggestions to those who themselves were sexually abused as children, or who are involved in raising such children.

Chapter Seven , also prepared by Dr. Herl, has to do with the role of clergy in helping people deal with substance abuse and addiction. Dr. Herl goes into considerable detail in terms of such key topics as how to assess/evaluate such abuse and effectively intervene.

In Chapter Eight , Professor Karen Scheel and her co-contributors go into detailed explanations/descriptions of depression and suicide. Of equal importance is their presentation of ways that clergy can assist congregants in alleviating their suffering.

Chapter Nine , authored by Dr. Paula E. Hartman-Stein, focuses on the kind of knowledge that clergy should have in order to provide pastoral care to older adults. This includes how they can recognize signs of dementia, as well as emotional problems among the aged.

In Chapter ten , Dr. Martha Lansing, who is a medical doctor, explores chronic illnesses and how it affects people not only physically, but also emotionally and spiritually. She offers suggestions to clergy concerning how they can help such persons as well as their relatives and caretakers deal with the situation.

Chapter Eleven , written by Dr. Kevin P. Kaut , et al, deals with how clergy can minister to persons who are dying, in addition to their loved ones. In part this entails educating people as to the nature of the illness, and helping prepare the patients and those close to them for the death of the former.

Chapter Twelve , prepared by Reverend Daniel H. Grossoehme, targets the grief experienced by children and adolescents whose sibling, parent, grandparent, or other key person in their life has recently passed away. Reverend Grossoehme points out how grief on the part of the young survivors can be effectively dealt with by clergy.

In Chapter Thirteen, Dr. Christopher Alan Lewis and Conor McGuckin provide a contemporary overview of school bullying phenomenon and youth aggression. In addition, they deal with such important issues as he link between bullying behaviors and religiosity, and what clergy can do in terms of intervention.

In Chapter Fourteen , Dr. Jennifer S. Ripley along with Stephanie D. Kemper write about the single most common problem faced in pastoral care. This has to do with helping couples and families. They emphasize a community-based approach rather than a counseling approach. One of the most important topics dealt with is determining the needs of couples and families in the neighborhood, as well as the resources each community has to help them meet their needs.

Chapter Fifteen, written by Professor Julie Juola Exline and Christine Smith , looks at forgiveness from a variety of perspectives. For example, what does it mean to forgive, what are the potential benefits of forgiveness, and how can clergy help people acknowledge their limitations and wrongs.

In Chapter Sixteen, Amy B. Wacholtz and Professor Kenneth I. Pargament talk about the long history of association that meditation has with spiritual and religious practices. They particularly relate to the functions of meditation in pastoral counseling. They point out such important matters as the ability of meditation to lower heart rate and blood pressure.

The last and third section of the book is entitled: *Issues for Clergy Wellness: Maintaining Bridges for Strength & Minimizing Morbidity*. This portion of the book emphasizes the pressures that clergy often operate under, and how they can deal with these in order to avoid excessive stress as well as considerable loss of personal energy. As psychologists, we are very concerned with the topic of clergy well-being and believe this topic is often not confronted more openly.

Dr. Mark L. Berman, author of Chapter Seventeen , presents information about the role of clergy as Universal Donors, how being a Donor can impact personal energy and stress levels, and ways that clergy can deal with such pressures.

Chapter Eighteen , also written by Dr. Berman, provides information to help clergy determine how to measure their personal energy as well as their stress levels, and how to maximize personal energy and minimize stress.

In Chapter Nineteen , authored by Reverend Leslie J. Francis and Reverend Douglas Turton, the main objectives are to distinguish between two key components of burnout among clergy, and discuss ways that clergy can reduce the incidence of burnout among them.

We recognize the diverse interests and needs of clergy and church associates within the domain of pastoral care and guidance. Our intent and hope is that the scope and range of topics presented strengthens pastoral care functions in ways that reduce human suffering and pain and fosters spiritual/religious growth along with emotional and psychological well-being. This is only possible with the depth and quality of knowledge and experiences shared by the contributing authors.

We trust the reader will benefit from this collaborative effort and that whatever bridges in the future are constructed that they bring optimal strength, integrity, and sustained vitality to pastoral care in navigating over the troubled waters which encumber so many parishioners.

SECTION ONE:

FOUNDATIONS OF PASTORAL CARE

Chapter 1
Spirituality, Religion & Psychology:
Core Concepts for Building Bridges for the
Troubled Parishioner / Congregant

by David Herl, Ed.D.

"I know God will not give me anything I can't handle. I just wish he didn't trust me so much."

Mother Teresa (1910-1997)

TENDING TO FOUNDATIONS IN CONTRUCTING BRIDGES:
OPPORTUNITIES IN RESPONDING TO THE CALL

In selecting desirable and worthwhile content for this chapter, I reflected upon the experience years ago that led to the idea for this book. Little did I know that over three decades ago, a mental health seminar I participated in for clergy would be the catalyst that poignantly illuminated some of the core concepts felt to be important in pastoral care and guidance.

During the late 1960's, I was a doctoral psychology student in Arizona completing a clinical internship at a psychiatric hospital and outpatient clinic. One of our licensed psychologists and an ordained pastor organized a small group seminar for clergy and several church associates/lay leaders to guide them in providing pastoral care for parishioners who were depressed and/or at possible risk for suicide.

The seminar was "process oriented," allowing clergy to interact amongst peers as well as mental health professionals, the group leaders. I was invited to attend and participate as a co-facilitator.

The seminar included some didactic discussion of reactive and clinical depression, grief, and symptom patterns of youth and elderly. Clergy participants consisted of very diverse denominations, both conservative and liberal.

What impressed me was the open disclosure of many of the clergy members' struggles in providing pastoral care for parishioners with despair and hopelessness, and in coping personally with parishioners who had tragically taken their own lives. A particular clergy's experiences were especially poignant and illustrate some of the core concepts to be discussed in this book. A clergy member in his fifties related that he had "dealt with lots of tragedy" in his church, but felt "I'm loosing it now." With his eyes staring vacantly, as if in a trance, he revealed that he had married a couple who met each other at church as young teens. Briefly, both were college graduates and had very promising careers. They had an eight year old daughter. However, marital problems evolved because the husband developed an addiction to alcohol and drugs. The wife was subsequently diagnosed with breast cancer that was refractory to treatment. After her untimely death, the husband became severely despondent and committed suicide half a year later. A note was discovered which stated that their daughter would have a "better life" with a family member because he feared a protracted psychological and physical decline leading to destitution. He added, "Why should I drag this out?"

The clergy gentlemen sobbed heavily after relating his personal feelings of emptiness, helplessness, anguish, and guilt over not being able to "offer more" and to sense deeper psychological turmoil in this parishioner and take preventative action.

This case illustrates a number of concepts important in caring for troubled parishioners. Religion involves not only doctrine, instruction/scriptures, etc., but the explicit and implicit roles of clergy with the church, as well as the nature of helping relationships with parishioners.

Spiritual issues now emerged for him as he questioned the meaning and significance of his calling and ministry. For the surviving family of the couple, a plethora of spiritual issues were salient –Why did this happen? How will this tragedy change or alter our purpose in life? Can we get over these losses? Psychological disruptions existed now with three family systems (clergy's family and the spouses' surviving families, including the child's multiple losses).

Fortunately, other clergy group members were readily empathic and supportive. This sharing was followed with some group problem-solving, in terms of future pastoral care planning. Despite divergent denominations among group members, a common bond united them in heart, mind, and spirit. For all of us, this experience was exceedingly valuable and exemplified the benefits of a collaborative journey between psychology and religion.

Mother Teresa's compassion and sensitivity towards those who suffered and were weighted down with life's burdens, led her to acknowledge incredible perceived needs which could not be easily ignored or cast aside. She certainly recognized the extent of demands and pressures in the calling for pastoral care.

Likewise, in July 2003 the Wall Street Journal's front page article ("For the Clergy, Flock's Troubles Become Their Own") dealt with the vulnerabilities of clergy in responding to pastoral care requests and needs. The article discusses how church members are increasingly seeking out pastoral counseling and guidance for "real world problems," particularly during stressful times.

Pastoral care, of course, is not liminal by any means. In fact, pastoral care origins can be found in the Old Testament, for instance, in Exodus Moses sought helpers for providing moral direction to the Israelites. Spiritual and religious beliefs are still very much salient, particularly in America. The Gallup Organization (1991) discovered that 96% of Americans believed in God or universal spirit, 75% felt religious faith is very important, and 90% said they pray. Similarly noteworthy is that Americans expressed interest in spiritual growth with 82% in 1998 contrasted to 58% in 1994 (Myers, 2000).

More recent data (Gallup Organization, 2003) indicated less "engaged" (i.e. "fully spiritually committed") congregation members than the previous survey data suggests. Engaged members of the congregations of all faiths comprised 28% while 55% were "not engaged". A minority (17%) of congregants, although notable, were found to be "actively disengaged".

Those engaged have a strong "psychological connection" to the congregation they belong to and are intensely loyal. Those not engaged are not psychologically connected, even though they may attend services regularly (Gallup Organization, 2003).

Another ongoing trend is found between gender and religion. More women than men are finding meaning and purpose in life through religion as well as inner peace and a belief that religion can be a resource in solving today's problems (Gallup Organization, 2003).

One last finding is that only 45% have a "great deal/quite a lot of confidence" in organized religion, while 52% (range 47%-58% depending on political ideology) rate honesty and ethics of clergy very high. Approximately 62% believe "religion can answer today's problems" (Gallup Organization, 2003).

Another interesting scientific study of church members, found that religious coping was a significant predictor of adjustment (Hill et al., 1990). The researchers found that more than 70% of members mobilized religion to cope with a stressful life event.

In looking to the future, George H. Gallup Jr. (Gallup Organization, 2002) points out that the U.S. revival among religion and churches will be undertaken by three groups: 1) African-Americans, 2) "Millennials" (graduates from high school beginning 2000), 3) "pre-retirement Army-Builder Generation."

African-Americans were discovered to fit the profile of "highly spiritually committed" at high incidence. Millennials, of which 40% are 19 years of age and younger, desire and seek spiritual growth in everyday life and have strong interests in assisting the poor and "less fortunate."

The third group, consisting of 20% of the population and ranging from ages 50-64, have exceptionally strong religious values with 7 in 10 indicating that religion is the most important or a very important influence in their lives.

What conclusions and implications can be made from such data with respect to clergy or congregation/faith community leaders?

First, the potential for religious institutions and churches to engage a very significant portion of the population exists. However, the need to enhance engagement levels will likely result in more effective and stronger churches or faith communities. Interventions for men that better meet their needs are indicated. Somehow, U.S. congregations are not reaching men at the level women's personal needs are being met.

Secondly, it seems important to build on the perception that religion can be a viable resource and "answer" to today's problems. The three groups of individuals with high religiosity are an excellent pool to focus upon. The lives they touch can have a contagion effect.

Thirdly, clergy must be sensitive to how they are perceived by congregants in terms of honesty and ethics. This entails a code of ethics and professional standards of care in dealing with congregants. Important too is the awareness of the interactional aspects of "relational boundaries" and clergy authority and transference ("power dynamics"), beautifully discussed in depth by Doehring (1995).

In assessing satisfactory role performance (Krause, Ellison, & Wulff, 1998), the authors point out that clergy are required to: 1) offer spiritual advice and solace to persons confronting problems, 2) preach and teach religious doctrine to church members, and 3) live exemplary spiritual and personal lives.

Actually, the foundations for effective and fulfilling pastoral care begin with clergy and lay leaders. Clergy self-care issues are very important considerations. We, the editors, have included several chapters in this book devoted to this topic. When I was in graduate school completing coursework and advanced practicums for the doctoral degree, a supervisor and professor with a penchant to "tell it like it is" told us: "Think of yourselves as an instrument in the helping relationship process. You need to be functioning well and in touch with yourselves - you are going to leave here before too long with your degrees and during your careers you'll be touching and influencing many lives, for better or for worse - hopefully, always for the better. So above all, care for yourselves - be good to yourselves or you won't be worth a damn to those you treat or offer psychotherapy." Very inspirational, and a truism even after three decades of clinical experience!

PASTORAL CARE & INTERFACE WITH PSYCHOLOGY

"Science without religion is lame, religion without science is blind."
Albert Einstein (1879-1955)

Historical Developments

Pastoral care, of course, is not liminal by any means, but a more comprehensive integration of psychology with religion/spirituality may well be, particularly as it is manifested in collaboration and mutual consultation.

Most scholars would agree that a strained relationship existed for some time between the religious community and professional psychology. Nevertheless, in the very early 1900's William James, the founder of American psychology, wrote about religious experiences linking religion and spirituality. His ideas were felt by behavioral science historians to be precursors for major developments in psychology's psychotherapy orientations.

Perhaps the most significant development of psychology's interface with religion was the emergence of humanistic psychology, also known as the Third Force in psychology, with the First Force being psychoanalytic psychotherapy (psychoanalysis), and the Second Force being behaviorism.

Briefly, premises of this movement, which included Maslow and Rogers as well as existential religious philosophers (Buber, Tillich), included a focus on holism, man's creative powers, an anthropomorphic conceptualization of man, a teleological approach, subjectivity (perceptual/phenomenological orientation), and a belief in the healing and curative aspects of the therapeutic relationship.

Transpersonal psychology, or the Fourth Force, was due to Maslow's influences that dealt with spirituality and includes other phenomenon of inner experiences and states.

During the past decade or so, scholars examined the religious, spiritual, and global mental health value of health/social human service professionals. Bergin and Jensen (1990) found that the percent of therapists or counselors who regularly attended religious services varied from 32% (psychiatrists) to 50% (marital & family therapists). Most attempted to embrace their religious or spiritual beliefs in daily life. The authors concluded that there was a substantial interest in spirituality (when broadly defined), including routine participation in traditional religious practices and beliefs.

For clinical psychologists, most believe spirituality is personally relevant and are affiliated with organized religion (Shafranske & Malony, 1990). Also, in the past few years, a number of psychologists have published in the domain of spirituality and religion, tackling some areas previously conceptualized as "out of bounds" and "too fuzzy".

Another significant, fairly recent trend, has been the interest in developing a positive psychology which examines topics of wellness, life satisfaction, happiness, spirituality, serenity and hope, for example, while de-emphasizing pathology and negative aspects of life.

These developments and trends are valuable in preparing the terrain for further clergy-psychologist collaboration and utilizing the multifaceted strengths and synergy this Gestalt can offer both professionals and, most importantly, troubled parishioners.

PASTORAL CARE FUNCTIONS & OPPORTUNITIES FOR INTEGRATING BEHAVIORAL SCIENCE

My intent is to revisit the traditional four major functions of pastoral care and guidance with respect to how psychology and the behavioral sciences can contribute to their operational characteristics in meeting troubled parishioners' needs.

Historically, the four major functions of pastoral care are: A. Healing, B. Sustaining, C. Guiding, and D. Reconciling (Clebsch & Jaekle, 1964).

A. Healing involves restoration, with the goal and hope that the troubled soul becomes more integrated and whole, and reflects a higher degree of spiritual growth and possible maturity than previously held. Interventions may include anointing with oil, prayer, charismatic healing, use of relics, and exorcism.

B. Sustaining seeks to support individuals be helping them cope and endure, and to subsequently elevate them to a realm of functioning above events and circumstances in which they perceive having little or no control.

Interventions are designed to inoculate against stress, instill hope and feelings of belonging, mobilize strengths and resources resulting in integration and "regrouping," while facilitating a renewed quest for life.

C. Perhaps the more contemporary guiding function was most strongly influenced by psychology. It has to do with assisting parishioners in decision-making, which leads to "cure of the soul" and a journey empowered with valued and congruous meaning, as well as direction.

The influence of Carl Rogers and non-directive psychotherapy and counseling became embraced during the 1940's and 1950's, reflecting an educative method of guidance. Utilizing this approach afforded increased opportunities for self-exploration and self-discovery. This development was in stark contrast to the traditional method of clergy authority and religion resources through prescribing scripture teachings.

D. The fourth function, reconciling, pertains to renewing or establishing productive and beneficial relationships, both between troubled and alienated parishioner with others, and with the individual and God.

Essentially, forgiveness and discipline are the salient yet interdependent modes of reconciling (Clebsch & Jaekle, 1964). The authors concluded that this function, with "extraordinarily rich heritage, should and will become integrated with healing." Their receptivity to psychology is notable in that they state that a "transformed" pastoral care can be "...continuous with the history of pasturing, integrated with the churches' theological formulation, open to new psychological insights, and able to meet creatively the aspirations and needs of modern men and women" (Clebsch & Jaekle, 1964, p.81).

A critical and exciting interface between psychology and pastoral care is the multipotentiality of church and lay associates for facilitating both growth enhancing psychological/emotional experiences and spiritual well-being and maturity. Such fulfillment and mastery of needs essential in adaptive and higher functioning personality development will bring about well-being and enhance mental health.

Considerable research has been conducted on three proposed key, innate psychological needs (Ryan & Deci, 2000) which are felt to be paramount in optimizing mental health. The researchers discuss the importance of satisfying the basic needs for competence, autonomy, and relatedness during the lifespan for health and well-being and minimization of psychopathology and "ill-being". For example, it was concluded by the authors (Ryan & Deci, 2000) that low support for these needs contributes to alienation and emotional problems (ill-being).

Church leaders and lay staff can assist in preventing protracted distress by observing how these needs are possibly thwarted and unmet satisfactorily in both youth and adults. Such a developmental "life span" orientation entails intervention at various times, particularly when life events are perceived as disruptive, distressful, possibly overwhelming, and often of crisis proportions.

Exploring areas of pastoral care functions wherein psychology may have opportunities to optimize and enhance pastoral interventions should be an ongoing collaborative process.

Skill and knowledge domains in psychology which can be integrated with pastoral care functions include:

1. Diagnosis and assessment of troubled parishioners: These functions are often vital in more serious and complex parishioner issues and problem presentations. Included could be risk assessments for determining potential harm or injury to oneself or others. Collaboration and integration of spiritual assessments provided by clergy are highly desirable.

2. Communication and relationship building: Psychology can offer both knowledge and insight in enhancing the quality of the pastoral relationship/alliance to optimize clergy effectiveness in reaching goals within each pastoral function. Actualizing clergy or religious communities' strengths, which are manifest or latent, is a consultive psychological skill and function.

3. Coping with stress and adversity: Psychological approaches and techniques can smoothly be dovetailed with religious and spiritual interventions to often potentiate resolution, mastery, and both spiritual/religious and psychological growth and well-being.

As a consultant to clergy, I have had opportunities to intervene with parishioners I had been seeing for psychotherapy and to work in tandem with clergy, each of us having specific roles. In some cases, my focus was to utilize language which increased parishioner receptivity to religious and spiritual teachings and messages from their clergy.

Such an approach both expands and enriches the armentatorium of problem-solving resources. In these cases, the sum of both psychological and religious interventions was greater than each respective discipline's impact on problem resolution.

4. Dynamics and mechanisms of "healing": We are truly at a liminal moment at the millennium as the behavioral and neurosciences discover new linkages between mind and body. Fortunately, we are at the stage of cognitive complexity where referring to the mind (psyche) and body (soma) as separate entities is provincial and archaic.

Internal conflict, anxiety, and stress can complicate a parishioner's ability to heal and resolve various symptoms and illnesses. Psychological defenses may cause resistance or barriers to overcoming physical and/or mental disorders. Psychology can offer approaches to more effectively deal with resistance and enhance motivation to change. Some of the specialized interventions are discussed in some depth in the chapter pertaining to addictions by this author.

In addition, psychological research is helping determine and understand how religion/spirituality can promote healing and improve health and well-being. For example, Powell, Shahabi, & Thorensen (2003) have utilized a "levels of evidence" approach to determine how religion and/or spirituality can have preventative, protective, and curative effects on health.

The authors conclude that such religious or spiritual interventions may protect against disease/death in healthy people and moderate disease present. Also, another interesting finding cited is that intercessory prayer appears to improve recovery from acute illness (such as cardiac disorder, AIDS).

Continued exploration and studies of mind-body relationships and the impact of religion/spirituality on healing and health will be exciting. Combining both psychological and religious interventions to possibly potentiate curative and positive outcomes is an area of inquiry certainly worth pursuing.

CORE CONCEPTS AS FOUNDATIONS FOR BUILDING BRIDGES

In preparing foundations for the bridges which allow for pastoral care functions to be optimized for troubled souls, I will discuss some select concepts and terms useful in the helping relationship.

A. Spirituality/Religion

Extensive writing on these topics abound, sometimes with confusion. Most scholars would agree to some overlap and some distinct differences between the terms. Certainly they are multifaceted, complex, and defy comprehensive definitions.

Both spirituality and religion can be seen as ways of being and living in a world to be sought and experienced. Together, they may be regarded as salient in influencing and structuring behavior, human experience, beliefs, values, and formulated destinations in life.

While religion generally connotes belief in God or higher power and institutional beliefs and practices (such as church affiliation or membership), spirituality may reflect beliefs, experiences and practices involving a person's relationship with the universe, sacred, or higher being. Also, spirituality may be conceptualized by some as an anchoring experience as well as a search or quest for meaning, purpose, and direction in life.

A useful concept for both clergy and psychologists is spiritual well-being. Ellison (1983) noted that psychologists, who have studied well-being indices and quality of life, have either overlooked or ignored the spiritual dimension of human experience. He has proposed that this concept of well-being include the satisfaction of a set of needs he labels "transcendence." For Ellison, this involves discovering and committing to purposes involving ultimate meaning for life.

Maslow likewise conceptualized a differentiated need hierarchy. The need for the highest level of self-actualization is in essence a spiritual quest forcing one to dissociate and transcend the "self" and demonstrate a steadfast and systemic ultruism towards mankind (i.e. typified, for example, by the lives of Albert Schwitzer and Mother Teresa). For Maslow (1970), "man has a higher and transcendent nature, and this is part of his essence, i.e. his biological nature as a member of a species which has evolved" (p.89).

A useful instrument is the Spiritual Well-Being Scale (Ellison, 1983) that provides a global measure of spiritual well-being on a continuum. A distinct qualitative advantage is that the instrument consists of factors for both religious and existential well-being. Furthermore, the author explains the scale is non-sectarian and has potential for being utilized by a range of diverse religions and denominations.

Ellison's concept of spiritual well-being is valuable in approaching human suffering, pain, conflicts, and anguish ("angst") in a holistic and integrative style which draws both from religion and psychology.

B. Pastoral Care

The word "pastoral" is derived form the Latin word "pascere," meaning "to feel." The response to troubled parishioners is pastoral, implying a compassionate, empathetic nurturance of others. It involves agape as well as belief and faith in the acts of supporting, understanding, and intervening to those who suffer and are in pain or distress, whether physical, emotional/psychological, or spiritual.

A related concept has to do with the nature of the pastoral relationship. The reader is invited to explore and embrace Doehring's notion of covenant (evolves from a pastoral contract, implicitly or explicitly) which, she explains, is a "rich and complex metaphor for a pastoral counseling or care relationship characterized by congruence with both divine and human faithfulness" (Doehring, 1995, p.163).

C. Agape

"Love in all its forms is ecstatic. The moment of love is a moment of self-transcendence."

Paul Tillich (1886-1965)
Theologian, Religious philosopher

Four types of love have been described. The libido type culminates in sex, while the eros type reflects a mystical union. Philia pertains to a love which culminates in friendship. Agape, which is central in climate building for personal change and growth (spiritual and psychological), pertains to and is manifested in a Christian, divine/virtuous type of love, rooted in a charitable, merciful perception of others.

By embracing and manifesting agape, Tillich believed one conveys to others both charitable forgiveness and potential fulfillment. With such an organizing principle, unconditional positive regard and genuine acceptance prevail, allowing the pastoral caregiver to create a climate which encourages openness to experience and sharing, as well as authenticity (Rogers, 1951).

D. Salutogenesis

The term, conceptualized be Antonovsky (1979), is derived from "salus", Latin for health and well-being. Essentially, this orientation (salutogenic model) is congruent with positive psychology that espouses global well-being, resilience, and a flexible adaptiveness due to a strong sense of coherence.

A salutogenic vision encourages clergy and lay members to examine what is self/health enhancing and wholesome within the religious and faith community. Similarly, identifying and creating opportunities for parishioners to meet the key, innate psychological needs discussed previously (i.e. competence, autonomy, and relatedness) can be integrated with both religious teachings and spiritual growth/well-being.

E. Beliefs and Expectations as Foundations for Effective Pastoral Care

Belief in the process of pastoral care as being curative and therapeutic in fostering spiritual and psychological integration is vital. An essential substrate underlying the belief in positive resolutions and outcomes reflects trust and faith in the pastoral care process.

Trust in oneself as an instrument for catalyzing change, healing, and integration is critical as one undertakes pastoral care. Another dimension is possessing faith and belief in the potential for parishioners to embrace life and discover new meanings, directions, and sense of purpose and worthwhileness.

RESPONDING TO THE CALL: TOWARDS COMPREHENSIVE COLLABORATION FOR BUILDING BRIDGES OF STRENGTH

"It is a calling to work together (clergy and mental health professional) to develop a psychology of the community that will protect those who are endangered by emotional stresses, and enhance the potential of human beings through the development of sound mental health."

Glenn E. Whitlock, Ph.D.
Pastor, Psychologist, Author

The majority of individuals experiencing emotional difficulties seek out clergy first before physicians and mental health professionals. This trend is not likely to change. A Joint Commission on Mental Illness & Health Report in 1960 revealed that 42% of people consulted clergy in times of domestic or emotional difficulties while 29% consulted physicians and 18% sought out psychiatrists and psychologists. Only 10% contacted other social agencies or clinics.

Interestingly, clergy usually see similar mental health problems as do mental health professionals. Benner (1992) identified the five most frequently reported and presented concerns to clergy by parishioners: marriage and divorce (84%), depression (64%), addictions (44%), grief (38%), and guilt and forgiveness (37%).

The relationship between psychology and theology is vital since theology's focus is upon both God and man. Essentially, the behavioral sciences provide clergy contemporary knowledge of human suffering and problems, which enhances the relevance and impact of religious intervention and support.

Several excellent examples are in the behavioral domains of addictions and mood disorders or depression. A lengthy time elapsed before addictions were understood as much more complex and multi-determined than reflecting hedonism, "weak willpower," or the hackneyed "they can stop if they really want to." Depression, likewise, was not understood as a disorder often with both biological and psychological etiologies.

Important contributions to theology and religion by behavioral sciences have been identified by Whitlock (1973). The following appear historically relevant:

1. A view of the individual as devoid of "simple moralism" with understanding in terms of "estrangement or alienation" from which the person requires intervention and assistance.
2. Relating to the whole individual "seriously" by recognizing the total implications of alienation from self, God, and others.
3. A dynamic view of the individual beyond rationality and with an understanding of the multifaceted nature of human behavior with conscious and unconscious dimensions to life.
    The author emphasizes that churches heavily embracing "logic and reason to their theological approach" would do parishioners better by "rediscovering the Biblical understanding" that knowledge is not only intellectual (cognitive), but is inclusive of the "total person" where experiencing "the moment of truth" and fresh, newly realized insights and understanding evolve.
4. Individuals are known solely in relationships. A goal of pastoral care is to help "restore wholeness through a rediscovery of a sense of community."
5. Religious convictions may express sickness as well as health.
6. A deeper understanding by theologians as to the importance of the individual's relationship with "primary authority figures" and potential

for "irrational images" that may exist in perceptions of both God and authority figures (such as omnipotents).

Theology teaches those in the behavioral sciences that religious faith cannot be reflected entirely by psychological investigation and that dimensions of reality go beyond the reach of science. One humbling discovery in astronomy at the millennium is the knowledge of the universe and discovery of infinite galaxies that dwarf current scientific knowledge and thinking.

David Barthgate (2003), an Australian psychiatrist, has asked for psychiatry and behavioral sciences to "look to widen our understanding (of human life) by exploring the possibilities for renewed dialogue that would encompass both scientific and religious/spiritual viewpoints" (p.284).

He adroitly adds: "If in modern times religion has come down out of the sky, so too must psychiatric understanding move out beyond its skull – encapsulated, anthropocentric view of mind, to a broader understanding of human life" (p. 285).

A resounding consensus now exists among psychologists and educators in pastoral counseling, that clergy and/or church associates or lay members are involved to varying degrees in the mental health of their parishioners, either overtly (explicitly and acknowledged) or covertly (implicitly or not acknowledged).

Such an increased interface and union reinforces the Gestalt view that together both are synergistic and truly much more than the sum of each discipline's offerings and talents.

At this juncture, it may well behoove us to learn from the ageless story, the Wizard of Oz. The essence of the story being that among ourselves, we have the potential within to create all the ingredients and dimensions to provide a standard of pastoral care which will meet human needs and foster both psychological/emotional and spiritual/religious integration and growth. That is, we have the intellect ("brain", as desired by the scarecrow), the empathy and passion to tend to the "hearts" (wished for by the Tin Man) and "souls" of troubled parishioners, and the most challenging being the "courage" (desired by the lion) to confront and resolve any barriers and conflicts in developing and maintaining a working alliance.

The reader may also recall how oil given to the Tin Man by Dorothy and the other cohorts drastically improved his quality of life. Perhaps our "oil" is faith and trust that will enable quality pastoral care to be provided with efficiency, alacrity, speed, and agility.

Enriched resources from the joint collaboration between the religious community and psychology will go a long way in building well-designed and enduring bridges for assisting troubled parishioners/congregants who face contemporary life issues and problems. As mortal individuals who have chosen a life engaged and involved in the "helping relationships," we owe parishioners the best we can marshal as we tend and commit to "the business of the angels."

REFERENCES

Antonovsky, A. (1979). *Health, stress, and coping: New perspectives on mental health and physical well-being.* San Francisco: Jossey-Bass

Barthgate, D. (2003). Psychiatry, religion, and cognitive science. *Australian and New Zealand Journal of Psychiatry, 37*, 277-285.

Benner, D.G. (1992). *Strategic pastoral counseling: A short-term structure model.* Grand Rapids, MI: Baker.

Bergin, A.E., & Jensen, J.P. (1990). Religiosity of psychotherapists: A national survey. *Psychotherapy, 27*, 3-7.

Bernstein, E., & Landers, P. (2003, July 31). For the clergy, flock's troubles become their own. *The Wall Street Journal*, p. A1.

Clebsch, W.A., & Jaekle, C.R. (1964). *Pastoral care in historical perspective.* New Jersey: Prentice-Hall.

Doehring, C. (1995). *Taking care: Monitoring power dynamics & relational boundaries in pastoral care & counseling.* Nashville: Abingdon Press.

Ellison, C.W. (1983). Spiritual well-being: Conceptualization and measurement. *Journal of Psychology & Theology, 11*, 330-340.

Gallup Organization. (1991). Church/synagogue membership. (In the Gallup Report). Washington, D.C.

Gallup Organization. (2002). Wide ideology gap evident in religious index. (In the Gallup Poll Tuesday Briefing). Washington, D.C.

Gallup Organization. (2003). New congregational engagement figure released. (In the Gallup Poll Tuesday Briefing). Washington, D.C.

Hill, P.C., Pargament, K.I., Hood, R.W. Jr., McCullough, M.E., Swyers, J.P., Larson, D.B., et al. (1990). God help me: I. Religious coping efforts as predictors of the outcomes to significant negative life events. *American Journal of Community Psychology, 18*, 793-824.

Krause, N., Ellison, C.W., & Wulff, K.M. (1998). Church based support, negative interaction, and well-being. *Journal of the Scientific Study of Religion, 73*, 725-741.

Maslow, A.H. (1970). *Religions, values, and peak-experiences.* Viking.

Myers, D.G. (2000). *The American paradox: Spiritual hunger in an age of plenty.* New Haven, CT: Yale University Press.

Powell, L.H., Shahabi, L., & Thorensen, C.E. (2003). Religion and spirituality: Linkages to physical health. *American Psychologist, 58*, 36-52.

Rogers, C.R. (1951). *Client-centered therapy.* Boston: Houghton Mifflin.

Ryan, R.M., & Deci, E.L. (2000). Self-determination theory and the facilitation of intrinsic motivation, social development, and well-being. *American Psychologist, 55*, 68-78.

Whitlock, G.E. (1973). *Preventive psychiatry and the church.* Philadelphia: Westminster Press.

Chapter 2
Caring for the Soul & the Self:
Perspectives on Pastoral Helping

by C. Kevin Gillespie, S.J., Ph.D.
Department of Pastoral Counseling, Loyola College in Maryland

In recent years it seems that the word "soul" has had a resurrection. Books ranging from to Thomas Moore's *Care of the Soul* to the religious recipes found in the series, *Chicken Soup for the Soul*, have made it to the bestsellers list. Moreover, an internet search for the word "soul" produces more than 6,000 titles! "Soul" certainly sells. The culture's fascination with the soul and spirituality in general suggests that a multiplicity of meanings have emerged.

Understanding of the soul has come a long way since Aristotle articulated a description of how the soul, *psuche*, represents the first principle of life housed by the body. He developed this understanding in distinguishing the vegetative soul of plants from the sensitive souls of animals from the rational souls of human beings. The ancient Jews, meanwhile, described soul or *nephesh*, as the breath given by the Breath or *Ruah*. The Christian view of soul, on the other hand, as developed by St. Paul and then by the early Church, added a new dimension to the soul in interpreting the implications of believing in the resurrection of Jesus. In this respect, every soul is given the opportunity to share in the immortality of Christ, but a possibility requires the believer to live a life with the intention of saving one's soul. The challenge to fulfill this possibility subsequently became a moral responsibility that was reinforced and supported by means of the Church's systematic soul-care through sacraments and sermons.

Soul-care moved into this sacramental system through the writings of St. Gregory of Nazianzus (d. 390) who was the first to develop the notion of the "cura animarum", whereby the ordained were charged with the responsibility to nurture the souls of believers. Later in his *Pastoral Rule*, St. Gregory the Great (d. 604) applied the notion of *cura animarum* in promoting the pastoral theology of sacramental care. Throughout the Middle Ages this sense of the *cura animarum* became one of the major manifestations of the Church's ministry. In fact, Gregory's *Pastoral Rule* was often given the bishops as they assumed their office.

Centuries later the responsibilities for the *cura animarum* was challenged by Luther and later Zwingli who saw soul care in terms of *seelsorge*, which was the responsibility of all baptized believers and not only the ordained. A few centuries later, with the emergence of the Enlightenment, the care of the soul became secularized into the care of the self.

No longer were a person's life struggles seen only in terms of saving one's soul. Religion's various and at times conflicting responses of caring for the soul in Western secular societies became perceived as inadequate. The rise of science and secular consciousness brought forth later in the nineteenth century psychiatry and psychoanalysis. These spoke more of the "self" than the soul with some suggesting that soul was no longer needed in understanding human being.

During the first half of the twentieth century, therefore, there was often a conflicted relationship between psychology and religion. Such a conflict began to dissipate after World War II as a rapprochement developed between the two areas. No less an authority than Pope Pius XII in 1953 lauded and blessed the work of psychotherapists, and spoke of religion and psychology as being engaged in a common project, a seeking "for the knowledge of the soul".

In the last decade the sacred and secular caring for the soul has found a new impetus. Research involving such areas as coping, forgiveness, stress and wisdom has shown how psychology and the theology can complement each other. The emergence of first humanistic, and then positive psychology, and the efforts of religious authorities to bridge the fields, has enhanced the conversation. Even the crisis and scandal of clerical abuse suggest the necessity for such conversations.

This brief historical overview of the development of understanding and caring for the soul may help us to appreciate how there has emerged a virtual lexicon of distinctions and nuances. For the minister of pastoral care, whose role historically has been described as one who cares for the soul of the other (*cura animarum*) the various formulations of "soul" may lead to confusion and at best ambiguity in one's ministry. Moreover, pastoral ministry in the twentieth century has appropriated strategies of caring for the soul from various psychological schools that have served to deepen and expand the psychological dynamics of pastoral care. From the psychoanalysis of Sigmund Freud through the client-centered methods of Carl Rogers to the cognitive theory of Aaron Beck, pastoral care and counseling have developed different psychological pathways to an understanding of the self, which in turn have implications for a sense of the soul. Psychology's diverse approaches to the self represent a challenge. Indeed as Holifield (1983) suggests, instead of the salvation of their souls many believers and their caregivers have placed more emphasis upon their self-realization. Nevertheless, for those who seek to care for the contemporary soul, a certain amount of psychology is necessary so as to inform and enhance one's pastoral strategies. In the remainder of this chapter I will offer what may be termed a matrix for the contemporary care of the soul by providing an assortment of principles and strategies for those who are engaged in ministerial caregiving. Through this matrix I present an overview of ministry that will help one offer effective responses to pastoral situations. The matrix is based upon Cheston's (2000) paradigm of three "ways" of counseling, namely, a way of being, a way of understanding, and a way of intervening.

By "a way of being" Cheston means the boundaries set, the degree of empathy exhibited, the values demonstrated, and the overall sense of presence that a counselor convey. Theories of counseling, personality and human development represent for Cheston "a way of understanding." Cheston also believes that a "way of intervening" involves specific strategies and techniques, listens and at times interrupts a client's expressions of feelings and thoughts. By considering the constituents of each of these three ways I intend to offer the interested reader descriptions and distinctions that may help the pastoral minister toward more effective approaches of caring for the soul.

Way of Being: Burnout/Balancing/Boundaries

Since the 1980s, with the first lawsuits against clerical abuse, a fair amount of clinical and pastoral literature has been written on the subject of boundaries. Not only have some members of the clergy been confronted with ethical violations of boundaries, but counselors and physicians have as well. In one of the first books on the subject, *Sex in the Forbidden Zone* (1989), Peter Rutter argues that one of the great professional secrets has been the violations of the trust that care recipients have in their professional caregivers. Today's caregivers, therefore, must become cognizant of the boundaries of a caregiving relationship, and what constitutes an ethical violation. By boundaries we mean the ethical guidelines in responding to someone who entrusts himself or herself to our care. Such guidelines include a mandate not to go beyond one's competence. Whatever our abilities as caregivers are we must recognize the limits of our competence and not mislead a person by going beyond the limits. In this respect we need to know when and how to refer someone in our care.

Certainly many of the demands of caregiving and pastoral ministry in general require the spontaneity of The Good Samaritan such that the needs of a person in need are responded to without worrying about one's level of professional competence at the time. To do so risks making ministry too professionalized. On the other hand, as Moessner (1991) points out in her exegesis of Lk.10:29-37, the care of the Samaritan demonstrated the proper use of boundaries. As related by Jesus, the Samaritan cared for the person by responding to the immediate needs of the victim and then took him to someone who could watch over him. The Samaritan then went about his business and later returned to make sure that the victim was properly cared for. The Samaritan did not extend himself to the point of creating chaos in his own life. In this respect, in his caregiving The Good Samaritan did not go beyond his level of competence or his capacity to communicate himself to the care of the victim which may very well have thrown his own personal projects out of balance and have resulted in undue stress. The Samaritan was not only compassionate and good, but also competent and effective without burning himself out.

A caregiver, professional and lay, often needs to make decisions as to respond to a person with compassion and competence and at the same time respecting the boundaries of a relationship and attend to one's own need for balance. Scott Peck in his popular bestseller, *The Road Less Traveled* (1978), speaks eloquently of the need for balancing and suggests that it involves the discipline of giving up. How often have caregivers, when faced with several choices of doing good, had difficulty in giving up one good for the other. So often we tend to choose all of them and enter into the frenetic quest of multitasks that can lead us to fatigue, stress and possible burnout.

Ignatius of Loyola in his *Spiritual Exercises* demonstrates how contemplation can exist amidst the activities of a busy life by suggesting exercises designed to help one to choose the greater good. For Ignatius most of life decisions are not choosing a good versus an evil, but rather choosing a good versus another good. He, therefore, developed a discipline of discerning whereby one comes to have a felt sense of choosing a greater good versus a good. In this respect Ignatius conceived that at times a good is an enemy of a greater good. When put into practice such discernment can help one to prioritize motivations and actions and lessen the fatigue and stress of an active life of caregiving.

More recently, Wicks (2001) in writing about a variety of ways to reduce stress suggests developing "safe zones" and goes on to list a variety of them: time for meditation; spiritual and recreational reading –including the diaries and biographies of those whom we admire; some light exercise; opportunities to laugh offered by movies and by cheerful friends; a hobby, e.g. gardening; phone calls to family and friends who tease you; and involvements in projects that renew.

Way of Understanding

As a youth I longed for the day when I could drive a car. Like any adolescent I considered that obtaining a license to drive would signal a major step toward maturity and independence. In my family before one obtained a license or even signed up for the driving exam, one had to first pass a series of tests given by my father. You see my father was a seasoned truck driver and he knew quite a few of the challenges and strategies of safe driving.

One Saturday morning Dad allowed me to drive his 1966 stick shift Chevy Impala. As we drove along I came upon a familiar hill with a steep incline, which had at the top a light that changed to red as I approached. How often had I traveled this way to school on the bus without realizing what a challenge the light at the top of the hill represented for my abilities as a new driver. Indeed that day on that hill with that light became one of the supreme tests of my adolescence.

As I waited for the light to turn to green I noticed that a large truck had pulled up close behind me. I began to sweat, knowing that I would have to quickly coordinate my feet: by letting go of the clutch pedal with my left foot and releasing the brake pedal with my right foot, and then almost instantaneously but not too forcefully placing the same foot on the accelerator. As I prepared to do so I looked in the rear view mirror at the face of the truck driver behind me and the truck driver Dad beside me. It almost seemed that both drivers had teamed up into some kind of conspiracy of men. Then, the truck driver beside me advised, "Son, this is what separates the men from the boys." The light turned green and I hesitated at first, and then somehow managed to move both feet with split second coordination. With my left foot I released the clutch and with my right released the brake and hit the accelerator. But I had to be careful how hard to hit the accelerator. Too little and the car would fall back into the truck behind me, too much acceleration and the car would lunge ahead and might put my Dad through the windshield. Somehow I managed to successfully complete the maneuver for the first time in my life. As I did so I noticed that the truck driver behind me was smiling and had given me a thumps-up. More important, the man beside me had a smile on his face. Having coordinated the tricky driving maneuver, I had arrived at an understanding not only about driving but about myself as a young adult.

To arrive at a practical and not just a theoretical understanding of pastoral caregiving requires us to make coordinated maneuvers. In some ways, caregiving resembles driving a car with a stick shift. As we listen to a person in need, we need to be prepared to make subtle shifts in our responses. Such responses include reflecting the person's feelings, paraphrasing his/her statements or making summarizations. These responses are important ways of communicating to the person-in-need that we are listening attentively and that we are focused on what is being said. Here is one example:

Vignette 1:

Description: After worship a middle-aged man seeks out his pastor and confides in him some of the struggles that he is having in his marriage. Their conversation includes the following responses.

Person-in-Need: "I am really tired of the way my wife treats me. She never asks me about what is happening in my life or what is worrying me at work." Pastor's Paraphrase: "By your wife's not asking you about your life and work, you feel neglected and you are tired of it?"

Pastor's Reflection of feeling: "You feel frustrated and perhaps angry about her not seeming to care about you."

After about 15 minutes of listening and making such responses, the pastor makes a summary statement and then shifts the conversation into another gear by asking an open question.

Summarization: "Tom, you have been telling me how angry and frustrated you are with your wife, and how she leads you to feel neglected. I wonder if you would help me to understand more fully by telling me more about the ways in which you and wife communicate."

Understanding the Unconscious: Projections and Transferences

To be effective as a pastoral caregiver one must face the challenge of oneself. That is to say, I must know myself well enough so that my own needs and wounds do not get in the way of responding to the needs of the other. We may find comfort in Henri Nouwen's beautiful description of the caregiver as a "wounded healer." At the same time, in recognizing myself as a "wounded healer," I must be careful not to become a "healer who wounds." In this light, I recall the words of one of my supervisors who cautioned me to monitor my own needs so that my emotions do not "leak" in the presence of the person-in-need. Freud in his psycho-analytic system recognized the significance of this awareness in writing exten-sively of the phenomena of countertransference. In fact, he made the phenomena one of the cornerstones of his psychoanalytic methods. We need not be psycho-analysts, however, to monitor our feelings toward a person or the issues that a person brings to us. It is important though to sense when and how a person's issues flow into our own issues or prejudices.

> Vignette 2 On her first day as a chaplain intern Susan, whose mother had recently passed away, walked into a room where a family had assembled to say goodbye to their mother and grandmother. In greeting the family Susan suddenly found herself overcome with grief and even tearing up, and within a few minutes politely excused herself from the room. In reporting this event to her supervisor the next day, Susan admitted that while she could readily identify with the family's sorrow, their pain brought back the pain that she was still feeling and working through.

Of course, it is easy for us to understand the vulnerability in which Susan found herself. We might say that she was too close to her own "wounds" to be of much assistance to the family. On the other hand, Susan having over time pro-cessed her own loss, might be especially effective in a similar situation. Having faced the sorrow and sadness of the loss of her mother, she may become uniquely qualified to help those going through such a process. In this respect, she may be not only sympathetic (feeling-with) in identifying with a family, but also empathic in feeling-for them. What's more, she may be able to generalize the wounds that she has worked through as an instrument for other situations. The psychoanalyst Heinz Kohut, who described the generalized empathy as "vicarious introspec-tion," developed this use of self as an important form of empathy. Essentially such empathy involves using one's imagination to "experience-near" the emotions of the person-in-need by recalling one's own difficult emotions in facing a similar type of experience. While never the same, a caregiver can introspect imagina-tively and vicariously so as to understand a person's pain at an emotional, and not just at a cognitive, level. However, when using one's own experience as an instru-ment for the other, it should be emphasized that it is generally unwise to disclose one's own experience.

Vignette 3:
Todd serves as a campus minister. He was asked to speak with a second semester college senior, listed in fair condition, who had been in a serious car accident over the weekend. The student, Todd was informed, was quite upset and anxious about his future. When he met and listened to the stu-dent, Todd, who had never had a serious accident, did recall some of the anxieties that he had experienced as a senior, and also recalled some of the

worries that he had when his sister had faced serious health problems. In recalling and feeling his own past emotions, Todd was able to speak more empathetically to both the student and his family.

Hunches and Hypotheses

Pastoral care actually involves several disciplines and may be compared to winemaking, which combines art and science and requires a great amount of patience and endurance over time. Pastoral care does require a certain amount of science. Not only does the caregiver require a capacity to make some judgments based on science (e.g. distinguishing some of the basic psychopathologies), but also some knowledge of the scientific method. For example, in evaluating the issues presented by a person-in-need, it is helpful for the caregiver to formulate systematically what the problem is and what the proper responses might be. This does not mean that one formulates a full-fledged diagnosis, but a putative pastoral diagnosis can be formulated for the purpose of the caregiving exchange so as to answer the questions at hand. In this respect, a caregiver may wish to formulate a working hypothesis as to the reasons behind the central concerns presented by the person-in-need. Just as a scientist is curious as to what makes things tick, a caregiver may be curious as to how this person is having this problem at this time of life.

At the same time, a caregiver may also want to have the attitude of an artist who imagines the world that the person-in-need recreates and intuits new possibilities. After listening to the person's concerns, the caregiver-as-artist may intuit an insight or wonder if the person has imagined other ways to look at the issues. Moreover, the caregiver may listen for the way that the person-in-need tells his/her story through metaphors and specific words. In Murray's (1974, p. 482) eloquent description, listening is seen as an exercise of attending to someone's way of metaphorizing life experiences. A couple may describe their marriage as one which "moves slowly but definitely from that imagining of life together as a bind, an imprisonment, a drudgery, a merry-go-round to an imagining of marriage as a delightful game of see-saw, an ongoing education in the subtleties and beauties of intimate relationships, a liberation from the horrors of loneliness, or a launching pad from which they leap together and brave the unknown of life's future with the strength that is derived from each other other's presence.

Cox and Theilgaard (1987) share with Murray the belief that metaphor has transformative capacities. Applied within the caregiving context the metaphors, which persons-in-need choose to express their reality, indicate how they see their life story unfolding. The phenomenologist Paul Ricoeur asserts that such disclosure begins with the event of language. Following Ricoeur we might ask, what happens when a person-in-need speaks and the caregiver listens? Ricoeur (1975) makes a phenomenological distinction between the noetic and noematic. He thereby allows us to conceive that the role of a caregiver is not only to listen to what a person intends (the noetic) but to listen for the meaning behind the sentences spoken (the noematic). That is to say, we seek to listen to the meaning that is greater than what the person actually intends. Through Ricoeur's approach, we can understand the therapeutic-client encounter as an interactive exchange whereby through the speaking and the listening of each person the meaning of experience is transferred. Such a transfer of meaning, for Ricoeur, is enhanced by means of metaphor and, at times, even more profoundly performed by means of symbol. Ricoeur's theory of metaphor, moreover, suggests that the condition that takes on the transformative power of metaphor possible is the infinite potential of a sentence. It is through the sentence, whose structure allows for an infinite use of finite means, that metaphor's potential to transcend occurs. Such linguistic transcendence, in effect, allows for psychological transformation. That is to say, the metaphor's capacity to transcend allows for it to have a transformative role in therapy. The same may be said of the symbolic. Its transcendent capacity and transformative role, if we follow Ricoeur and Murray, would be at a more profound level linguistically and psychologically speaking.

For example, a person might describe her life situation as chaotic with everything in her future thrown up in the air. In response a caregiver might ask what the experience of things being "up in the air" is like and might she need to look at ways in which her life could become "less up in the air" and "more grounded."

Murray's presentation of word, metaphor, symbol and myth seems to be an application and an extension of Ricoeur's theory of language. In effect, Murray suggests that the capacities of language at each of these levels may transform a client's self-understanding away from disintegration and towards integration. Cox and Theilgaard (1987, p. xxvi) also view therapy as a transformative or mutative capacity of metaphor. For them metaphor helps a client to tell her disturbing story and is the vehicle whereby a therapist helps the client to "call something new into existence" (*poesis*) so that a new understanding of her story may be brought forth.

The Swiss philosopher, Max Picard, in his beautiful work, *The World of Silence*, describes the various ways silence creates a language in life. In lines that border on the poetic Picard believes deeply in the language of silence. For instance, in a chapter about "silence as the origin of speech," Picard (1952, p 25) writes:

> *When two people are conversing with one another...a third is always present: Silence is listening. That is what gives breadth to a conversation: when the words are not moving merely within the narrow space occupied by the two speakers, but come from afar, from* the place where silence is listening. That gives the words a *new fullness. But not only that: the words are spoken as if it were from the silence, from that third person, and the listener receives more than the speaker alone is able to give. Silence is the third person in such a conversation.*

Silence, then, may be seen as not only another modality of language, but

the modality from which all other modalities emerge. Indeed, concerning the therapeutic context, it has been said that silence is where the communication between
the client and therapist really happens.

In addition to the modality of silence and the previous ones, which have
been discussed, words, metaphor, symbol and myth, another modality is evident
within the therapeutic context. This is the language of gesture. Over the past two
decades the psychological literature has been filled with reams of information
about body language. Most significant has been the analysis of Maurice Merleau-
Ponty who in his masterpiece, The Phenomenology of Perception (1962, p. 197),
states:

> *It has always been observed that speech or gesture transfigure the body,
> but no more was said on the subject than that they develop or disclose
> another power, that of thought or soul. The fact was overlooked that, in
> order to express it, the body must in the last analysis become the thought or
> intention that it signifies for us. It is the body which points out, and which
> speaks.*

Gesture then represents the language of physiognomy and as such cannot
be discounted as an important vehicle for communicating meanings intended and,
especially, unintended between one person and another. Indeed, the pastoral psychologist Anton Boisen suggested as much when he spoke of the person as "the
living human document."

Whether through silence, gesture, words, metaphor, symbol or myth, a
client may be seen by a therapist as a living human document to be read and
interpreted in order to understand. The therapist, on the other hand, has the challenge to understand the living human document better than the document or client
understands himself or herself. Such is the quest of the therapeutic encounter and,
for such a quest to be undertaken and accomplished, different modalities of language need to be communicated and must be heard.

We have then in silence-gesture-word-metaphor-symbol-myth a chain of
language modalities that may be associated with one another almost like a symphony. The ears of the caregiver, then, must listen both selectively and compre-
hensively as if he/she were listening to a symphony. At first, words are heard and
then a metaphor, then perhaps a gesture and then silence and maybe a sudden
symbol is brought forth which in turn may suggest a person's myth. These are
different modalities of language, to be sure, but each modality provides an avenue
whereby one human being can listen and enter into the language world of another
for the purpose of a shared understanding.

Pastoral caregiving offers a unique dimension to the helping professions,
for it allows the caregiving interaction to include conversation about religious
concerns. Within the context of our discussion, we might say that pastoral caregiving
recognizes that the language of the Holy, while not necessarily directly spoken, is,
nevertheless, always implied in the therapeutic encounter. For the pastoral caregiver

this would suggest that within the framework of silence-gesture-word-metaphor-symbol-myth schema, there exists a willingness to listen to and for the Word of God revealed incarnationally in and through the language of the therapeutic encounter. Such a listening stance need not be explicit. Generally it is not. There, nevertheless, can exist for the caregiver an implicit awareness, that through a language modality, the Holy breaks in and becomes present. This awareness may lead to recognition by the pastoral caregiver that a deeper drama of discourse is taking place not only between the client and himself or herself, but between God and each of them. The language event of therapy may indeed be seen as a salvific event disclosed through different modalities at this time in this place between these two human beings. In this respect, the language modalities of silence-gesture-word-metaphor-symbol-myth are manifestations of the healing and salvific events of God's revelations being told in and through the language of caregiving.

Pastoral Insights via Correlational Method

An important strategy that serves to make caregiving pastoral is the use of the correlational method first developed as the method of critical correlation by Paul Tillich and later revised by David Tracy. As eloquently described by Charles Gerkin (1994) in his important work, *Living Human Document: Re-visioning Pastoral Counseling in a Hermeneutical Mode*, the correlational method involves comparing a caregiving context with a context in Scripture or another form of inspirational or wisdom literature. It need not and often should not be articulated to the recipient. However, by reflecting to oneself how a caring encounter might resemble a situation from Scripture, the caregiver may draw from his/her tradition of inspirational resources. For example, a caregiver formed in the Judaic-Christian tradition may turn to a passage in the Bible to correlate themes. So, for example, in helping a person-in-need to find hope one may recall something like Paul's words from Romans 8:25 ff on hope so as to support the caregiver's hope for the person-in-need. In order to provide hope the caregiver must believe that there is hope and a scriptural passage such as Romans 8:18-25 can provide and sustain such hope. Another instance may be found in Mt 10:7, where the caregiver as a "wounded healer" may find ministerial motivation in the phrase "what you have received as gift, give as gift" (New Jerusalem translation).

As may be seen, pastoral correlation involves the process whereby the caregiver engages both the experience of the person-in-need as well as his/her own experience with a wisdom tradition. Kinast (2000) describes this process as involving a retrieval whereby one recalls wisdom literature passages that serve to inspire a richer presence to the one in need.

Moreover for Kinast, the correlation process may also involve a reconstruction of a wisdom tradition, whereby a larger issue social issue may fit the context of concerns that faces the person-in-need. Such retrieval and reconstruction can serve as a means of befriending the tradition of one's pastoral presence to fit more effectively the situation at hand. For example, in serving a homeless woman, it may be helpful not only to retrieve for oneself a Scripture passage such as Mathew 25, but also to reconstruct the passage in light of contemporary culture, whereby the woman's homelessness may be seen as the product of an unjust system. In this respect, justice concerns may become important ingredients of one's caregiving context. A listening presence might not be adequate to the situation. A pastoral presence that engages by means of the correlational process of retrieval and reconstruction adds a broader context to serving the person-in-need. Indeed, it is one of the important constituents that make one's pastoral presence in caregiving uniquely pastoral in both breadth and depth..

Way of Intervening

Strategies of intervention are what make caregiving communication different from ordinary conversations and exchanges. Wicks and Rodgerson (1998) speak of caring for someone as a caring exchange that is formed around an intentional conversation. By this they mean that the conversation is not superfluous, but has a direction and purpose. With such a purpose in mind it would be helpful to discuss some of the important ways in which a caregiver's interventions respond to a person-in-need. These involve the following:

Advice Interventions

To give advice to a person-in-need is the quickest way to respond to a particular need. If a person is asking us for a suggestion or a recommendation about what to do, to respond with specific advice may be the quickest way to support the person. How easy it is to instruct a person as to what they should or should not do. Even easier is to tell them, this is what I would do if I were you. Such responses may be useful when speaking with a family member or a friend, but for caregivers it generally is the least effective form of responding. Sometimes advice-giving is simply based upon our opinion or worse, our prejudice. Even when our advice is founded upon solid information it might not be a form of caring exchange, for it may lead the person-in-need to act according to our will and not their own. This is especially important to consider when dealing with emotional exchanges. How often have each of us been tempted to reduce the anxiety around an emotional decision by acting primarily because of someone's suggestions and not according to our desires or beliefs. This is not to say that the caring exchanges of ministry do not involve the giving or receiving of advice. Competent care gives advice sparingly and with the intention of helping the person-in-need to make decisions based upon his/her capacity to choose, rather than depending upon me as a decision maker. As a general rule, when a person seeks advice that entails specific cognitive information in an area of the caregiver's competence, it is helpful to give it. The more emotional the need, however, the more cautious one should be in giving advice.

The same may be said about the urge to problem-solve. People who come to a caregiver with emotional needs do not so much seek answers to solve problems as responses to help them resolve their issues. Problem solving is fine for the calculus classroom or the chemistry laboratory, but not for a pastoral encounter where feelings and values are at stake. Within such an encounter it is important to keep in mind the wise words of the philosopher, "life is mystery to be lived, not a problem to be solved." Obviously the advice we receive as well as give is a source of guidance in the mystery of life, but just as important are the responses without advice. That is to say, the ways in which we respond to a person-in-need serve as an indication of guidance and involve more than what we say. A brief overview of some helpful responses will serve to make this clear and how they reveal the competence of a caregiver.

The Appropriateness of Self-disclosure

Since Freud first developed the art of listening it has been an axiom that a counselor should never self-disclose. Indeed, as noted above, what makes listening as a caring professional different from listening as a friend is that one brackets one's own concerns and needs for the sake of the client. In recent years however, with the emergence of feminine approaches to therapy, appropriate self-disclosure has been given serious consideration.

As presented by Jordan et.al. (1991) and by Walsh et.al.(2002), a case can be made for mutual self-disclosure or "mutual empathy" when such self-disclosure is viewed to be in the interest of the client. As we noted before, it is important that the pastoral caregiver not "leak" his or her emotions to the client. On the other hand, on occasion it may be strategically helpful to disclose one's own experience to a care recipient. In the eyes of "mutual empathy" proponents, such disclosure is especially useful between women as it typifies "woman's ways of knowing."

Questioning: Closed and Open

One of the most common mistakes in pastoral care centers around questions. So often a well-intentioned caregiver falls short of establishing an effective presence by asking too many questions. It is as if the caregiver equates caregiving with the amount of information that one can "dig out" of the person-in-need. In such cases a caregiver becomes like the detective "Joe Friday" who seeks and gets "just the facts" when feelings should be the focus. True, it is important to obtain some essential facts from the person-in-need so as to establish a sense of context, but one should seek to obtain such facts by asking questions carefully and sensitively. The difference between seeking facts and seeking feelings is seen in the distinction between closed and open questioning.

It should also be noted that questions could prove to be too open and lack specificity. This is especially true in cases when a caregiver asks the question, "Why?" Like lawyers, counselors should be wary of "why" questions, as there can be an almost limitless series of causes and determinants. Instead, in seeking to determine some of the reasons for behaviors or emotions, a caregiver might simply ask "How is it that…" or "Help me to understand how." Or "Would you tell me more about this experience?"

The following are some other examples of helpful and unhelpful questions:

Helpful Closed Question: Are you married? What sort of work do you do?
Unhelpful: Do you feel sad?
Helpful: Could you tell me how you felt?
Unhelpful: Are you angry at your spouse?
Helpful open question: Help me understand your anger at your spouse.
Unhelpful: Why are you feeling this way?
Helpful: How is it that you are feeling this way?

Having examined how significant closed and open questions can be we turn now to consider when it may be important to ask direct questions.

Caring Confrontation

Pastoral caregiving requires a great amount of emotional sensitivity so as to encourage a person-in-need to express her/his worries and wounds. At the same time, while emotional expressivity represents a path toward a person's growth, such a path may, at times, require a caregiver to consider the recipient's sense of responsibility. In recent years, some writers have challenged the counseling culture for allowing persons-in-need to examine and decide according to the criteria of their individual growth without taking into account the consequences of their decisions and actions. Some writers, such as Lasch (1991) and Vitz (1994), have accused counseling and therapists of having contributed to the creation of a culture of narcissism. Pastoral caregivers must be alert to such criticism so that the person in their care does not speak of issues without taking into account the moral context of their lives and the lives of others. That is to say, we must not allow for freedom without responsibility. Caring confrontation interventions are designed to help a person to face both the freedoms and responsibilities of decisions and actions. Once again the science and art of caregiving is revealed in the criteria for such interventions.

It is helpful to see caring confrontations as simply offering another perspective, both emotional and intellectual, to the person-in-need's situation. The challenge for the caregiver is to make such an offering without becoming authoritarian or telling the recipient what should or should not be done. Instead, one seeks to introduce perspectives that address values and virtue into the conversation by having the person explore the priorities and responsibilities that guide his/her life. In this respect, the caregiver wishes to empower the person-in-need with authority. That is to say, the caregiver seeks to help the person-in-need to examine and own those values and virtues that promote creativity and courageous responsibility for the decisions and actions of life.

Obviously, such a caring and confrontative process requires a certain amount of trust between the caregiver and the person-in-need. Consequently, the caregiver needs to evaluate carefully what to say and when to introduce it. The following vignette may be helpful in this regard.

Vignette 4:
Client Description: For several weeks Larry has been meeting with his pastor Louise about issues at work. He claims that his depression is only temporary and he does not need to see a therapist. He feels it has been helpful to speak with Louise and would like to see her once or twice more. Louise, however, has suggested that Larry see his primary care physician for a physical so that she can be sure that there is nothing physiological involved in his distress. That is to say, she recognized the importance of ruling-out any organic explanations to Larry's problems. At the beginning of their meeting Larry has informed her that he still has not called for an appointment.
Larry: " I know you have advised me to see my doctor, but I just don't think it is necessary."
Louise: "Larry, I wonder if we might look at your distress and your reluctance to call the doctor for an appointment in a different way. For example, suppose one of your employees had been calling in sick for a week or so and reported that he was not exactly sure what was wrong. He also related to you that he did not think a doctor's appointment was necessary. I wonder how you might respond to him."

It is important to note that Louise is attempting to present Larry with a different perspective as a means of inviting him to see his own issue from a broader perspective. Of course, Louise may be concerned and even annoyed by Larry's resistance to her suggestion. In her response, she seeks to refrain from criticizing his behavior. By making her suggestion she hopes to allow Larry to imagine how he would respond if someone resisted similar evidence coming from him.

Timing Interventions
How often have we felt someone say just the right thing at just the right time? We may have felt confused and a person's response led us to move toward clarity. Often friends and family members who know us well make an effort to time their remarks so that we may hear them with receptivity. The same is true in pastoral caregiving. We may feel strongly about what a person-in-need's problem pattern is, but it may not be the right time to make our intervention. What we have to say may be dead right, but the timing may all wrong. In a sense, telling the truth involves not just what is said, but how and when it is said. I do not mean to suggest that we should lie or become deceptive. I am saying that as pastoral caregivers we take into account the context and the content of our communication.

The interventions that we have considered represent just a few of many intervention strategies common in pastoral caregiving. As we have described above, attentive listening often means listening metaphorically. At the same time, the caregiver needs to consider the central issues requiring a response and then ask, Do I have the competence to respond effectively to the issues being expressed? If so, what strategies of listening would be effective? Are some of the person's issues beyond my competence and, if they are, how do I introduce the referral process without conveying a sense of rejection to the person-in-need? Such questions, as they are carefully considered and nuanced, demand the systematic approach of the scientist and the intuitive attitude of an artist.

Conclusion

This chapter's presentation of pastoral care has offered an approach, a method and various constitutive elements to foster a caregiver's presence to the contemporary soul. Certainly contemporary caregivers are faced with the enormous challenge of responding to persons in need within an increasingly complex context. The paradigm of responses proposed in this chapter is organized around Cheston's tripartite template of way of being, a way of understanding and a way of intervening. In addition, this paradigm is situated within a particular historical context of caring for the soul. The paradigm is admittedly from a Western perspective, but it should be noted that developments of caring for the soul and the self are also emerging from non-Western cultures. While beyond the purpose and parameters of this chapter, it is, nevertheless, important to mention that the future of pastoral ministry will be measured by the extent to which cross-cultural and interfaith perspectives of the soul are incorporated into pastoral models. Through such cross-cultural developments not only will the self be better served psychologically, but the pastoral care for the soul will be broadened and deepened. By so doing, pastoral caregivers of the present and the future will serve to fulfill the words of Paul to the Ephesians, "you will have the strength to grasp the breadth and length, the height and the depth until…you are filled with the utter fullness of God." (Eph. 3:18-19).

References

Cheston, S. (2000) A new paradigm for teaching counseling therapy and practice. *Counselor education and supervision* Vol. 39,254-269.

Cox, M. & Theilgaard A. (1987) *Mutative metaphors in psychotherapy: The aeolian mode* (New York: Tavistock, 1987).

Gerkin, C. (1994) *Living human document: Re-visioning pastoral counseling in a hermeneutical mode* (Nashville: Abingdon).

Holifield, E. B. (1983) *A history of pastoral care in America; From salvation to self-realization* (Nashville: Abingdon Press, 1983)

Jordan, J.V., Kaplan, A.G., Miller, J.B., Stiver, I.P., & Surrey, J.L. (Eds.) (1991) Women's growth in connection: Writings from the Stone Center. (New York: Guilford.)

Kinast, R. L. (2000) *What are they saying about theological reflection?* (New York: Paulist).

Lasch, N. (1991) The culture of narcissism: American way of life in an age of diminishing expectations.(New York: W.W. Norton).

Moessner, J. S. (1991) "A new pastoral paradigm and practice" in M.Glaz, & J.S. Moessner (Eds.), *Women in travail and transition: A new pastoral care* (Minneapolis: Fortress) 198-225.

Picard, M. (1952) The *world of silence* (Chicago: Henry Regnery Company, 1952).

Merleau-Ponty, M. (1962) *The phenomenology of perception* (New York: The Humanities Press.

Murray, E. L (1974) "Language and the integration of personality." *Journal of phenomenological psychology.* 480-495.

Murray, E.L. (1986) *Imaginative thinking and human existence* (Pittsburgh: Duquesne University Press).

Reuter, P. (1989) *Sex in the forbidden zone* (New York: J.P. Tarcher).

Ricoeur, P. (1975) *The rule of metaphor*, Toronto: University of Toronto Press.

Vitz, P. (1994) Psychology as religion: The cult of self-worship (Grand Rapids: W.B.. Eerdmans).

Walsh, B.B. Gillespie, C.K., Greer, J. M., & Eanes, B.E. (2002) Influence of dyadic mutuality on counselor trainee willingness to self-disclose clinical mistakes to supervisors. *The clinical supervisor.* 83-98.

Wicks, R.W. (2001) Safe zones. *The Catholic Herald* (June 28, 2001) http://www.catholicherald.com/wicks/01wicks/wicks0628.htm

Wicks, R.W. & Rodgerson T.E. (1998) *Companions in hope: The art of Christian caring* (New York: Paulist).

ABOUT THE AUTHOR:

Having received his doctorate in Pastoral Psychology from Boston University, Rev. C. Kevin Gillespie, S.J., Ph.D. serves as the Director of the M.A. program in Spiritual and Pastoral Care at Loyola College in Maryland. He is the author of the book, *Psychology and American Catholicism: From Confession to Therapy* (Crossroad, 2001). An Associate Professor in Loyola's Department of Pastoral Counseling and a Fellow in the American Association of Pastoral Counselors, Fr. Gillespie's ministerial experiences include pastoral counseling, spiritual direction and chaplainry.

Chapter 3
Cultural Diversity Perspectives in Pastoral Care & Counseling

by K. Elizabeth Oakes, Ph.D. Loyola College in Maryland

The Importance of Culture in Pastoral Caregiving

      Nearly two decades ago, Howard Clinebell observed, "The vigorous process of internationalization within the pastoral care movement in the last fifteen years has made it increasingly multicultural" (cited in Augsburger , 1986, p.8). Since then, the processes of globalization has made cultural significance a prevailing fact of life which we can no longer minimize or ignore in our understanding of the worldwide human condition. Judith Vallimont (1995) has written on the subject of cultural diversity and the unity of the church in the United States and concludes that one of the major challenges to this unity in contemporary times is bridging the gaps in Christian community created by a multicultural and pluralistic society.

      Vallimont (1995) voices a reality that is becoming a pressing need for pastoral communities to address. She writes:

> *We as church in the United States provide pastoral services to a population that is globally representative of the world. More specifically, we attempt to respond realistically to the "new immigrants" as well as to those groups already present, including those frequently referred to as "minority populations." Critical to this pastoral care is our concern to preserve the values of the cultural or ethnic groups while building a sense of community belonging. But how do we as church bridge differences and build one church?* (p.17)

      One fundamental premise is foundational to bridging differences – accepting that culture is holistic. We know intuitively and empirically that culture contributes to the psychosocial, religious, and physical dimensions that define us as individuals. In acquiring culture through the processes of enculturation within family and acculturation within society, we acquire our individual values, beliefs, social identity and worldview. David Augsburger (1986), author of *Pastoral Counseling Across Cultures* – a classic textbook and distinguished authority on its subject – states, "Culture is given to the human person. It simply is in our origins" (p.18).

      In the specific case of providing pastoral care to culturally different individuals, we may believe ourselves to be in strange company, indeed, when the persons who ask us for help are not like us in very important ways. These persons call us out of our psychological comfort zones and invite us to examine the limits of our compassion, tolerance, and attitudes toward the culturally-different. This special case of providing pastoral help to persons who are of a different gender, ethnicity, race, physical fitness, or age from ourselves also speaks to the quality of our training to provide such help. Therefore, when a clergy member or pastoral counselor is engaged by a person seeking counseling support or spiritual care, it is not *just* the presenting emotional problem or the family conflict or the relationship issue that the caregiver needs to understand, but he or she must have also a skilled awareness and understanding of the cultural context in which the problem exists.

If, for example, a Christian Armenian American mother whose family immigrated to the United States from Iran during the country's Islamic revolution in 1979 seeks pastoral help for depression after recently giving birth, it is not enough that the pastoral helper has good basic counseling skills and is knowledgeable about the symptoms of post-partum depression. The pastoral helper will want to understand how the woman's immediate and extended family determines and defines parenting roles within the adopted American culture. To provide relevant pastoral support for this individual, the caregiver needs to have an understanding of how cultural and historical religious beliefs may be contributing to the woman's distress. Of course, if it is determined that the woman needs psychotherapy and the helper is not trained as a clinical therapist, then an appropriate referral must be made.

The pastoral caregiver should know that enculturation begins at the moment of birth and, arguably, even before birth, where the mother's prenatal and postnatal experiences are all related to cultural practices associated with pregnancy and childbirth. Wimberly (1982) sees understanding the developmental aspects of culture as crucial and states:

> [I]mportant in . . .[cultural] understanding . . . is the recognition that families serve as the primary shapers of reality and meaning for newborn children. The quality of care within the home influences the way the child will become oriented to reality, develop a sense of identity, control impulses, learn cultural language symbols and values, and lay the foundation for developing meaning and a religious perspective on life. (p. 99)

In addition, within the context of cultural development is religious development, which is considered an important dimension of acquiring culture. Kliewer (1987) observes, " Just as who we are as individuals is determined to a great degree by our families of origin, so our religious identity is formed by our religious 'family of origin'" (p.9). It is this understanding of the developmental aspects of enculturation as well as the broader, cultural determinants of society (acculturation) that enables the pastoral caregiver to bring a culturally-enhanced perspective to the pastoral helping relationship.

The Interrelationship between Culture and Identity

As the pastoral helper increases in cultural understanding, two basic determinants of individual identity become paramount – worldview and cultural identity. There is a broad body of clinical and empirical literature on these two subjects (see Pedersen, Draguns, Lonner, and Trimble, 2002), so a brief overview is provided here for definitional purposes only. When a pastoral helper begins a counseling relationship, it is first important to recognize that the pastoral caregiver and the person seeking help are both defined by their respective cultures. An individual's worldview is developed over a lifetime of acquired attitudes, stereotypes, and biases, which define and sustain cultural identity. Worldview is supported by specific values and beliefs that are, for the most part, unconscious and influence the mutual perceptions of the pastoral helper and the helpseeker in the pastoral care relationship.

When we consider worldview, it is understood to mean one's conceptual framework or philosophy about life. It essentially speaks to how one thinks the world works. Worldviews have to do with how people perceive, value, and understand the passing of time, human activity, social relationships, and the relationships between humans and nature. It is apparent that people who have grown up under sociopolitical and economic oppression or conflict will develop worldviews defined by that reality.

Within the specific context of culture, the pastoral helper must be aware of the "etic" and "emic" cultural perspectives of worldview. An etic perspective views culture as universal and all encompassing. An emic perspective views culture as specific and unique. Because cultural awareness is largely unconscious and therefore "invisible", both the pastoral caregiver and the care receiver will likely view the world through an emic lens (which a dominant culture will also believe is "normal"), and will find it difficult to see the etic or wider, more universal aspects of culture.

However, every person embodies the universal, the cultural, and the unique. Augsburger (1986) emphasizes that each of us is like every other and more alike than we are different. Modern science has discovered no difference in the genetic makeup for humans and it is well documented that we share most of our biological heritage with other primates. Paradoxically and in contrast, each of us is defined by the cultural community in which we developed, and at the same time, each of us is uniquely individual, possessing a unique worldview and sense of identity. Augsburger addresses the paradox in this fashion:

> *Only when the universal is clearly understood can the cultural be seen distinctly and the individual traits respected fully; only when the person is prized in her or his uniqueness can the cultural matrix be seen clearly and the universal frame be assessed accurately. The universal unites us as humans, the cultural identifies us with significant persons, and the individual affirms our identity. (pp. 49-50)*

Exploring biblical tradition, DeYoung (1995) makes a clear case for the inclusion of both etic and emic perspectives:

> *While the Bible begins with the unity of humanity, it clearly demonstrates that God values the diversity that emerged within the human family. God honors by inclusion people who represent the wide range of cultural ex-*

pressions that continue to develop in this one human family. This rich mosaic of people is acknowledged and celebrated by the biblical authors. (p.2)

To become truly effective in assessing the etic and emic aspects of culture, the pastoral helper must consider the important and central dimension of worldview – cultural identity development. Understanding cultural identity development is pivotal to becoming a culturally-aware pastoral helper. Despite the lack of genetic differences between human groups and the lack of scientific evidence corroborating the existence of distinct, biologically determined racial groups, racial origin has been used as a primary factor in defining cultural identity development. In fact, racial identity is sometimes equated with cultural identity, especially in sociopolitical systems which distribute social and economic power based on skin color or other physical attributes.

The significance of racial identity development grew out of the seminal work of Bailey Jackson and William Cross, who developed Black Identity Development models in the early 1970s (see Sue & Sue, 1990; also Atkinson, Morten, & Sue, 1989). Their research interest during this time was precipitated by the social upheavals sparked by the combination of the civil rights movement, the Black power movement, and the feminist movement. Jackson's work subsequently seeded the research of several doctoral students who developed cultural identity development models of their own, including Jewish, Asian, Gay and Lesbian models.

Today, there are many identity development models, at least one for every affected minority or oppressed cultural group (eg. for the physically impaired and the elderly). A foundational model applied in research and clinical practice today is the Minority Identity Development Model by Atkinson, Morten, and Sue (1989). This model is a theoretical guide to understanding cultural identity development in oppressed minority groups in general. There are three counselor education objectives for the model: 1) to help counselors become familiar with the strong influences of socioeconomic, religious, and political discrimination on identity development in oppressed groups; 2) to become aware of the cultural differences *within* minority groups as well as differences between minority groups; and 3) to provide strategies for helping clients to change negative or maladaptive behavior associated with racial identity development.

There are also specific White identity development models available (see Hardiman and Jackson, 1997; also Helms, 1995). Rita Hardiman conducted the original research in this area when she studied under Bailey Jackson as a graduate student. Hardiman's research experience is informative. Hardiman initially attended a multicultural issues class taught by Jackson where he asked her why she had chosen the course. Hardiman who, at the time, had been working with Black and Hispanic juvenile offenders answered that she wanted to understand what made her charges 'tick'. Jackson's response was, "To do that you need to understand yourself."

This question propelled Hardiman into the racial identity development field and today she is a leading expert in White identity development. As a result of her research, Hardiman has provided both empirical and practical knowledge which shows how White people in the US (also known as European Americans) learn to internalize the dominant cultural values that relate to ethnic, racial, and gender identity. Similar to the Black identity development model, Hardiman's White identity development model consists of five stages: 1) the initial stage or "naïve" stage (presocial consciousness) of early childhood where racial distinctions are nonexistent; 2) the acceptance stage where family, friends, and media help to form the beliefs and value systems of the dominant culture which includes acceptance and maintenance of racial stereotypes and cultural biases (most White Americans are socialized to remain at this stage); 3) the resistance stage (or rejection stage) where the individual (after direct experience) starts to question the beliefs and values of the acceptance stage; 4) the identity redefinition stage where the individual begins to question self-identity as major beliefs of the acceptance stage are dismantled; and 5) the internalization or integration stage where the individual begins to apply a new awareness to living and experience, and is open to embracing the ideal of cultural/racial interdependence.

The ideal of cultural interdependence runs counter to the Western ethnocultural ideals of individualism and independence, which the pastoral helper must personally explore thoroughly in order to become an effective cross-cultural caregiver. Augsburger (1986) has written that the Western perspective prizes the development of autonomy and supports the individualistic values of freedom of choice and socioeconomic laissez-faire. Of themselves, these values of independence are worthwhile, but in a system of sociopolitical and economic oppression, they contribute to social isolation, loneliness, and competitive violence. These values, remarkably, also reinforce the phenomena of cultural encapsulation which characterizes Hardiman's acceptance stage in White identity development.

DeYoung (1995) provides a biblical perspective for the sense of normalcy derived from European American cultural dominance:

> Unfortunately, the oneness of the human family and the universality of God's love have been distorted in postbiblical times. Instead of living as one human family with many cultural expressions, we have divided ourselves by many classifications. By way of example, the modern invention that we call "racism" created a system of racial hierarchy that undergirded the superiority of one "race" of people, white Caucasian Europeans, for the purpose of cultural and economic domination. . . . One result of this artificial racial hierarchy has been the portrayal of the majority of people in the Bible as members of the . . . Caucasian race . . . [and] led to the belief that the important people in the Bible had to be white. (p. 6)

The fruit of racial and economic dominance for European Americans is the sense of belonging to a monolithic, "normal" culture which contributes to a deeper sense of cultural encapsulation. Augsburger (1986) has discussed cultural encapsulation at length and warns of its negative influence on the ability of pastoral counselors to effectively help persons who are culturally different. He warns:

> . . . *As in a fused family, the culturally encapsulated counselor is surrounded by a rubber wall of boundary assumptions from which new ideas effectively rebound. The person with few independent reflective ideas may function effectively and empathically with others who share the identical cultural perspectives and so facilitate appropriate adjustment within that culture, but such a counselor will be culturally oppressive to persons from another world of experience. (p. 23)*

Related to Augsberger's warning, DeYoung (1995) concludes, "In today's context of racial and ethnic fragmentation, it is essential to rediscover the wide cultural diversity of biblical peoples if we are ever to find our way back to the oneness of the human family" (p. 7). It becomes important, then, for the pastoral caregiver to become knowledgeable about his or her own worldview and cultural identity, the cultural identity of the care receiver, and how the interaction of the two impacts the helping relationship.

Cultural Differences and the Helping Relationship

When the pastoral caregiver begins to earnestly study different cultures, he or she may initially think that issues of difference, of diversity, exist only *between* cultural groups. It is important, however, for pastoral helpers to be aware of the fact that different cultural groups are also diverse *within*. This diversity within diversity, for example, can be overwhelming and confusing to new immigrants who, struggling to accommodate their own cultural differences within their acculturation process, discover that the host culture is anything but monolithic.

Wicks and Estadt (1993) have observed that pastoral helpseekers who have just moved from one country to another or from one region to another will most likely experience both emotional and psychological upheaval upon entering a new and unfamiliar culture. They note that cultural differences exist within the same country and, when these differences are also directly affected by varying political and economic conditions, the stress of acculturation increases. Wicks and Estadt conclude: "Therefore, even the cultural variances within countries must be noted by ministers if the pastoral care undertaken is to be meaningful. Knowing this, we can begin to see the great import, and sense the potentially significant interpersonal rewards, of being attuned to the nuances of cultural diversity" (p. vi).

Offering another, insightful perspective, Hickson and Kriegler (1996), working in South Africa, have made both similar and contrasting observations about cultural diversity. In their experience, they note that culture did not explain all the differences that existed between indigenous South Africans. People in the same ethnic group describe their experience of culture differently. The stereotype that all black South African men are alike is particularly unfounded. They have written:

A distinction between individual differences and cultural differences is important and must be adopted in order to have an accurate multicultural perspective. . . .Individual characteristics and cultural predispositions must not be confused. In understanding individual versus cultural differences, it must be remembered that all individuals are embedded in societies that forge their identities. (p.10)

When we wish to determine the influence of cultural differences on the nature of the helping relationship, pastoral counselor John Rieschick who works in Kenya, recommends we consider the essential elements of motivation, ability, and functioning for assessing the culturally-different helpseeker in a pastoral helping relationship. Rieschick (cited in Wicks & Estadt, 1993) based his recommendation from his work with native Kenyans who sought counseling out of significant need after unsuccessfully using their community support systems, or after finding none available. The importance of community is integral to identity in many African countries as well as to others. With respect to African self-identity, John Mbiti (1980) equates it to community identity: "I am because we are, and since we are therefore I am (p. 56)."

That Judeo-Christian theology and tradition also have their roots in community is posited as biblical fact, according to DeYoung (1995), who writes:

The Bible has much to say about community. In the very act of creating humanity, God initiated community. When God created humanity, the spiritual aspect of community began (God and human forging a relationship). In creating Adam and Eve, God initiated human community. From the beginning, God determined that community is indeed "the native climate of the human experience. (p.155)

By extension, Howard Thurman (as cited in DeYoung, 1995) understands that without community, people are bereft and long for togetherness with others and belonging to group. Both Thurman and DeYoung agree that life is empty of meaning when the experience of community is lacking. Thurman concludes, "Every person is at long last concerned with community. There is a persistent strain in the human spirit that rejects the experience of isolation as being alien to its genius ...community is the native climate of the human spirit" (in DeYoung, 1995, p. 155).

Yet, despite the truth of the necessity of human community, actual experience bears out to the contrary. Again citing DeYoung (1995), who poignantly observes:

Although we may be one family, it is easy to demonstrate that "community" is a rare experience in society. In many parts of the world, we find people isolated by the unique aspects of their humanity. Men and women, even in marriage, can find themselves lonely for someone who truly understands their journey. Parents and children under the same roof often live in worlds with dramatically different value systems. The opportunities of the rich versus those of the poor, the experiences of whites versus those of people of color, the perspectives of East versus those of the West, and the histories of indigenous peoples versus those of immigrants – all contribute to a multitude of differing worldviews. Our lifestyles are barely comprehensible to each other. These different, and sometimes conflicting, ways of understanding human existence have led to an experiential separation by race, culture, nationality, gender, age, economic, and the like. The breakup of the human family leads to using the "other" as a scapegoat for all the world's problems. It has brought us ethnic cleansing, holocaust, genocide, and a host of other ills. Discovering a humane and beloved community in the midst of such human diversity is indeed an imposing proposition. (pp. 153-154)

Furthermore, the Western values of individualism, independence, and egalitarian relationships run counter to the collectivistic values of tribalism, filial piety, hierarchical relationships, and community or tribal dependence. Consequently and by way of example, Rieschick (in Wicks & Estadt, 1993) understands that, as a matter of custom, value, and belief, the Kenyan seeks help from his community network of family and tribesmen before seeking personal help outside of it.

Augsburger (1986) also noted the importance of community and concludes that the implications for counseling and caregiving to individuals from collectivistic cultures are quite clear. He provides an optimistic perspective:

Where personalities are sociocentric rather than egocentric, where familial esteem is more crucial than self-esteem, where identity is more rooted in village (land), in tribe (kinship), in patrilineal solidarity (filial piety) than in self-actualization, counseling and care will have different beginning points, processes, and ends. Pastoral care around the world is, as it must be, as varied as the human family. (p. 16)

It would appear that diversity within and between cultures will lead the pastoral helper to discover diverse solutions in helping. Returning to the specific work of Riescheck in Kenya (cited in Wicks & Estadt, 1993), he notes that when tribal and family support is not available, Kenyans will generally enter counseling under acute stress, but nevertheless, are highly motivated to do counseling. Under these circumstances, Rieschick cautions that caregivers must be alert to the helpseeker's expectations. Since they have sought help outside the conventions of community support, Kenyans may view pastoral counseling interventions with superstition and expect a "magical cure." The caregiver must determine the helpseeker's *capacity* to participate usefully within a helping relationship, which normally includes the capability for self-awareness and self-insight. Depending on the receptivity of the helpseeker, Augsburger (1986) might add further that the pastoral helper must also be open to consulting with and, where appropriate, including traditional tribal healing practices to augment the helping relationship.

Further, Kacela (2003) addresses the potential conflict between the worldviews of the helpgiver and the helpseeker:

[A] skillful pastoral counselor can find ways of discerning points of connection between cultural worldviews that may be in conflict. By sorting through the conflicts individuals may find ways of developing solutions to difficult problems. I find [this] suggestion congruent with Christian experience. The commandment to love our neighbor as self accepts the necessity of making another's reality just as precious as our own rather than forcing our reality upon others. Moreover, a willingness to consider unknown experiences as valid goes a long way to understanding deep-rooted problems that are difficult to navigate. (p. 26)

There are specific and practical helping methods that are useful in working with the culturally-different help seeker. Rieschick (in Wicks & Estadt, 1993) advises against rapid-fire questioning and quick problem-solving. Consistent with the traditionally defined elements of pastoral presence, patience and acceptance are key methods for both encouraging and supporting the helpseeker. Carl Rogers' (1961) has observed, ". . . I find that the more acceptance and liking I feel toward [a client], the more I will be creating a relationship which he can use" (p. 34). Rogers went on to define the central element of acceptance – warm, positive, and unconditional regard – as invoking a sense of security in the helpseeker, inviting trust, and establishing rapport.

Additionally, Miller (1999) includes a unitive understanding of acceptance derived from both Eastern and Western religious perspectives, ". . . acceptance is the developed capacity to fully embrace whatever is in the present moment. It requires a spacious mind, an open heart, and strength to bear one's experience (p. 200)." The root meanings of acceptance refers from a Western perspective, according to Miller, to receiving, seizing, and catching God's Will; and from an Eastern view, seizing and catching reality as it is.

Yet, there is the stark reality that acceptance is difficult to cultivate. As Kliewer (1987) has remarked:

There is clearly a negative side to diversity as it is present in a human community and we must know what can go wrong when we bring dissimilar or heterogeneous types together. . . . "A large group of studies indicate that like people group together. Unlike ones do not. Heterogenity often reduces potential interaction to zero . . . ." The conclusion is clear. The more diversity, the less interaction. . . . Homogenity encourages intimacy and community; heterogeneity does not. (pp. 10-11)

Even so, Kliewer (1987) also acknowledges the positive impact of diversity. He sees diversity as providing conditions that lead to the cultivation of tolerance and to opportunities for "creative dialogue" (p. 13). Kliewer asserts that conflicts precipitated by diversity, when handled creatively, leads to conditions of acceptance. The larger pastoral experience is that conflict explored and negotiated leads to forgiveness, trust, and reconciliation. Resolution of conflict is an important understanding for healing within broken communities and for cultivating acceptance within the pastoral helping relationship.

Related to the pastoral helping requirement of acceptance, the pastoral helper must be skilled in his or her ability to gauge the helpseeker's current level of functioning and adaptability. This skill is helpful in determining the helpseeker's capacity to tolerate the affective tension (conflict) that arises when the helpgiver is culturally different. Wicks and Estadt (1993) also emphasize the need for the helper to be competent in basic helping skills that use open-ended questioning and paraphrasing which enables the helpseeker to explore areas of their lives that may be difficult for them to discuss. If the caregiver listens carefully and assesses the daily functioning of the helpseeker, this contributes usefully to understanding the extent to which the pastoral care and counseling will be helpful.

Cultivating a Culturally Sensitive & Cross-Culturally Effective Pastoral Presence

"Ethnic, cultural, religious, and racial backgrounds can become heritages to be prized, protected, nourished and cherished, as guides for life-style, but not as boundaries, barriers, or blocks to communication and cooperation between peoples" (Augsburger, 1986, p. 19). The degree to which the pastoral caregiver is open, culturally-aware, and can pastorally explore the contribution of culture to the problem, the helping encounter may approximate Martin Buber's (1970) "I – Thou" relationship. However, when negative cultural preconceptions and perceptions, stemming from unconscious elements of the pastoral caregiver's worldview and cultural identity, are allowed to unconsciously operate within the encounter, the relationship becomes what may be referred to as "I-You." The pastoral helper must also be aware of the potentially negative biases and stereotypes embedded in the worldview and cultural identity of the helpseeker which can work against building an effective helping alliance.

The helpseeker's biases, however, are mitigated by the depth of the caregiver's cultural sensitivity and cultural effectiveness. Hickson and Kriegler (1996) make these observances about the necessity for counselor sensitivity:

Many of the [cross-cultural training] models . . . encourage self-exploration and an awareness that practitioners are themselves a product of their own culture, class, language and experience. From this perspective there is a need to be aware and accepting of one's own cultural baggage and how it can impact on the helping encounter. Encapsulated theories and practices should be discarded and more appropriate interventions used that are grounded in respect for diverse clients' cultural beliefs and values.

In sum, both a sensitivity to the possession of an ethnocentric world-view and an awareness of how this will block authentic interaction are needed. (p. 12)

In the context of the larger community, the pastoral helper can contribute to the community's growing awareness and openness to diversity. Kliewer (1987) argues:

The reason openness is so crucial has something to do with the problem of resolution. Openness may lead to anger, but it also leads to communication. It is true that often people involved in dialogue may be angry, furiously angry at each other, but at least they are talking. And that is important, for dialogue creates the possibility of resolution. Undisclosed diversity and conflict cannot be resolved. They are like an undiagnosed illness which slowly but surely destroy the body they inhabit. (p. 28)

Without an authentic, open dialogue with our personal and community issues of diversity, we cannot become culturally sensitive. Additionally, Hickson and Kriegler (1996) believe that developing cultural sensitivity involves the need to become socially proactive. A pastoral helper cannot be blind to the problems within modern society and must assume responsibility for taking a social justice position in support of those who come for help. This view is especially relevant in American society where the dominant European American worldview, as Goodman (2001) observes, ". . . overtly and covertly promotes the normalcy and superiority of the 'advantaged' group and that group's right to domination and privilege" (p. 35).

Despite the increasingly popular movement to embrace diversity within the United States, Goodman (2001) concludes that the privileged worldview of the dominant European American culture (which is largely unconscious) is generally unaware and insensitive to its perpetuation of oppressive cultural biases and prejudices against racially and ethnically different cultural groups. As such, the conclusion drawn by Hickson and Kriegler (1996) regarding cultural sensitivity is especially relevant, "[T]he cross-cultural caregiver should . . . meet the world and the people in it in depth and to share in the same reality in a collaborative endeavor to effect change" (p.12). Further, the pastoral helper must rigorously examine his or her own cultural identity and courageously explore existing personal beliefs about people who are culturally different.

Goodman's conclusions about a privileged cultural group echoes the warnings of Augsburger and Hickson and Kriegler about the myopic effect and destructive encapsulation that results in a monocultural worldview. Augsburger (1986) argues: "One who knows but one culture, knows no culture. . . . To become culturally effective is a gift, a gift received through learning from other cultures, through being teachable in encounters with those who differ, and through coming to esteem other worldviews equally with one's own" (p. 18).

While becoming culturally effective is a challenging task for caregivers with a monocultural worldview, there is one central condition to effective pastoral helping - empathy - that is also the central condition for both cultural sensitivity and cross-cultural effectiveness. Empathy is a complex affective process that many erroneously believe they understand. Augsburger (1986) makes clear distinctions between empathy, sympathy, and a word of his own creation, "interpathy." All three have the Latin root term "pathos" which means "feeling with." Augsburger defines sympathy or simpatico as projective pathos which can be described as, "I feel the way you feel." With empathy, Augsburger discerns an intuitive pathos, which can be described as, "If I were having your experience, I'd feel to the way you feel." With interpathy, however, Augsburger , defines an imaginative pathos or, "If I believe as you do, lived in your culture and had your experience, I would feel the way you feel."

Empathy is at the heart of pastoral presence and it is the therapeutic motive force in the Rogerian way of being in counseling. This way of being is characterized in the counselor as unconditional regard for the helpseeker, authenticity of presence, nonjudgementalness, and emotional transparency. Deep empathy in the caregiver emanates peace, safety, and deep respect to the helpseeker, thereby promoting trust and willing self-disclosure in her or him.

However, empathy without cultural knowledge is empty and ineffective. While the culturally-different helpseeker may feel affirmed and supported during a helping session, they will come away still feeling misunderstood. Therefore, cultural knowledge becomes an important addition to empathy when one is cultivating a culturally effective pastoral presence. Cultural knowledge refers to the caregiver's awareness and education about cultural differences and about the influence of culture on behavior and functioning. The need for the pastoral helper to be open to continuing education is most important, especially in light of the rapidly growing and diverse immigrant groups that use pastoral services. Recommended resources in multicultural training are included at the end of this chapter.

Empathy, cultural knowledge, and cultural sensitivity approximates Augsburger's critical notion of interpathy. He explains that the culturally effective and intepathic pastoral caregiver has ". . . differentiated a self from the culture of origin with significant perceiving, thinking, feeling, and reflecting freedom to recognize when values, views, assumptions, and preferences rise from an alternate life experience" (Augsburger, 1986, p.23). In other words, the caregiver will acknowledge that his or her own cultural worldview is distinct from that of the careseeker, and will both honor and accept the careseeker's distinctiveness. Augsburger believes culturally-effective caregivers will have gained a personal interior freedom and flexibility that enables them to sit with persons of starkly contrasting, even oppositional, ideas and beliefs without prejudice, reactivity, or defensiveness.

As an example of interpathy, we can view Bonhoeffer as a case in point (cited in DeYoung, 1995):

> *Dietrich Bonhoeffer, a German-Christian martyr during the Nazi regime, developed a way of seeing the world through the eyes of others he called "the view from below." . . . Bonhoeffer's commitment to be faithful to God's call on his life to work reconciliation and social justice led him to understand the importance of solidarity with the oppressed. For Bonhoeffer, solidarity was not merely living with the oppressed; it was comprehending life from the perspective of the person who suffered. The "view from below" meant having the ability to see the world through the eyes of one who was being oppressed. (p. 178)*

In addition to "feeling with" helpseekers, helpgivers must also acquire effective cultural knowledge in order to gain comparative understandings of culturally-based spiritual belief systems. For example, Fukuyama and Sevig (1999) examine the relationship between worldview and spiritual journey for women, African Americans, and Native Americans. From a feminist worldview perspective, the authors conclude that women's spirituality ". . . emphasizes personal experience, empowerment, and liberation in the context of patriarchal values" (p.39). African American or Afrocentric spirituality derives from a worldview greatly influenced by West Africa, in which existence derives meaning in relation to God, nature, spirits, and the rhythms of life. As has become well-known, Native American spirituality is Earth-based and linked to a worldview that values the sacredness and spiritual universality of life.

Fukuyama and Sevig's (1999) understanding of Native American spirituality is consistent with DeYoung 's (1995) assertion that the process of *koinonia* can be instrumental in addressing diversity within the faith community:

> *. . . A spirit of koinonia brings great freedom. Individuals can be set free from the emptiness of material prosperity or the desperation of poverty by meeting at the common ground of koinonia. . . . [Koinonia] is "a cooperative sharing of talents and spiritual gifts toward the creation of an integrated, healed, and whole body." The koinonia community is embodied in the Native American understanding of the circle. The symbol of the "circle is self-defining; it defines the limits of the people." (p. 164)*

Fukuyama and Sevig (1999) also explore the spiritual journey from the perspective of three developmental models: 1) faith development (adapted from Fowler, 1981); 2) optimal identity development (a spiritual development adaptation of the minority identity development model cited earlier); and 3) stages of mystical awakening (adapted across Eastern, Western, and Sufi spiritual traditions). These developmental models emphasize the relationship between ego transformation and transcendence, and spiritual maturation.

Ethnocultural Assessment:
A Method for Collecting Cultural Information in Pastoral Caregiving

So far, the discussion has explored the need and rationale for cultivating cultural empathy, knowledge, understanding, sensitivity and effectiveness. As a practical matter, the culturally effective pastoral caregiver needs a method for sensitively collecting cultural information during a pastoral helper encounter. Returning to an earlier example - the Christian Armenian American mother and the contingent determination that the pastoral caregiver will be able to help her - an ethnocultural assessment is a good initial step in gathering information about her cultural background. Making specific reference to Armenian American subculture, Vontress, Johnson and Epp (1999) emphasize the importance of knowing that Armenian immigrants from Iran suffered significant religious oppression and ethnic discrimination during the Islamic revolution and also during the Iran-Iraq war when 100,000 Armenians fled the country. Further, Armenian refugees settling in the United States brought with them a cultural history rife with social, political, and religious conflict, including a brutal genocide at the hands of the Turks.

Additionally, the Armenian American subculture is defined by a collectivistic worldview which places high value on filial piety. In other words, the new Armenian American mother will likely embrace the Armenian cultural value that requires primary allegiance to the immediate and extended family, even at the expense of having established her own separate family. For this helpseeker and others like her, the ethnocultural assessment is useful in capturing information about cultural history and important ethnic values.

Information for the ethnocultural assessment can be collected while gathering information for a genogram. By definition, a family genogram reflects cultural history and, in developing one, the pastoral caregiver can explore significant cultural mores and values with the helpseeker as they relate to the presenting problem. According to Wimberly (1982), the genogram is an essential model for compiling the family's interactional history and is defined as, ". . . a structural diagram of a generational relationship (p. 121)." It includes the names of family members, their ages, and the specific dates of marriages, births, deaths, and divorces. While developing a genogram, the pastoral helper can explore important events and crises in the evolution of the family's history. It is during this process that particular patterns, connections, and traditions are identified as contributors to the general cohesion between family generations. The ethnocultural assessment can be adapted as an integral part of the genogram development.

There are five basic stages in an ethnocultural assessement as conceived by Frederick Jacobsen (1988): a cultural biography of the helpseeker, determination of the helpseeker's immigrant status and sociopolitical adaptation, the socioeconomic status of the helpseeker's family, the helpseeker's worldview and cultural identity stage, and a consideration of the pastoral helper's ethnocultural background and its likely contribution to the helping relationship. The Jacobsen model is to be used as a suggested guideline, not as a rule for cultural assessement and, as already mentioned, is ideally used in conjunction with developing a family genogram.

The use of ethnocultural assessment must be used sensitively and with the helpseeker's agreement. It is most effective with first- and second-generation immigrants, but is indicated for later-generation immigrants to further define the problem for which the person seeks help, or when the person is currently in a transcultural or a new acculturation process. Language differences between the helper and the helpseeker may present a major barrier to effective assessment. Ideally, the assessment should occur in the helpseeker's native tongue, which can capture the authentic emotional quality of the helpseeker's explanations.

Kacela (2003) also emphasizes the need to find a reconciling "future" story for careseekers who have been culturally oppressed. Citing his direct experience with African Americans, Kacela recommends:

Finding a future story is often the key to overcoming and transcending perceived troubles and realizing the prospects for change. African American parishioners can especially benefit from finding new stories for their future that may be hidden away. With pasts that are often mired in the hurt and pain of oppression and sequestered opportunities, black people are anxious for new ways of envisioning the future. Pastors that recognize the existing possibilities in one counseling session have the potential for initiating great change and imaging new futures with unlimited possibilities. (p. 34)

The Culturally-Competent Caregiver

As another matter of actual practice, the pastoral caregiver will find the identification of specific skills for cross-cultural counseling competency both instructive and adaptive in the helping relationship. David Augsburger is a pioneer in concretely defining those attitudes and behaviors a pastoral helper should adopt in order to become interculturally competent in caregiving. Augsburger's (1993) typology of cultural competencies is related to his exposition on the quality of pastoral presence and its application in providing care across cultures. Regarding presence, Augsburger (1986) has written:

. . . Presence requires an integration of self-awareness with an awareness of the other. The consciousness of being "with" another is not a superficial association but an openness from the center of one's existence. . . . Presence is central to all forms of ministry. Being and doing are inseparable. It is being which authenticates doing, doing which demonstrates authentic being. (pp. 37-38)

As a basis for counseling competency, an authentic, pastoral presence is the motive force beneath truly effective caregiving. It is this presence that underscores the "five measureable and teachable characteristics" that Augsburger (1986) uses to define culturally capable counselors. He lists these characteristics as follows:

1. Culturally aware counselors have a clear understanding of their own values and basic assumptions.
2. Culturally aware counselors have a capacity for welcoming, entering into, and prizing other worldviews without negating their legitimacy.
3. Culturally aware counselors seek sources of influence in both the person and the context, both the individual instance and the environment.
4. Culturally aware counselors are able to move beyond counseling theory, orientation, or technique and be effective humans.
5. Culturally aware counselors see themselves as universal citizens, related to all humans as well as distinct from them.

(p. 21)

Lastly, it is important to note that, in 1992, Derald Sue and colleagues published multicultural counseling competencies intended for adaptation and practice by clinical counseling practitioners. These competencies were divided into the three categories of cultural self-awareness, awareness of cultural worldviews of clients, and application of appropriate counseling interventions and techniques. Since 1992, these competencies continue to be refined and are in the process of being clinically operationalized (see Arredondo, et. al., 1996) along the original three categories, and each of these, in turn, are explained according to specific attitudes and beliefs, cultural knowledge, and counseling skills.

Summary
The importance of diversity in the church and in pastoral care has taken on more salience as globalization becomes a fact of everyday life. Pastoral caregivers are encouraged to become more effective in pastoral ministry by increasing personal awareness, acceptance, and sensitivity to careseekers who are culturally different. Biblical tradition and examples of pastoral care within other cultures point to the power of community and communication in multicultural encounters. Further, pastoral care and counseling across cultures should be characterized by embracing universal values and beliefs, and celebrating different customs and traditions.

Cultural identity and worldview are critical to cultural understanding, so the pastoral caregiver needs to become familiar with the developmental aspects of worldview and identity. The caregiver is also cautioned against cultural encapsulation and the detrimental effects it has on helping relationships with people from other cultures. The basic and most instrumental skill in helping across cultures is empathy. In addition, strong helping skills are conducive to inviting openness and trust. The caregiver will also need to determine the careseeker's motivation and capacity for engaging in a helping relationship.

The pastoral helper may find it useful to collect information about culture by conducting an ethnocultural assessment. Further, there are specific multicultural counseling competencies that can be adapted to helping relationships as they are designed to augment helping skills with diverse helpseekers. Pastoral caregivers are strongly encouraged to seek additional information and training in multiculturalism.

Where To Go For More Information
1. *Microtraining and Multicultural Development* – Videos, Tapes, and Books
   Microtraining Associates
   25 Burdette Avenue
   Framington, MA 01702
   Telephone: 888-505-5576; e-Mail: info@microtraining.com;
   Web Address: www.emicrotraining.com
2. *National Multicultural Conference and Summit 2005*
   c/o American Psychological Association
   750 First Street, NE
   Washington, DC 20002-4242
   Contact: Wendy Anderson, c/o Multicultural Summit 2005
   686 S. Arroyo Parkway, Suite 221
   Pasadena, CA 91105
   Telephone: 626-683-8243; e-Mail: www.wowproductions2@earthlink.net
3. *Association for Multicultural Counseling and Development*
   and *Association for Gay, Lesbian, and Bisexual Issues in Counseling*
   c/o American Counseling Association
   5999 Stevenson Avenue
   Alexandria, VA 22304
   Telephone: 800-347- 6647
4. *California Newsreel* – Films and Videos for Social Change
   500 Third Street, #505, San Francisco, CA 94107
   Telephone: 415-284-7800; e-Mail: contact@newsreel.org;
   Web Address: www.newsreel.org

References

Arrendondo, P., Toporek, R., Brown, S. P., Jones, J., Locke, D.C., Sanchez, J., & Stadler, H. (1996). Operationalization of the multicultural competencies. *Journal Multicultural Counseling and Development*, 24, 42 – 78.
Atkinson, Donald R., Morten, George & Sue, Derald Wing. (1989). *Counseling American minorities: A cross-cultural perspective.* (3rd ed.). Dubuque, IA: Brown Publishers.

Augsburger , David W. . *Pastoral counseling across cultures.*
Philadelphia: The Westminster Press. (1993). Cross-cultural pastoral psycho-
therapy. In R.J. Wicks & R.D. Parsons (Eds.), *Clinical handbook of pastoral counseling: Volume 2* (pp. 129-143). New York: Paulist Press.

Buber, Martin. (1970). *I and thou.* New York: Simon & Schuster.

DeYoung, Curtiss P. (1995). *Coming together: The Bible's message in an age of diversity.* Valley Forge, PA: Judson Press.

Fowler, James W. (1981). *Stages of faith: The psychology of human development and the for meaning.* San Francisco: Harper Collins.

Fukuyama, Mary A. & Sevig, Todd D. (1999). *Integrating spirituality into multicultural counseling.* Thousand Oaks, CA: Sage Publications.

Goodman, Diane J. (2001). *Promoting diversity and social Justice: Educating people from privileged groups.* Thousand Oaks, CA: Sage Publications.

Hardiman, Rita & Jackson, Bailey. (1997). Conceptual foundations for social justice course. In M. Adams, L. Bell, & P. Griffin (Eds.), *Teaching for diversity and social justice : A sourcebook* (pp. 16-29). New York: Routledge. Westport, CT: Greenwood Publishers.

Hickson, Joyce and Kriegler, Susan. (1996). *Multicultural counseling in a divided and traumatized society.* Westport, CT: Greenwood Press.

Jacobsen, Frederick M. (1988). Ethnocultural assessment. In L. Comas-Diaz & E. H. Griffith (Eds.), *Clinical guidelines in cross-cultural mental health* (pp. 135-147). New York: John Wiley.

Kacela, Xolani (2003). One session is enough: Pastoral counseling for African American families. *American Journal of Pastoral Counseling,* 6(3), pp. 21-36.

Kliewer, Stephen (1987). *How to live with diversity in the local church.* Washington, DC: The Alban Insitute.

Mbiti, John. (1970). *African religions and philosophy.* Garden City, NY: Doubleday & Company.

Miller, William R. (Ed.) (1999). *Integrating spirituality into treatment: Resources for practitioners.* Washington, DC: American Psychological Association.

Pedersen, Paul B., Draguns, Juris G., Lonner, Walter J., & Trimble, Joseph E. (Eds.) (2002). *Counseling across cultures.* Thousand Oaks, CA: Sage Publications.

Rogers, Carl R. (1961). *On becoming a person.* Boston: Houghton-Mifflin.

Sue, Derald W. & Sue, David. (1990). *Counseling the culturally different: Theory and practice. (3rd Ed.).* New York: John Wiley & Son.

Sue, Derald W., Arredondo, P., & McDavis, R. J. (1992). Multicultural counseling Competencies and standards: A call to the profession. *Journal of Counseling and Development,* 70, 477 – 483.

Vallimont, Judith. (1995). Unity beyond all understanding: being church today. *The Catholic World,* 238(1423), pp.17-22.

Vontress, Clemmont E., Johnson, Jake A., & Epp, Lawrence R. (1999). *Cross-cultural counseling: A casebook.* Alexandria,VA: American Counseling Association.

Wicks, Robert J. & Estadt, Barry K. (Eds.) (1993). *Pastoral counseling in a global church: Voices from the field.* Maryknoll, NY: Orbis Books.

Wimberly, Edward P. 1982. *Pastoral counseling & spiritual values: A black point of view.* Nashville: Abingdon.

ABOUT THE AUTHOR:

Dr. Oakes has a broad generalist background covering more than 30 years of professional experience in academia, government, business, ministry, and counseling. She is currently assistant professor and director of academic operations in the pastoral counseling graduate program at Loyola College in Maryland. She has published articles on spirituality and counseling, and her current research is in the counseling areas of cultural diversity, spirituality and addiction rehabiltation.

Chapter 4
Religion as a Meaning System:
Implications for Pastoral Care & Guidance

by Israela Silberman Ph. D. Columbia University

"I sometimes think of religion in terms of medicine for the human spirit. Independent of its usage and suitability to a particular individual in a particular condition, we really cannot judge a medicine's efficacy"
                    The Dalai Lama, *Ethics for the New Millennium*

      The goal of this chapter is to describe the view of religion as a system of meaning, and to discuss some relevant implications of this view to pastoral care and guidance. The chapter starts with an example of the different meanings religion can give to coping with adversity. The second part describes the concept of meaning systems and their development, and the view of religion as a somewhat unique system of meaning. The third part describes possible positive and negative impacts of religion as a meaning system on individual and societal well-being — particularly on self esteem, self efficacy, emotional well being, coping, and on interpersonal relations. The chapter concludes with a discussion of implications of the view of religion as a meaning system for pastoral care and guidance.

      In his best-selling book "When Bad Things Happen To Good People", which was written following the death of his young son, Rabbi Harold Kushner (1989-a) says that in his interactions with members of his congregation the most important and most frequently asked question is: "Why do bad things happen to good people?" He suggests that the psychological/ theological basis to this question is the fact that the following three religiously based claims are not consistent: 1) "God is good;" 2) "God is responsible for everything that is happening in the world;" 3) "Bad things happen to good people." Kushner's solution to this seeming inconsistency is to change the second claim. Instead of it he proposes the principle that God neither causes or prevents tragedies. Tragedies are caused by other people or by some randomness in the universe. The role of God, according to Kushner, is to give hope, courage and the perseverance to overcome difficulties. God encourages people to help each other by utilizing their intelligence, love and compassion.

      Rabbi Shloma Majeski (1995), who struggles with the same issue in his book "The Chassidic Approach To Joy", describes the more traditionally religious approach to the issue. He proposes to solve the seeming contradiction by refining and modifying the third claim: "Bad things happen to good people". Instead of that claim he proposes the principle that "Everything that happens is positive in nature". Rabbi Majeski states that there are two kinds of goodness: goodness that is openly apparent, and goodness that is disguised. When the goodness seems to be disguised he suggests remembering that life is a large puzzle with many pieces, of which human beings, unlike God, possess only a small portion. He adds that occurrences that appear negative are merely tests that could enable people to reach a higher spiritual level. In other words, when things seem negative it is because human beings with their limited understanding of reality do not understand God's plan for them or for the universe. A known metaphor in this context (Kushner, 1989-a) is that an ignorant person observing a surgical procedure would suspect that the surgeon is torturing the patient instead of understanding the reality in which the surgeon is trying to save the patient's life.

According to Rabbi Majeski, the internalization of these principles would help individuals cope when seemingly undesirable things happen. The denial of these principles would mean, according to him, that a person does not accept God's plan. That, in turn, would lead to sadness, depression, hopelessness and anger. Kushner (1989-a), on the other hand, criticizes the traditionally religious approach, which has been represented here by Rabbi Majeski, by saying that it involves denial of the reality of negative events, teaches people to blame themselves, and might increase unhealthy and unjustified guilt feelings. He adds that this approach is meant to protect God, not to relieve suffering, and that in actuality it may make people hate God.

Both Rabbi Majeski and Rabbi Kushner are deeply religious individuals who are considered to be influential spiritual leaders. Both of them have helped numerous individuals in their efforts to cope with adversity. Their different approaches exemplify the power religion can have as a source of meaning in people's lives. They also demonstrate the wide range of meanings religion can offer in the context of coping with adversity.

Within the context of pastoral caring and guidance, which of the above approaches should be encouraged? Based on the following analysis of religion as a meaning system, as well as on varied reactions of students and of mourning friends to these two approaches, I would like to suggest that the answer to this question would not be easy, and that this question demonstrates the challenging role of clergy in the context of pastoral care.

Religion as a Meaning System

In their everyday lives, individuals operate on the basis of personal beliefs or theories that they have about themselves, about others, about the world of situations they encounter and their relations to it. These beliefs or theories form idiosyncratic meaning systems that allow individuals to give meaning to the world around them and to their experiences, as well as to set goals, plan activities and order their behavior (e.g., Bowlby, 1969; Dweck, 1996, 1999; Epstein, 1973, 1985, 1990; Higgins, 1989, 2000; Janoff-Bulman, 1992; Janoff-Bulman & Frieze, 1983; Kelly, 1955; Lerner, 1980; Loeb (Silberman) et. al., 1994, 1998; Mischel, 1973; Pepper, 1942; Silberman, in press-a; Whitehead, 1929; 1938).

Meaning systems usually contain descriptive beliefs as well as motivational or prescriptive beliefs. The major descriptive postulates of a meaning system are concerned with the nature of the person (a self theory; e.g., "I am competent"), the nature of the world (a world theory; e.g., "the world is just"), and propositions relating the two (e.g., "I can change the world"). Such postulates may also include contingencies and expectations regarding the world, other people and the self. e.g., "good people should get awarded" or "the world will improve in the future". Major motivational or prescriptive postulates are broad generalizations about how to behave in the future in order to obtain what one desires and avoid what one fears (Epstein & Erskine, 1983, Higgins, 2000). It has been suggested that the construction of such meaning systems is necessary for humans to function in the world. Epstein (1985), for example, explains that meaning systems develop in order to fulfill four basic motives; namely, to maintain the stability and coherence of a personal conceptual system, (while assimilating the data of experience), to maintain a favorable balance of pleasure and pain over the foreseeable future, to maintain a favorable balance of self-esteem, and to maintain a favorable relationship with significant others.

A growing line of research has supported the idea that people's meaning systems are very important in everyday life and may be of particular importance in predicting general patterns and individual differences in coping with adversity. Religious and optimistic beliefs, as well as beliefs about a just world, personal vulnerability and malleability of self and others are some of the beliefs that are important in this context (e.g., Dweck, 1999; Janoff-Bulman, 1992; Janoff-Bulman et. al., 1983; Lazarus & Folkman, 1984; Loeb (Silberman) et. al., 1994, 1998; McIntosh, Silver & Wortman, 1993; Perloff , 1983; Rubin and Peplau, 1975; Pargament, 1990, 1992, 1997; Pargament et. al., 1990, 1992; Pargament, Magyar & Murray-Swank, in press; Park, in press; Park & Folkman, 1997; Scheier & Carver, 1985; Silberman, in press-a, Silver, Boon & Stones, 1983).

In similar ways to any other non-religious meaning systems (e.g., Higgins, 2000 for a review of basic cognitive processes in social cognition), religion functions by serving as a lens through which reality is perceived and interpreted (McIntosh, 1995). Like other meaning systems (e.g., Epstein, 1990; Higgins, 2000; Janoff-Bulman, 1992; Silberman, in press-a), religion can also influence the formation of goals for self-regulation, affect emotions and influence behavior (e.g., Batson & Ventis, 1982; Emmons, 1999; Geertz, 1973; James, 1902; Pargament, 1992, 1997; Park et. al., 1997; Silberman, in press-a; silberman, in press-b; Silberman et. al., 1999, 2000, in press).

The Uniqueness of Religion as a Meaning System

Yet, religion as a meaning system is unique in that it centers on what is perceived to be sacred, such as conception, experience, or expression of higher powers, transcendent forces or Personal Beings (cf. Pargament's definition, 1992). This connection to the sacred can be shown, as demonstrated below, in each of the components of the meaning system, namely, beliefs, contingencies, expectations, and goals, as well as in prescriptive postulates regarding emotions and actions (see Pargament et. al., in press; Silberman, in press-a).

Self and World Beliefs: When religion is incorporated into the meaning system of a person, conceptions of the sacred are connected to beliefs about the nature of people, of the self, of this world, and of whatever may lie beyond it. E.g., different religious systems may include beliefs about humans as being sinful or Godly, and of the world as being evil or holy.

Contingencies and Expectations: Religious meaning systems often include beliefs regarding contingencies and outcome expectations. One of the most common contingencies is that righteous people should be rewarded for their good deeds, while sinners should be punished for their actions. Such systems of meaning may also teach the circumstances under which people need to apply certain rules. For example, the circumstances under which one needs to treat others in loving and compassionate ways, versus the circumstances under which one needs to punish, fight or kill others (Hunsberger & Jackson, in press; Oman and Thoresen, 2003; Tsang, McCullough & Hoyt, in press). Such systems may include self-efficacy expectations regarding the ability of individuals to change themselves and the world around them (The Dalai Lama, 1999; Thurman, 1998). They may also include positive or negative expectations regarding the future of the world, ranging from predictions of utopian redemption to destructive apocalypses (Silberman, Higgins & Dweck, in press).

Goals: On the level of goals, religious systems basically encourage the ultimate goal of connecting or adhering to the sacred, but any goal, ranging from benevolence (Schwartz & Huismars, 1995), forgiveness (McCullough & Worthington, 1999), and altruism (Batson et. al., 1982) to goals of destruction and supremacy (e.g., Hunsberger et. al., in press) could take on religious value by virtue of connection to the sacred (Silberman, in press-a).

Actions: On the level of actions, religious systems usually prescribe actions that are considered to be appropriate or inappropriate (Pargament, 1997). While some actions are perceived as prototypical religious or spiritual (e.g., the act of praying), each and every aspect of human life may become connected to the sacred and receive a special power through the process of sanctification (e.g., Pargament, et. al., in press).

Emotions: Religious meaning systems may influence emotions in several ways. They may directly prescribe appropriate emotions and emotional levels or they may include beliefs, goals or actions that may impact emotions (e.g., Pargament et. al., 1995; Pargament et. al., 2000; Sethi & Seligman, 1993; Silberman, in press-a, Silberman, Higgins & Dweck, 2001).

Religion as a meaning system that is centered around the sacred is one of the few types of meaning systems that can meet the basic organismic need for self-transcendence (Sheldon and Kasser, 1995), a striving that has especially strong relations with well-being (Emmons, 1999 and in press; Emmons, Cheung & Tehrani, 1998).

Beyond that, religion as a meaning system is unique in its ability to facilitate the fulfillment of an exceptionally wide range of basic needs in addition to the spiritual one — the search for meaning in the world and for the self, a search for comfort that includes a search for shelter from the world as well as a shelter from human impulses, a search for physical health and a search for a community, which includes both a search for intimacy and a search for a better world (Pargament, 1997).

This comprehensiveness of religion is consistent with the description of spiritual strivings as instrumental for accomplishing other strivings. It is also consistent with the view of religion or spirituality as able to give unity to all other concerns (Tillich, 1957), and to serve as an integrating framework which reduces the overall amount of conflict within a person's goal system and fosters coherence in personality (Emmons, 1999 and in press; Emmons et. al., 1998; Pargament et. al., in press).

The description of the uniqueness of religion as a meaning system can not be complete without an emphasis on its special power of meaning-making that is exceptional both in terms of its comprehensiveness and in its quality; i.e., the type of meaning that it offers. In terms of comprehensiveness, religion offers meaning to history from the moment of creation until the end of time, as well as to every aspect of human life from birth to death and beyond (Emmons, in press; Pargament et. al., in press; Silberman et. al., 2000; Silberman et. al., in press).

Religion, as a source of meaning-making, has also been described as qualitatively unique in its ability to propose answers to life's deepest questions (Myers, 2000, Pargament et. al., in press) and, unlike other philosophical meaning systems, to do that in a way that satisfies "the need to know that somehow we matter, that our lives mean something, count as something more than just a momentary blip in the universe," and in a way that brings hope (Kushner, 1989-a,1989-b). Beyond that, religion has been described as a powerful source of meaning even under the most testing circumstances when stressful events can not be repaired through problem solving strategies, and where other basic personal beliefs, such as the belief in personal invulnerability, the perception of the world as meaningful and comprehensible and the view of ourselves in a positive light may be shattered or at least seriously questioned (Jannoff-Bulman, 1992; Jannoff-Bulman et. al., 1983 on the effect of victimization on basic beliefs; Park, in press; Park et. al., 1997; Pargament, 1997 and Pargament et. al., in press, on the role of religion in coping).

In sum, religion as a meaning system is similar to other systems in its structure and functioning, yet it is unique in being centered around what is perceived to be the sacred, in the many basic needs that it seems to be able to fulfill, and particularly in its unique ability to fulfill the need for transcendence, and in the comprehensive and special way in which it fulfills the quest for meaning.

The learning, development and change of meaning systems

The learning of meaning systems involves the learning of the contents of the systems, namely, beliefs, contingencies, expectations and goals, as well as prescriptive postulates regarding emotions and actions (Silberman, in press-a). In addition, such learning can involve knowledge about how to connect to the meaning system. For example, one can learn how to connect to religious meaning systems in internal, external, quest or fundamentalistic ways.

Connecting to a religious meaning system in an intrinsic way is considered to be more mature, stemming from an internalized, committed and sincere faith. Connecting in an extrinsic way is associated with religious immaturity, involving an externalized, consensual, utilitarian orientation to religion (Allport & Ross, 1967). Connecting in a quest orientation involves a questioning, doubting, open and flexible approach to religious issues (Batson et al., 1993). Connecting in a fundamentalistic way suggests closed-mindedness, and the belief that one has access to absolute truth (Altemeyer & Hunsberger, 1992).

Meaning systems, religious or non-religious, are dynamic systems (Silberman, in press-a) that can be learned, developed and changed in several ways. One way involves development through direct explicit teaching of the basic postulates of the system. For example, religious or spiritual leaders, educators, philosophers, authors, journalists, family members or friends can express and teach in explicit ways their beliefs about God, and about the nature of the world or of human beings. Such explicit teaching can be done in formal or non-formal ways, in the form of public presentations, or as parts of individual interactions.

A second way of developing meaning systems involves learning through observation. Oman et al (2003) describe spiritual modeling as an important component of traditional religious development. They suggest that religious and spiritual traditions are often taught through formal and informal observation of persons serving as exemplars of how to live a spiritually meaningful life. Silberman (2003) adds that the archetype of spiritual role modeling within major religious systems would be the emulation of God. For example, the major three Western religions, Christianity, Islam and Judaism, call people to imitate God's forgiveness (Rye, Pargament, Ali, Beck, Dorff, Hallisey, Narayanan & Williams, 2000; Tsang et. al., in press). Beyond the description of God and community leaders as spiritual role models, Judaism suggests that a wise person can be defined as one who learns from every person (Ethics of the Fathers, 4(1)). In other words, every person can serve as a role model to teach people how to improve themselves. The Baal Shem Tov, for example, said that seeing certain deficiencies in other people should teach a person to correct his own deficiencies (Schochet, 1990). Jewish sources suggest that one can learn from animals, not only from people. For example they recommend learning vicariously from ants how to work hard (Proverbs 6,6), and from oxen how to know one's owner (Isaiah 1,3). Beyond that, the Baal Shem Tov and other Jewish spiritual leaders teach that every phenomenon in life is our teacher. A diamond, for example, "could teach people the value and preciousness of the soul; a soul that lies deeply embedded in rock and which, when it emerges, shines with unprecedented brilliance and fire" (Jacobson, 1995).

A third way in which meaning systems can change and develop is by accommodating to observed phenomena that seem to disconfirm the basic postulates of the meaning system. For example, during the process of coping with adversity, changes in the meaning system can occur in order to decrease the discrepancy between the situational meaning of challenging events and the general system of meaning. In other words, it is usually agreed that the basic postulates of a meaning system are often constructed unwittingly by individuals, and in the course of their development come to function as subconscious or implicit theories. However, events such as criminal victimization, terrorist attacks, accidents, natural disasters, and disease can shatter these basic implicit theories and force people to recognize, objectify, and modify these basic postulates (e.g., Dweck et. al., 1988; Epstein, 1973, 1985, 1990; Janoff-Bulman, 1992; Janoff-Bulman et. al., 1983; Park et. al., 1997).

According to Park, (in press) a discrepancy between one's global system of meaning (e.g., the beliefs that God is good and that God is responsible for what happens in the world) and one's perception of a situational meaning (e.g., the sudden death of my children was a tragic unjust event) can cause significant psychological distress. Such distress can be decreased through changing the global meaning systems, which tend to resist change, by changing the perceived perception of the situation, or by changing both the global and situational meanings.

Possible positive and negative impacts of religious meaning systems on individual and communal well-being.

Religious meaning systems can have both positive and negative impacts on individual and societal well-being (e.g., Batson et. al., 1982; Beith-Hallahmi & Argyle, 1997; Paloutzian, 1996; Paloutzian & Kirkpatrick, 1995; Pargament et. al., in press; Silberman, 2003; Silberman, in press-a; Silberman, in press-b, Wulff, 1997). This section describes possible impacts of religion on several variables that may be of particular interest for both clergy and for psychologists or other health care professionals.

Self-esteem: Religious meaning systems often include messages that can impact the self-esteem of individuals in both positive and negative ways. On the one hand, religious systems have portrayed human beings as images of God. This has been done often on the basis of biblical verses such as "And God said: Let us make man in our image, after our likeness" (Genesis, 1:26). This idea that man is endowed with some Godly element, which sets him apart from all other creatures, has been interpreted as suggesting that human beings are the pinnacle and focal point of creation. More precious to God than any other creature (Ethics of the Fathers 3(18)). This religious idea implies that each person matters, each person is irreplaceable (Jacobson, 1995). It underlies in the eyes of many people the basic principle of the sanctity of human life, which according to Gopin (2000) is common to many religious systems of meaning. On the other hand, religious meaning systems can include messages that emphasize the inferiority, sinfulness and nothingness of human beings (e.g., The Ethics of the Fathers, 3(1), 4(4); Pargament, 1997; Pargament et al., in press). Such statements can lead according to Fromm (1950) to "despising everything in oneself" (p. 36).

It is important to note in this context that some religious meaning systems seem to be aware of the dangerous impact that negative portrayal of human beings may have on the self esteem of individuals, and offer protective measures against such dangers. For example, within Judaism, the Talmudic tractate, 'Ethics of the Fathers', instructs "do not judge yourself to be a wicked person" (2, 18). The logic behind this instruction is that a person's standard of behavior is to a large extent influenced by his self-image, and one may become a prisoner of his self-image, unable to free himself from the burdens of his past. In other words, one who perceives himself as an evil person has no psychological safety net to prevent him from committing the worst of sins. He can tell himself the following: 'I'm a wicked person anyway. Why should I not indulge my basic instincts?'

How can the negative portrayal of human beings be consistent with positive self esteem? One religious approach to this issue involves the religious distinction between self-esteem, self-obsession (defined as arrogance), and selflessness. According to Rabbi Majeski (1995) for example, it is important for a person to have a positive self-image. A person should feel strong, confident, and able to respond to situations. Selflessness, which means nullification in front of God, and focus on goals and objectives, rather than on the self, is strongly recommended. Arrogance, on the other hand, or obsession with the self, is discouraged. According to this approach the negative portrayal of human beings aims at increasing selflessness and decreasing arrogance, without hurting one's self-esteem. A second religious approach that is relevant to this issue emphasizes the opportunities that are given to individuals within religious systems of meaning to change and improve themselves (Silberman, 1998). This topic will be discussed next in the context of self efficacy.

Self efficacy: Religious meaning systems seem to often imply and encourage beliefs in self efficacy by suggesting that individuals can change and improve themselves and the world around them (Silberman, 1998; Silberman, Higgins & Dweck, in press).

Self-change

The possibility of changing and improving the self is mentioned and encouraged in many major religious systems. The Dalai Lama (1999) for example, says that the spiritual qualities of love and compassion, patience, tolerance, forgiveness and humility are most easily developed within a religious context. He adds that religion can play a leading role in encouraging people to develop a sense of responsibility toward others, and the need to be ethically disciplined. Seyyed

Hossein Nasr (2003), in his book on Islam, says that one of the main goals of Islam is the creation of spiritual realization based on the inculcation of the spiritual virtues within the inner being of men and women.

Within Judaism the basic concepts of the commandments and of repentance suggest the possibility of self-change and improvement. An analysis of the reasons that are offered for the commandments suggest that they aim at the improvement of the self and the society. The concept of repentance, which involves the two basic stages of moving away from evil and moving toward good, is also interpreted as a call for people to change and improve themselves (Silberman, 1998).

World-change

The prevailing view in social science is that religion tends to preserve the status quo and to justify the existing social order. An alternative view, which is based on the analysis of religions as systems of meaning, suggests that religions often encourage radical changes and improvements in the world (Sethi et. al., 1993; Silberman et al., 2000; Silberman et. al., in press). Within this approach, many theologians view the struggle for political and social equality as a spiritual struggle, an attempt to realize God's kingdom on earth (Spilka and Bridges, 1992; Walzer, 1982). Exemplary figures of faith such as Martin Luther King, Jr., Mahatma Gandhi and Mother Theresa, can be described as trying to put this theology into practice.

In this context, the Dalai Lama (1999) is calling for a spiritual/ethical revolution, and Thurman (1998) explains that the principle that is in the heart of the Buddha's social revolution is that helping the individual transform himself or herself is what transfers society. According to Nasr (2003), one of the main goals of Islam is the creation of a moral order in human society.

Within Judaism all religious trends call for human action to take part in the effort to change the world and repair it (Silberman et. al., in press). The traditionally religious view of the future world is revolutionary in predicting a radical change in the world toward a messianic utopia. This future messianic world is described as a world of universal peace and harmony, characterized by awareness and knowledge of God and by the absence of evil and sin, as well as by the end of suffering and death (Schochet, 1990). The less traditional Jewish thought tends to view the future in less mystical ways. Yet they believe that human beings, acting in harmony to exercise the full range of their potential, could create a better world. Maimonides (1973) summarizes the power of the individual and the encouragement of self-efficacy within Judaism in a strong and parsimonious way. He recommends for each person to believe that both in his own life and in the world as a whole there is a balance between good deeds and negative actions. If a person conducts one more sin he would damage both himself and the world significantly. If a person conducts one additional good deed that person could redeem with this one action both himself and the world.

Coping and emotional well-being: Religion as a meaning system may have effects on emotions. First, it may directly prescribe appropriate emotions and emotional levels. For example, within Judaism, people are required to love God with all of their hearts (Deuteronomy, 6:5) and to serve God with joy (Deuteronomy, 28: 47). Second, religious beliefs that are part of the meaning system may have a causal effect on emotions (e.g., Pargament et. al., 1995; Pargament et. al., 2000; Sethi et. al., 1993). For example, a belief about a loving personal God may have a positive effect on emotional well-being, while a belief about a punitive vengeful God may have the opposite effect. Third, religion may offer the opportunity to experience a uniquely powerful emotional experience of closeness to a powerful spiritual force (Otto, 1928; Pargament, 1997).

Considerable research has been conducted on the relation between religion, well-being and coping. This research suggests, on the one hand, that religion and spirituality are often linked positively to well-being (Emmons, in press; Maton, Dodgen, Sto. Domingo, & Larson, in press; Pargament et al, in press). Emmons et al., (1998), for example, found that an increased proportion of spiritual strivings (i.e., goals that are oriented toward the sacred) was associated with higher levels of subjective well-being, especially to greater positive affect and to both marital and overall life satisfaction. In a similar way, research on coping suggests that religious coping can make a significant and unique contribution to the prediction of adjustment to stressful life events beyond the effects of non-religious coping (Pargament et. al., in press).

On the other hand, religion can be a source of unique distress. For example, certain forms of negative religious coping, such as questioning God's love for the individual, perceiving God as punishing, appraising a situation as an act of denial, and feeling abandoned by God, was significantly predictive of mortality (Pargament, Koenig, Tarakeshwar & Hahn, 2001).

In sum, religious meaning systems can contribute significantly to the well-being of individuals and to their efforts to cope with adversity. The positivity or negativity of the impact seems to depend to a certain extent on the specific contents of the religious systems (Silberman, in press-a).

Interpersonal and intergroup relations: Religious meaning systems often include a wide range of messages that can either facilitate or inhibit peaceful interpersonal or intergroup relations. Most religions, for example, encourage forgiveness (Rye et. al., 2000) yet they also seem to fuel resentment, conflict and revenge (Tsang et al, in press). Similarly, in the context prejudice, research shows that religion seems to both reduce and exacerbate prejudice (Allport, 1966). In their comprehensive review of the research on the relationship between religion and prejudice, Hunsberger and Jackson (in press) suggest that this relationship is complicated and depends on several factors. They suggest that it depends on the religious orientation of a person (intrinsic, extrinsic, quest or fundamentalistic), on the target of the prejudice (e.g., racial/ethnic prejudice versus prejudice towards gays and lesbians) and on whether the prejudice is perceived as having been pro-scribed by one's religious group.

Implications for pastoral care and guidance

The view of religion as a system of meaning has several important impli-cations for pastoral care and guidance: First, this approach emphasizes individual differences in the contents of the idiosyncratic religious meaning systems that individuals have, and in the ways individuals connect to these systems. It suggests that in order to work with individuals and to help them, clergy would often need to go beyond knowing the formal definition of individuals as religious or non-reli-gious, as Christians, Jews or Muslims, as endorsing the meaning systems of Bud-dhism, Confucianism or Hinduism, as Ultra-Orthodox, Orthodox, Conservative or Reform Jews, as Catholics or Protestants, as belonging to Sunni or Shiite Islam. They would need to explore the basic postulates that constitute the religious meaning systems of the individuals and how these postulates impact the emotions and the actions of those individuals.

Second, the meaning system approach to religion suggests that religious meaning systems can impact individual and communal well-being in both positive and negative ways. It is recommended for clergy to explore in their work with congregants how the basic postulates of the religious systems of these individuals impact their emotions and actions in both positive and negative ways.

It is important in this context to mention that there is a tendency in both scientific and popular writings to distinguish between religion, which is described as organized, substantive and negative, in contrast to the personal, functional and positive spirituality. This tendency has been criticized by many scholars in the psychology of religion, who have emphasized the need to acknowledge the fact that spirituality, like religion, can have both positive and negative potentials (Hill, Pargament, Hood, McCullough, Swyers, Larson & Zinnbauer, 2000; Silberman, 2003; Zinnbauer, Pargament, & Scott, 1999), and have suggested that individual differences exist in the perceived distinction between religion and spirituality (Zinnbauer et. al, 1999).

Third, the meaning-system approach to religion suggests that religious systems often include within themselves a variety of messages that can have both positive and negative impacts on individual and communal well-being. It suggests that since such systems are dynamic in nature, they can be changed and re-di-rected in different directions that emphasize different messages (Gopin, 2000; Hunsberger et al., in press; Silberman, in press-a; Tsang et. al., in press). Histori-cally, religious and spiritual leaders have used their influence to both increase and decrease the well-being of their followers, and to increase both conflicts and con-flict resolution (Silberman, 2003). It is my personal belief that it is the responsibil-ity of clergy to direct or redirect the meaning systems of their congregants in positive ways that would increase not only the well-being of the congregants, but also their positive peaceful attitudes toward others within their community and outside of it.

Fourth, while religious-meaning systems are dynamic and can change it is important to realize that, like other meaning systems, they tend to resist change. This resistance can be understood considering the effort that is invested in their development over the life span, and their essential role of helping people function in the world. Considering the resistance of global meaning systems to change, clergy, in their efforts to educate congregants and help them to cope with adversity, need to be very sensitive to existing global systems that the individuals have, and need to take into account psychological and ethical considerations in that context (e.g., the Dalai Lama, 1999). For example, it seems to me that the decision whether to recommend the approaches of Kushner (1989-a) or Majeski (1995) to religious coping should depend to a large extent on the existing meaning-systems of the individuals who are being helped by the clergy.

Fifth, research on the development and the learning of religious-meaning systems describes spiritual modeling as an important component of traditional religious development (Oman et. al., 2003; Silberman, 2003). This line of research suggests that clergy should try and serve as positive spiritual role models in every aspect of their behavior (Herl, this volume).

Finally, the name of this book, as well as David Herl's introductory chapter, suggest that the role of clergy is challenging and involving the building of bridges between different worlds, the religious-spiritual world on the one hand, and the psychological-scientific world on the other side.

The meaning-system approach to religion emphasizes on the one hand the challenge that is facing clergy by suggesting that any interaction between two individuals involves an interaction between two idiosyncratic systems of meaning, and by suggesting that both the meaning systems of the clergy and of their congregants may include both religious and non-religious components.

On the other hand, the meaning system approach to religion, which compares and contrasts religion to other systems of meaning, implies that bridges between religious/spiritual and psychological scientific worlds are both necessary and possible. It implies that religious and non-religious systems may interact within individuals (e.g., the belief about the goodness of the world may have both religious and non-religious sources within an individual). Accordingly, this approach recommends collaboration between clergy who represent different religions, as well as collaborations between clergy and between psychologists or other health professionals in the effort to increase individual and communal well-being, and in order to bring about world peace (See Maton, et. al., in press; Pargament et al, in press; Richards & Bergin, 1997; Silberman, in press-a; Silberman, in press-b).

Author Note: Correspondence concerning this paper should be addressed to Israela Silberman, Department of Psychology, 406 Schermerhorn Hall, 1190 Amsterdam Ave., MC 5501, Columbia University, New York, NY 10027. E-mail: isl@psych.columbia.edu

References

Allport, G.W (1966). The religious context of prejudice. *Journal for the Scientific Study of Religion*, 5, 447-457.

Allport, G.W. & Ross, J.M. (1967). Personal religious orientation and prejudice. *Journal of Personality and Social Psychology*, 5, 432-443.

Altemeyer, B. & Hunsberger, B. (1992). Authoritarianism, religious fundamentalism, quest, and prejudice. *The International Journal for the Psychology of Religion*, 2, 113-133.

Beit-Hallahmi, B., & Argyle, M. (1997). *The psychology of religious behavior, belief and experience*. London and New York: Routledge.

Batson, C. D., Schoenrade, P. & Ventis, W. L. (1993). *Religion and the individual: A social-psychological perspective*. New York: Oxford University Press.

Batson, C. D. & Ventis, W. L. (1982). *The religious experience: A social psychological experience*. New York and Oxford: Oxford University Press.

Bowlby, J. (1969). *Attachment and loss*. vol1: Attachment. London: Hogarth.

The Dalai Lama (1999). *Ethics for the new millennium*. New York: Riverhead Books- A member of Penguin Putnam Inc.

Dweck C. S. (1996). Implicit theories as organizers of goals and behavior. In P. Gollwitzer & J. A. Bargh (Eds.) *The psychology of action: The relation of cognition and motivation to behavior*. New   York: Guilford.

Dweck, C.S. (1999). *Self theories: Their role in motivation, personality and development*. Philadelphia: Psychology Press.

Dweck C. S., & Leggett, E. L. (1988). A social-cognitive approach to motivation and personality. *Psychological Review*, 25, 109-116.

Emmons, R. A. (in press). Striving for the sacred: Personal goals, life meaning and religion. *Journal of Social Issues*,

Emmons, R. A. (1999). *The psychology of ultimate concerns*. New York: The Guilford Press.

Emmons, R. A., Cheung, C., & Tehrani, K. (1998). Assessing spirituality through personal goals: Implications for research on religion and subjective well-being. *Social Indicators Research*, 45, 391-422.

Epstein, S. (1973). The self-concept revisited, or a theory of a theory. *American Psychologist*, 28, 404-416.

Epstein, S. (1985). The implications of cognitive-experiential self theory for research in social psychology and personality. *Journal of the Theory of Social Behavior*, 15,3.

Epstein, S. (1990). Cognitive-experential self-theory. In L.A. Pervin (Ed.), Handbook of personality: Theory and research (pp. 165-192). New York: Guilford.

Epstein, S. & Erskine, N. (1983). The development of personal theories of reality from an interactional perspective. In D. Magnusson & V. L. Allen (Eds.), *Human   development: An interactional perspective*. New York: Academic Press.

Fromm, E. (1950). *Psychoanalysis and religion*. New Haven: Yale University Press.

Geertz, C. (1973). *The interpretation of culture*. New York: Basic Books, Inc., Publishers.

Gopin, M. (2000). *Between Eden and Armageddon: The future of religion, violence and peacemaking*. New York and London: Oxford University Press.

Herl, D. (in press). Spirituality, religion and psychology: Core concepts for building bridges for the troubles parishioner/congregant. In D. Herl & M. Berman (Eds.) Building bridges over troubld waters: Ehancing pastoral care and guidance.

Higgins, E. T. (1989). Self-discrepancy theory: What patterns of self beliefs cause people to suffer? In L. Berkowitz (Ed.), *Advances in experimental social psychology*,

Vol. 22. New York: Academic Press.

Higgins, E. T. (2000). Social cognition: Learning about what matters in the social world. European. *Journal of Social Psychology*, 30, 3-39.

Hill, P.C, Pargament, K.I., Hood, R.W., McCullough, M.E., Swyers, J.P., Larson, D.B., & Zinnbauer, B. (2000). Conceptualizing religion and spirituality: Points of commonality, points of departure. Journal for the Theory of Social Behavior, 30:1, 51-77.

Hunsberger, B. & Jackson, L. M. (In press). Religion, meaning, and prejudice. *Journal of Social Issues*

Jacobson, S. (1995). *Toward a meaningful life: The wisdom of the Rebbe Menachem Mendel Schneerson.* New York: William Morrow and Company, Inc.

James, W. (1902). *The varieties of religious experience.* New York: Longman.

Janoff-Bulman, R. (1992). *Shattered assumptions. Toward a new psychology of trauma.* The Free Press.

Jannof-Bulman, R. & Frieze, I. H. (1983). A theoretical perspective for understanding reactions to victimization. *Journal of social issues*, 39, 2, 1-17.

Kelley, G. A. (1955). *The psychology of personal constructs.* New York: Norton.

Kushner, H. S. (1989-a). *When bad things happen to good people.* New York: Avon Books.

Kushner, H. S. (1989-b). Who needs God. New York: Summit Books.

Lazarus, R. S., & Folkman, S. (1984). *Stress, appraisal, and coping.* New York: Springer Publishing.

Lerner, M. J. (1980). The belief in a just world: A fundamental delusion. New York: Plenum Press.

Loeb (Silberman), I. & Dweck, C. S. (1994). Beliefs about human nature as predictors of reactions to victimization. Paper presented at the Six Annual Convention of the American Psychological Society, Washington, DC.

Loeb (Silberman), I., Dweck, C. S. , Bhomia, G. K., & Novello, E. P. (1998). Beliefs about Human Moral Nature as Predictors of Reactions to anti-Semitism. Paper presented at the 10th Annual Convention of the American Psychological Society, Washington,DC.

Maimonides, M. (1973). *Sefer Mishneh Torah hu ha-yad ha-hazakah.* Hilchot Teshuva (Chapter 3). Jerusalem: N/A. (Original work published 1168).

Majeski, S. (1995). *The Chassidic approach to joy.* Brooklyn, NY: Sichos in English.

Maton , K.I., Dodgen, D., Sto. Domingo, M.R., & Larson, D. (in press). Religion as a meaning system: Policy implications for the new millennium. *Journal of Social Issues.*

McCullough, M. E., & Worthington, E. L., Jr. (1999). Religion and the forgiving personality. *Journal of Personality*, 67, 1141-1164.

McIntosh, D. N. (1995). Religion as a schema, with implications for the relation between religion and coping. International Journal for the Psychology of Religion, 5, 1-16.

McIntosh, D.N., Silver, R. & Wortman, C. B. (1993). Religion's role in adjustment to a negative life event: Coping with the loss of a child. *Journal of Personality and Social Psychology*, 65, 812-821.

Mischel, W. (1973). Toward a cognitive social learning reconceptualization of personality. *Psychological Review*, 80, 252-283.

Myers, D. G. (2000). The funds, friends, and faith of happy people. *American Psychologist*, 55(1), 56-67.

Nasr, S.H. (2003). *Islam: Religion, history, and civilization.* New York: HarperSanFrancisco-a Division of HarperCollins Publishers.

Oman, D. & Thoresen, C.E. (2003). Spiritual modeling: A key to spiritual and religious growth? *The International Journal for the Psychology of Religion*, 13(3), 149-165.

Otto, R. (1928). The idea of the holly: An inquiry into the non-rational factor in the idea of the divine and its relation to the rational. London: Oxford University Press.

Paloutzian, R. F. (1996). Invitation to the psychology of religion. MA: Allyn & Bacon-A Simon & Schuster Company.

Paloutzian, R. F. & Kirkpatrick, L. A. (Eds.). (1995). Religious influence on personal and societal well-being. *Journal of Social Issues*, 51(2).

Pargament, K. I. (1990). God help me-religious coping efforts as predictors of the outcomes to significant negative life events. *American Journal of Community Psychology*, 18, 793-824.

Pargament, K. I. (1992). Of means and ends: Religion and the search for significance. *The International Journal for the Psychology of Religion*, 2(4), 201-229.

Pargament, K. I. (1997). The psychology of religion and coping. New York: The Guilford Press.

Pargament, K. I., Ensing, D. S., Falgoat, K., Olsen, H., Reilly, B. Van Haitsma, K., & Warran, R. (1990). God help me: (I): Religious coping efforts as predictors of the outcomes to significant negative life events. *American Journal of Community Psychology*, 18(6), 793-824.

Pargament, K. I, Koenig, H. G., Tarakeshwar, N., & Hahn, J. (2000). Negative religious coping predicts mortality among medically ill elderly. Paper presented at the 108th Annual Convention of the American Psychological Association.Washington,DC.

Pargament, K. I, Koenig, H. G., Tarakeshwar, N., & Hahn, J. (2001). Religious struggle as a predictor of mortality among medically ill elderly patients: A two-year longitudinal study. *Archives of Internal Medicine*, 161, 1881-1885.

Pargament, K. I., Magyar, G. M. & Murray-Swank, N. (In press). The sacred and the search for significance: Religion as a unique process. *Journal of Social Issues*

Pargament, K. I., Olsen, H., Reilly, B., Falgoat, K., Ensing, D. S., Van Haitsma, K.(1992). God help me: (II): The relationship of religious orientations to religious coping with negative life events. *Journal for the Scientific Study of Religion*, 31(4), 504-513.

Pargament, K. I. & Park, C. L. (1995). Merely a defense? The variety of religious means and ends. *Journal of Social Issues*, 51(2), 13-32.

Park, C.L. (in press). Religion as a meaning-making framework in coping with life stress. *Journal of social issues*

Park, C. L. & Folkman, S. (1997). Meaning in the context of stress and coping. *Review of General Psychology*, 1(2), 115-144.

Pepper, S. C. (1942). *World hypotheses*. Berkeley, CA: University of California Press

Perloff, L. S. (1983). Perceptions of vulnerability to victimization. *Journal of Social Issues*, 39, 41-62.

Richards, P.S. & Bergin, A.E. (1997). *A spiritual strategy for counseling and psychotherapy*. Washington, DC: American Psychological Association.

Rubin, Z., & Peplau, A. (1975). Belief in a just world and reaction to another's lot: A study of participants in the national draft lottery. *Journal of Social Issues*, 29(4), 73-93.

Rye, M. S., Pargament, K.I., Ali, M.A., Beck, E.N., Dorff, E.N., Hallisey, C., Narayanan, V. & Williams, J.G. (2000). Religious perspectives on forgiveness. In. M.E. McCullough, K.I. Pargamnet, & C.E.Thoresen (Eds.). Forgiveness: Theory, research, and practice. New York and London: The Guilford Press.

Scheier, M. F., & Carver, S. C. (1985). Optimism, coping, and health: Assessment and Implications of Generalized Outcome Expectancies. *Health psychology*,4(3),219-247.

Schochet, J. I. (1990). *Chassidic dimensions: Themes in Chassidic thought and practice.* The mystical dimention, Vol 3: New York: Kehot Publication Society.

Schwartz, S. H. & Huismars, S. (1995). Value priorities and religiosity in four Western religions. *Social Psychology Quarterly,* 58, 88-107.

Sethi, S. & Seligman, M. E. P. (1993). Optimism and fundamentalism. *Psychological Science,* 4,(4), 256-259.

Sheldon, K. M. & Kasser, T. (1995). Coherence and congruence: Two aspects of personality integration, *Journal of Personality and Social Psychology,* 68, 531-543.

Silberman, I. (1998). Religiousness: Change vs. Status Quo: A review paper. Columbia University.

Silberman, I. (2003). Spiritual role modeling: The teaching of meaning systems. *The International Journal for the Psychology of Religion,* 13(3), 175-195.

Silberman, I. (in press-a). Religion as a meaning system: Implications for the new millennium. *Journal of Social Issues*

Silberman, I. (Ed). (in press-b). Religion as a meaning system. *Journal of Social Issues*

Silberman, I., Higgins, E. T., & Dweck, C. S. (in press). Religion and openness to change. *Journal of Social Issues*

Silberman, I., Higgins, E. T., & Dweck, C. S. (2000). The relation between Religiosity and openness to change. Paper presented at the 108th Annual Convention of the American Psychological Association. Washington, DC.

Silberman, I., Higgins, E. T., & Dweck, C. S. (2001). Religion and well-being: World beliefs as mediators. Paper presented at the 109th Annual Convention of the American Psychological Association. San Francisco, CA.

Silberman, I., Higgins, E. T., Dweck, C. S., Rohatgi, R., Bhomia, G. K., & Novello, E. P. (1999). Religiosity as a call for world change: Contradiction in terms or Messianism? Paper presented at the 11th Annual Convention of the American Psychological Society. Denver, Colorado.

Silver, R. L., Boon, C. & Stones, M. L. (1983). Searching for meaning in misfortune: Making sense of incest. *Journal of Social Issues,* 39, 81-101.

Spilka, B., & Bridges, R. A. (1992). Religious perspectives on prevention: The role of theology. In K. I. Pargament, K. I. Maton, & R. E. Hess (Eds.), *Religion and prevention in mental health: Research, vision, and action.* pp. 19-36, New York: Haworth Press.

Thurman, R. (1998). Inner revolution: Life, liberty, and the pursuit of real happiness. New York: Riverhead Books - a member of Penguin Putnam Inc.

Tsang, J.A., McCullough, & Hoyt, W.T. (In press). Psychometric and rationalization accounts for the religion-forgiveness discrepancy. *Journal of Social Issues*

Tillich, P. (1957). *Dynamics of faith.* New York: Harper and Row.

Walzer, M. (1982). The revolution of the Saints: A study in the origin of radical politics. Cambridg and London: Harvard University Press.

Whitehead, A. N. (1929). *Process and reality.* New York: Free Press.

Whitehead, A. N. (1938). *Modes of thought.* New York: Free Press.

Wulff, D. M. (1997). *Psychology of religion.* New York: John Wiley & Sons.

Zinnbauer, B. J., Pargament, K. I., & Scott, A.B. (1999). The emerging meanings of religiousness and spirituality: Problems and prospects. *Journal of Personality,* 67(6), 889-919.

About The Author

Israela Silberman received her B.A. from the Hebrew University of Jerusalem in psychology and philosophy and her Ph.D. (with distinction) in social-personality psychology in 1999 from Columbia University. She is currently an Associate Research Scientist at the Psychology Department of Columbia University and an Assistant Professor at the Department of Jewish Studies of Stern College — the Women's College of Yeshiva University. Dr. Silberman has written extensively on the relations between religion and individual and societal well-being, in general, and on the role of religion in recent world events, in particular. Her theoretical and applied research illuminates the importance of religion as a powerful system of meaning that can affect the lives of individuals in terms of their beliefs, motivations, emotions and behaviors, and can influence their interactions on both interpersonal and intergroup levels. She is the editor of a forthcoming special issue of the Journal of Social Issues on "Religion as a Meaning System", and is co-editing a book on the role of religion in national and international conflicts and their resolutions. Dr. Silberman received the Richard Christie Award for Research on Social Issues (1996), awards from the Memorial Foundation for Jewish Culture (1999, 2000) to support her research on the psychological worlds of American Jewry, a teaching grant from the Columbia University Center for the Study of Science and Religion (2002) for her seminar on the psychology of religion, and the Margaret Gorman Early Career Award (2004) from the American Psychological Association (Div. 36) for her research on the psychology of religion.

Chapter 5
Pastoral Care as Practical Theology:
Bridges for Theory & Practice at the New Millennium
by Carrie Doehring, Ph.D.

Chaplain Sally Lewis has been asked to visit Mrs. Jane McEwen, an eighty-five year old Caucasian woman who is recovering from hip surgery. Mrs. McEwen fractured her hip in a fall in her home, where she has lived alone since her husband died five years ago. She has asked that the chaplain visit her. Sally wrote the following verbatim of this visit, which she reconstructed afterwards.

Chaplain: Hello, Mrs. McEwen. I'm Sally Lewis, one of the chaplains here.

Jane McEwen: Oh, I'm so glad you've come. I've wanted to talk with one of the chaplains.

Chaplain: Yes, the nursing staff passed along your request to me. How are you doing?

Jane McEwen: This damn hip! (She clenches her hands and her face flushes.) I still can't believe that I was so clumsy and tripped over that mat in my kitchen. If only I hadn't been shuffling along. I hated it when my husband shuffled like that, instead of picking up his feet. I've told myself over and over again, pick up your feet.

Chaplain: You're pretty angry with yourself.

Jane McEwen: You bet I am. It's my fault that I've ended up in here with this busted hip. I guess I deserve what's coming next.

Chaplain: What's that?

Jane McEwen: They're going to ship me off to some rehabilitation center and then stick me in a nursing home. I'm never going home again.

Chaplain: Who's going to do this?

Jane McEwen: The doctors and my daughters. They've teamed up and decided it's not safe for me to live alone. When I picture my house, the kitchen table with my plants and the sun shining through the window in the morning, and sitting there with my coffee and reading the paper… And I won't ever do that again. (She leans back and clenches her eyes shut to hold back the tears.)

Chaplain: That's so sad. (She lays a hand on one of Mrs. McEwen's clenched fists. Mrs. McEwen's shoulders begin to shake and she starts to weep. A few moments of silence pass by.)

Jane McEwen: Thanks, Chaplain. I really needed that. I just keep all of my tears bottled up. Even when Frank died, I just kept holding back my tears all of the time.

Chaplain: It must be hard to let yourself cry when you have so much sadness.

Jane McEwen: Yes, I'm afraid that the dam will burst and I'll never stop crying. (Mrs. McEwen becomes teary, and gazes out the window for a time, wiping her tears occasionally.) I wanted to talk to a chaplain.

Chaplain: Yes.

Jane McEwen: I can't pray. I used to sit at my kitchen table every morning, and read the day's devotion from my little book, *The Upper Room*.[1] Then I would read one of my favorite psalms. "I lift up my eyes to the hills... (she recites the Psalm 121 from memory). Sarah, that's my eldest daughter, brought my devotional book and my bible here, but when I try to read, I get this tightness in my chest, and I can't breath. I have to put the books away and try to calm down....

I have abruptly stopped the verbatim at this point because the conversation could go in several directions, depending upon the chaplain's and patient's theological perspectives. The verb, to bridge, is useful to describe the tensions inherent in this moment. How will the chaplain and patient connect with each other as they talk about Mrs. McEwen's religious practices and her sense of where God is? They have already connected relationally by being responsive to each other. The chaplain has listened respectfully and with empathy. Mrs. McEwen has allowed herself to experience anger and sadness, and realized that neither she nor the chaplain are going to be overwhelmed by the intensity of these emotions. In their initial conversation a bridge has been constructed from the trust that each has experienced. Mrs. McEwen has started to trust that the chaplain is sensitive and empathic. The chaplain is putting her trust in the process thus far, and in Mrs. McEwen's engagement in this process.

The bridge, however, is still in the process of being constructed, when the conversation turns to a highly sensitive area: Mrs. McEwen's experience of God and the chaplain's response. At this moment, one or both of them may realize how little they know about the other. Mrs. McEwen may wonder about the chaplain, asking herself what the chaplain's religious background is. The chaplain knows from the medical records that Mrs. McEwen is Presbyterian, but she's not familiar with the congregation where Mrs. McEwen worships. She may wonder at this moment why Mrs. McEwen isn't speaking with a member of the pastoral care team at her church.

By casting ourselves in the chaplain's place, we have an opportunity to consider how we usually respond at moments in pastoral care conversations when there is explicit reference to religious practices and experiences believed to be of God, the sacred, the divine or some sense of a transcendent reality. In this chapter,

I present an array of ways to engage with Mrs. McEwen theologically. In order to explore such options, I will turn to Scalise's description of five models of practical theology. Before doing so, I would like to offer some working definitions of pastoral care and counseling, and practical and pastoral theology.

The term pastoral care[2] has a long history in the Christian tradition. It is the care offered by representatives of this tradition. Today this term usually indicates the ways in which a community of faith tends to the emergent needs—spiritual, psychological, material—of its member. Crisis and supportive pastoral counseling are an extension of community care by those who are specially trained and designated or ordained for this ministry. Those engaged in this ministry attend not only to emergent needs but also to underlying causes. For example, in crisis counseling, caregivers initially assess the suffering of careseekers and make decisions about what sort of help they need. Pastoral psychotherapists have further training. They can work in more intensive and long-term relationships in arenas like family dynamics that require more expertise and training.

Pastoral care, counseling, and psychotherapy can be contrasted with medical or psychological care by its use of religious sources of authority, like sacred texts, creeds, doctrines, religious/spiritual experience and the norms used for interpreting these sources. One set of norms are Biblical critical methods, which provide various ways of interpreting sacred texts. Theological perspectives can be used to interpret religious/spiritual experiences, especially in terms of the ways persons experience God and how God is symbolized.

In the verbatim that opened this chapter, as the chaplain and Mrs. McEwen turn to speaking about her religious faith, both begin to draw upon Christian sources of authority and norms for interpreting them. In institutional settings like hospitals, prisons, hospices, and nursing homes, chaplains are trained to respect and, when possible, work with the religious traditions of those for whom they care. When they cannot provide care that draws upon religious traditions other than their own, they are obliged to arrange for a visit with a representative of the careseeker's religious tradition. Many institutions and organizations accrediting chaplains are using the term spiritual care to acknowledge that patients seeking religiously-based care come from traditions other than Christian. Or, they may be persons who reject the use of any specific religious sources of authority and prefer to describe themselves as spiritual, not religious. In this chapter, since both the chaplain and patient are drawing upon Christian sources and norms of authority, I will continue to use the term pastoral care rather than spiritual care.

Pastoral care can draw upon its sacred texts, like the Hebrew Scriptures and the New Testament, or liturgical rites like confession, eucharist, or holy communion, in a variety of ways. Practical theology is the term used to describe the ways in which the practice of pastoral care is related to religious sources of authority and the norms for interpreting them. Pastoral theology is a form of practical theology. It can be focused upon the practice of pastoral care, and it can be distinguished from liturgical theology, which is related to the practice of liturgy and ritual, and homiletical theology, which is related the practice of preaching.

Scalise (2003) has aptly entitled his book on practical theology *Bridging the gap: Connecting what you learned in seminary with what you find in the congregation.* The gap between theological education and the practice of care could also be described as the gap that may open up at moments in pastoral care conversations, when caregivers and careseekers begin to draw explicitly upon particular sources of religious authority and ways of interpreting such sources. In this moment both Mrs. McEwen and the chaplain are engaging in practical theology. They are moving from Mrs. McEwen's religious practices to reflecting theologically upon these practices.

Mrs. McEwen has identified two sources of religious authority: her devotional text, *The Upper Room,* and the Book of Psalms. The chaplain at this moment is empathetically imagining how these sources of authority have helped Mrs. McEwen cope with stress, and what norms she might be using to interpret these sources. The chaplain is also wondering how the religious sources and norms that she usually uses might be similar or different from Mrs. McEwen's. Here is where Scalise's discussion of practical theology is most relevant, for he describes five models of practical theology, which I will describe in terms of how each draws upon and uses religious sources and norms. He has used the following names for these models: the regulative, performance, correlational, narrative and contextual models. After discussing each model, I will imagine how the pastoral conversation would continue if the chaplain were using the model under consideration.

In elaborating Scalise's descriptions of each model, I will note what happens when pre-modern, modern, and post-modern approaches to knowledge and truth are used. Pre-modern approaches to religious knowledge and truth were part of early and medieval Christian traditions in which religious leaders were given authority to name what was and wasn't true in all times and places. Nowadays some pastoral caregivers draw upon pre-modern approaches to religious sources, like biblical texts and doctrines, as a justification for using literalist norms for deriving single meanings from sacred texts. They believe that they are returning to some historical core or essence of the Christian tradition. In another contemporary use of pre-modern approaches to religious sources, particularly religious and spiritual experiences, authority is given to the individual to name religious experience as truly mediating a connection with what is identified as the transcendent, divine or sacred. For example, persons viewing the controversial film, *The Passion,* directed by Mel Gibson (2004), may use pre-modern approaches to describe how the film mediated a profound sense of connection with their experience of the suffering Jesus.

Those who work within modern assumptions about knowledge and truth assert that trans-historical and universal truth can be established through rational and empirical methods. Using scientific methods will result in more and more aspects of life becoming known. It is as though each scientific finding fills in a piece of the puzzle depicting "reality" or the way things really are. For example, in recent discussions about Gibson's film *The Passion,* reference was made to medical research of the details on Jesus' suffering on the cross, like descriptions of Jesus sweating blood. Medical studies are used to claim the "truth" of Jesus' suffering (Steinfels, 2004). In biblical studies, those using modern approaches believe that historical criticism, mainly form, tradition history, redaction, source and several other methods[3] can be used to establish when and by whom a biblical text was written, and what the author of a text intended the exact meaning of the text to be (Barton, 1998).

A postmodern approach to knowledge and truth assumes that knowledge is socially constructed in particular contexts out of traditions of understanding, and that such knowledge is provisional and contextual. Such knowledge is not true in terms of its one-on-one correspondence with "reality" but in terms of relevance, meaningfulness, and usefulness.[4] The effects of emerging post-modern approaches to knowledge were seen in biblical studies in the 1970s and 1980s when there was a shift away from historical methods and toward an array of new methods in many academic circles. Barton characterizes this shift as a questioning of the approach to knowledge used by Enlightenment thinkers: "The neutral, scientific pursuit of truth by a disinterested scholar has been shown (it is said) to be bankrupt (Barton, 1998, 13). This questioning of modern approaches to studying biblical texts generated skepticism about trying to determine conclusively what the author/s of any biblical text intended to communicate. More generally, postmodern discussions of truth claims have made many biblical scholars "somewhat more circumspect about their truth claims."[5]

Having distinguished these three approaches to knowledge and truth, I need to add that in their daily lives, most people use all three approaches, as though they are wearing tri-focal eyeglasses. As Lartey (2003, 2) says, "It is ... important to note that all of these conditions [of pre-modernity, modernity, and post-modernity] exist to different degrees all over the globe and that they do so simultaneously." In one moment, perhaps while participating in a religious service, they look upon the religious symbols through their "pre-modern" lens, as if, for example, God is truly present in the bread and wine of the Christian sacrament of communion. In another moment, when listening to the sermon, they might look through their modern lens, and use rational approaches to knowledge as they listen to the argument being made by the preacher. During the social hour after the worship they may use their post-modern lens to interact with a Muslim visitor who describes her religious tradition, in terms of what makes it unique and distinctive from Christian traditions. The image of perceiving life through tri-focal lens is itself reflective of post-modern sensibilities, and would be rejected by those who perceive their experiences of the God, the sacred, or transcendent realities solely through a pre-modern lens. A person committed to modern approaches to knowledge and truth might argue that we view the world through bifocal lens that include pre-modern and modern perspectives, but not postmodern perspectives.

I turn now to elaborating Scalise's five models of practical theology, and consider how the pastoral care conversation with Mrs. McEwen would continue, depending upon which model was used to relate theory—specifically theology—to the practice of care.

Regulative Model

The regulative model of pastoral theology is distinctive in the kinds of norms it uses to interpret religious sources of authority, like Hebrew Scriptures and the New Testament, and spiritual experiences, like communal worship experiences or individual devotional practices. In interpreting these texts and experiences, practitioners of this model look for core theological doctrines or symbols that are described as the essence of their religious tradition. This essence is like the deep structure of religious practices. Another distinctive norm is that practices ought to reflect what is believed to be the core or essence of a religious tradition. The term, regulative, refers to this norm. The essence or deep structure of the tradition should regulate its practices.

The terms Scalise uses to describe the regulative model of pastoral theology are drawn from Lindbeck's (1984) cultural linguistic approach to understanding the nature and role of doctrine in religious traditions and practices. Borrowing from linguistic studies, Lindbeck likens the essence or deep structure of religious practices to the grammar that shapes the way we use words to express ourselves. In a broad sense, grammar, like the essential doctrines and symbols of a religious tradition, can be understood to be the inherent rules that govern practice.

A pastoral theologian who works within the regulative model of pastoral theology is Thomas Oden. Oden's religious sources are the patristic writings on pastoral care (Oden 1984, 1992). Using the norms I have described above, he defines the "essence" of pastoral care in terms of the religious doctrines and symbols used by the early Church Fathers when they wrote about the practice of pastoral care. He proposes that what he has identified as the deep grammar of pastoral care can serve a regulative function, in that pastoral caregivers ought to understand their practices of care in terms of the kind of care practiced by the early Church Fathers.

How would the pastoral care conversation unfold if Mrs. McEwen is someone who has been raised in a Presbyterian tradition which draws upon the regulative model of pastoral theology? Could the chaplain in this particular setting provide care to Mrs. McEwen within such a model? It would be unusual for a chaplain to provide such care, unless he or she was in the same tradition as Mrs. McEwen and used the same model of care. If, for example, both were part of the Nazarene Christian religious tradition, and were committed to conserving what they described as the core of that tradition, and were in a hospital that was funded and run by the Nazarene Church, then it would be appropriate for the chaplain to provide such care if this is what Mrs. McEwen wished. Given that this is not the situation in this pastoral care scenario, then it will be up to the chaplain to talk with Mrs. McEwen about who would be the most appropriate caregiver for her. It is likely that Mrs. McEwen's own minister could provide such care, and the chaplain can carefully explore this possibility with Mrs. McEwen, especially in terms of whether this is what Mrs. McEwen wants right now. If this is what happens, then the chaplain can remain in contact with Mrs. McEwen, while not providing direct pastoral care, because the chaplain is a part of her care-giving team who is especially able to assess the extent to which Mrs. McEwen's religious faith helps her cope with her crisis. A pastoral caregiver using this model of pastoral theology might describe Mrs. McEwen's faith crisis in terms of alienation from God, likely using the word sin to describe this alienation. The core theme of sin will then be linked with other core themes like confession, repentance, God's mercy, forgiveness, and grace.

Performance Model

The performance model is distinct in that it draws upon religious sources like religious practices that, in their enactment or performance, can, it is believed, connect care-seekers with what they experience as the divine, the sacred, or transcendent realities. The norms used to interpret such practices are often implicit beliefs that if the liturgy is correctly enacted it has the power to mediate a sense of the sacred or the divine.

An example of such care is a visit from a representative of the Roman Catholic Church, who has been designated to bring hosts or bread, consecrated in the sacrament of the eucharist, to hospital patients. Other examples of the performance model of pastoral theology that often occur in hospital settings are the anointing of the sick and those who are dying, and baptizing infants. This model of pastoral theology is most often found in Roman Catholic, Orthodox, Lutheran, Episcopal and other traditions (like some Native American spiritual traditions) in which liturgy or ritual plays a central role. In a more general sense, the saying of prayers often functions as a kind of performance of one's faith that serves to connect people with what they believe to be God or the sacred.

As with the regulative model of pastoral theology, the performance model seems best suited to tradition-specific forms of pastoral care. For example, if the patient identifies herself as a member of a Navaho tribe, that is, a particular Native American spiritual tradition, the chaplain can talk with her about whether she wishes to speak with someone from her own tribe about her spiritual needs. Similarly, if Mrs. McEwen is Roman Catholic and has gone to Mass every week, she may most want to see her priest and partake of the sacrament of communion during this crisis in her life. The chaplain can stay in touch with such a patient if this is amenable to the patient, as a way of communicating to the patient that the hospital care team takes seriously her spiritual needs and sees them as part of her healing process.

As with the regulative model, it may initially seem as though the performance model is most often used by those drawing upon pre-modern approaches to knowledge and truth, in that they believe, for example, that the bread consecrated in the Roman Catholic sacrament of the eucharist is truly the body of Christ, which they take into their bodies, and which profoundly connects them with God. More sophisticated members of the faith community may draw upon modern approaches to knowledge used in systematic theologies that rationally explain the doctrine of transubstantiation, that is, how it is that the bread becomes, in substance, the body of Christ. Those using a postmodern approach to the performance model of pastoral theology qualify what happens in the receiving of the sacrament of communion as follows: it is *as if* the bread is God in a way that profoundly mediates the presence of God within us. Another way to say this is that in the experience of receiving communion a person can shift to a pre-modern form of knowledge and belief, in order to say in that moment that God is truly present in the bread and wine.

Pastoral theologians, like Elaine Graham (1996), using a post-modern approach to knowledge, see the performance model as a way to identify emergent forms of religious practices and beliefs that may challenge traditional beliefs. Examples of such practices are the liturgies being written and used to celebrate the unions, some say marriages, of homosexual persons. Experiencing the "goodness" of such ceremonies can lead those in attendance to reconstruct radically their theologies of marriage. Another example of religious practices that enact theologies at odds with the tenets of their religious tradition is the widespread practice of using birth control by Roman Catholics. They practice a theology that challenges the ecclesial authority of their tradition.

The performance model, either in its pre-modern, modern or post-modern form, is relevant to pastoral care with Mrs. McEwen. Mrs. McEwen describes how suddenly her religious practice of reading devotional material and psalms and praying are not ways in which she can connect with what she has experienced as God. In other words, her religious practices are not working; indeed they are causing her great distress. If the chaplain draws upon the performance model of pastoral theology, then there are several questions to explore. Are there other religious practices in which Mrs. McEwen engages regularly that might not cause such distress and mediate a connection with the sacred? For example, if Mrs. McEwen is a devout Roman Catholic who has found great comfort and solace in the rites of confession and the eucharist, might the use of such rites break the spiritual impasse in which she finds herself?

The chaplain could also explore whether Mrs. McEwen's religious practices are not working because her beliefs, like her symbols of God, have "broken" in the midst of this crisis, and have become false in ways that are terribly distressing.[6] For example, Mrs. McEwen's may often have experienced God as a loving father who takes care of her. The less conscious part of this symbol of God, however, may be that God takes care of her if she takes care of herself, like not shuffling her feet when she walks. The less conscious part of her relationship with God, namely its conditional nature, may have come to the surface in her recent crisis. Her physiological reactions when she tries to engage in her religious practices may arise from anger with God. If this is the case, then the performance model is helpful in discerning the religious beliefs (in this case, that God's love and care depend upon her ability to take care of herself) that are now being enacted in the practices. The chaplain can use this approach to explore further what is going on theologically for Mrs. McEwen. In this way the chaplain can assess whether Mrs. McEwen ought to try continuing her religious practices, try other liturgical rites for connecting with God, or try spiritual practices in which she can open herself up to experiencing God in new ways. Needless to say, the kind of exploration I am describing is best suited when the chaplain will have the opportunity to meet with Mrs. McEwen over a period of time.

Correlational Model

The correlational model is likely the most familiar to pastoral caregivers educated in theologically liberal seminaries and schools of theology. The term correlate refers to how disciplines, like theology and psychology, are brought into dialogue to reflect upon pastoral care conversations. For example, in describing how a trusting relationship between the chaplain and Mrs. McEwen was being built, I used psychological language to describe the role of empathy.

In the tradition of liberal Protestant theology in the twentieth century, Seward Hiltner (1958) was a pioneer in bringing psychological and theological perspectives into dialogue to reflect upon the practice of pastoral care. In its earliest form the correlational method was articulated by Tillich (1952), a theologian who envisioned bringing the questions that arose from existential experiences to religious sources of authority, which could be interpreted to formulate answers. Theologian David Tracy (1981) proposed a revised correlational method, in which the questions and answers of existence were engaged with the questions and answers that could be interpreted when drawing upon religious sources of authority like scriptures, doctrines, confessions, and spiritual or mystical experiences.

This method became a way of engaging theological perspectives more directly during the 1960s, 1970s and 1980s when many pastoral counselors were relying primarily on therapeutic psychological perspectives and techniques, like Carl Roger's (1951) therapeutic concept of unconditional acceptance in the practice of pastoral psychotherapy, and this became a dominant approach not only for pastoral psychotherapists, but for pastoral caregivers as well. The therapeutic paradigm, so-called by Patton (1993)[7] was pervasive among pastoral caregivers, counselors and psychotherapists. Then practical theologian Don Browning challenged his colleagues to use a correlational model of pastoral theology to engage theological and psychological perspectives equally in reflecting upon the spectrum of pastoral care practices. His work, *Fundamental practical theology* (Browning, 1991), and his leadership in using a correlational method to study religious understandings and practices[8] related to the family have been an enormously rich contribution.

As I noted earlier, many liberal Protestant and Roman Catholic pastoral caregivers draw upon psychological perspectives to reflect upon care. In what has been called a therapeutic culture (Reiff, 1966; Holifield, 1983) it is easy to neglect theological studies, even though the use of these perspectives is what makes pastoral care distinctive from other forms of care. Why is it so hard for liberal Protestant and Roman Catholic pastoral caregivers to reflect theologically upon their practices? The difficulty is that the use of religious sources and norms requires fluency in the specialized languages of theology and biblical studies. Many pastoral theologians have responded to this difficulty by becoming specialized in only one theological approach. For example, in the last half of the 20th century, those desiring to bring psychological and theological perspectives into dialogue often became fluent in using Tillich's systematic theology (Tillich, 1951-1963), because Tillich was interested in psychodynamic models of personality, and specifically Freudian theory. Tillich was a congenial conversation partner with Freud, and more generally post-Freudian models of personality, like the self psychology of Kohut.[9] The problem with this uni-lingual approach was that Tillich wasn't always the most relevant or pragmatically useful theologian for reflecting upon an array of pastoral care conversations, as became evident in the contextual model of pastoral theology that I will next discuss.

I have been discussing liberal Protestant and Roman Catholic pastoral theologies and their use of a therapeutic paradigm in the 1960's, 1970's and 1980's, and how use of the correlational method by practical theologians like Don Browning has challenged such pastoral caregivers to become fluent in theological perspectives. There was a reaction to the dominance of the therapeutic paradigm in the 1960s and 1970s by Christian pastoral caregivers and counselors who were committed to conserving what they saw as the essence of their religious traditions. Some conservative Christians reacted by using pre-modern approaches to knowledge that consisted of relying solely upon Hebrew and Christian scripture as sources of religious authority, and using literal norms, and doctrines like the inerrancy of Scripture to interpret biblical texts. The pastoral theologian who exemplifies this approach is Jay Adams whose texts, like *Competent to Counsel* (Adams, 1975), are widely used in pastoral care courses in conservative Christian seminaries. This approach has been called biblical counseling or *nouthetic* counseling (the term *nouthetic* is Greek for guidance). A common practice among them is to interpret a biblical text using literal norms that yield a single meaning, and then to use this meaning as an instruction or directive for people seeking salvation, a term interpreted using their doctrinal statements. Biblical or *nouthetic* counselors eschew the use of other disciplinary perspectives, like psychological perspectives for reflecting upon care, because of their pre-modern worldview that the source of true revelation comes directly from God, as revealed in the bible.

Obviously, a hospital chaplain could not use a biblical or *nouthetic* approach to reflecting with Mrs. McEwen on her spiritual crisis, since hospital chaplains are not ethically and theologically allowed to interpret religious sources using literal norms. If, however, Mrs. McEwen's Presbyterian church was part of this conservative approach to pastoral care, then her religious leaders might use this approach to understand her crisis. Likely they would describe her crisis as one in which her salvation is endangered, and biblical texts would be used in literal directive ways to "save" her.

Another approach to the use of Christian sources and norms that took shape in reaction to the dominance of the therapeutic paradigm in liberal Protestant and Roman Catholic pastoral care and theology was also among conservative Christians who were committed to using modern psychological and biblical critical methods in reflecting upon the practice of care. This approach draws upon a correlational model of practical theology, and often relies upon scientific approaches to psychology and/or biblical critical methods for interpreting sacred texts. Besides being committed to conserving what they see as the essence of their Christian tradition, they are committed to using modern approaches to knowledge, in the sciences or in biblical studies. Those relying upon science can be described as positivists who assume that there is a reality about which claims can be made that are true in all times and places. Christians committed to this modern worldview and specifically the scientific method meet in associations like the Christian Association of Psychological Studies (www.caps.net). They are also part of explicitly Christian doctoral programs in psychology that have been approved by the American Psychological Association. As psychologists of religion they are committed to using scientific methods rigorously to investigate the psychological function of religion. They do not often explicitly draw upon religious sources and norms of authority, and often only in journals that represent their explicitly Christian approach to psychology.[10] When they do use theological perspectives often they use theological terms reflecting current systematic theologies articulated by conservative Christians. They tend to be theologically uni-lingual in their use of a common conservative Christian theology in the ways that some liberal Protestant or Roman Catholics are uni-lingual in their use of Tillich or others.

The other conservative Christian approach to pastoral care that draws upon modern approaches to knowledge are those who rely upon the historical-critical biblical methods developed during the Enlightenment, to investigate the origins (when and by whom) of books of the Hebrew and Christian scriptures, and more generally the original meaning of the text.[11] The modernist assumption is that the original meaning is the true meaning. This approach is most clearly seen in debates on sexual orientation, in which the biblical texts on homosexual male behavior are the ultimate source of religious authority for dealing with sexual orientation issues. Historical-critical methods, along with conservative Christian theologies, are used to describe homosexual behavior as sinful, and to challenge social science sources and norms of authority that argue that homosexual orientations are not pathological.

In a hospital setting, in which social sciences and medical knowledge are often used with modernist assumptions about truth, it would be easy for the chaplain to rely heavily on these sources of authority to convince Mrs. McEwen that she must accept 'the reality" that she cannot live by herself in her own home anymore. The chaplain might then draw upon a psychological approach to understand Mrs. McEwen's spiritual crisis as fueled by anger. If she is operating out of a therapeutic paradigm, without bringing explicit theological perspectives to bear upon this pastoral care conversation, she will try to have Mrs. McEwen uncover or cathartically release her anger, in the hopes that this will clear the impasse in her relationship with God. If the chaplain were to draw upon correlational approaches in pastoral theology that bring psychological and theological perspectives into dialogue, she could look at Lester's (2003) *The Angry Christian*, if anger was an issue for Mrs. McEwen.

Narrative Model

The narrative model of pastoral theology is the model that is most often intuitively used by pastoral caregivers who are not committed to a regulative or performance model of pastoral care. In this model, caregivers immerse themselves in the careseeker's narrative, listening for how the suffering they are now experiencing reflects the story of their lives, especially as it is embedded in the stories of their family of origin, their community of faith, and their ethnic background.

Within this approach, caregivers can draw upon biblical stories, bringing the narratives of sacred texts into dialogue with the personal, family and communal narratives of careseekers. This approach is especially rich within ethnic religious traditions, like many African-American Christian communities. These sources of religious authority are biblical stories, particularly the story of the Exodus of the Israelites from Egypt, and also the stories of religious leaders or elders who have challenged racism. This model of pastoral care is reflected in the work of Wimberly (1991).

Various other models of narrative pastoral theology have been developed. Gerkin (1986) draws upon hermenetical philosophical perspectives and psychodynamic models of personality to propose a pastoral care approach that culminates in what Gerkin calls a fusion of the horizons of biblical narratives and personal/family/communal narratives. Anderson and Foley (1998) look at how narrative theological perspectives can be used alongside liturgies, resulting in strategies for care based upon liturgical celebrations of life cycle transitions like becoming married, becoming parents, marrying again, and so on.

Lester's (2003) approach to understanding the anger of religiously-committed persons, described previously in terms of the correlational model, also incorporates elements of the narrative model, in that faith narratives are a religious source of authority. In my use of films and novels as case studies depicting complex life experiences (Doehring 1997), I have drawn upon film studies and literary critical methods to open up the multiple meanings of these narratives.[12]

This discussion of the narrative model highlights the array of ways that narrative can be made central in pastoral care. In the verbatim of the pastoral care conversation between the chaplain and Mrs. McEwen, the chaplain can more intentionally use a narrative method to elicit more narrative details about Mrs. McEwen's life, and especially her relationship with God. A narrative approach to finding out more about her relationship with God could be a way of engaging empathically with Mrs. McEwen in what could be a difficult conversation. This narrative approach could also be used to interpret Mrs. McEwen's favorite psalms, in terms of how they describe relationships between peoples of faith and God.

Contextual Model

Those who use contextual models recognize and are explicit that their models of pastoral theology and care are contextual, arising out of particular contexts and describing persons in terms of their social identities, aspects of which interact to give them access to, or deny them social resources.[13] There are many examples of contextual pastoral theologies by those committed to reconstructing patriarchal, heterosexist, and racial aspects of their religious traditions. Some of these draw upon gender studies in elaborating pastoral theologies for women in particular contexts experiencing certain kinds of suffering (Neuger, 2001; Doehring , 1999; Gill-Austern & Miller-McLemore, 1999; Moessner,1996; Grieder, 1997; Bons-Storm, 1996), and for men of various classes and racial identities (Neuger & Poling, 1997). There are pastoral contextual theologies for various Asian ethnicities (Park, 1993), and for gay and lesbian persons (Marshall, 1997; Graham,1997). These contextual theologies usually draw upon cultural studies concerning various aspects of social identity (gender, race, sexual orientation, social class, and so on), and find congruent theological conversation partners in various feminist, gay or lesbian, African-American, Asian and other liberation theologies. These are oriented toward strategies of care that sustain persons, families, communities and minority groups in the face of oppression, and which seek to transform social, economic, and religious systems in which power is abused.

In using a contextual approach with Mrs. McEwen, the chaplain assesses the ways in which the various systems—cultural, religious, community, family— in which her life is embedded are helping her cope with or exacerbating her suffering (Doehring, 2004a). Social class, especially in terms of financial resources, will be an important aspect in considering Mrs. McEwen's options. Is she able to afford in-home care? Another aspect to do with culture is whether she is in a geographic area where an alternative elder care program can allow her to remain in her home and come for elder care during the day.

In discussing the correlational model earlier, I highlighted its limitations when modern assumptions are used to claim particular psychological and theological perspectives as true in all times and places. The contextual model, by its commitment to constructing contextual pastoral theologies, is most congruent with post-modern approaches to knowledge where truth claims are provisional, arising out the particularities of the context. Using a contextual approach, the chaplain in the case study will consider which theological and psychological perspectives meet the following criteria:

1. Contextual meaningfulness: do the theological and psychological perspectives under consideration help counselors explore more fully the complexity of religious/spiritual and psychological experiences they are studying, or do these perspectives simplify and close-down meanings?
2. Inter-disciplinary meaningfulness: can the theological and psychological perspectives that are being considered become lively conversation partners? Does cross-disciplinary conversation open up dialogue, or truncate it?
3. Pragmatic usefulness: Do the theological and psychological perspectives lend themselves to formulation of strategies for seeking care and justice? Is a perspective so abstract that it is difficult to understand and use? Does it remain in the stratosphere of theory so complex that it is difficult to relate to pragmatic strategies?

A chaplain providing care to Mrs. McEwen will ask herself whether the psychological or theological perspectives under consideration open up many rich ways of understanding Mrs. McEwen and her God. For example, she may decide that biblical theological perspectives on the psalms, particularly the psalms of lamentation, like Billman and Migliore's (1999) *Rachel's Lament*, would be highly relevant, meaningful, and useful in formulating strategies for care. This use of the bible as a source of authority is based on post-modern norms for interpretation, that assume that there are multiple, sometimes conflicting meanings that become evident in biblical studies of the Book of Psalms. Billman and Migliore's (1999) theological reflections on biblical laments can be brought into dialogue with cultural studies on aging that articulate and critique attitudes toward the frail elderly, and how these attitudes inform care. The chaplain can also draw upon gender studies of frail elderly women, and psychological studies of aging, and particularly the function of religion for the frail elderly, or how frail elderly persons use religious courses to cope with stress (Koenig & Weaver, 1997).

Conclusions

In elaborating Scalise's five models of pastoral theology I have described a rich and perhaps bewildering array of ways to bridge the gap between theory and practice when pastoral care conversations become explicitly theological. When such models are discussed in terms of pre-modern, modern and post-modern approaches to knowledge, readers may feel that they are the rarified stratosphere of abstract theory. Such mind-stretching and perhaps mind-numbing discussions of post-modern approaches can appear to be intellectual exercises. In turning to practice I have outlined what pastoral care might look like with many of these pastoral theological models.

One conclusion that can de drawn from this discussion of the array of pastoral theologies and practices that arise from Scalise's five models of pastoral theology and their pre-modern, modern and post-modern versions is that there are many ways of bring theology into dialogue with other disciplinary perspectives and with various practices of pastoral care.

A second conclusion is that pastoral theologians and caregivers are accountable for knowing their assumptions concerning religious sources and the norms they use to interpret these sources. As the history of Christianity demonstrates, such sources have been used by those in authority to abuse their power in breath-takingly violent ways. In order to not participate in this inglorious history, pastoral theologians and caregivers are accountable for how they use religious sources and norms of authority.

A third conclusion is that theological education, whether in training for ministry or continuing education for pastoral caregivers, ought to be opportunities to reflect critically upon one's assumptions about the use of religious sources and norms, and the pastoral theological method one uses to bridge theory and practice. Education must also include continued opportunities to become literate and fluent in theological, cultural, and social scientific perspectives that are relevant, meaningful, and pragmatically useful in one's practice of care.

The final conclusion is that the challenges of practicing pastoral care and constructing pastoral theologies are enormous. Being engaged in such ministry involves life- long learning. The benefits of such learning are that pastoral caregivers and theologians are engaged in using theological perspectives in dialogue with other disciplinary perspectives in ways that open up the richness of practice.

References

Adams, J. (1975). *Competent to counsel.* Philadelphia, PA: Presbyterian and Reformed Publishing Company.

Anderson, Herbert & Edward Foley. (1998). *Mighty stories, dangerous rituals: Weaving together the human and the divine.* San Francisco: Jossey Bass

Barton, John. (1998). Historical critical approaches. In Barton, John (Ed.)*The Cambridge companion to biblical interpretation,* pp. 9-20. Cambridge, England: Cambridge University Press.

Bons-Storm, Riet. (1996). *The incredible woman: Listening to women's silences in pastoral care and counseling.* Nashville: Abingdon.

Browning, Don. (1976). *The moral context of pastoral care.* Philadelphia: Westminster.

Browning, Donald. S. (1991). *A fundamental practical theology: Descriptive and strategic proposals.* Minneapolis: Fortress.

Doehring, Carrie. (1995). *Taking care: Monitoring power dynamics and relational boundaries in pastoral care and counseling.* Nashville: Abingdon.

Doehring, Carrie. (1999). A method of feminist pastoral theology. In Brita Gill-Austern & Bonnie Miller-McLemore (Eds.), *Feminist and womanist pastoral theology* (pp. 95–111). Nashville: Abingdon Press.

Doehring, Carrie. (1997). Enlivening models of pastoral care: Relating theory to the complex life experiences depicted in fiction. *Pastoral Psychology* 46 (Summer): 19-33.

Doehring, Carrie. (2002). Theological literacy and fluency in a new millennium: A pastoral theological perspective." In Rodney L.Petersen with Nancy M Rourke (Eds.) *Theological literacy for the twenty-first century* (pp. 311 – 324). Grand Rapids: Eerdmans..

Doehring, Carrie. (2004a). *Theologically-based care: A post-modern approach.* Accepted for publication by Louisville: Westminister/John Knox.

Doehring, Carrie. (2004b). *Pastoral care of Bess in Breaking the Waves: A contextual practical theological approach.* Submitted for publication.

George, Mark. (2004). Personal communication.

Gerkin, Charles V. (1986). *Widening the horizons: Pastoral responses to a fragmented society.* Philadelphia: Westminster.

Gill-Austern, Brita & Bonnie Miller-McLemore, (Eds.) (1999). *Feminist and womanist pastoral theology.* Nashville: Abingdon Press.

Graham, Elaine. (1996*). Transforming practice: Pastoral theology in an age of uncer tainty.* New York: Mowbray.

Graham, Larry Kent. (1997). *Discovering images of God: Narratives of care among lesbi ans and gays.* Louisville: Westminster John Knox.

Greider, Kathleen. (1997). *Reckoning with aggression: Theology, violence and vitality.* Louisville: Westminster John Knox.

Holifield, E. Brooks. (1983). *A history of pastoral care in America.* Nashville: Abingdon.

Hiltner, Seward . (1958). *Preface to Pastoral Theology.* Nashville, Abingdon.

Hunter, Rodney J. (1995). The Therapeutic Tradition of Pastoral Care and Counseling, in Pamela D. Couture and Rodney J. Hunter (Eds.) *Pastoral care and social con flict,* 17-31. Nashville: Abingdon..

Hunter, Rodney J. and John Patton. (1995). "The Therapeutic Tradition's Theological and Ethical Commitments Viewed through its Pedagogical Practices: A Tradition in Transition," in Pamela D. Couture and Rodney J. Hunter (Eds). *Pastoral Care and Social Conflict,* 32-43. Nashville: Abingdon.

Johnson, Eric L. (1997). Christ, the Lord of psychology, *Journal of Psychology and The ology* 25, no. 1: 18.

Koenig, Harold George & Andrew Weaver. (1997). *Counseling troubled adults: A hand book for pastors and religious caregiver.* Nashville: Abingdon.

Lartey, Emmanuel Y. (2002). Embracing the Collage: Pastoral Theology in an Era of 'Post-Phenomena'. *Journal of Pastoral Theology,* 12:2, 1-10.

Lester, Andrew. (2003). *The angry Christian: A theology for pastoral care and counsel ing.* Louisville: Westminster John Knox.

Lindbeck, George A. (1984). *The nature of doctrine: Religion and theology in a Postliberal Age* Philadelphia: Westminster.

Marshall, Joretta. (1997). *Counseling lesbian partners.* Louisville: Westminster John Knox.

Moessner, Jeanne. (Ed.). 1996. *Through the eyes of women: Insights for pastoral care.* Minneapolis: Fortress.

Neuger, Christie Cozad. (2001). *Counseling women: A narrative, pastoral approach.* Minneapolis: Fortress.

Neuger, Christie Cozad & James Newton Poling, (Eds.). (1997). *The care of men.* Nashville: Abingdon.

Neville, Robert C. (1996). *The truth of broken symbols.* Albany: SUNY Press.

Oden, Thomas, C. (1984). *Care of souls in the Classic tradition.* Philadelphia: Fortress.

Oden, Thomas C. (1992). The historic pastoral care tradition: A resource for Christian psychologists, *Journal of Psychology and Theology* 20: 137-146.

Park, Andrew Sung. (1993). *The wounded heart of God.* New York: Maryknoll.

Patton, John. (1993). *Pastoral Care in Context: An Introduction to Pastoral Care* Louisville: Westminster/John Knox..

Religion, Culture and Family project. http://divinity.uchicago.edu/family

Rieff, Philip. 1966. *The triumph of the therapeutic: Uses of faith after Freud.* New York: Harper & Row,

Rogers, Carl R. (1951). *Client-centered therapy: Its current practices, implications, and theory.* London, Constable.

Schlauch, Chris. (1995). Faithful companioning. Minneapolis: Fortress.

Steinfels, Peter. (2004). Beliefs. *The New York Times*, February 28.

The Upper Room: Daily devotional guide. www.upperroom.org.

Scalise, Charles. (2003). *Bridging the gap: Connecting what you learned in seminary with what you find in the congregation.* Nashville: Abingdon.

Tillich, Paul. (1952). *The courage to be.* New Haven: Yale University.

Tillich, Paul. (1951-1963). *Systematic theology.* 3 Volumes. Chicago: University of Chicago.

Tracy, David. (1981). *The analogical imagination: Christian theology and the culture of pluralism.* New York: Crossroad.

Wimberly, Edward. (1991). *African-American pastoral care. Nashville: Abingdon.*

NOTES:

[1] *The Upper Room* is a monthly periodical published at www.upperroom.org..

[2] In this definition I focus on Christian and Jewish pastoral care, and not on care provided by religious professionals and volunteers in other religious traditions, since the vast majority of literature on pastoral care has, until recently, arisen with Christian contexts.

[3] Mark George, a scholar of the Hebrew Bible, clarified my understanding of the shift from modern to post-modern approaches to knowledge in biblical studies.

[4] See Doehring (2004a) for a further discussion of pastoral care and pre-modern, modern, and post-modern approaches to knowledge and truth

[5] Conversation with Mark George (2004)

[6] See my use of Neville's (1996) *The truth of broken symbols* in Doehring (2004a and 2004b).

[7] See also Hunter (1995) and Hunter and Patton (1995).

[8] see the web site for the Religion, Culture and Family Project, http://ivinity.uchicago.edu/family.

[9] Schaluch's (1995) Faithful companioning is a good example of a correlational model of pastoral theology that brings Kohut and Tillich into dialogue to reflect upon the practice of pastoral psychotherapy.

[10] For an example of an article that draws explicitly on religious sources see Johnson

(1997)

[11] "Very sophisticated philological and linguistic studies could be brought to bear on obscure texts, in order to establish what the original author could have meant in his own historical period" (Barton, 1998, 10).

[12] I have used the literary work of John Updike, Toni Morrison, Raymond Carver, and Iris Murdoch on reflecting upon power dynamics and relational boundaries (Doehring, 1995), a novel by David Lodge to discuss theological fluency in pastoral care (Doehring 2002), and the films *Affliction* (Doehring, 2004a) and *Breaking the waves* (Doehring, 2004b).

[13] This chapter offers a contextual understanding of pastoral theology and care, in that it is constructed using disciplinary perspectives like social constructionism and postmodern approaches to theological studies, in a context of theological education where these approaches are valued. It will be most relevant and meaningful to those working in similar contexts.

ABOUT THE AUTHOR:

Carrie Doehring is an assistant professor of pastoral care and counseling at Iliff School of Theology. She is ordained in the Presbyterian Church, U.S.A., licensed as a psychologist in Massachusetts, and a diplomat in the American Association of Pastoral Counselors. *Her forthcoming book,* Theologically-based Care: A Postmodern Approach *will be published by Westminster/John Knox. Carrie Doehring can be reached at cdoehring@iliff.edu.*

SECTION TWO:

CARING FOR PARISHIONERS

Chapter 6
Stormy Weather:
Understanding Domestic Violence & Child Sexual Abuse

by Stephen A. Dean Ph.D.

Domestic violence appears to be one of the most serious problems facing society today. One-third of women report being kicked, hit, choked, or harmed by their partners (Gazmarian et al., 2000). Similarly, Straus and Gelles (1990) reported that 30 percent of couples experience physical aggression at least once in their marriage. Domestic violence is not confined to marital couples. Leonard and Senchak (1996) reported that one-third of men in their study used physical violence against their fiancés in the previous year. Domestic violence seems to be even more probable in couples who are in counseling. O'Leary, Vivian and Malone (1992) reported that more than 50 percent of husbands had been physically aggressive with their wives within the past year.

Many of the batterers that I have worked with often complain that their partner is physically aggressive with them. Some researchers have reported that violence appears to be reciprocal in low levels of physical aggression. Cascardi, Langhinrichsen, and Vivian (1992) reported that 86 percent of partner aggression was reciprocal. So why has so much attention been focused on men's aggression and not on women's aggression? It appears that women are more likely to sustain more serious injuries than men following acts of domestic violence. According to the American Medical Association, 15 to 30 percent of emergency room visits by women are due to acts of domestic violence. In a study of military couples referred to a treatment program for domestic violence, 38 percent of the couples reported that wives were injured while the husband received no injury (Cantos, Neidig, and O'leary, 1994). However, in the same study there were only five percent of couples in which the husband received injury and the wife was not injured. Langhinrichsen-Rohling, Neidig and Thorn (1995) reported that two-thirds of husbands stated that they received no injuries following marital violence, whereas only 35 percent of women stated they were not injured.

Another reason why men's violence is more often the focus of intervention is because women are more likely to incur psychological injuries as well as physical injuries following acts of domestic violence. Stets and Straus (1990) noted that women reported more depression and stress following husband violence than men reported following wife violence. Women's self-esteem also seems to be more negatively impacted than men's after incidents of domestic violence. Men's violence is also more often studied because it appears to be motivated by differing factors than women's violence. Men are more likely to report using violence as a means of controlling their partners (Hamberger, Lohr, and Bonge, 1994) whereas only women listed self-defense and escape as reasons for using violence.

Impact of Domestic Violence

Victims of domestic violence appear to be negatively impacted in a variety of ways. A number of studies have shown that battered women are vulnerable to developing Post Traumatic Stress Syndrome (PTSD) (Houskamp and Foy, 1991, Gleason, 1993, Astin, Lawrence and Foy, 1993). Some of the more prominent PTSD symptoms noted by battered women include numbed affect, startle response, sleeping problems, eating difficulties and nightmares. The likelihood of a victim developing PTSD seems to increase as the severity of the violence increases. The development of PTSD also appears to be negatively correlated with the level of support a victim receives following domestic violence (i.e. greater levels of support are associated with less risk of developing PTSD and vice versa). Thus, it appears that a victim's support system can help buffer the deleterious effects of domestic violence.

Some women experience severe distress after being assaulted by their partner. Riggs, Kilpatrick and Resnick (1992) compared groups of women who had been raped by their husbands, raped by a stranger, assaulted by their husband, or experienced some other type of assault. They concluded that there were no group differences between the four different groups of women, and that victims of domestic violence were no less traumatized than women who were victimized by others.

A number of studies suggest that victims of domestic violence are at risk for developing clinical depression. Andrews (1995) reported that 61 percent of women who were victims of marital abuse suffered from depression. Sato and Heiby (1992) found that 47 percent of battered women qualified for a diagnosis of depression. The risk of depression for women who are victims of domestic violence seems to increase with the frequency and severity of violence. Being physically abused by one's partner also appears to lower one's self-esteem. Most studies suggest that battered women have lower self-esteem. However, the self-esteem of battered women may improve once they are no longer in a relationship with a batterer. Aguilar and Nightingale (1994) reported that women who had not been with an abusive partner for at least one year had higher self-esteem than women who were involved in a relationship with an abusive partner.

One common misnomer is that victims of domestic violence continue to stay in abusive relationships. It appears that domestic violence is often a precursor to the ending of marriages. Heyman, O'Leary, and Jouriles (1995) found that premarital aggression predicted a woman seeking divorce and overall lower marital satisfaction. Schwartz (1988) reported that out of 2,254 women in a national crime survey, 32 percent were divorced and 47 percent were separated. Interestingly, in the same study, women who had been assaulted by strangers were divorced only 19 percent of the time and separated only 11 percent of the time. Similarly, Herbert, Silver and Ellard (1991) found that 66 percent of women had left an abusive relationship prior to the interview by researchers. Although women do leave abusive relationships, they may have multiple separations prior to ending a relationship. Okun (1986) completed a study using 187 women who lived in a domestic violence shelter. The average number of separations of women who returned to their partners was two, whereas the number of separations of women who ended the relationship was five. One of the factors that appear to affect the decision to leave an abusive relationship is economic independence. A six-year study by the US Maternal and Child Health Bureau and the National Institute of Mental Health reported that 60 percent of very low- income mothers had experienced severe physical abuse. Okun (1986) reported that 55 percent of the women who had a better income than their husbands ended their marriage immediately. Only 28 percent of woman who had earned the same level of income or less income than their husband ended their marriage immediately.

Another factor that may influence a woman's decision to leave an abusive relationship are the attributions she makes regarding the abuse. In general, it appears that most women tend to blame their partners for the abuse rather than themselves. Perhaps a more important attribution may be the perception of the likelihood of a partner being violent again. Holzworth-Monroe, Jacobson, Fehrenbach, and Fruzzetti (1992) reported that women believed that their husbands being violent with them in the future was less likely than other negative nonviolent behavior. Women appear to blame external factors for partner violence such as drinking and stress rather than internal factors of their partners such as personality characteristics. Women who perceive domestic violence as being unstable (i.e. unlikely to occur again) are less likely to leave an abusive relationship.

Women are not the only ones who are negatively impacted by domestic violence. Children appear to suffer considerably from the witnessing of domestic violence. The number of children who have witnessed domestic violence is staggering. Carlson (1984) estimated that " at least 3.3 million children yearly are at risk of exposure to parental violence" (p.160). Carlson believed that her estimate is likely to be low because it only includes exposure to violence likely to cause injury, and because her estimate excluded families with children under the age of three. Straus (1992) estimated that as many as ten million teenagers a year are exposed to parental violence. He obtained his estimate by asking adults " whether, during their teenage years, their father had hit their mother and how often " (p.98) as well as if they had witnessed their mother hit their father. Strauss reported that 13 percent had memories of a violent incident between their parents, with 50 percent recalling their father striking their mother, 19 percent recalling their mother hitting their father, and 31 percent recalling witnessing both parents hitting one another. The adults who recalled witnessing domestic violence reported seeing an average of nine incidents of domestic violence during their teenage years.

Other researchers have also noted the large number of children who have witnessed domestic violence. Silvern, Karyl, Waelde, Hodges, Starek, Heidt, and Min (1995) asked college students if they had witnessed violence between their parents. Forty one percent of women and 32 percent of men reported having witnessed domestic violence. Part of the difficulty in obtaining more accurate estimates of children who witness domestic violence is that parents often believe that they have somehow shielded their children from the violence within their homes. O'Brien, John, Margolin and Erel (1994) found that 78 percent of the time in which a child reported that he or she had witnessed domestic violence, at least one parent denied the occurrence of any violence or stated that their children had not witnessed violence.

Witnessing domestic violence is emotionally harmful to children and is considered as psychological maltreatment by the American Psychological Association. Children may be subjected to domestic violence in ways other than being an eyewitness to physical violence. Examples include a father taking a child hostage to force a mother to return to the home, using a child as a spy, threatening a child's mother, and interrogating a child about a mother's activities. Children can be used as pawns in domestic disputes by telling them that the mother is responsible for the breakup of the family.

The extent of a child's suffering seems to depend on a number of variables. The probability of harm to children appears to increase with both the frequency and severity of domestic violence. O'Keefe (1994) reported that " children showing more severe disturbance were more likely to have witnessed a greater frequency/severity of marital violence " (p.72). Children who are physically abused and witness domestic violence also appear to fare worse than children who witness domestic violence without being physically abused. There seems to be a greater risk for children being abused in a home where there is domestic violence. Holtzworth-Monroe, Smutzler, and Sandin (1997) noted that " Strauss et al. (1980) found that there was a 129% greater chance of child maltreatment in a home where conjugal violence was present " (p.89).

One of the more insidious outcomes of domestic violence is that neither parent may be emotionally available for their children. Mothers may be emotionally unavailable because they may be overwhelmed, depressed, and/or suffering from PTSD. Fincham, Grych and Osborne (1994) note that " fathers in particular may tend to withdraw from their children when they're dissatisfied with their marriages " (p.134). Children's sense of security is likely to be impacted when parents are emotionally unavailable to them. Davies and Cummings (1994) put forth a concept they labeled as the " emotional security hypothesis, " which says that children develop a sense of emotional security from positive parent-child and husband-wife relationships. A number of researchers have posited that having at least one good parent-child relationship or having support outside the immediate family (e.g. friends, grandparents) seems to provide a buffer against parental conflict and helps mitigate any negative impact on a child's development.

Boys tend to react differently to domestic violence than girls. Boys tend to externalize or act out their emotional difficulties, and are more likely to have behavior or conduct problems at school and home. Boys are also more likely to imitate any violence perpetrated in the home. Carlson (1990) found that adolescent males exposed to marital violence were more likely to hit their mothers than females. Spaccarelli, Coatsworth and Bowden (1995) studied 213 adolescents incarcerated for violent crimes. Adolescents exposed to family violence endorsed more than others in the study that " acting aggressively enhances one's reputation or self-image " (p.173). However, there have been studies that suggested that girls exposed to family violence tend to display more aggressive behavior especially as they get older (Spaccarelli, Sandler, & Roosa, 1994).

Children who witness domestic violence also show what has been labeled as " internalized '' behaviors. A number of studies have shown that children exposed to family violence are more likely to" show anxiety, depression, trauma symptoms and temperament problems " (Edleson, 1999, p.846) than children who did not witness violence in the home. Children who have been exposed to domestic violence also appear to be less socially competent (Adamson & Thompson, 1998). They tend to be less skilled at conflict resolution and have less effective problem-solving ideas.

Some researchers have attempted to examine the long-term effects of children who witness domestic violence. Silvern et.al (1995) found that witnessing violence, as a child was associated with "adult reports of depression, trauma-related symptoms, and low self-esteem among women, and trauma-related symptoms in men " (Edleson, 1999, p. 861). There has been limited research on the association between witnessing domestic violence as a child and perpetrating domestic violence as an adult. However, Rosenbaum and O'Leary (1981) reported that male batterers were more likely to have been exposed to family violence. They also note though that 82 percent of the sample were also physically abused, which may have accounted for the perpetration of domestic violence. In a somewhat different vein, Spaccarrelli et al., (1995) reported that witnessing domestic violence and being abused were significantly associated with teenagers' use of violence.

What is Domestic Violence

From a psychological perspective, domestic violence encompasses far more than physical aggression. It is quite possible and even likely that others will be harmed in a significant way through behaviors that do not constitute severe physical aggression (e.g. punching, choking, kicking). Seventy-two percent of women who had been severely battered reported that emotional abuse was more damaging to them than physical abuse (Follingstad, Rutledge, Berg, Hause, & Polek, 1990). Psychological aggression (e.g. name calling, verbal insults, swearing) has been reported to be so prevalent among couples (e.g. 89-97 percent of couples seeking marital therapy) that some researchers have questioned whether it makes sense to label such behavior as abusive (Holzworth-Munroe, Smutzler, & Sandin, 1997). They suggested that psychological aggression may be considered abusive when it reaches certain levels of frequency and severity.

There is no single definition of what constitutes psychological, emotional, or verbal abuse. Follingstad and DeHart (2000) attempted to define more specifically what constitutes psychological abuse. They provided 449 psychologists with a questionnaire in which they were asked to rate specific behaviors as either " a) the behavior was never abusive, no matter what the circumstances ("no"); b) the behavior might be considered abusive in some contexts or under some conditions ("maybe"); or c) the behavior was always abusive, no matter what the circumstances ("yes"), (p.902). They found that the psychologists' responses were clustered into five different groups. The first group they described as threats to physical health. The following constitutes the first group of items along with the percentage of psychologists who responded " yes ":

Threatened to disfigure her permanently	98%
Threatened to hurt her	99%
Prevented her from getting necessary medical care	95%
Threatened to hurt her family or children or friends	99%

The second group of items were described as control over physical freedoms (isolation/restriction, degradation). The following are the items in that group along with the percentage of psychologists who responded " yes ":

Would not let her sleep	89%
Would not let her leave the house	94%
Wanted to use her as a prostitute	93%
Forced her to eat from a bowl on the floor	100%

The third group of items were described as general destabilization (intimidation, degradation, isolation/restriction/monopolizing, destabilizing perceptions).

The following are the items and the percentage of psychologists who respond " yes ":

Harassed her at work (e.g. called often, showed up unexpectedly interfered with what she had to do at work)	95%
Damaged her personal belongings	80%
Threatened to hurt a pet	86%
Physically abused a pet	77%
Threatened to hurt himself	52%
Threatened to take the children away from her	83%
Called her derogatory names (e.g. slut, bitch, whore)	93%
Forced her to beg for something essential	94%
Treated her like she was stupid, inferior to him	85%
Demanded obedience to his every order; whatever he said he expected her to obey	94%
Would not let her go anywhere without him	88%
Did not let her socialize with female friends or family	83%
Tried to turn family, friends, and children against her	88%
Controlled flow of information into/out of the house by limiting phone/car use	85%
Threatened to have her committed to a mental institution	79%
Tried to make her believe that she was crazy	92%
Tried to convince her family, friends, or children that she was crazy	78%
Denied her access to money	80%
Threatened to deny her economic support	72%

The fourth group of items were referred to as dominating/controlling (jealousy/ suspicion, isolation/restriction/monopolization, control of personal behavior, emotional withholding / blackmail, verbal abuse, treatment as inferior). There was less agreement amongst psychologists in this cluster of items as to whether a behavior was always abusive. I have therefore listed only the items that were endorsed 50 percent or more of the time as always being abusive.

Would not allow her to speak to or look at other men	80%
Expressed jealousy of any men who came into contact with his wife	51%
Checked her belongings looking for confirmations of his suspicions	61%
Listened in on telephone conversations when she did not know	70%
Followed her when she was away from home	65%
Monitored her time; made sure he knew where she was at all times	66%

Made her account for her whereabouts at all times	80%
Forced her to discuss past sexual relationships	68%
Insisted that she answer any question he asked	65%
Denied her any private time	52%
Intruded in her work with demands that she do things for him immediately	68%
Refused to let her work outside the home	65%
Kept her from engaging in self-improvement (e.g. exercise class, continuing education, volunteer work)	71%
Was rude to guests to discourage visitation in their home	56%
Chose her friends	77%
Decided what activities she could engage in	77%
Decided whether she could smoke or drink	66%
Decided what makeup and clothes she wore	63%
Decided what she could eat	78%
Blamed her for his own problems	63%
Blamed her for things that were totally unrelated to her	74%
Stayed angry until she cooperated	55%
Threatened to reveal secrets that she had told him	64%
Would not let her talk about her feelings	51%
Left for long periods of time during the day or night with no explanation	60%
Threatened to have an affair	52%
Swore at her	52%
Criticized her sexual performance/attractiveness	61%
Insulted her in front of others	81%
Threatened to humiliate her in public	83%
Treated her as inferior to himself	65%
Played cruel jokes on her	61%
Threw tantrums, breaking objects in the house	76%
Made her ask him every time she needed money	73%
Used money that the family needs for his own addictions/hobbies	57%
Refused to pay his fair share to maintain the family & household	54%

The fifth group of items were labeled as ineptitude (rigid gender roles, role failure). No item within the fifth group was endorsed by 50 percent or more of psychologists as always being abusive. However, on all but one item in the fifth group, more than 50 percent of psychologists rated an item as either always abusive or as possibly abusive under some conditions (i.e. " maybe "). Thus, it's important to evaluate any potential abusive behavior within the context of the situation.

Appendix 1 is a copy of a form that is used during intakes with men referred for domestic violence at the Voyager Program in Canton, Ohio. Clinicians use the form as a guide to assess the potential of abusive behaviors. Men are asked to rate themselves as to how often they in engage in the listed behaviors. They are not given the form to complete, but are asked directly by a therapist. Appendix 2 is a form that has been periodically used at the Voyager Program and Melymbrosia Associates when completing evaluations with women who are suspected of having been abused by their partner. These forms have been listed in the appendices to assist clergy in trying to determine if abusive behavior is present within a relationship.

Considerable attention has been devoted to psychological abuse not only because of its harmful effect on others, but because it also seems to generally precede physical violence. Less than one percent of women had indicated that physical aggression had occurred without some form of verbal aggression (Stets, 1990). Malamuth, Linz, Heavey, and Acker (1995) (reported in Holzworth-Monroe, Smutzler, and Sandin,1997) stated that "men's use of verbal aggression was the only direct predictor of their use of physical non-sexual aggression toward women " (p.193). Other studies have shown that psychological abuse early within a marriage tended to lead to physical abuse within the first years of marriage (Murphy & O'Leary, 1989, O'Leary, Malone, & Tyree, 1994).

Characteristics of Batterers

A number of demographic variables are correlated with an increased risk of battering. Age appears to be negatively correlated with the risk of marital violence. As one gets older the risk of domestic violence decreases. Pan, Neidig and O'Leary (1994) found that the risk of mild physical aggression decreased more than 70 percent for every increase in age of 10 years. Perhaps more significantly, they found that severe physical aggression decreased by more than 80 percent for every increase in age of 10 years. Similarly, Hampton and Gelles (1994) reported that couples under 30 years old had rates of severe violence that were three times greater than couples over 40 years of age.

Income level appears to be another demographic variable related to domestic violence. Holzworth-Monroe, Smutzler, and Bates (1997) reported that most studies that examined income have found that social class is negatively correlated with violence. The higher a couple's income or social class, the less the risk for domestic violence. Holzworth-Munroe et al. state that there are some studies that have not found a connection between income level and violence. However, they also point out that while income may not be related to violence in some studies, other related variables such as " financial stress" may be associated with domestic violence. They cite a study by Neff, Holaman, and Schluter (1995) in which income was not a predictor of violence, but men's perceptions of "financial stress " was predictive of violence.

Unemployment appears to be a risk factor for domestic violence. Kaufman-Kantor, Jasinski, and Aldarondo (1994) reported that one's employment status was predictive of husband violence. Being unemployed and young may be especially pernicious. Howell and Pugleisi (1988) found that the probability of violence was more than six times greater for men who were unemployed and under 40 compared to men who were unemployed and over 40.

Race has been reported to be related to domestic violence. Holzworth-Munroe et al. (1997) reported that "rates of domestic violence are higher among minority couples than among their White counterparts" (p. 288). In a national survey of family violence, Straus and Gelles (1986) reported that the rate of domestic violence was higher for African-Americans than for Caucasians. Economic differences between African-Americans and Causasians does not appear to adequately account for the difference in rates of domesticviolence between them. McLaughlin, Leonard, and Senchak (1992) and Neff, Holamon, and Schluter (1995) both controlled for socioeconomic status and found that African-American women were still at higher risk for domestic violence than Caucasian women.

Kaufman-Kantor et al. (1994) did not find a significant difference in the level of domestic violence between Anglo couples and Hispanic couples. They did however find significant differences in the level of violence between subgroups of Hispanic couples. Husband violence was virtually nonexistent among Cubans, whereas 20 percent of Puerto Rican men were reported to have engaged in violence against their wives. Acculturation into the United States also appears to increase the risk for domestic violence. Individuals born in the United States were more at risk for domestic violence than individuals who immigrated to the United States (Kaufman et al., 1994). Sorenson and Telles (1991) reached a similar conclusion. They reported that Mexican-Americans born in Mexico had significantly less domestic violence than Mexican-Americans and Caucasians who were born in the United States.

Couples who live together without being married appear to be at an increased risk for domestic violence. Stets and Strauss (1989) discovered that rates of violence were 35 percent for couples who cohabitated versus only 15 percent for couples who were married. Couples in the study who were neither married or living together (i.e. dating) were reported to have a violence rate of 20 percent. McLaughlin et al. (1992) found a similar difference between women who lived with their partner and women who were married. Women who lived with their partner reported rates of violence that were two and one-half times higher than married women. Age alone does not appear to be the sole reason for the difference in domestic violence between married couples and couples who live together. Stets and Strauss (1989) found that a significant difference still existed after controlling for age, education and occupational status.

Violent husbands evince a number of personality characteristics in addition to demographic factors. In my work with men who commit domestic violence, I have found them to often exhibit signs of depression. They are often gloomy and pessimistic and appear to expect the worst from others. Men who perpetrate domestic violence have consistently shown higher rates of depression (Holzworth-Munroe, Bates, Smutzler, and Sandin,1997). Pan, et al. (1994) found in their study of nearly 12,000 men that violent men had more depressive features than nonviolent men. Furthermore, men who committed more severe acts of violence showed more depressive features than men who committed more mild acts of violence. They stated that the risk of being mildly aggressive rose by 30 percent for every 20 percent increase in depressive symptoms. The likelihood of being severely aggressive rose by 14 percent for every 20 percent increase in depressive symptoms.

Men who commit domestic violence are likely to be defensive. They tend to be insecure and feel threatened quite easily. Therapeutic work with men who commit domestic violence is time consuming because they usually have a great deal of difficulty receiving feedback and become angry quickly. O'Leary et al. (1994) showed that husbands' physical aggression was predicted by their scores on the impulsivity, defended and aggression scales of the Jackson Personality Research Form. It has been my experience that men who are violent in their homes react quickly (i.e. are impulsive) and are easily offended (i.e defended). They especially react quickly to what they perceive as criticism, and struggle to accept responsibility for their behavior. Scott and Wolfe (2000) studied men who were deemed by their partners and therapists as having changed their abusive behavior. Men who were considered as having changed " displayed a great deal of honesty about and responsibility for their past abuse.....an important part of treatment was learning to recognize their own abusive behavior " (p.834).

Some researchers have suggested that many batterers are overly sensitive to being abandoned by others. Men who are violent can experience feelings of abandonment from such benign events as their partner wanting to spend time with their friends or family. Their hypersensitivity to being abandoned is likely to stem from poor relationships with batterers' parents. This creates disturbed or insecure attachment to their parents, which carries forth into other relationships. Dutton, Saunders, Starzomski, and Bartholomew (1994) reported that maritally abusive men had higher scores than nonviolent men for fearful and preoccupied attachment. Abusive husbands may be become violent when they perceive their partner as being rejecting of them, or when they feel threatened that their partner may leave them. This may help explain why women are two to four times more likely to be killed when they separate from their partners (Wilson & Daly, 1993). Batterers' insecure attachment with their partners also helps to explain their controlling behavior. Most professionals who treat men who are abusive to their partners believe that control is one of the primary motivations for men's abusive behavior. Abusive men may try to restrict a partner in an effort to help them feel more secure. Men who are abusive to their partners are often very insecure. Their insecurity is likely to be manifested by feelings of jealousy and mistrustfulness.

Batterers' insecurity also is reflected by their tendency to be emotionally dependent on their partners. Men who are violent may attempt to present themselves as being independent and not needing anyone. However, many of them are terrified about being alone, and appear to need someone to help them cope with their sense of inadequacy. Batterers often see their partners as extensions of themselves, and do not recognize that their partners have their own feelings and needs which may be different from their feelings and needs. Men who are violent often feel threatened when their partner disagrees with them or feels different about an issue. Scott and Wolfe (2000) reported that men who appeared to have changed their abusive behavior seemed to be less dependent on their partners. Abusive men who appeared to have changed " realized that their partner had a right to their feelings and to decisions they make about discussing those feelings " (p.836).

Dutton (1995) hypothesized that men who are abusive often suffer from borderline personality disorder. The following is the diagnostic criteria for borderline personality disorder as described by the Diagnostic Statistical Manual III - Revised:

1. frantic efforts to avoid real or imagined abandonment.
2. a pattern of unstable and intense interpersonal relationships characterized by alternating between extremes of idealization and devaluation.
3. identity disturbance: markedly and persistently unstable self-image or sense of self.
4. impulsivity in at least two areas that are potentially self-damaging.
5. recurrent suicidal behavior, gestures, or threats, or self-mutilating behavior.
6. affective instability due to a marked reactivity of mood.
7. chronic feelings of emptiness.
8. inappropriate, intense anger or difficulty controlling anger.
9. transient, stress-related paranoid ideation or severe dissociative symptoms.

One needs to have five or more of the aforementioned symptoms to qualify for a diagnosis of borderline personality disorder. Men who are violent with partners are likely to have symptoms 1 and 8. As discussed earlier, batterers are also more likely to suffer with depression (symptom 6) and to be dependent on their partner (symptom 3). They also have difficulty being alone (symptom 7), and tend to be impulsive (symptom 4). Some of their thinking is paranoid in nature at times (i.e. reading evil intent into otherwise benign behavior, symptom 9). It is not unusual for batterers to alternate between devaluing their partner (i.e. verbally and physically abusing them) and adoring them (symptom 2). Walker (1979) described a cycle of abuse by men, and stated that many couples go through a " honeymoon phase " following acts of domestic violence in which the man is very loving and promises to never be abusive again. Some women have trouble leaving their partner because of his ability to act in a loving and caring manner following his abusiveness.

Another factor that increases the probability of men being impulsive and violent with their partners is the use of drugs and alcohol. O'Farrell and Murphy (1995) found that alcoholic men were six times more at risk for domestic violence than nonalcoholic men. Alcoholic men were also found to engage in more frequent and more severe violence with their partners. Pan et al. (1994) reported similar findings and stated that men with alcohol problems were 70 percent more likely to engage in acts of severe violence than men who do not have alcohol problems. They found that the use of drugs also increased the risk of severe violence by more than 120 percent. Men who are not necessarily alcoholics, but engage in periodic binge drinking, also seem to be at greater risk for violence against their partners. Kaufman-Kantor and Strauss (1987) discovered that binge drinkers were three times more at risk of being violent with their wives.

Men's attitude towards violence seems to be a risk factor for domestic violence. It's hard to believe, but there appear to be men who endorse being violent with their partners. In my therapy sessions with batterers, I have heard a number of men make such comments as " if you act like a man, I'm going to treat you like a man " (i.e. you hit me, I'm going to hit you back). Stith (1990, as reported in Holzworth-Monroe, Bates, Smutzler, and Sadin, 1997) reported that " men's approval of marital violence was the best predictor of their use of marital violence " (p.78). In another study, Dibble and Strauss (1980, as reported in Holzworth-Munroe et al., 1997) reported that men who believed " that slapping one's spouse was necessary, normal and good " (p.78) were four times more likely to have been violent with their wives. Kaufman et al. (1994) stated that husbands who endorsed slapping their wives in certain situations were at more than twice the risk of domestic violence.

A number of studies have examined the relationship between perpetrating violence against a partner and having witnessed domestic violence as a child. Most studies have found a positive relationship between committing domestic violence and witnessing domestic violence as a child. Hotaling and Sugarman (1986) for example, reviewed 16 studies and found that 14 of them showed a positive correlation between partner violence and witnessing violence as a child. Men who commit acts of severe violence are likely to have witnessed more acts of domestic violence as children. They are also more likely to have been physically abused as children. Caesar (1988) found that 62 percent of batterers in his study were physically disciplined with items such as a belt or switch versus only eight percent of nonviolent men.

Evidence appears to be mixed as to the role of stress and domestic violence. Some studies have found a relationship between stress and domestic violence while other studies have not found a relationship between them. Stress may interact with other variables in increasing the risk of domestic violence. Seltzer and Kalmus (1988) found men who had childhood exposure to family violence (i.e. had been victims of childhood abuse and had witnessed domestic violence) and had high levels of stress were 31 times more likely to commit acts of domestic violence than men who had not been exposed to family violence or had high levels of stress. Thus, the combination of childhood exposure to violence along with stress seems to create a much more dangerous situation than stress by itself or early exposure to violence by itself.

Assessing for Domestic Violence

Perhaps the most critical role that clergy can play with domestic violence is establishing the existence of domestic violence. Parishioners are likely to feel more comfortable discussing personal issues with clergy than with others. However, it is important to recognize that some parishioners are still hesitant to discuss domestic violence even with clergy. Domestic violence is often embarrassing and shameful for both the victim and perpetrator of domestic violence. O'Leary, Vivian, and Malone (1992) discovered that only six percent of women had indicated that they had been victims of domestic violence on an intake form. However, 44 percent reported that their husbands had been violent when they were directly questioned about domestic violence during an interview. Thus, one of the most useful interventions for clergy is to become comfortable with asking about the presence of violence and abuse between couples.

In addition to asking about the presence of domestic violence, it is vital to ask about the presence of domestic violence when the male partner is not present. This is especially important when men are perpetrating severe violence against their partners. A woman may fear the repercussions that might ensue following her disclosure of domestic violence, and is likely to be less forthcoming when a violent partner is present. An important variable to measure when meeting separately with a female partner is how safe she feels within the relationship. Weisz, Tolman, and Saunders (2000) asked women whose partners had been court-ordered to domestic violence treatment, " How likely would you say it is that your partner will become violent with you during a dispute in the next year " (p. 79). Victims were asked to rate the probability of future violence using a scale between 0 and 10, with 0 being " no chance of this happening, " and 10 being " sure to happen " (p.79). Weisz et al. (2000) found that asking victims the aforementioned question was the best predictor of future violence four months later. Other significant predictors of future violence listed in the study included " more violent disputes between focal incident and court date, he threatened her to get her to drop charges, kicked or bit or hit her with something, forced her to have sex, choked or strangled her, she got a personal protection order before the focal incident, she was treated for injuries from a dispute with her partner ever before the focal incident, he told her she could not leave or see certain people, he restricted her use of phone or car, and he accused her of an affair ".

Another variable to assess is the frequency and severity of any violence. Most researchers seem to agree that more frequent and more severe violence elevates one's potential for further violence. Quigley and Leonard (1996) reported that the best predictor of future violence was the initial severity of violence. When the presence of domestic violence has been established, it is vital to consider if a woman is in a potentially lethal situation. Seventy percent of murdered woman are murdered by their current or estranged partners (Campbell, 1995). One needs to be especially cautious if a man has threatened to kill or threatened to seriously harm a woman. Campbell (1995) also stated that any threats to hurt a partner is a risk factor for killing a partner. Other risk factors enumerated by Campbell for men murdering their partners include other life threatening injuries in prior assaults by a partner, prior criminal history, violence outside the home, fantasies of homicide and suicide, forcing a partner to have sex, and extreme jealousy and dominance.

Assessing for the presence of substance abuse is also essential. Numerous studies have shown an association between substance abuse and domestic violence. Drugs and alcohol increase the risk for the disinhibition of behavior and domestic violence. The risk for more severe violence also increases with the use of drugs and alcohol. Campbell (1995) listed the abuse of drugs and alcohol as a factor that increases the risk of a woman being killed by her partner.

Other criminal behavior seems to be another risk factor to assess when there is domestic violence. In particular, it is important to look for any history of violence that occurs with others outside of the home. As noted earlier, Campbell lists violence outside the home as a risk factor for men who murder their partners. In addition, Holtzworth-Munroe and Stuart (1994) suggested that one of the core dimensions for classifying batterers is the generality of violence or the presence of extra-familial violence. Some examples of extra-familial violence include fighting at work or a bar, arrests for assault, disorderly conduct, resisting arrest, rape, kidnapping, criminal damaging, or sexual assault. I also have found it useful to ask batterers how they feel about fighting. Interestingly, some men indicate that they actually enjoy fighting.

Assessing for the presence of any verbal, emotional, or environmental abuse (e.g. breaking of partner's personal items, throwing objects, punching holes in walls) is very important. I have provided two questionnaires (Appendix 1 & 2) that can be used with both men and women in trying to discern the existence of verbal, emotional or environmental abuse. Verbal and emotional abuse has been reported by battered woman to be as damaging or more damaging than physical abuse. In addition, abuse other than physical abuse appears to portend physical abuse.

When children are struggling emotionally or behaviorally, it is often useful to assess for the presence of domestic violence. I am often asked to assess children who are struggling in school and/or at home. I quite often find that there is a history of domestic violence against the mother with these children. If domestic violence is present in a child's home, it is critical to assess if he or she is also being abused. Straus, Gelles, and Steinmetaz (1980, in Holzworth-Munroe, Smutzler, and Sandin) " found that there was a 129% greater chance of child maltreatment in a home where conjugal violence was present " (p.203).

Interventions for Domestic Violence

Assuming that clergy are aware of domestic violence, they are left with a number of options. If a woman is fearful for her safety, it would be prudent to refer her to the local women's shelter who would be able to provide a victim with available options. Women's shelters can provide legal advice, assistance with housing and employment, as well as assist a woman with safety planning should she feel she is in jeopardy of being harmed again. They also can link women up with therapy services if necessary. Marital therapy is not warranted if a woman feels that she is in danger. A necessary prerequisite for any couple in therapy is that they feel comfortable being open and honest with one another. When a woman feels threatened, it would be more appropriate to refer her partner to a batterers treatment program.

Marital therapy does also not appear to be a good option if a man who is being violent is actively abusing drugs and alcohol. He must first be treated for his substance abuse problem prior to any couples therapy. Couples therapy is also most likely contraindicated if there has been any history of severe violence. Any injury that requires medical attention could constitute severe violence. If a woman has been the victim of severe violence it would be more prudent to refer her partner to a batterers treatment group and to refer her either to a support group for battered woman or to the local domestic shelter. Marriage therapy is also inappropriate if a husband refuses to acknowledge his abusiveness and if he is unwilling to work towards ending his abusiveness.

When referring men for batterers treatment, it is very important to refer to an agency that uses a long-term treatment model. Many treatment providers offer a 10 to 12 week anger management program which is primarily designed to teach abusive men new skills. However, abusive men need more than new skills. Much of their abusive behavior is likely to be rooted in a desire to control their partner and stems from feelings of insecurity and inadequacy. Anger management programs do not address these issues. It has also been my experience that most abusive men generally deny their abusive behavior when they start treatment, and usually do not begin to accept they have a problem until they have been in treatment for at least three months. Abusive men are defensive and look outside themselves to explain any abusive behavior (i.e. blame others or situations). Given that many anger management programs are only 10 to 12 weeks in length, it seems unlikely that they would be able to help men accept accountability for their abusive behavior.

Research is scant on the optimum amount of time for treatment for men who are violent with their partners. The Voyager Program requires a minimum of 52 group sessions. Most men who successfully complete treatment at the Voyager Program require more than 52 sessions, and the average length for treatment is 15 months. We are currently in the process of completing an outcome study to determine the rate of recidivism for men who successfully complete the Voyager Program. In addition to the length of treatment, it is important to consider the format of treatment for batterers. Most therapists who treat batterers use group therapy. Individual therapy does not appear to be as effective as group therapy. I have found that men who are further along in their treatment are often able to be helpful to other men who are newer to treatment. Group treatment allows men to discuss behavior that is shameful to them in an open and honest manner.

In summary, it is important for clergy to have good referral sources to assist both the victims and perpetrators of domestic violence. Marital therapy should be entered into with a great deal of caution when domestic violence is present. Marital therapy should not be undertaken when there is severe violence, a partner is concerned about her safety, or when a partner is actively abusing drugs and/or alcohol.

Understanding Child Sexual Abuse

The prevalence of child sexual abuse is disheartening. Some authors have estimated that one out of four females and one out of eight males are sexually misused as children. Gazmarian et al. (2000) reported that 27 percent of women stated that they had suffered childhood sexual abuse. Childhood sexual abuse often has long lasting and profound consequences. One factor related to the impact of sexual abuse is the extent of the sexual activity perpetrated on a victim. In general, the more advanced the level of sexual activity with a victim, the greater potential for harm. For example, victims who are fondled are likely to suffer less than victims whose perpetrators have intercourse with them. Another factor related to the sequela of childhood sexual abuse is the relationship of the perpetrator to the victim. Usually, when there is a close relationship between a perpetrator and their victim, there tends to be more harm inflicted than when there is a more distant relationship between a perpetrator and victim. For example, a victim molested by a parent is likely to have more long lasting consequences than a victim molested by a stranger. Frequency of sexual abuse appears to impact the level of harm to victims. Victims who are subjected to multiple incidents of abuse generally fare worse than victims who are sexually abused on one occasion.

The impact of sexual abuse also seems to depend on how parents react to their child's disclosure that they have been abused. Children whose parents are supportive of them are likely to be harmed less. Parents can further traumatize their children by denying that their children were sexually abused. Some women who have been sexually abused themselves are unable to acknowledge the existence of sexual abuse to their children because of their struggle with being abused. Parents can also create further damage to their children by blaming them for the sexual abuse. Some parents fail to recognize the inherent power difference that usually exists between a perpetrator and a victim, and may ask such questions as " why didn't you stop him ", or " why didn't you tell him no ". Children who have been molested by one parent may be treated by the non-offending parent as if she somehow seduced the perpetrator. Perpetrators are likely to attempt to avoid the legal and moral consequences of their actions by portraying their victim as soliciting or seeking sexual activity from them.

Unfortunately, children do not always directly inform others that they have been sexually abused. Some children because of their age or lack of knowledge may not even know that they have been abused. Some children do not disclose their abuse because they have been threatened by their perpetrator. Perpetrators naturally want to keep their victims quiet, and tell their victims not to tell anyone because they will get in trouble. Perpetrators may also use their relationship with their victim to keep them from disclosing by informing a victim that the perpetrator will go to jail if they tell. Another reason why victims don't disclose is because of the intense level of shame they often feel. In my work with sex offenders, it is often easier for them to discuss their sexual offenses than it is for them to discuss their own sexual abuse as a child.

Some of the symptoms of children who have been sexually abused is similar to children who have witnessed domestic violence. Children who are sexually abused often exhibit signs of PTSD. Thus, they may have trouble sleeping, difficulty with attention or concentration, numbed affect, startle responses (i.e, jumpy at sudden noises or unexpectedly being touched), are fidgety and have trouble sitting still, nightmares, withdrawal from others and decrease in appetite. Greydanus, Patel and Pratt (2003) described a study that compared girls who had been sexually abused to a control group of girls who had not been sexually abused. Behaviors that were listed as differentiating sexually abused girls from non-sexually abused girls included " difficulty getting to sleep, noticeable changes in behavior, fear of being left with a particular person, fear of males, becoming withdrawn, unusual self-consciousness, changes in school performance, difficulty concentrating, enhanced sexual knowledge, and unusual interest or curiosity about sexual matters " (p.929). There are fewer studies with boys who have been sexually abused. Boys have been shown in a few studies to evidence greater behavioral difficulty at school and home, and are more likely to be aggressive. Children who have been sexually abused also appear to be at greater risk for depression and suicide.

One of the more important markers of sexual abuse is a child's sexual behavior with other children. Understanding what differentiates normal from abnormal sexual behavior for children can be very helpful in determining if a child has been sexually abused. Children who exhibit advanced sexual behavior for their age may have been sexually abused. For example, an eight year old girl who is caught performing fellatio on a six year old is cause for concern. It is important to note that the aforementioned example does not necessarily mean that the eight year old girl was sexually abused. She may for example, have been exposed to pornographic material and was reenacting that which she had seen. The proliferation of pornography via the Internet has exposed many children to sexual material that was not available even a few years ago. I often advise parents I work with to insure that they have parental controls on the Internet, and that they supervise any use of the Internet by their children.

Other sexual behaviors that raise concern for possible sexual abuse to young children (i. e. 7 years and younger) include touching or rubbing genitals in public after being told many times not to do this, sexual knowledge too advanced for age, showing oneself in public after being reprimanded numerous times, playing or smearing of feces after being scolded, forcing other children to remove their clothing or to play doctor, simulated or real intercourse without clothes, engaging in oral sex, and placing objects in genitals or rectum of self or others after being told not to do so (note: this does not include a child who puts an object into their genitals or rectum for curiosity or exploration prior to being told not to do so).Gil and Johnson (1993) noted that normal sex play between children includes "spontaneity, joy, laughter, embarrassment, and sporadic levels of inhibition and disinhibition " (p.32). Problematic sexual behavior has distinctly different qualities and appears to be stilted. Sexually abused children may want to engage in sexual behavior to the exclusion of other normal play activity. Their sexual behavior is not likely to be modified and may not change even after parental prohibitions against such behavior.

Most people have little difficulty understanding that sexual behavior between a child and an adult is exploitive and abusive. However, many people seem to struggle with defining what constitutes sexually abusive behavior between children. Gil and Johnson (1993) provided some guidelines for distinguishing sexual behavior between children that may or may not be abusive. The age difference between two children is important to consider, because an older child is likely to have an advantage over a younger child in their physical, emotional, and intellectual development. Gil and Johnson suggested that any sexual behavior where there is a discrepancy of more than three years between children should be explored. However, they also point out that more than age alone needs to be considered. The second criterion they list is size difference between children. Children may be of the same age, but a child who is significantly bigger than another child may be able to coerce another smaller child into sexual activity.

The use of force or coercion is an indicator of sexual abuse. However, it is important to recognize that a child may not have to be physically forced into sexual activity but may have been mentally manipulated into sexual activity by someone who is in a position of power. A younger child who is being baby-sat by an older child may feel compelled to engage in sexual behavior. Some children may be able to manipulate other children through the use of bribes such as money, candy or toys.

Intervening with Children Who Have Been Sexually Abused

Sexual abuse has the potential to be very damaging to children. When allegations of sexual abuse are made one needs to be particularly careful. It is important to define one's role and what one is able to do and not do. One needs to be clearly aware of one's ethical and legal requirements when sexual abuse allegations are made. For most clergy, there is an ethical and legal obligation to report disclosures of sexual abuse. Perhaps the most important intervention for clergy when a child or parent discloses child sexual abuse is to notify authorities (i.e. child protective services) about the alleged abuse because it provides the opportunity for both the perpetrator and victim to receive help. It would be inappropriate and dangerous to try to work with a child and their perpetrator in trying to ameliorate any sexual abuse. It has been my experience that both adolescent and adult sex offenders are not likely to desist from their offending without participating in sex offender therapy. Sex offenders do not typically seek help on their own, but instead are caught committing sexual offenses. Sex offenders need to be mandated to therapy, and this does not happen unless they are brought under the jurisdiction of the legal system.

Victims of child sexual abuse should be referred to a therapist who has been trained to work with such individuals. It may be a good idea for parents to participate in counseling, as they may struggle with blaming themselves for the abuse and may not understand how to respond to their child who has been sexually abused. Clergy can be helpful to the families of victims where there has been child sexual abuse by offering support. It is important not to rush victims or their families to forgive their perpetrator, and instead validate any negative feelings they may have. Clergy should also be alert to victims or their families blaming themselves for the abuse, and help them to understand that people who commit sex offenses are in need of considerable help.

Appendix 1

1	2	3	4
Never	Occasionally	Sometimes	Frequently

A. Not Physically Abusive
  1. Discussed the issue calmly
  2. Given the silent treatment, withheld affection, or withdrawn
  3. Ignored your partner's feelings
  4. Criticized your partner's cooking, cleaning, childcare, etc.
  5. Pouted or tried to talk your partner into sex when she said no
  6. Threatened to leave or told your partner to leave
  7. Took car keys or money away
  8. Used your partner's history to threaten/taunt her
  9. Called your partner names, put her down, humiliated her

B. Indirect Threats of Abuse
  1. Made your partner feel guilty when she socialized with her family or friends
  2. Felt abandoned when your partner socialized with her family or friends
  3. Kept your partner awake to finish an argument
  4. Told your partner she's a bad parent/threatened to take away the kids
  5. Threatened to harm yourself

C. Direct Threats of Abuse
1. Threatened to hit or throw something at your partner
2. Threw, hit or kicked objects, or punched walls
3. Broke her favorite things
4. Drove recklessly when angry
5. Punished the children when you were angry at your partner
6. Directed anger at/threatened the pets to hurt your partner's feelings

D. Direct Violence
1. Threw objects at your partner
2. Pushed, carried, restrained, grabbed, shoved, wrestled your partner
3. Held your partner to keep her from leaving after an argument
4. Locked your partner out of the house
5. Slapped, hit or thrown your partner

E. Severe Violence
1. Choked or strangled your partner
2. Physically forced sex on your partner
3. Punched or kicked your partner
4. Abandoned your partner where she had to get her own ride
5. Kicked / punched your partner in the stomach when she was pregnant
6. Beat your partner unconscious
7. Intimidated with guns, knives, or other weapons

Appendix 2

Does your partner ...
____ embarrass you in front of people ?
____ belittle your accomplishments ?
____ make you feel unworthy ?
____ constantly contradict himself to confuse you ?
____ do things for that you are constantly making excuses to others or yourself ?
____ isolate you from many of the people you care most about ?
____ make you feel ashamed a lot of the time ?
____ make you believe he is smarter than you and therefore more able to make decisions ?
____ make you feel that it is you who is crazy ?
____ make you perform acts that are demeaning to you ?
____ use intimidation to make you do what he wants ?
____ prevent you from common-place activities such as shopping, visiting friends and family, talking to other men ?

____ control the financial aspects of your life ?
____ use money as a way of controlling you ?
____ make you believe you cannot exist without him ?
____ make you feel there is no way out and that "you made your bed and must lie in it" ?
____ make you find ways of compromising your feelings for the sake of peace ?
____ treat you roughly - grab, pinch, push or shove you ?
____ threaten you - verbally or with a weapon ?
____ hold you to keep you from leaving after an argument ?
____ lose control when your partner is drunk or using drugs ?
____ get extremely angry, frequently without an apparent cause ?
____ escalate his anger into violence - slapping, kicking, etc.
____ not believe that he hurt you nor feel sorry for what he has done ?
____ physically force you to do what you do not want to do ?

Do You ...
____ believe that you can help your partner change the abusive behavior if you were only to change yourself in some way, if you only did something differently, if you really loved him ?
____ find that not making your partner angry became a major part of your life ?
____ do what your partner wants you to do rather than what you want to do out of fear ?
____ stay with your partner only because you're afraid he might hurt you if you tell ?

If you have said yes to many of the above questions, you are likely to be in an abusive relationship and need to seek help and advice.

References

Adamson, L.A., & Thompson, R.A. (1998). Coping with inter-parental verbal conflict by children exposed to spouse abuse and children from nonviolent homes. Journal of Family Violence, 13, 213-232.

Aguilar, R.J., & Nightingale, N. N. (1994). The impact of specific battering experiences on the self-esteem of abused women. Journal of Family Violence, 9, 81-95.

Andrews, B. (1995). Bodily shame as a mediator between abusive experiences and depression. Journal of Abnormal Psychology, 104, 277-285.

Astin, M.C., Lawrence, K.J. & Foy, D.W. (1993). Post traumatic stress disorder among battered women: Risk and resiliency factors. Violence and Victims, 8, (1), 17-27.

Caesar, P. L. (1988). Exposure to violence in the families-of-origin among wife-abusers and maritally nonviolent men. Violence and Victims, 3, 49-63.

Campbell, J. (1995). Prediction of homicide of and by battered women. In J. Capmbell, (Ed)., Assessing dangerousness: Violence by sexual offenders, batterers and child abusers. California: Sage Publications.

Cantos, A. L., Neidig, P. H., & O'Leary, K. D. (1994). Injuries of women and men in a treatment program for domestic violence. Journal of Family Violence, 9, 113-124.

Carlson, B.E. (1984). Children's observations interparental violence. In A.R. Roberts (Ed)., Battered women and their families (pp.147-167). New York: Springer.

Carlson B. E. (1990). Adolescent observers of marital violence. Journal of Family Violence, 5, 285-299.

Cascardi, M., Langhinrichsen, J., & Vivian, D. (1992). Marital aggression: Impact, injury, and health correlates for husband and wives. Archives of Internal Medicine, 152, 1178-1184.

Davies, P. T., & Cummings, E. M. (1994). Marital conflict and child adjustment: An emotional security hypothesis. Psychological Bulletin, 116, 387-411.

Dutton, D. G., Saunders, K., Starzomski, A., & Bartholomew, K. (1994). Intimacy-anger and insecure attachment as precursors of abuse in intimate relationships. Journal of Applied Social Psychology, 24, 1367-1387.

Dutton, D. G. (1995). Intimate Abusiveness. Clinical Psychology: Science and Practice, 207-224.

Edleson, J. L. (1990). Children's witnessing of adult domestic violence. Journal of Interpersonal Violence, 14, 839-869.

Fincham, F. D., Grych, J. H., Osborne, L. N. (1994). Does marital conflict cause child maladjustment ? Directions and challenges for longitudinal research. Journal of Family Psychology, 8, 128-140.

Follingstad, D. R., Rutledge, L. L., Berg, B. J., Hause, E. S., & Polek, D. S. (1990). The role of emotional abuse in physically abusive relationships. Journal of Family Violence, 5, 107-120.

Follingstad, D. R., and DeHart, D. D. (2000). Defining psychological abuse of husbands towards wives. Journal of Interpersonal Violence, 15, 891-920.

Gazmarian, J., Peterson, P., Spitz, A., Goodwin, M., Saltzman, L., & Marks, J. (2000). Violence and reproductive health: Current knowledge and future research directions. Maternal and Child Health Journal, ,4, 79-84.

Gil, E., & Johnson, T. C. (1993). Sexualized Children. Assessment and treatment of sexualized children and children who molest. Launch Press, Rockville, MD.

Gleason, W. J. (1993). Mental disorders in battered women: an empirical study. Violence and Victims, 8, 53-66.

Greydanus, D. E., Patel, D.R., & Pratt, H. D. (2003). Behavioral Pediatrics: Part I. Volume 50, Number 4. W. B. Saunders Co., Philadelphia, PA.

Hamberger, L. K., Lohr, J. M., & Bonge, D. (1994). The intended function of domestic violence is different for arrested male and female perpetrators. Family Violence and Sexual Assault, 10, 40-44.

Hampton, R. L., & Gelles, R. J. (1994). Predicting mild and severe husband-to-wife physical aggression. Journal of Consulting and Clinical Psychology, 62, 975-981.

Hebert, T. B., Silver, R. C., & Ellard, J. H. (1991). Coping with an abusive relationship: How and why do women stay. Journal of Marriage and the Family, 53, 311-325.

Heyman, R. E., O'Leary, K. D., and Jouriles, E. N. (1995). Alcohol and aggressive personality styles: Potentiators of serious physical aggression against wives. Journal of Family Psychology, 9, 44-57.

Holzworth-Munroe, A., Bates, L., Smutzler, N., and Sandin, E. (1997). A brief review of the research on husband violence: part I: Maritally violent versus nonviolent men. Aggression and Violent Behavior, 2, 65-99.

Holzworth-Munroe, A., Jacobson, N. S., Fehrenbach, P. A., & Fruzzetti, A. (1992). Violent married couples' attributions for violent and nonviolent self and partner behaviors. Behavioral Assessment, 14, 53-64.

Holzworth-Munroe, A., Smutzler, N. & Bates, L. (1997). A brief review of the research on husband violence: part III: sociodemographic factors, relationship factors, and differing consequences of husband and wife violence. Aggression and Violent Behavior, 2, 285-307.

Holzworth-Munroe, A., Smutzler, N., Sandin, E. (1997). A brief review of the research on jusband violence: part II: The psychological effects of husband violence on battered women and their children. Aggression and Violent Behavior, 2, 179-213.

Holzworth-Munroe, A., & Stuart, G. L. (1994). Typologies of male batterers: Three subtypes and the differences among them. Psychological Bulletin, 116, 476-497.

Hotaling, G. & Sugarman, D. (1990). A risk marker analysis of assaulted wives. Journal of Family Violence, 5, 1-13.

Houskamp, B. M., & Foy, D. W. (1991). The assessment of posttraumatic stress disorder in battered women. Journal of Interpersonal Violence, 6, 367-375.

Howell, G., & Pugleisi, K. (1988). Husbands who harm: Predicting spousal violence by men. Journal of Family Violence, 7, 309-319.

Kaufman-Kantor, G. K., Jasinski, J. L., & Aldarondo, E. (1994). Sociocultural status and incidence of marital violence in Hispanic families. Violence and Victims, 9, 207-222.

Kaufman-Kantor, G. K., & Strauss, M. A. (1987). The "druken bum" theory of wife beating. Social Problems, 34, 213-230.

Langhinrichsen-Rohling, J., Neidig, P., & Thorn, G. (1995). Violent marriages: Gender differences in levels of current violence and past abuse. Journal of Family Violence, 10, 159-176.

Leonard, K. E. & Senchak, M. (1996). Prospective prediction of husband marital aggression within newlywed couples. Journal of Abnormal Behavior, 105, 369-380.

Malmuth, N. M., Linz, D., Heavey, C. L., Barnes, G., & Acker, M. (1995). Using the confluence model of sexual aggression to predict men's conflict with women: A ten year follow-up study. Jouranl of Personality and Social Psychology, 69, 353-369.

McLaughlin, L., Leonard, K., and Senchak, M. (1992). Prevalence and distribution of premarital of aggression among couples applying for a marriage license. Journal of Family Violence, 7, 309-319.

Murphy, C. M., & O'Leary, K. D. (1989). Psychological aggression predicts physical aggression in early marriage. Journal of Consulting and Clinical Psychology, 57, 579-582.

Neff, J. A., Holman, B., & Schulter, T. D. (1995). Spousal violence among Anglos, Blacks and Mexican-Americans: The role of demographic variables, psychosocial predictors, and alcohol consumption. Journal of Family Violence, 10, 1-21.

O'Brien, M., John, R. S., Margolin, G., & Erel, O. (1994). Reliability and diagnostic efficacy of parents' reports regarding children's exposure to marital aggression. Violence and Victims, 9, 45-62.

O'Farrell, T. J., & Murphy, C. M. (1995). Marital violence before and after alcoholism treatment. Journal of Consulting and Clinical Psychology, 63, 256-262.

O'Keefe, M. (1994). Linking marital violence, mother-child/father child aggression, and child behavior problems. Journal of Family Violence, 9, 63-78.

Okun, L. E., (1986). Woman abuse: Facts replacing myths. Albany, NY: State University of New York Press.

O'Leary, K.D., Malone, J., & Tyree, A. (1994). Physical aggression in early marriage: Prerelationship and relationship effects. Journal of Consulting and Clinical Psychology, 62, 594-602.

O'Leary, K. D., Vivian, D., & Malone, J. (1992). Assessment of physical aggression against women in marriage: The need for multimodal assessment. Behavioral Assessment, 14, 5-14.

Pan, H., Neidig, P., & O'Leary, D. (1994). Predicting mild and severe husband-to-wife physical aggression. Journal of Consulting and Clinical Psychology, 62, 975-981.

Quigley, B. M., & Leonard, K. E. (1996). Desistance of husband aggression in the early years of marriage. Violence and Victims, 11, 355-370.

Riggs, D. S., Kilpatrick, D. G., & Resnick, H. S. (1992). Long-term psychological distress associated with marital rape and aggravated assault: A comparison to other crime victims. Journal of Family Violence, 7, 283-296.

Sato, R. A. and Heiby, E. M. (1992). Corrrelates of depressive symptoms among battered women. Journal of Family Violence, 7, 229-245.

Schwartz, M. D. (1988). Marital status and women abuse theory. Journal of Family Violence, 3, 239-248.

Scott, K., & Wolfe, D. (2000). Change among batterers. Examining men's success stories. Journal of Interpersonal Violence, 15, 827-842.

Seltzer, M. L., & Kalmus, D. (1988). Socialization and stress explanations for spouse abuse. Social Forces, 67, 473-491.

Silvern, L., Karyl, J., Waelde, L, Hodges, W. F., Storek, J., Heidt, E., & Min, K. (1995). Retrospective reports of parental partner abuse: Relationships to depression, trauma symptoms and self-esteem among college students. Journal of Family Violence, 10, 177-202.

Sorenson, S. B., & Telles, C. A. (1991). Self-reports of spousal violence in a Mexican-American and Non-Hispanic white population. Violence and Victims, 6, 3-15.

Spaccarelli, S., Coatsworth, J. D., & Bowden, B. S. (1995). Exposure to serious family violence among incarcerated boys: Its association with violent offending and potential mediating variables. Violence and Victims, ,10, 163-182.

Spaccarelli, S., Sandler, I. N., & Roosa, M. (1994). History of spouse violence against mother: Correlated risks and unique effects in child mental health. Journal of Family Violence, 9, 79-98.

Stets, J. E. (1990). Verbal and physical aggression in marriage. Journal of Marriage and the Family, 52, 501-514.

Stets, J. E., & Strauss, M. (1989). The marriage license as a hitting license. A comparison of assaults in dating, cohabitating and married couples. Journal of Family Violence, 4, 161-180.

Stets, J. E., & Straus, M. (1990). Gender differences in reporting marital violence and its medical and psychological consequences. In M. A. Strauss and R. J. Gelles (Eds.), Physical violence in American families: Risk factors adn adaptation to violence in 8145 families. New Brunswick, NJ: Transaction Publishers.

Strauss, M. A. (1992). Children as witnesses to marital violence: A risk factor for lifelong problems among a nationally representative sample of American men and women. Report of the 23rd Ross Roundtable. Columbus, Oh: Ross Labortatories.

Strauss, M. A., Gelles, R. J., & Steinmetz, S. K. (1980). Behind closed doors: Violence in the American family. Garden City, NY: Doubleday Press.

Walker, L. E. (1979). The battered woman. New York: Harper and Row.

Weisz, A. N., Tolman, R. M., & Saunders, D. G. (2000). Assessing the risk of severe domestic violence: The importance of survivor's predictions. Journal of Interpersonal Violence, 15, 75-90.

Wilson, M. & Daly, M. (1993). Spousal homocide risk and estrangement. Violence and Victims, 8, 3-16.

About The Author

Steve Dean received his doctorate degree from The Ohio State University in 1995. He currently works at Melymbrosia Associates as the clinical director. As clinical director Dr. Dean is responsible for supervising other therapists who treat batterers and sex offenders. Part of his duties at Melymbrosia Associates is to complete psychological evaluations of batterers and sex offenders as well provide treatment to them. Dr. Dean also works as a adolescent sex offender group at Community Mental Healthcare.

Dr. Dean has a strong interest in providing training to clergy. He has co-facilitated seminars for the Steubenville and Youngstown Dioceses of the Roman Catholic Church and for the Northern Ohio Diocese of the Episcopal Church. Dr. Dean has also taught at the Josephenium Potifical College.

Chapter 7
Trapped in the Undertows & Cross-Currents:
Overconing Substance Abuse & Addictions

by David Herl, Ed.D.

"I count him braver who overcomes his desires than him who conquers his enemies, for the hardest victory is the victory over self."

Aristotle (384-322 BC)
Philosopher, Educator, Scientist

INTRODUCTION

My first exposure to substance abusing patients was early in my psychology internship in the late 1960's when Woodstock was being advertised but wasn't yet "a happening of the century" in America. Woodstock, I discovered, was not necessary to call attention to the extensive amount of substance abuse among youth in particular, and the deleterious effects of "trips 'n highs." Needless to say, these were tumultuous times for America and whatever the sociological, psychological, and political forces at play, there emerged a serious drug epidemic.

Parents were frantic, confused, and perplexed as to how to cope with their drug-seeking and abusing family members, many of whom overdosed, became ill, and/or entered the criminal justice system.

My orientation to the grim realities of drug abuse included witnessing a drug psychosis and being impacted by the sheer horror in the hospitalized young adult in turmoil due to a mood-altering drug which caused shadowing of reality boundaries and a swift vaporization of his self-identity.

More disconcerting was the "fall out" or relapses of drug dependent individuals who were in treatment programs and who seemingly were from intact families. I recall speaking with a number of such youth who impressed me as being bright, socially poised, and with articulated goals of pursuing potentially rewarding careers.

Rather quickly, my idealistic perceptions of treatment being effective (they "talked the talk" I later discovered) were derailed beyond belief when I learned of the youth who overtly appeared to be "going straight" died from either accidental overdose or suicide.

Substance abuse is a major health problem in the United States. Some National Institute of Drug Abuse (NIDA) estimates of the cost of substance abuse are between 240 to 300 billion dollars. Alcohol abuse alone is approximately 185 billion with 6 million misusing alcohol and 8 million dependent on it. Also, in 1999 there were an estimated 14.8 million Americans using illicit drugs and 3.5 million dependent on them. Also, in 1999 there were 4 million, age 12 or over, using sedatives, stimulants, tranquilizers, or opiates for non-medical reasons.

To generate more gloom, it has been estimated that two-thirds of Americans with serious substance abuse treatment needs are not being treated. The challenges in reducing substance abuse and addictions are great, however this chapter will discuss what has been helpful and how clergy/church associates can intervene to deal with substance abuse among parishioners.

SUBSTANCE ABUSE AND ADDICTION

Addiction as a Specialty in Treatment

The historical development and background of understanding and treating addictions has been fraught essentially with much trial and error. During the 1940's and 1950's, there was a predominantly psychoanalytical approach, which involved the emotional processing of conflicts and unmet needs, especially dependency longings and "oral hunger." This orientation, sadly, often led to an exacerbation of substance abusing and treatment limited in terms of ease and accessibility.

Interestingly, the first major treatment model, 12-Step (Alcoholics Anonymous), was developed by non-professionals by default, in that many professionals were not that interested in the field of addiction. Perhaps this was the result of both dismal treatment outcomes and the lack of a sound, integrated knowledge base.

Fortunately, during the past decade there has been an appreciation of the multifaceted dimensions to addiction, resulting in various research avenues which include brain-behavior links and multi-modal prevention and treatment approaches. However, attaining integration and solid viable factual information has been slow in evolving and controversies exist. There is however a strong consensus that addictions are a complex biobehavioral disorder which negatively impacts body, mind, and spirit.

Mechanisms and Dynamics of Addiction Development

Addictive behaviors share some common denominators and exist on a continuum. Addiction causes reduced levels of functioning due to deficits or impairments in physical health and psychological well-being (mental health).

Addictions involve a central and circumscribed focus of attention and preoccupation with the substance for which there is a dependency or compulsion to ingest or from which to derive short-term pleasure or satisfaction.

In addition, the addictive behaviors are automatic, impulsive in nature, and the reason for the behavior is outside the awareness of the individual. In essence, addictions develop as "a life of their own" over time, with the origins and dynamics of their stimulus-seeking behaviors/addiction being obscure.

This feature of addiction is characterized metaphorically as being snarled in dangerous cross-currents and undertows which potentially could result in death, sudden or prolonged.

Paradoxically, the individual with a "full blown" or florid addiction may well acknowledge the negative consequences of their behaviors and the pain which impacts themselves and others. However, they remain inert, ineffectual, and seemingly unable to take purposeful action or steps to curtail or abstain from the addictive behaviors.

With respect to addictions to substances or psychoactive drugs, neurobiological changes accompany the transition from voluntary to compulsive drug or substance usage. Addictive drugs (such as alcohol, cocaine, heroin, amphetamines, and nicotine) modify the pleasure circuits in the brain. In fact recent research suggests that an unusually rapid shift and increase in a neurochemical (dopamine) occurs both before and after a pleasurable act (United Press Intern. – April 9, 2003). Such a finding may help better understand the triggering signals which influence the compulsive habit leading to addiction.

A psychological dynamic felt to explain the development of an addiction has to do with complex learning and the existence of deficits in the individual's regulation and modification of emotions. Basically, the utilization of the substance, which becomes addictive, alters aspects of the individual's coping abilities and functioning with respect to external stress and/or internal (intrapsychic) discomfort and disruption.

Initially, the learning is largely incidental in nature in that the ingestion of a psychoactive substance (alcohol, drugs, tobacco) alters a mood state which is felt and perceived as highly reinforcing and pleasure enhancing. Then, over time the substance seeking and using takes on "a life of it's own" which no longer provides the emotional modulation (i.e. soothing, comforting) that it originally afforded the individual.

The insidious development of an addiction or dependence to alcohol is brilliantly discussed in a probably not well known work by Vernon Johnson (1980). Johnson describes how alcohol "always moves the drinker in the right direction (p.11)" with mood shifting, initially, in the drinking experience (first phase), to pleasure and relaxation.

However, with consistent use and increase in the amount of alcohol ingested to attain a desired effect, the mood state of the individual, in reality, actually dips lower than the prior baseline mood state. Essentially, it then takes more of the substance to elevate the mood. At this stage, tolerance is becoming salient and, unfortunately, the addictive cycle is well underway. The biphasic properties illustrated with alcohol are unique and, therefore, render alcohol potentially exceedingly addictive, as well as lethal.

It is important to acknowledge one other common characteristic of addictions, and that is their tenacity to persist, episodically, resulting in lapses and eventual relapse. Staying or remaining abstinent from addictive substances is often incredibly difficult for many. In studies of habit change, numerous attempts with failures are more the rule than the exception. In fact, the folk hero Mark Twain once remarked: "A habit is habit and not to be flung out the window but coaxed down stairs a step at a time."

ASSESSING AND EVALUATING SUBSTANCE ABUSE

In pastoral care settings, it is family members or concerned significant others who will likely call attention to the problem. Often the individual with a substance abuse problem or dependency will not openly acknowledge the degree to which the problem exists. Rationalizations, externalization of blame, denial, and minimization are characteristic defenses when confronted with the negative consequences of abusing the substance (drugs, alcohol) and/or the amount of substance(s) ingested.

It is helpful to have access to several assessment devices which can clarify the extent to which substance use (especially alcohol because of its prevalence and social acceptance) is problematic and risk-taking.

The following brief measures have been found to be reliable and valid indicators of significant problems associated with alcohol use.

One widely recommended and popular instrument is the CAGE questionnaire (Mayfield, McLeod, & Hall, 1974). Each letter is an acronym for a particular question. These include: C ("Have you ever felt the need to Cut down on your drinking?"), A ("Have you ever felt Annoyed by criticism of your drinking?"), G ("Have you ever felt Guilty about your drinking?"), E ("Have you ever taken a drink (i.e. Eye opener) first thing in the morning?"). A positive response on two (2) or more questions out of four (4) is considered problematic and suggesting further professional assessment to rule out a psychoactive substance use disorder.

Asking straightforward questions about frequency and quantity of alcohol use can help sort out current abuse or dependence from a status of being in remission.

Another recommended assessment tool is the Alcohol Use Disorders Identification Test (AUDIT), developed by the World Health Organization (Saunders, Aasland, Babor, De La Fuente, & Grant, 1993) correct to assist in the early detection of problem drinking in primary care medical settings. The AUDIT consists of ten (10) items. A distinct advantage to this device is its presence on the internet (www.alcoholscreening.org), whereby an individual can respond to the questions and have it scored instantaneously.

An additional noteworthy assessment tool is referred to as the modified T-ACE questionnaire (McQuade, Levy, Yanck, Davis, & Liepman, 2000). The authors found this instrument to be the most effective screening instrument for both men and women when contrasting it to the CAGE and AUDIT. Basically, the T-ACE is the CAGE device minimally modified, in that the guilt question is replaced by a question involving tolerance (i.e., "How many drinks does it take to make you feel high?").

The authors recommend assigning one (1) point to the tolerance question (resulting in more than one drink) while keeping a criterion of two (2) or more of the possible four (4) questions for a positive finding for problem drinking. Furthermore, the authors' research was effective in identifying a cluster of risk factors which predicted, with very impressive accuracy, the diagnostic criterion of alcohol abuse or dependency (i.e. positive family history of alcohol abuse, age 30-39, two or more depressive symptoms, and indicating a lack of satisfaction with one drink).

Clergy and others working in the religious community of the church who offer pastoral care and encounter substance (alcohol) abuse among congregants may well want to examine their own knowledge of alcohol.

Miller and C'DeBaca (1995) have made an interesting and valuable contribution by developing a questionnaire entitled Knowledge of Alcohol Problems: A Questionnaire (KNAPSA Q). The 50 multiple-choice items assess a broad array of content involving scientific findings pertaining to alcohol and subsequent abuse/dependence. Items vary in degree of difficulty.

I recommend this questionnaire for the helper or change agent and applaud the authors for pointing out the unfortunate deficits in training for many professionals in counseling and mental health in substance use disorders. Such knowledge can be exceedingly valuable in assisting troubled parishioners in "coming to terms" or recognizing problems with alcohol.

TREATMENT ISSUES FOR ADDICTIONS/SUBSTANCE ABUSE: CONSTRUCTING BRIDGES THAT ENDURE

Common Ingredients in Effective Treatment

In considering treatment approaches and strategies, it is worthwhile to reflect on the lyrics in the song Everyday People, "different strokes for different folks." That is to say, there is no one superior or "best" treatment for addictive behaviors despite much research.

What psychologists do know is that people change as a result of a sequence of stages. These stages may evolve and progress at highly variable rates. I am reminded of a 10 year old girl I treated for rather severe asthma attacks determined to be exacerbated by various stressors.

Briefly, her father remained resistant to curbing or eliminating his excessive drinking which resulted in marital tension and his tobacco addiction which contributed to his daughter's asthma attacks due to second hand smoke. Confrontation by physicians, spouse, and concerned others seemingly encapsulated and bolstered his denial and resistance to change ("Lots of parents smoke and drink – she'd still have those asthma attacks if I stopped cigarettes.") He finally, and rather abruptly, abstained from tobacco after his daughter had a severe and near death asthma episode while on vacation, remote from any medical facilities. He had been smoking in the car with the children in the back seat. Several years had elapsed before he finally took action to deal with his addictive behavior. Asked why he made the decision, he retorted: "My little girl is worth much more to our family than any damn cigarettes." Seemingly, the harsh reality of losing his daughter was necessary to propel this parent into the action phase.

Read, Kahler, & Stevenson (2001) have nicely summarized essential considerations for rendering treatment for substance abuse, regardless of the approach utilized. These include: Address Motivational & Reinforcing Factors, Use a Nonconfrontational Approach, Teach Specific Skills to Facilitate Changes in Substance Abuse, Promote Active coping & Goal Setting, and Target Socioenvironmental Factors.

Another very significant and impressive finding with respect to treatment is that less is often best! Researchers such as Bien, Miller, & Tonigan (1993) discovered that brief treatment outcomes for alcohol abuse tend to be comparable to outcomes from more lengthy treatment. Also, it is known that highly predictable positive outcomes for problem drinkers are directly related to therapist or counselor empathy (Miller & Baca, 1983).

Miller (2000) has poignantly analyzed, with great alacrity, the contributions of agape as an Ancient Greek term, which he points out emerged during early Christianity to describe "a selfless, accepting, sacred form of loving" (Miller, 2000, p.12).

These findings have important implications for the pastoral caregiver whose time may be limited due to numerous demands. Thus, the impact clergy and church associates can potentially have in brief interventions can be highly significant, particularly during early stages of change.

Stages of Change and Motivational Enhancement Treatment

Psychologists (Prochaska, DiClemente, & Norcross, 1992) have performed extensive research on various stages of change which are highly predictable among both individuals who seek change on their own (self-changers) and those seeking assistance through a treatment program or professional.

They have documented a highly significant rate of treatment failures in those individuals who were poorly matched for the treatment approach at that time. In essence, treatment success (either self-initiated or sought out) depends on the best fit or match of the individual and the particular strategy employed.

The transtheoretical model of stages of change (Prochaska et al., 1992) is empirical and characterizes motivation to change as a spiral continuum. Motivational enhancement treatments developed by psychologist William R. Miller and colleagues (1991), fosters change in a supportive and non-threatening atmosphere. As you will see, the technique of motivational interviewing dovetails nicely with stages of change concepts.

Briefly, the first stage of Precontemplation is where the individual sees no need for change and is not thinking about it. Denial is often present, which permits an active dismissal of evidence of a problem or need for change.

The goal for pastoral intervention at this stage is to increase awareness of a possible problem, create self-doubts or concerns, and mobilize ambivalence. It is helpful for clergy, at this stage, to express concerns in the context of positive regard and what is happening in terms of specific negative consequences of the addictive behavior. Avoiding arguments is helpful in minimizing resistance and a defensive stance.

Gently leading the parishioner to talk about their own concerns is a critical, pivotal development – tipping the scales towards the next stage, Contemplation.

An illustration of "leading," in the context of agape, might be: "John, your family is very concerned that you may be harming yourself by drinking to excess. I know that you don't see much of a problem now, but I wonder if you have been aware of anything about yourself that makes you think about possible future difficulties? Is their anything that looks like it might get to be a problem unless you do something about it? I want you to know that I am concerned about you and am here with you and care for you. John, would you be willing, at this stage, to see a professional to get an opinion as to your alcohol use and patterns? Perhaps after an evaluation you can share with me where you are with respect to life in general, OK?"

The value of pastoral intervention at the Precontemplation stage offers an exceptional opportunity to assist the parishioner moving into the next stage and, according to some authorities, doubling the chance of changing addictive behavior over the next year.

The next stage of Contemplation includes the awareness of a problem. The individual is seriously thinking about overcoming it and they are ambivalent, as they are basically pondering the advantages (pros) and disadvantages (cons). Here, pastoral intervention can be very valuable in attempting to elicit reasons the parishioner/congregant may have for changing the addictive behavior(s) and also in highlighting incongruities between the individual's purported life goals and the apparent consequences of addictive behavior/substance abuse.

Miller and Rollnick (1991) discuss a variety of strategies of questioning in order to explore any concerns an individual may have about substance use. These include:

1. Ask about substance use in detail.
2. Ask about a typical day (including use of substances).
3. Ask about lifestyle and stresses.
4. Ask about health, then substance use.
5. Ask about good things, then the less good things (about their substance use/addictive behavior).
6. Ask about substance use in the past and now.
7. Provide information and ask, "What do you think?"
8. Ask about concerns directly.
9. Ask about the next step.

During the contemplation stage an emphasis is also placed upon individual responsibility and freedom of choice ("No one can really force you to change. It's really up to you."). Also, clergy can be inspirational and supportive to help "jump start" self-efficacy and the process of attaining personal control. For example, pointing out the difficulties and prior tendencies to fail or relapse as universal (with addictive behaviors) which involves a process of sequential learning in order to eventually succeed, can be highly reassuring and foster hope.

With some Christian patients in treatment, I have been impressed with the degree of relief and reduction in self-loathing and self-derogatory beliefs when I have framed the difficulties of overcoming addictive behaviors as a reminder that Christians acknowledge that life on Earth will have "trials and tribulations" and life events which challenge one's faith and successful journey to salvation and ultimate forgiveness. The phrase: "God works in mysterious ways," I have found can be utilized to stimulate the scanning of possibilities and options in resolving addictive behaviors or reducing harm to self.

An illustration will also depict the meaning of the quote by William Coffin Jr. – "Hell is truth recognized too late." A Christian attorney with severe alcohol and tranquilizer dependency I saw remarked after discussing the concept of "trials and tribulations" as a mortal test – "My drinking has been a huge challenge for me. It ruined my marriage and hurt my health and almost got me disbarred from practicing law, but after some serious praying here I am talking with you about my problems, being more honest than I have ever been." At this juncture of treatment (Determination Stage), we were well on the road to moving into the Action phase of change and the implementation of a plan leading, in this case, to abstinence from psychoactive substances.

The Action phase involves actual behavior change from a period of one day to six months and the implementation of chosen strategies and effort. After six months, the Maintenance stage involves consolidating gains and preventing relapse by stabilizing behavior changes.

Pastoral interventions can be helpful during the last two stages discussed. It is important to know that even as congregants begin and appear to have made some definitive changes in resolving their addictive behaviors/substance abuse, many often remain ambivalent and require a strong continued support network for their resolution to change.

In this context, clergy and church associates can function in ways to bolster and maintain hope. Some individuals will obsessively dwell on negative aspects of past experiences and relationships. By fostering a hopeful outlook, pastoral care interventions can include rejecting the notion that one is powerless over tribulations and negative, even painful, life events.

Another strategy is to explore the meaning of any perceived painful and/or negative, undesirable experiences and sometimes, inadvertently, discover a "silver lining." Such was the case in the previous illustration of the attorney patient. As we subsequently explored the meaning of the struggles and demise surrounding substance dependence, the patient reflected: "You know, as a result of all of what

I've been through, I've gotten closer to who I really am and to my Heavenly Father too." Interestingly, the patient discovered in psychotherapy a core of unhappiness and non-fulfillment in career choice and subsequently entered a legal position which was much more rewarding and enjoyable. Although earning far less remuneration, this consequence was totally irrelevant in the patient's recognized values and spiritual hierarchy.

Specific Effective Treatments

During the Determination phase of change, the individual is preparing for taking action often within a month or so. Selection of specific approaches and strategies are required. At this juncture, the person with substance abuse or addictive behaviors should feel free to select approaches which will "fit" the person's expectations for change.

The following table developed by Jennifer Read and colleagues (2001) is comprehensive in summarizing both spiritual and secular approaches and includes treatment approaches which are the most common and effective. Although specific reference is made to alcohol dependence, the concepts and methods employed have excellent generalizability to substance use (psychoactive drugs).

See Table 1: Description of Interventions for Alcohol Dependence

---

Note: AA=Alcoholics Anonymous

Reprinted with author permission & American Psychological Association (journal: *Professional Psychology: Research & Practice*)

Table 1: Description of Interventions for Alcohol Dependence

Treatment	Defining characteristics	Objectives	Methods used
Coping and skills training	Grounded in social-cognitive learning theory. Conceptualizes drinking problems as a function of deficits in interpersonal and coping skills	Condition more adaptive responses to drinking-related cues. Basic skills for coping, achieving, and maintaining sobriety.	Behavioral self-control training, social skills, cue exposure, relapse prevention, drinking triggers assessment, functional analysis
Motivational enhancement	Evolved from brief intervention tradition Nonconfrontational Client-centered Emphasis on motivation or readiness of change	Develop safe, nonthreatening environment to explore substance use and consequences Evaluate whether and how behavior change should be made Reinforce client's self-efficacy for behavior change	Open-ended questions, reflective listening, avoiding labeling and argumentation, decreasing resistance, affirmation, eliciting self-motivational statements, expressing empathy, cost-benefit analysis of drinking behavior
Community reinforcement approach	Based in cognitive-behavioral theory Emphasis on building on client's support systems to facilitate recovery process	Develop and strengthen social support systems and incorporate these systems into recovery Examine interaction between drinking and environment	Skills training (e.g. sobriety sampling, functional analysis, social skills training, mood monitoring, recreational counseling, vocational counseling, drink refusal training), relationship counseling, treatment compliance monitoring, "buddy systems"
Behavioral marital and family therapy	Builds on social-cognitive learning theory Considers dyadic and family functioning to be integral to achieving and maintaining sobriety	Decrease or eliminate problem drinking by including partners and families in treatment Improve dyadic and family functioning Delineate structural roles of patient and family in the recovery process	Develop "house rules" for recovery, include spouse or family members in alcohol treatment adherence, decrease "relationship triggers" for drinking, participate in communication and problem-solving skills training, reinforce positive dyadic and family interactions

Table 1: Description of Interventions for Alcohol Dependence (Cont.)

Treatment	Defining characteristics	Objectives	Methods used
Disulfiram	Prescribed medication Inhibits aldehyde dehydrogenase (ALDH), which breaks down alcohol in the blood stream	Alcohol use becomes associated with aversive side effects Prevent alcohol use by causing nausea, vomiting, other aversive side effects when alcohol is ingested	Drug is ingested daily, compliance measures help to enhance outcome
Naltrexone	Prescribed medication Blocks opiate receptors in the brain, prevents positive effects of alcohol that make consumption rewarding	Alcohol consumption less rewarding Decreases urges to drink Prevents relapse following initial drink	Drug is ingested daily, compliance measure help to enhance outcome
Alcoholics Anonymous	Based on disease model - views alcoholism as progressive, chronic illness 12 traditions provide organizational structure 12 steps offer framework for the recovery process Spiritual orientation Introspection, self-understanding, and making amends with self and others critical to recovery process Membership is free	Accept alcoholism as a disease over which one is powerlessness Achieve and maintain sobriety through continued active involvement in the program, spirituality, and group support	"Working the steps," belief in a "Higher Power," acceptance and surrender, slogans and metaphors, receiving support and guidance (for newer members), from a sponsor attending meetings
Other 12-step approaches	Disease model Supportive fellowship revolving around 12 recovery steps Facilitated by a treatment professional Enhances involvement and use of 12-step programs such as AA Spiritual orientation	Accept alcoholism as a disease over which one is powerlessness Achieve and maintain sobriety through continued active involvement in the program, spirituality, and group support	Facilitator works with client to benefit from AA, working the steps, belief in a Higher Power, acceptance and surrender, receiving support from sponsor, attending meetings

PASTORAL CARE, SPIRITUALITY & ADDICTIONS:
A MATCH MADE PERHAPS IN HEAVEN

Those offering pastoral care and guidance within religious communities have unique advantages, specifically, in contrast to secular professionals and licensed/certified clinicians. First, referrals by self (parishioner) and/or concerned others are more likely to be initially with clergy. Secondly, integrating spirituality into treatment can be complicated for the professional involving ethical issues surrounding dual relationships wherein the clinician attempts to be both a therapist and spiritual mentor to the person with addiction problems.

Clergy can be effective by utilizing both religious and spiritual intervention in helping addicted parishioners search for meaning, purpose, and value in their lives as a result of being alienated from themselves in the progression of giving addiction(s) "center stage."

Bennett (1998) has nicely summarized research findings, despite limitations in assessing spirituality and religion, of spirituality related to addictions. Although much is still not known about the relationship, the researcher points out that less substance abuse exists among those adults and youth with religious and/or spiritual involvement or affiliation in their lives. Also, positive perceptions and views of God as accepting and forgiving are related to less substance abuse (Pardini, Plante, Sherman, & Stump, 2000). Pardini and colleagues also note that those who have a negative view of God as rejecting and punitive tend to assess themselves as being more spiritual than "religious."

The researchers have also determined that non-denominational religious faith, in the form of a sense of guiding faith, prayer, and belief in God, includes much in the conceptualization of spirituality as perceived by the majority of recovering individuals (from substance abuse/addictions). This finding is, according to the researchers, due to their exposure to 12-Step (self-help) programs which indeed have many beliefs and prescriptive behaviors associated with organized religions.

A sound assessment tool which measures non-denominational religious faith, as well as beliefs and salient behaviors associated with numerous organized religions and 12-Step recovery programs, is the Santa Clara Strength of Religious Faith Questionnaire (Plante & Boccaccini, 1997).

This measure can be useful in pastoral care. By increasing a parishioner's religious faith, it can be expected that they will manifest higher stress resilience, greater perceived social support, greater optimism in life orientation, and less anxiety (Pardini et al., 2000) all of which can help maintain recovery and maintenance as well as minimize relapse.

Tending to one's spirituality and religious faith can be a viable objective, as much as "working the 12-Steps," in being able to buffer triggers which could potentially lead to pernicious undertows and cross-currents, causing relapse and drifting from the maintenance stage of change.

I believe that another unique advantage of pastoral care and guidance in the addiction arena is to restore self-worth, dignity, hope, and faith should a parishioner relapse or "fall off the wagon." Commonly, they will experience shame, guilt, and self-loathing, and be hesitant or even refrain from wanting to commit to behavioral change.

In these instances, it is most beneficial for the parishioner to know that in conquering addictive behaviors, more often than not, persistent efforts and hard work are required during the journey. Aversive sequelae or "fall out" from apparent "wheel spinning" (i.e. numerous attempts or trials at self-change) can certainly be dealt with effectively through pastoral interventions based upon agape and motivational enhancement. Such a climate fosters both behavioral mastery and spiritual growth. Such outcomes are glorious to behold.

RECOMMENDATIONS AND GUIDELINES

Those involved as pastoral caregivers for the parishioner experiencing substance abuse or addiction can be very effective in mobilizing changes. Flexibility and resourcefulness are essential ingredients in assisting in the process of change and growth.

Clergy and associates should become familiar with some of the diverse but effective treatment interventions reviewed in this chapter (Table 1) which include both faith-based and science-based or secular approaches. Such flexibility in leading troubled parishioners, family members, and significant others can minimize resistance to treatment as well as reduce conflicts over religious faith.

By choosing from options, an individual is afforded an opportunity to engage with the approach, take responsibility, and reinforce a sense of autonomy.

Many individuals with addiction problems resent stereotypes and dictums. A good intentioned pastor told a parishioner I saw eventually for psychological consultation: "You are ruining your marriage and family. You have got to admit you are a very sick alcoholic.....and, you can only make it if you go to AA (Alcoholics Anonymous)." The pastor became frustrated and resentful after the parishioner stated: "I know, Pastor, that I drink too much sometimes, but I'm not an alcoholic! AA is for drunks. I hold a job and take care of my family ..... I'm not a bum on skid row."

As the reader may well surmise by now, a horrific power struggle ensued, with the parishioner becoming even more resistant and entrenched in the very early stages of change. Most interesting, from a clinical perspective, is that if a parishioner's or congregant's selection(s) fail initially, they will often make successive choices which likely lead to greater success or self-mastery of the stated goal(s).

It is strongly suggested that those rendering pastoral care for this population develop a trusting alliance with a professional (psychiatrist, psychologist, clinical counselor/social worker) who is licensed and credentialed in, ideally, both mental health and substance abuse/chemical dependency. Such a professional will be equipped to consult with individuals having co-morbid or co-existing conditions (i.e. substance use disorders as well as emotional problems such as anxiety, depression, personality disorders, etc.). Consultation is extremely valuable should clergy surmise at any time the potential for the parishioner causing serious harm to themselves or others. In some instances, in-patient psychiatric treatment or court-ordered (involuntary commitment) treatment may be required depending upon the severity and nature of the disturbance being manifested.

Other suggestions for clergy and church associates include:

1. Encourage and promote educational activities to increase consciousness and awareness of the potential for abuse of substances.
2. Maintain role boundaries, being aware of the potential for enabling and fostering dependency. Administer realistic support, active listening, and empathy with an emphasis upon the parishioner's freedom of choice in decision-making.
3. a.) Serve as a catalyst in recognizing and building spiritual strengths by incorporating secular teachings which accentuate the importance, value, and meaning of coming to terms with human weaknesses and vulnerabilities. Bolster religious faith and hope.

    b.) Explore the troubled parishioner's past for clues in terms of spiritual or religious teachings and/or experiences that have had an impact in altering their beliefs, attitudes, values, actions, or feelings and generalize and expand upon those in facing current issues and problems.

For too many of those addicted, the sands of time will sadly run out prematurely. Others will be tossed about aimlessly in the depths of cross-currents and undertows along the river of life's journey – their lives increasingly shattered with ensuing emotional and spiritual impoverishment.

We know that self-change and recovery are possible either slowly over time or more rapidly with some. With enlightened pastoral care and timely, appropriate professional consultation, we can only hope and pray that change, with lasting recovery, is sooner, rather than later.

RESOURCES FOR FUTURE INFORMATION

A. MOTIVATIONAL INTERVIEWING
Internet site : www.motivationalinterview.org
Motivational Enhancement Therapy Manual: A Clinical Research Guide for Therapists Treating Individuals with Alcohol Abuse & Dependence. National Institute in Alcohol Abuse & Alcoholism (Project MATCH, 1999).

B.   SUBSTANCE ABUSE

National Institute of Alcohol Abuse & Alcoholism (Internet site: www.niaaa.nih.gov)

National Institute on Drug Abuse (Internet site: www.drugabuse.gov)

Office of National Drug Control Policy (Internet site: www.whitehousedrugpolicy.gov)

Substance Abuse & Mental Health Service Admin. for Substance Abuse Treatment
(Internet site: www.samhsa.gov)

Substance Abuse Among Older Adults: A Guide for Treatment Providers, Concise Desk
Referene Guide (CDRG). Substance Abuse & Mental Health Services Adminis
tration, U.S. Dept. of Human Services.

C.   SELF-HELP ORGANIZATIONS

Faith-Based:

Alcoholics Anonymous (AA World Services, 1980)

Twelve Steps and Twelve Traditions (AA World Service, 1978)

Secular and Science-Based*:

Moderation Management (MM): a self-control program for problem drinkers based upon
scientific , cognitive-behavioral approaches. (Internet site: www.moderation.org)

Rational Recovery (RR): a secular program suited for those with any aversion towards
Alcoholics Anonymous (AA). (Internet site: www.rationalrecovery.org)

Secular Organization for Sobriety (SOS): a secularized version of the 12-step fellowship
program, not affiliated with AA.

Self-Management & Recovery Training (SMART Recovery): goal is abstinence from any
harmful addictive behavior with issues of spirituality and faith for individual exploration.

Women for Sobriety (WFS): a secular, empowering, affirming program.
(Internet site: www.womenforsobriety.org)

* The author wishes to express gratitude and thanks to Dr. Henry Steinberger for his contribution of identifying and describing these secular/science-based organizations.

REFERENCES

Bien, T.H., Miller, W.R., & Broughs, J.M. (1993). Motivational interviewing with alcohol out-patients. *Behavioral and Cognitive Psychotherapy, 21*, 347-356.

Johnson, V.E. (1980). *I'll quit tomorrow.* (Rev.Ed.). San Francisco: Harper & Row.

McQuade, W.H., Levy S.M., Yanck, L.R., Davis, S., & Liepman, M.R. (2000). Detecting symptoms of alcohol abuse in primary care settings. *Arch Fam Med, 9*, 814-823

Miller, W.R. (2000). Rediscovering fire: Small intervention, large effects. *Psychology of Addictive Behavior, 14*, 6-18.

Miller, W.R., & Baca, L.M. (1983). Two-year follow-up of bibliotherapy and therapist directed controlled drinking training for problem drinkers. *Behavior Therapy, 14*, 441-448.

Miller, W.R., & C'DeBaca, J. (1995). What every mental health professional should know about alcohol. *Journal of Substance Abuse Treatment, 12*, 355-365.

Miller, W.R., & Rollnick, S. (1991) *Motivational interviewing: Preparing people to change addictive behavior.* New York: Guilford Press.

Pardini, D.A., Plante, T.G., Sherman, A., & Stump, J.E. (2000). Religious faith and spirituality in substance abuse recovery: Determining the mental health benefits. *Journal of Substance Abuse Treatment, 19(4)*, 347-354.

Plante, T.G., & Baccaccini, M.T. (1997). The Santa Clara strength of religious faith questionnaire. *Pastoral Psychology, 45*, 375-386.

Prochaska, J.O., DiClemente, C.C., & Norcross, J.C. (1992). In search of how people change. *American Psychologist, 47*, 1102-1114.

Read, J.P., Kahler, C.W., & Stevenson, J.F. (2001). Bridging the gap between alcoholism treatment research and practice: Identifying what works and why. *Professional Psychology: Research & Practice, 32(3)*, 227-238.

Saunders, J.B., Aasland, O.G., Babor, T.F., De La Fuente, J.R., & Grant, M. (1993). Development of the alcohol use disorder identification test (AUDIT): WHO collaborative project early detection of persons with harmful alcohol consumption – II. *Addiction, 88*, 791-804.

Chapter 8
In the Depths of Murky Waters:
Depression & Suicide

by Karen R. Scheel, Ph.D.;
Christopher J. McNally, M.A.;
Cynthia A. Yamokoski, M.A.; &
James L. Werth, Jr., Ph.D.
The University of Akron

Please address correspondence to the first author at:
Department of Counseling, The University of Akron, Akron, OH 44325-5007
E-mail: kscheel@uakron.edu

In the Depths of Murky Waters: Depression & Suicide
A Case Example: Stephanie

Stephanie is a 26 year-old biracial (European-American / African-American) female, currently beginning her first year of graduate school, studying to be an orthopedist after working for a number of years as an elementary school teacher. Stephanie is the youngest of five children and the remaining members of her very traditional, tightly knit family all live nearby. Belonging to the same Apostolic faith as the majority of her extended family, Stephanie has forged strong bonds within her church community. Her family has a long history of religious involvement, as well as an impressive tradition of civic influence and accomplishment in local business.

Stephanie excelled academically as an undergraduate Education major, while also distinguishing herself as a student athlete and remaining quite active within her church. Stephanie met Derek, a 25 year-old African-American businessman and her longtime boyfriend, while playing volleyball as an undergraduate. Derek was one of two athletic trainers who worked directly with Stephanie's team and, shortly following their graduation, the two began a romantic relationship that has lasted more than four years. Derek works for a local sports management company and he has been extremely supportive of Stephanie's move into the field of orthopedics and sports medicine.

Stephanie pursued a degree in orthopedic medicine against her parents' wishes and against the tenets of their religious faith, which ascribes very narrow vocational and social roles for women. Stephanie's previous work as a teacher met with general approval from her family, but her own enthusiasm for the field of education was never significant. Secretly, she had always hoped to become a physician. Through her relationship with Derek, Stephanie realized the strength of her conviction, finally deciding to pursue a lifelong dream by applying to medical school. Only upon admission did she inform her family of her future plans.

Since informing her family of this decision, Stephanie has become increasingly irritable and impatient and, more recently, has experienced excessive fatigue. She has been uncharacteristically asocial, often choosing to remain home in the evenings rather than attend campus sports events with Derek. She has been eating very little and, in Derek's opinion, seems frighteningly unaffected by her lack of sociability and her diminishing appetite. To Derek's surprise, she has also been demonstrating a lack of interest in her academic work, despite her known interest in this material. She has become prone to excessive ruminating, constantly questioning whether her choice of a career change was wise and whether her family will accept her as a successful physician. Though her parents have expressed concern and have asked that she speak with an Elder of their church, this support has seemed strangely superficial to Stephanie. Her career interests have forced her to question many aspects of her upbringing, including her religious faith. She finds herself extremely conflicted regarding her family and the faith that has always been her "rock" and her primary source of identity, security, and belonging in the world. She finds herself becoming increasingly reliant upon Derek, which makes her nervous despite her acknowledged love for him.

Sensing that her condition is worsening, Derek has suggested that Stephanie visit with a campus counselor or, if she wishes to discuss her faith-related struggles, with the Chaplain of the university medical center. When Derek and Stephanie originally began discussing the possibility of engagement and marriage, they met with this Chaplain to discuss various options regarding the wedding ceremony. Following this discussion, Stephanie came to the difficult and painful realization that her family would never accept a wedding outside of their own church. Now, it appears that her dream of becoming a physician is unexpectedly resulting in similar stress and conflict, but on an even grander scale. This has caused her to withdraw and isolate. She attends her classes only sporadically and spends most of her time at home, experiencing feelings of loss, abandonment, and – perhaps for the first time in her life – significant grief.

Introduction

Depression, often accompanied by suicidal thoughts and behaviors, occurs with high prevalence in today's society and brings great suffering to those affected. As Stephanie's case illustrates, it has become vital for clergy[1] to understand the various phenomena related to depression and suicide so that they may helpfully respond to affected members of their faith communities. In the chapter that follows, readers will be introduced to depression—its definition, its prevalence, and its numerous forms. Current treatment approaches for depression are presented, with a particular emphasis on criteria for diagnosis and the discernment of potential suicidality. Common myths about suicide are discussed, as are common reactions and needs of those bereaved by a loved one's suicide. Finally, attention is given to the impact of a church member's suicide on clergy themselves. Practical tips and guidelines for intervention are provided throughout the chapter, and a list of further resources and related readings is located at the chapter's conclusion.

Depression

Although most people have felt "down or "blue" at one time or another, clinical depression is actually a much different condition. In this section we will describe and differentiate various types of depression, outline a number of prominent treatments for these conditions, and provide practical guidelines for intervention.

Types and Prevalence of Depression

Two predominant methods have been utilized for describing various forms of depression. One method involves distinct description of different types of depressive disorders, while the other views depression as existing on a continuum. In determining appropriate interventions and treatment for those who suffer from depression, it is helpful to be both proficient in the description of specific types of depression and capable of differentiating this depression from grief, stress, anxiety, and other disorders of mood. Rather than attempting to provide detailed instructions for establishing such fine-grained distinctions, a more general approach to diagnosis is provided here, in the interest of facilitating knowledgeable referral to qualified mental health professionals.

The *Diagnostic and Statistical Manual of Mental Disorders, 4th edition*, (or, *DSM-IV*, published by the American Psychiatric Association in 2000; all referenced pagination and accompanying descriptions of psychiatric conditions within this subsection are taken from this source) is commonly used to determine whether a person is experiencing a diagnosable mental health condition. Depression is classified as a *mood disorder* in the *DSM-IV*. The primary types of mood disorders are (a) major depressive disorder, (b) dysthymic disorder, (c) bipolar disorder, (d) cyclothymic disorder, and (e) substance-induced mood disorder. Bipolar disorder (referred to in the past as "manic depression") is characterized by swings of mood, between periods of time where one feels very depressed and periods of time where one feels very energetic (i.e., "manic"). Cyclothymia is a less extreme version of bipolar disorder, while substance-induced mood disorder - as its name implies - occurs when depression or mania results from substance abuse. Due to their less frequent occurrence and the decreased likelihood of clergy encountering these disorders, they will not be discussed in detail.

Major depressive disorder (pp. 349-356, 369-376) - also referred to as "major" or "clinical" depression - has a very distinct meaning for mental health professionals. In order to receive a diagnosis of major depression, a person must experience depressed mood and/or loss of interest/pleasure in nearly all activities, as well as four of the following seven additional symptoms (or three of the following seven, if depressed mood *and* loss of interest/pleasure are present):

- Significant weight loss or decrease in appetite

- Insomnia or oversleeping
- Objectively observable agitation or retardation of physical activity
- Fatigue or loss of energy
- Feelings of worthlessness or inappropriate guilt
- Indecisiveness and/or diminished ability to think or concentrate
- Recurrent thoughts of death or suicide-related thoughts/behavior

Each symptom must be present for a period of at least two consecutive weeks (with each symptom present nearly every day, for the majority of each day). In addition, this cluster of symptoms must be accompanied by significant distress or impairment in various aspects of life (e.g., social functioning, work, etc.). Symptoms must not be associated with a natural period of bereavement (i.e., two months) following the loss of a loved one, unless the symptoms are atypical for grief, such as excessive feelings of guilt or worthlessness.

Among different racial/ethnic groups, symptoms demonstrated by those experiencing major depression may be interpreted a variety of ways. For example, some cultures interpret depression as primarily an expression of physical symptoms (e.g., "nerves," "imbalance," "problems with my heart," etc.), focusing on these symptoms almost exclusively. Others focus primarily on affect (e.g., "blue") and, in some cases, cognitive functioning (e.g., "down"). Similarly, different age groups may manifest depressive symptomology in different ways. For example, children may display more active irritability and social withdrawal, while older adults may simply become disinterested or apathetic. Medical conditions may be equally significant, with approximately 20-25 percent of individuals with chronic or severe medical conditions believed to experience concurrent major depression.

Community-based research indicates that the lifetime risk for major depression is 5-12% for men and 10-25% for women (p. 372), with an average age of onset in the mid-20's. These prevalence rates do not appear to vary by ethnicity, education, income, or marital status, although, as can be seen, they do vary by sex. The reasons for the higher prevalence of depression among women are likely complex. Biological differences between men and women might account for some of the discrepancy in rates, as might sociocultural differences relating to life in a male dominated society and gender role socialization patterns affecting how distress is manifested and communicated (e.g. as guilt versus anger). Prevalence rates also vary by family; the condition appears to be 1.5 – 3.0 times more common for people with a first-degree biological relative who has experienced either major depression or dysthymia.

Dysthymia is a less severe form of major depression, differing primarily with regard to duration and persistence (pp. 374, 376-381). In order to receive a diagnosis of dysthymia, a person must experience depressed mood for most of each day and for more days than not, for at least two years. Additionally, two or more of the following six symptoms must be present:

- Poor appetite or overeating

- Insomnia or excessive sleeping
- Low energy or fatigue
- Low self-esteem
- Poor concentration or difficulty making decisions
- Feelings of hopelessness

These symptoms must be present for at least ten months each year and cause significant distress or impairment. Additional, less central criterion for this diagnosis are beyond the scope of this chapter. An individual diagnosed with dysthymia may also experience periods of major depression; this phenomenon has sometimes been referred to as "double depression." The likelihood of an individual diagnosed with dysthymia being diagnosed with major depression within five years is high, up to 75% in clinical settings.

The lifetime prevalence of dysthymia is approximately 6%, with women, again for likely complex reasons, being two to three times more likely to develop the disorder than men. Dysthymia also appears to be more common among people with first-degree biological relatives who have experienced major depression or dysthymia.

Although not a *DSM-IV* diagnosis, the term "minor depression" has been used to describe depressive episodes where less than five of the above symptoms are exhibited. Depending upon specific circumstances, this condition may be formally diagnosed as "Adjustment Disorder with Depressed Mood." Adjustment disorders are characterized by significant emotional or behavioral symptoms in reaction to single or multiple stressors (either recurrent or continuous) (pp. 679-683). These symptoms must develop within three months of a stressor's onset and must be distinguishable from bereavement. A marked distress over and above what would typically be expected must be present, along with significant impairment in social or occupational/academic functioning. The level of disturbance should not rise to the level of other disorders, such as major depression.

Adjustment disorder with depressed mood may be impacted by sociocultural beliefs and experiences to a greater degree than major depression and/or dysthymia. Women receive the diagnosis twice as often as men. The rate of prevalence for this diagnosis has been reported at 2-8%, with people who experience stress related to their living conditions (e.g., impoverishment, lack of resources) appearing to be more at risk.

Treatment and Intervention for Types of Depression

This subsection highlights various approaches to the treatment of depression, dysthymia, and adjustment disorder with depressed mood. This information is not intended to be comprehensive or instructional with regard to specific treatments, but is intended to support effective foundational work with clients and to enable knowledgeable referral to qualified mental health professionals.

Typically, an untreated episode of major depression lasts for four months or longer, with 5-10% of these untreated cases lasting more than two years. Follow-up studies indicate that 40% of those who suffer from major depression retain symptoms warranting the diagnosis one year after original diagnosis. By the same token, 20% of these individuals no longer meet full criteria and 40% are in full remission. The spontaneous remission rate for dysthymia is comparatively low, estimated to be only 10% per year. By definition, people experiencing adjustment disorder with depressed mood will experience symptom remission within six months of the stressor's conclusion. If symptoms persist, a different diagnosis may be warranted.

For individuals experiencing adjustment disorder with depressed mood, counseling interventions quite familiar to clergy may prove sufficient. Helping to normalize reactions, providing empathic listening, engaging social support, and motivating people to remain involved rather than retreating into isolation—all can be very helpful and highly appropriate for individuals struggling to adjust to significant stressors.

Successful treatments for dysthymia are typically more involved, often requiring a mental health background that is more extensive than the training received by most clergy. Recent research indicates that approximately half of all individuals diagnosed with dysthymia respond positively to a mixture of antidepressant medication and traditional forms of psychotherapy. Due to the chronic nature of dysthymia and the generalized loss of interest and/or pleasure that is often evidenced in these cases, working to generate renewed hopefulness and optimism on the part of the client may be challenging. Integrative or eclectic approaches to therapy are frequently utilized for this purpose, as their context-focused frameworks provide a highly adaptive and receptive forum for discussion of client concerns. Treatment of dysthymia may often involve a detailed assessment of client history, for purposes of determining the origin of client suffering and the potential impact of trauma and/or significant loss. Existential-humanistic approaches to therapy, including active interpretation of the individual's prevailing worldview, have demonstrated effectiveness in these cases. Fairly prolonged intervention is often necessitated, due to a considerable incidence of relapse when treatment is terminated.

Due to the fact that individuals who experience major depression often contemplate suicide, with a significant percentage actively attempting to end their lives, providing professional assistance as soon as possible becomes imperative. Several treatment approaches have demonstrated effectiveness for individuals experiencing major depression, including behavior therapy (Craighead, Hart, Craighead, & Ilardi, 2002), cognitive therapy (e.g., Craighead et al.; Young, Weinberger, & Beck, 2001), interpersonal therapy (e.g., Craighead et al.; Gillies, 2001), and medication (e.g., Nemeroff & Schatzberg, 2002). Successful therapeutic treatment of major depression further supports the assertion that psychological treatment effectiveness is equivalent to that of medication, with combined approaches perhaps better than either type alone (Craighead et al.).

Referral

For clergy meeting with individuals who appear to be experiencing major depression, dysthymia, or adjustment disorder with depressed mood, referral to a mental health professional is a primary option. A licensed professional counselor, social worker, psychologist, or psychiatrist has typically received training that permits a thorough and accurate diagnosis of the individual's condition. Psychiatrists remain the primary group called upon to prescribe medication in these situations, though increased demand has more recently resulted in primary care physicians prescribing more anti-depressant medications. Psychologists have typically received extensive training in assessment, individual psychotherapy, group psychotherapy, and in some cases may specialize in couples therapy or family systems therapy. All of these approaches may be adapted for use with depressed individuals in a wide variety of settings. Social workers typically receive comprehensive training regarding community resources and entitlements, while professional counselors have increasingly become front-line service providers for many organizations.

Regardless of professional affiliation or specialization, mental health professionals frequently utilize a "common factors" approach to therapy with depressed and/or suicidal clients. The common factors approach (Frank & Frank, 1991) acknowledges the existence of countless therapies, all seeking to affect positive change for the client in a prescribed manner. While acknowledging an enormous therapeutic diversity, the common factors approach suggests that all therapies – regardless of technique – necessitate a meaningful relationship between client and helper aimed at clarifying problems, inspiring hope, and supporting the client's sense of competence and mastery. By inspiring the client emotionally, a common factors approach also seeks to alleviate the client's sense of powerlessness, moving them toward active change within their environment.

As many depressed individuals tend to withdraw and isolate, it may be useful to intervene by encouraging involvement with other people and participation in leisure activities that require socializing. Depressed individuals often state: "I'll do something when I feel better". Though an obvious statement in many ways, the reverse is frequently true—people often feel better after doing something! Research indicates that volunteering may be an effective intervention for depressed individuals, not only because it involves interaction with others but because it often enables the depressed persons to gain useful perspective regarding the relative degree of difficulty in their current situation. Others may be worse off, illustrating not only that there is much good work to be done, but that one's condition could be much worse. Finally, due to the fact that depression has a physical component, encouraging people to exercise (even moderately) may be an effective intervention, resulting in alleviation of depressed mood. In one form or another, all of these interventions incorporate a common factors approach to healing, moving the client toward a place of greater personal insight and facilitating active growth within the client's current context.

Suicide

Introduction

Just as there are many different definitions and forms of depression, there are many different definitions of suicide and multiple ways to classify the various types of suicidal behavior. The definition of suicide is not solely a mental health issue, but also a legal matter. The general consensus among mental health and legal experts is that a death may be defined as a suicide when an individual intentionally dies from self-inflicted injuries. The term "suicidal behavior" refers to a wide variety of behaviors, including much more than the act of killing oneself. Additional forms of suicidal behavior include non-fatal deliberate self-harm with or without wanting to die; suicidal communications, including suicide threats; and - most commonly - suicidal thoughts or "ideations." It is generally agreed that these suicidal behaviors fall along a continuum of severity, ranging from general risk-taking behaviors and thoughts of death to the most extreme act of intentional fatal self-injury.

Aspects of Suicidal Behaviors

Two of the most important aspects of suicidal behaviors are *intent to die* and *lethality of action*. Existence of intent serves to differentiate between various types of suicidal behaviors. If an individual engages in an action that is purposefully harmful to self, but does not wish to bring upon death, a *parasuicide* is said to occur. Though the individual in question does not intend to die, parasuicide is frequently included in the spectrum of suicidal behaviors due to the very real possibility that the individual involved may die "accidentally" or grow in his or her wish to die intentionally. If an individual inflicts self-harm with the intent to die, but the self-harm does not prove to be fatal, the behavior is labeled a suicide attempt. Suicide itself occurs when an individual's self-harm does intentionally end his or her life. The expression "completed suicide" is sometimes used, although it is generally preferable to simply say "died by suicide." The expression "committed suicide," with its connotations of sin and crime, is insensitive at best and should be avoided.

Factors that may determine the lethality of an attempt are method choice (e.g., cutting, overdose, gunshot to head), reversibility of action, probability of discovery, and location of attempt (see Maris, Berman & Silverman, 2000, chapter 2). In the United States, approximately 30,000 individuals die by suicide each year, with estimates of annual suicide attempts ranging from 240,000 to 750,000. These figures indicate that most people who attempt suicide do so with non-lethal actions. Suicidal thinking ranges from general thoughts about death (e.g., believing that it would be easier to be dead than alive) and suicide (e.g., reactions of others if suicide were attempted), to current plans and/or active wishes to die by suicide. Quite frequently, depressed individuals will communicate their thoughts about suicide to others. Suicidal ideation is not always followed by self-harm, but it remains quite difficult to differentiate between individuals who will actually follow through on their suicidal thoughts and those who will not.

In conclusion, individuals broadly considered to be "suicidal" may demonstrate a wide array of behaviors with very different purposes and intents. While "suicidal behavior" does not represent a single phenomenon, it does always represent cause for concern and intervention by those who care for the sufferer.

Myths of Suicide

In Western society, suicide has historically been a phenomenon shrouded in secrecy, superstition, and fear. With so little light shone into these "murky waters," it is not surprising that myth and misconception continue to this day. The following list contains common misbeliefs regarding suicide, all of which carry the potential to negatively influence perceptions and helping efforts when a suicide or potential suicide occurs within a faith community.

Myth #1: *Asking troubled people if they are thinking of suicide will 'put the idea into their heads.'* There is no evidence that this common fear has any basis in reality. To the contrary, gently but directly asking distressed individuals if they are thinking of taking their own life conveys concern and caring. Isolation and pessimism (including pessimism about being helped) are common characteristics of suicidal people. Reaching out in a warm and caring manner invites disclosure and connection and may ultimately decrease the likelihood of suicide.

Myth #2: *People who threaten suicide and/or make non-fatal suicide attempts are not the people who actually kill themselves.* Consistent with the previous discussion of the suicidal continuum, individuals who have threatened suicide, particularly those who have made a past attempt or attempts, are at higher risk for eventually dying by suicide than those who have not. In practice, this means that every suicidal statement and behavior must be taken seriously. However, it does not mean that relying solely on suicidal statements and behaviors is sufficient for determining whether someone is at risk for suicide. While most people who eventually die by suicide do communicate their suicidal thoughts to others and have often made prior suicide attempts, some complete suicide without ever providing any direct warning, either in word or behavior. Others provide warning only indirectly, in the form of such behaviors as giving away valued possessions or making a will.

Myth #3: *You have to be 'crazy' to kill yourself.* When people say "crazy," they are typically referring to psychosis as manifested in the disorder schizophrenia. Although people diagnosed with schizophrenia do exhibit a higher than average rate of suicide, most people who die by suicide are not schizophrenic. A large majority of individuals who die by suicide (approximately 90%) do appear to have exhibited symptoms indicating a diagnosable mental illness. However, this is most commonly a mood disorder, such as depression or bipolar disorder. Alcohol and substance abuse, frequently in conjunction with a mood disorder, are also common among those who die by suicide. A substantial portion of the 10% or so of individuals who die by suicide but do not appear to have had a mental illness may be vulnerable individuals who experienced what seemed to be a cataclysmic loss to their sense of self, relationship, or the world.

Suicidal individuals are not generally "crazy" in the sense of being grossly out of touch with reality, although psychotic states may occur in depression, bipolar disorder, and other mental illnesses frequently associated with suicide. While typically not psychotic, the suicidal condition *is* commonly associated with cognitive distortion and "tunnel vision." Thinking becomes rigid, problem-solving abilities deteriorate, a dark hopelessness pervades perception, and suicide appears to be the only solution.

A small final group represents those who died by what are termed acts of *rational suicide*. Typically, members of this group are individuals who had painful incurable illnesses and who made considered, clear-minded decisions to hasten their own deaths. Although rational suicide is controversial, it is difficult to call it "crazy."

Myth #4: *Suicidal people are committed to dying.* To the contrary, most suicidal people are considerably ambivalent. They may not wish to die, but they desperately hope to escape an experience of pain that feels unbearable and exceeds their coping capacity. Suicidal threats and non-lethal suicidal behaviors truly *are* cries for help. Thankfully, a better solution is found for most. The pain abates and life goes on. For some - especially those with severe and chronic psychological conditions - pain, crises, and thoughts of suicide may ebb and flow for many years, perhaps even for a lifetime. And finally there are those - on average, 11 or 12 of every 100,000 persons in the United States each year – who, with or without help, simply cannot find their way out and drown in the murky waters.

Guidelines for Intervention with Suicidal Individuals

Given the high degree of overlap between suicidality and depression, treatment and intervention issues overlap significantly. As these topics were previously discussed in relation to depression, they will not be dealt with at length here. Work with depressed individuals who are also actively suicidal is, of course, especially demanding and challenging, and referral to a qualified mental health professional is almost always necessary. Clergy play an invaluable role in suicide prevention by being perceptive "front line" helpers, actively following up on their concerns regarding members of their faith communities and connecting those in need to appropriate mental health providers.

At times this "front line" work will require skill in crisis intervention, as when a clergyperson interacts with someone at imminent risk of self-harm. Providing guidelines for crisis intervention is beyond the scope of this chapter, and clergy are encouraged to seek training in this area if it has not already been received. In general, when intervening in a suicidal crisis it is important to warmly and directively help the individual bring negative affect and agitation under control, while also agreeing on a plan for safety. If the individual is unwilling or unable to convincingly agree to a safety plan, it may be necessary—as a last resort—to contact law enforcement to escort the individual to a hospital.

After the immediate crisis has passed, it is important that the clergyperson continue to build a relationship with the suicidal individual. Doing so may help to position the clergyperson to successfully influence a reluctant individual to seek professional treatment or an ambivalent one to continue it. Having the social support of the clergyperson is also invaluable in itself, as the troubled and often isolated individual seeks to make sense of his or her life and pain.

Role of the Clergy in the Aftermath of Suicide

Even with the best helping efforts, there are times when suicide nevertheless occurs. These tragic endings may usher in a multitude of tragic beginnings, as loved ones embark upon the long and painful process of grieving and understanding their loss. It has been estimated that every suicide intimately affects at least six additional people, leaving over four million suicide *survivors* in the United States (see Jobes, Luoma, Hustead, & Mann, 2000, p. 537). Given the sheer number of lives touched by members of the clergy, it seems nearly inevitable that most will be called upon at some time, perhaps many times, to minister to those grieving the loss of a loved one to suicide. Because supporting the bereaved falls in clergy's purview as much or more than mental health professionals,' particular attention is given to this topic.

This work may be relatively common, but it is rarely easy. What helpful words could the Chaplain say to the family of the woman described at the opening of this chapter if her despair ultimately led her to suicide? What does a concerned clergyperson say to a terrified and angry woman who wants to know how God could possibly have permitted her husband, the father of her young children, to take his own life? To a teenager haunted by images of his friend, dead on the ground after shooting himself? To a mother desperate to understand what she did "wrong" and what has happened to the soul of her beloved child?

These are just a few of the many heart wrenching and immensely challenging suicide-related scenarios faced by clergy every day. To a large extent, the skills gained through ministering to individuals grieving other types of death apply here as well. Reactions to the loss of a loved one to suicide have a great deal in common with bereavement in general, particularly bereavement following sudden or unexpected deaths. Clergy may expect to encounter the familiar denial, anger, bargaining, and acceptance originally described by Kubler-Ross (1969). It should be noted, however, that grief reactions following loss from any cause are often complex and rarely follow the linear, sequential stages described in many interpretations of Kubler-Ross's work.

Though commonalities exist between the grief that occurs following suicide and grief that follows other deaths, there are also important differences. The unique aspects of grief after suicide have a number of implications for clergy wishing to support those bereaved by suicide. The most immediately striking difference between bereavement following suicide and bereavement following death from other causes is the pervasiveness of guilt among suicide survivors. Survivor guilt may only fleetingly nag at the corners of the mind, or it may be ever-present and overwhelming. It is perhaps most painfully and enduringly present for those whose social role in relation to the deceased included care taking and protection. However experienced and expressed and however irrational this guilt may seem to outsiders, few survivors appear to escape it entirely.

A related difference in grief experiences is the pervasiveness of anger and blame among suicide survivors. Anger seeks a villain, and the inexplicable seeks an explanation. Nameless, formless anger is often a primary emotion for the recently suicidally bereaved, though for some anger may emerge only slowly or not at all. Asking "Why?" begins early and ends late in the grieving process for most survivors, and the first attempts at answering this haunting question often involve blame. In addition to providing a focus for anger, the placing of blame may fundamentally serve to maintain an illusion - that all events result from causes that are clearly knowable and ultimately controllable. Sadly, this illusion may subject the suicide survivor to both overt anger and covert criticism from anyone from unsettled acquaintances to other bereft intimates of the deceased. Concurrently, this same suicide survivor may at least temporarily blame others for the loss. Perhaps for similar underlying reasons, suicide survivors often describe a process of endlessly reviewing their loved one's final days in a search for clues to what went wrong and what they, others, or simple chance could have done to avert the disaster.

Not surprisingly, survivor anger toward the deceased may also be especially pronounced. To an individual suffering the incredible pain and hardship of losing a loved one, the loved one's choice to take his or her own life may seem unbelievably selfish. Survivor anger may result in guilty feelings, as innumerable questions persist. How could the loved one have failed to hang on? How could he or she have ignored how grief-stricken those left behind would be? Eventually, the survivor may understand that in the distorted "tunnel vision" of the suicidal state, depressed individuals often genuinely believe that they are doing their loved ones a favor by ending their lives. Conversely, their vision may be so restricted that they do not think at all about the way their death will impact loved ones. Indeed, clinical experience suggests that if they survive the suicidal crisis, these individuals are often shocked, in retrospect, by this cognitive omission. For the newly bereaved, however, understanding of these issues and a related dissipation of anger is typically well down the road.

To be shaken. Survivors may feel angry at or abandoned by God. They may question how a compassionate God could possibly be presiding over a universe where this type of senseless loss occurs. An utter collapse of one's religious beliefs, when those beliefs previously provided a central meaning system for the understanding of both life and death, may be as terrifying and disorienting as the suicide itself. The survivor who maintains his or her belief system may face a different problem of faith. The image of a loved one's soul returning to rest in the hands of God, perhaps eventually to be reunited with the souls of those still living, brings profound comfort to many bereaved individuals. This comfort may feel denied to some suicide survivors. Those from certain traditions may find that the comforting image of rest and reunification in the afterlife is replaced by a torment-ing one of their loved one's damnation.

Last, but certainly not least, is the enduring *stigma* of suicide. Hearts are broken by the loss of a loved one to any cause, and there is no weighing one heartbreak against another. Still, those bereaved following other causes of death are unlikely to encounter the whispers, the social awkwardness, and the outright avoidance that all too often compound the grief of the suicide survivor. The result can be shame, isolation, and loneliness at a time when the comfort of others is needed most.

Lessons in Helping and Healing

In the process of healing, every suicide survivor follows an individual course and timetable. There is no "normal" pattern of healing and no predictable chain of reactions. As any experienced member of the clergy surely knows, there is simply no prescription for the "right" thing to say or do. In the following sec-tion, an attempt is made to pass along a number of general lessons in helping learned by suicidologists, therapists, and suicide survivors themselves. Ideas are organized around loose time frames before and after a suicide. Following this section, additional thoughts are offered regarding the special demands of helping child survivors.

Lesson #1: *Find your own bearings.* Before helping someone lost at sea to shore, one first must find one's own bearings. Ideally, this occurs before any ac-tual encounters with suicide survivors. Finding your own bearings means many things. Working "from the top down," it means understanding the theological po-sition of your particular Church on suicide, and understanding it in a way that can be compassionately conveyed to searching suicide survivors. The Bible itself pro-vides little specific, direct guidance. Although several suicides are recorded, without disapproval, there are no statements that specifically condemn or condone the act. Maris, Berman, and Silverman (2000) report that Christianity was several centu-ries old before an official position against suicide was taken, based on interpreta-tion of the sixth commandment, "Thou shalt not kill." In the centuries since, many different understandings and positions have evolved in the varying Christian tra-ditions. At heart are interpretations of central Christian issues. Among these are questions about who has the right to end a life, the purpose of human suffering, whether God ever *does* give us more than we can bear, the meaning of compassion and forgiveness, and the boundlessness of God's grace.

In addition to reflecting upon your Church's perspective, it is important to reflect upon the expectations of the laity. Given the harsh condemnation of suicide and the general stigma surrounding it in the lore of the early Church (and State), many survivors expect a judgmental response from their religious institution when they actually would receive a compassionate one. If this is suspected, proactive efforts to reach out and reassure survivors might be called for.

In addition to living in theological contexts, clergy and laypersons also live within cultural contexts. In ways both in and out of awareness, cultural lenses may color responses to suicide. Individuals of African, Asian, European, Latino, and American Indian descent may collectively hold different culturally-based beliefs about suicide. Within these very broad racial/ethnic groupings are even *more* subcultural differences and, within these, individual differences as well. It is important that clergy bring to light the culturally based suicide beliefs they themselves hold and familiarize themselves with the traditional suicide beliefs of the cultures represented in their local faith community. Doing so may help avoid misunderstanding and inadvertent offense at a most sensitive time.

Lastly, finding your own bearings in these murky waters means knowing yourself. Suicide evokes strong reactions, even for the most seasoned helping professionals. Common reactions include sorrow, anger, horror, fear, compassion, guilt, judgment, and withdrawal. Ministering to those who are grieving a suicidal loss requires the ability to be fully present as these individuals experience their own intensely strong reactions. Suicide survivors are often painfully aware of even the most veiled discomfort on the part of their "helpers," whether that discomfort be related to the suicidal act itself or to the survivor's own expressions of grief about it. If coping with personal reactions or those of survivors proves difficult, further reflection, training, or consultation is recommended. Those who fear that their beliefs, personal experiences, and/or emotional reactions regarding suicide may lead to a less than healing response may find it helpful to focus on their role as ministers to living, grieving survivors in the short term, rather than focusing on personal reactions to the suicide itself. If efforts to overcome difficulties with reactions to suicide prove unsuccessful in the long term, finding a willing pastoral colleague or mental health professional with related expertise is recommended. Referring suicide survivors to this individual may be the most genuine expression of compassion available.

Lesson #2: *Provide shelter from the storm.* When an individual discovers that a loved one has taken his or her own life, this individual is cast into stormy waters. The waters are even rougher for those who witnessed the suicide or found the body firsthand. Figuratively and at times literally, clergy may become persons to hold onto as the first terrible waves of anguish crash over the suicide survivor. Commonly, the survivor initially feels shocked, disbelieving, numb, and disoriented. During this time, simply "empathically being" with the bereaved is most valuable. Complicated attempts at explanation and reassurance are offered in vain when the recipient is overwrought, but the comfort of a strong, caring, "grounding" presence can be immense.

While the reactions mentioned above are common, it is especially important when approaching the survivors of a suicide to avoid making any assumptions about how they will or "should" feel or behave. Any reaction is possible. Survivors might, for example, feel relief if the suicide followed a prolonged and painful physical or mental illness.

As with most deaths, practical assistance from clergy and the church community via death notifications, burial plans, meals, and other necessities of life is generally appreciated. Extended family members or friends are oftentimes welcome and available for many of these functions. However, intimate survivors are not always immediately prepared to bring in even trusted "outsiders." Arranging to keep the ship afloat while intimates have time to absorb the news and prepare themselves for interaction with friends and extended family can be extremely helpful.

From a research perspective, little is known about the impact of clergy behavior on survivor coping. Anecdotally, the pastoral response – particularly that of the Church leader officiating at the funeral service - seems quite important. The value of the typical practice of consulting with willing friends and family prior to a funeral cannot be overstated. Tension and interpersonal discord within the social network of the deceased may occur (e.g., between blood relatives and in-laws, etc.), and the impact of the completed suicide may ripple through schools, workplaces, and various community groups. Thus, one or two spokespersons are seldom enough to craft a meaningful and healing ceremony for all who have been affected.

Given the frequent pervasiveness of guilt and blame in the aftermath of suicide, special care needs to be given to the way in which events seen as precipitating the suicide are described in the service, if they are described at all. It is soberingly easy for survivors to interpret innocently composed statements as confirmation of their own guilt or that of another. Generally, if explanations are offered, it is wise and more fitting to portray the suicide as the result of multiple, complex influences over time, rather than a single precipitating event. To the greatest extent possible within the bounds of the individual Church's belief system, reassurance should be provided regarding the repose of the deceased's soul. Finally, the manner of death should neither be romanticized nor overemphasized. The individual died a sad and unfortunate death. That person's life was bigger than his or her death, however, and reflections on the individual's activities, loves, achievements, and the joy he or she brought others are, as always, appropriate.

In the days and weeks following a suicide, attention of the clergy will understandably be directed primarily towards the individual's loved ones. However, it is important to maintain a watchful eye over the rest of the flock. Although we (the authors) are personally unaware of any cases of suicidal "contagion" within a congregation or parish, suicides are often seen to cluster during the time period immediately following a publicized suicide or a suicide in an institution such as a school. The span of time following a suicidal death within a church community may be a vulnerable time for fragile church members, regardless of the degree to which they experienced a personal connection with the deceased.

Lesson #3: *Shine a beacon on the shore.* After the initial storm has passed, a long journey to healing begins. Suicide survivors may easily feel lost and alone on this journey. However, there are many things that clergy and others within the church community can do to help ease the slow return to shore.

It is often helpful to gently encourage the survivor's gradual return to routine, starting with basic routines of eating, showering, exercising, and sleeping. Survivors need to take good care of their physical health in order to sustain the hard emotional work of grieving of a suicide. Routine itself tends to be comforting. Resuming previous activities and responsibilities at a pace that fits the individual and his/her circumstance often helps recently bereaved survivors to begin to understand that, while they will never forget the deceased, life does go on for the living. It may also be helpful to assure the survivor that it is okay to take breaks from grieving to engage in pleasurable and distracting activities.

Similar to other trauma survivors, a large number of suicide survivors find themselves needing to repeatedly recount and process their traumatic experience. Social support, so important throughout the entire bereavement period, takes on a special importance here. More specifically, survivors attempting to heal via a recounting of their experience need patient and empathic listeners. Some survivors will find themselves fortunate enough to locate such listeners among their family and friends. The shame, stigma, and social awkwardness of suicide survival can, however, makes such listeners hard to come by, as can post-loss divisiveness among family and friends. For others, the listening support of associates is available, but not accessed because the survivor wants to shield them from his or her pain. Inviting suicide survivors to talk about their loss experience can be a way for clergy to help fill these social gaps. Church members who fear saying or doing the wrong thing might also be encouraged to approach the suicide survivor with the same solicitous attention that they would any bereaved among them. While valuable, social overtures on the part of clergy and others in the faith community do need to be accompanied by close attention to the survivor's cues for needed privacy.

In talking with suicide survivors, it is generally facilitative to adopt a warm and involved demeanor, as opposed to the more passive and detached style of some traditional forms of counseling. It is important to allow survivors to freely express their thoughts and emotions. While this may sound simplistic, it is often quite difficult to remain "present" when emotions such as guilt, shame, and anger arise. There is a tendency to rush to provide reassurance or concrete advice. This tendency may spring more from listeners' needs to feel helpful than the actual needs of survivors, and giving way to it can easily shut survivors down. If that occurs, survivors are again left alone with their "unspeakable" thoughts and feelings. If, however, a survivor has been allowed to thoroughly explore (or "confess") his or her thoughts and feelings, and if the survivor has recognized that those thoughts and feelings have been accepted by the listener with empathy and understanding, then offering thoughtful reassurance, new perspectives, and other words of wisdom can be both helpful and impactful.

The preoccupation, confusion, and emotional intensity associated with bereavement after suicide can be so intense that some survivors fear they are "going crazy." Over time, conversations that are accepting and supportive may help to bring peace as survivors talk through and let go of anger and guilt, find whatever forgiveness they may need for self and others, and begin to come to a new understanding of the suicide. As alluded to above, acceptance of the suicidal death can mean coming to terms with the limits of human control and the existential issues that go along with them. Much as we would prefer that things be different so that we could save our loved ones from pain and suffering, no one ultimately *can* be responsible for the life or death of another.

In this deeply reflective "stage" of healing, suicide survivors may begin to slowly integrate their experience of the suicidal death into their larger understandings of self, relationship, and the world. Such a process is one of meaning-making, and previously held meaning systems may no longer offer the assured answers that they once did. As it may be difficult to resist the impulse to quickly provide reassurance to the newly bereaved, it can be equally difficult to resist the impulse to quickly provide meaning-based explanations to those in this highly reflective state. Superficial answers, whether drawn from folk wisdom or theology, are unlikely to be satisfying to those whose worlds have been profoundly shaken by the suicide of a loved one. Deeper understandings that might bring peace must be personally meaningful to survivors themselves. Clergy might best provide companionship and consultation to the survivor in his or her search for understanding and meaning and - at last - a warm helping hand, leading the survivor back to shore.

Unsuccessful Bereavement and Referral

What if this hoped for outcome does not occur, and a suicide survivor's journey seems to proceed in endless, painful circles? It is difficult to differentiate between "normal" bereavement following suicide, in all its varying time frames and expressions, and bereavement that is "stuck." If a suicide survivor is experiencing debilitating grief (i.e., grief that is seriously interfering with his or her social or occupational functioning), and this debilitation shows little sign of abating over time, referral for more intensive mental health treatment may be in order.

Another difficulty in determining the type and level of help needed by suicide survivors is accurately assessing whether they have become suicidal themselves. Depressive symptoms and *passing* thoughts of suicide (to escape the pain of bereavement or to join the deceased in the afterlife) are not at all uncommon following the loss of a loved one to any cause of death. These thoughts do not always represent a significant "at risk for suicide" status. On the other hand, the risk level of suicide survivors might be somewhat higher than bereaved individuals generally, as social exposure to suicide and family history of suicide are both risk factors for suicide. Thus while it remains important for clergy to be attentive to the occurrence and persistence of suicidal thoughts on the part of any bereaved, it may be especially important with the suicidally bereaved. If suicidal thoughts are found to be present, suicidal intent must be assessed, followed by appropriate mental health referral.

Ongoing couple or family conflict and tension may also indicate a need for referral. Similar to other traumatic events, suicide appears to either bring couples and families closer together or to drive them further apart. If the latter begins to occur, the assistance of a marriage and family therapist who has experience with suicidal bereavement may be indicated.

Breaking the Silence

In recent decades, a considerable amount of silence around suicide survival has been broken, as suicide survivor organizations, web sites, and support groups have been established. Involvement in survivor organizations and support groups appears to be extremely therapeutic for many survivors. Knowing that one is not alone can be quite comforting, with the concern and compassion of people who share a common experience providing additional solace. Communicating with survivors who are further along in the grieving process may instill hope for eventual healing in the more recently bereaved. At the conclusion of this chapter, a list of organizations that directly sponsor suicide survivor activities and/or help individuals locate survivor groups is provided. In referring survivors to support groups, the survivor's ability to attend to the pain of others without being overwhelmed must be closely considered. Sensitivity to timing and individual differences in the grieving process will likely result in more successful referrals.

Helping Child Survivors of Suicide

Helping child survivors of suicide has all the challenges, and more, of helping adult survivors. It is difficult to offer reasonable guidelines in this area, as many childhood reactions and the helpfulness of responses to them depend upon complex factors, such as the child's age, developmental level, and relationship to the deceased. A brief, general summary of common reactions and suggestions is provided below. However, clergy are referred to other resources, some of which are listed at the conclusion of this chapter, for in-depth guidance.

Children dealing with the suicidal death of a loved one may experience the full range of reactions experienced by adults. Denial may be more pronounced, reflecting either "unsophisticated" efforts to cope by children who are overwhelmed by grieving or a developmental inability to fully grasp the finality of death. Children experiencing the sharp grief and yearning of bereavement may not realize that the acuteness of their pain will fade in time, and that they will not always feel as they do currently. Developmentally normal childhood "egocentrism" and "magical thinking" often leave children especially vulnerable to believing that they caused the suicide by something they felt, thought, or did. When the deceased was a loved adult, the child's dependence upon others, often combined with a lack of experience with death, may lead to increased fear of death or abandonment by other adult caretakers. If the deceased was a child, especially a sibling, the child survivor may fear that the same thing will happen to him or her. Ironically, young children may keep their hurts and fears to themselves to protect grieving adults from further pain and worry.

Child suicide survivors may evidence innumerable reactions in addition to those mentioned above. The most important point for present purposes is that it falls upon the adult helper to draw out the child's individual concerns and to respond to them in straightforward and developmentally appropriate ways. At the same time, of course, the child must be surrounded with love and support. As with adults, it is important to permit children to freely express their thoughts and feelings, assuring them that any (non-destructive) reactions they may have - regardless of whether they are like or unlike those of the people around them - are understandable and acceptable.

Clergy as Survivors

Clergy, like the children and adults that they serve, also may suffer from suicidal loss. Unfortunately, it is relatively common for professional helpers to lose someone with whom they worked to suicide. Surveys indicate that nearly 50% of all psychiatrists and 25% of all psychologists will lose a client to suicide (Jobes & Berman, 1993). Little data is available regarding the incidence of suicide among those seeking pastoral care, though the general consensus is that active religious involvement works as a protective factor against suicide. This suggests a decreased likelihood that clergy will experience such difficult deaths on the parts of those that they serve. On the other hand, congregations are usually much larger than caseloads, so it is difficult to know, overall, whether clergy are actually less likely than mental health professionals to experience suicidal deaths. Whatever the relative frequency of such losses, it would be expected that clergy would respond to those that do occur with strong and painful reactions similar to those found among mental health professionals.

When helping professionals are faced with a client's suicide, the experience of grief and mourning may be quite similar to that experienced over the loss of a loved one. Clients and helpers form meaningful relationships over time, so the loss that helpers experience is in part a personal one. Helpers also, however, respond like professionals who have lost a client. The combination of these two responses often results in a difficult, complex, and confusing grief experience. This experience may be even more emotionally and professionally complicated for clergy, who often are ministering to the grieving family and friends in their church community while simultaneously grieving themselves.

When distressed individuals die by suicide, the helpers who had worked with them may blame themselves and feel as if they failed. They may also become concerned that others are directing blame towards them. Many survivors, despite their confusion and pain, maintain only gratitude towards helping professionals who were involved with their loved one before the suicide. For other survivors, however, acts of omission or commission by professional helpers may be safe and likely targets for the anger and blame that are frequent components of survivor grief. Self-blame and the real or perceived blame of others commonly lead to loneliness, isolation, shame, and embarrassment among helpers, much as they do among surviving loved ones. Resources and support for helper survivors are available from some of the organizations listed at the end of this chapter.

Helping professionals' sense of competence and self-efficacy may plummet after a suicide by one under their care. While clergy may be helping grief-stricken loved ones to understand that it is impossible to entirely predict or control another individual's behavior, they may find that they also need to remind themselves of this same wisdom. After experiencing a traumatic suicidal loss, many helping professionals temporarily do not wish to work with suicidal individuals. Some may seek further training in this area, to help ensure that they have the necessary knowledge and skill for effective intervention. All are urged to actively consult with trusted colleagues to work through personal feelings about the experience and regain a comfort level permitting future productive work with suicidal individuals and their loved ones. Revisiting and deeply reflecting upon personal and theological beliefs about suicide may also be necessary.

Throughout this difficult process of consultation and reflection, clergy are encouraged to show themselves the same care and compassion that they do others. It is those clergy who again find their own emotional and spiritual bearings who can most confidently and compassionately guide others to shore.

Conclusion:

Stephanie Revisited:

The case of Stephanie produces a number of challenging dilemmas for clergy, who may be called upon to assist this young woman in her current dilemma. Initial assessment of Stephanie's condition must include a close consideration of her physical, behavioral, and affective symptoms. She has not been herself of late, with many of her recent symptoms pointing to a developing depression and an "at risk" situation with regard to suicidality. Clergy would be wise to address the faith history of Stephanie's family, its impact upon her life choices, and the conflict that this appears to currently elicit within her. Stephanie's relationship with Derek appears to be central to her emerging identity, as does her work in orthopedic medicine. Where Stephanie's church community and her family once provided a foundation for her worldly endeavors, her relationship with Derek and her career development now appear to be central. What does this mean to Stephanie? Why is she unhappy, with so many positive developments occurring in her young life?

The developmentally appropriate transitions that Stephanie is undergoing must be examined closely and with empathy. Processing her recent experience with an understanding and knowledgeable member of the clergy may afford Stephanie an opportunity to openly discuss her attempts to balance foundational beliefs of her family and church with the adult self that she finds herself becoming. Within this context, the guidelines described above may facilitate accurate assessment of depressive symptoms and inform further dialogue. By gaining a solid foundation of knowledge about depression and suicide, clergy may perform this assessment with reasonable reliability and refer to qualified mental health professionals as indicated.

Suggestions for Further Information
National Hopeline

The primary national suicide prevention and local referral hotline is: 1-800-SUICIDE (784-2433). The hotline is provided by the Kristin Brooks Hope Center, National Hopeline Network. www.livewithdepression.org www.hopeline.com

Organizations

The following organizations provide information about depression and suicide, suicide prevention and intervention materials, information for and about suicide survivors, information about support groups, newsletters, and/or suggested reading:

American Association of Suicidology, Suite 310, 4201 Connecticut Avenue, N.W.,, Washington, D.C. 20008; 202-237-2280; www.suicidology.org

American Foundation for Suicide Prevention, 120 Wall Street, 22nd Floor, New York, NY 10005; 212-363-3500 www.afsp.org

National Organization for People of Color Against Suicide, 4715 Sargent Road, N.E., Washington, DC; 1-866-899-5317 (toll free), 202-549-6039 (business); www.nopcas.com

National Resource Center for Suicide Prevention and Aftercare, 348 Mount Vernon Highway, N.E., Atlanta, GA 30328; 404-256-2919 www.thelink.org

National Youth Violence Prevention Resource Center, P.O. Box 6003, Rockville, MD 20849 1-800-243-7012 www.safeyouth.org

Organization for Attempters and Survivors of Suicide in Interfaith Services (OASSIS) 101 King Farm Boulevard, #D 401, Rockville, MD 20850; 240-633-3055 www.oassis.org

Suicide Awareness/Voices of Education (SAVE), 7317 Cahill Road, Suite 207 Minneapolis, MN 55439-2080; 952-946-7998; www.save.org

Suicide Information and Education Center; 201-1615 10th Avenue, Calgary, Alberta Canada T3C0J7; 403-245-3900; www.siec.ca

Suicide Prevention Action Network (SPAN); 5034 Odin's Way, Marietta, GA 30068 1-888-649-1366 (toll free); www.spanusa.org

Suicide Prevention Resource Center, Education Development Center, Inc., 55 Chapel Street, Newton, MA 02458; 877-438-7773; www.sprc.org

The Compassionate Friends (for bereaved parents and siblings), P.O. Box 3696, Oak Brook, IL 60521; 877-969-0010 (toll free); www.compassionatefriends.org

The Jason Foundation; 116 Maple Row Boulevard, Suite C, Henderson, TN 37075 1-888-881-2323 (toll free) www.jasonfoundation.com

Trevor Helpline (GLBT Youth); 8950 West Olympic Boulevard, Suite 197, Beverly Hills, CA 90211; 800-850-8078 (hotline), 310-271-8845 (business) www.thetrevorproject.org

Further Reading

Alvarez, A. (1973). *The savage god: A study of suicide*. New York: Random House.

Bolton, I., & Mitchell, C.) (1983). *My son…my son…A guide to healing after death, loss, or suicide*. Atlanta: Bolton Press.

Burns, D. (1999). *The feeling good handbook*. New York: Plume/Penguin Books.

Clark, D.C. (Ed.) (1993). *Clergy response to suicidal persons and their family members*. Chicago: Exploration Press.

Dunne, E.J., McIntosh, J.L., & Dunne-Maxim, K. (Eds.) (1987). *Suicide and its aftermath: Understanding and counseling the survivors*. New York: Norton.

Gotlib, I.H., & Hammen, C.L. (Eds.) (2002). *Handbook of depression*. New York: Guilford.

Maris, R.W., Berman, A.L., & Silverman, M.M. (Eds.) (2000). *Comprehensive textbook of suicidology*. New York: Guilford.

Shneidman, E. (1996). *The suicidal mind*. New York: Oxford Press.

Solomon, A. (2001). *The noonday demon: An atlas of depression*. New York: Scribner/ Simon & Schuster.

Switzer, D.K. (1986). *The minister as crisis counselor*. Nashville, TN: Abington Press.

Whybrow, P.C. (1997). *A mood apart: Depression, mania, and other afflictions of the self*. New York: Basic Books.

Yapko, M.D. (1988). *When living hurts: Directives for treating depression*. Philadelphia: Brunner/Mazel

.

References

American Psychiatric Association. (2000). *Diagnostic and statistical manual of mental disorders* (4th ed., text revision). Washington, DC: American Psychiatric Press.

Craighead, W. E., Hart, A. B., Craighead, L. W., & Ilardi, S. S. (2002). Psychosocial treatments for major depressive disorder. In P. E. Nathan & J. M. Gorman (Eds.), *A guide to treatments that work* (2nd ed.) (pp. 245-261). New York: Oxford University Press.

Frank, J.D. & Frank, J.B. (1991). *Persuasion and healing: A comparative study of psychotherapy*. Baltimore, MD: Johns Hopkins University Press.

Gillies, L. A. (2001). Interpersonal psychotherapy for depression and other disorders. In D. H. Barlow (Ed.), *Clinical handbook of psychological disorders* (3rd ed.) (pp. 309-331). New York: Guilford.

Jobes, D.A., Luoma, J.B., Hustead, L.A.T., & Mann, R.E. (2000). In the wake of suicide: Survivorship and postvention. In R.W. Maris, A.L. Berman, & M.M. Silverman (Eds.). *Comprehensive textbook of suicidology* (pp. 536-562). New York: Guilford Press.

Kubler-Ross, E. (1969). *On death and dying*. New York: Macmillan.

Maris, R.W., Berman, A.L., & Silverman, M.M. (Eds.) (2000). *Comprehensive textbook of suicidology*. New York: Guilford Press.

Nemeroff, C. B., & Schatzberg, A F. (2002). Pharmacological treatments for unipolar depression. In P. E. Nathan & J. M. Gorman (Eds.), *A guide to treatments that work* (2nd ed.) (pp. 229-243). New York: Oxford University Press.

Young, J. E., Weinberger, A. D., & Beck, A. T. (2001). Cognitive therapy for depression. In D. H. Barlow (Ed.), *Clinical handbook of psychological disorders* (3rd ed.) (pp. 264-308). New York: Guilford.

Notes

[1] The term "clergy" is broadly used in this chapter to refer to faith leaders of all religious traditions.

About The Authors

Karen R. Scheel received her Ph.D. in Counseling Psychology from the University of Iowa in 1999. She is currently an Assistant Professor in the Department of Counseling at the University of Akron. Dr. Scheel's scholarly interests include suicide prevention and postvention, as well as clinical training issues and self-efficacy in the natural sciences. Dr. Scheel serves on the editorial boards of *Suicide and Life-Threatening Behavior* and *The Journal of Mental Health Counseling.*

Christopher J. McNally, M.A. is a doctoral student in the Collaborative Program in Counseling Psychology at The University of Akron and a pre-doctoral intern at Counseling and Consultation Service of The Ohio State University. His interests include postmodern/constructivist approaches to therapy and integration of the social sciences and humanities. He has co-authored Explorations in Counseling and Spirituality: Philosophical, Practical, and Personal Reflections (Wadsworth, 2001).

Cynthia A. Yamokoski, M.A., is a doctoral student in the Collaborative Program in Counseling Psychology at The University of Akron. Her professional interests include suicide, diversity, and therapist self-care and wellness.

James L. Werth, Jr. received his Ph.D. in Counseling Psychology from Auburn University in 1995 and his Masters of Legal Studies from the University of Nebraska - Lincoln in 1999. He was the 1999-2000 American Psychological Association William A. Bailey AIDS Policy Congressional Fellow where he worked on aging and end-of-life issues in the office of United States Senator Ron Wyden (D - OR). He has been employed as an Assistant Professor in the Department of Psychology at The University of Akron since August 2000; he is also the pro bono psychologist for the local HIV services organization where he provides counseling and supervises graduate students.

Chapter 9
Pastoral Care & the Older Adult:
What Clergy Need to Know

by Paula E. Hartman-Stein, Ph.D.

A middle-aged woman called her father's minister one evening, sounding desperate and overwhelmed. "Reverend Dan, I need your help. My Dad fell again yesterday, the second time in the past few weeks. I live over an hour away, and when I stopped by to visit on Saturday, Dad was in obvious pain. He was unable to get out of a chair on his own, and my mother could barely help him up. He said he tripped in the basement, but we don't know what really happened. He has two fractured ribs. What concerns me the most is that he did not call anyone. My mom said that my father told her he'd be all right and not to worry the children. I don't know why they did not call '911.'

I just got back with Dad from the emergency room. He has to wear a monitor to check his heart for a few days. He is sleeping now, and as I am sitting here I noticed he has bills scattered throughout junk mail all over his kitchen table. Several bills are overdue, and there is a notice from the gas company threatening to turn off his service. My mother used to take care of such things, but she has had noticeable memory impairment for at least two years, and Dad has become her caregiver. He used to be so sharp, but I noticed last summer he seems to be slipping too. Neither of them will accept paid help in the home. Dad seems grumpy, often yelling at my Mom when she loses things. I suggested that I need to help out more, you know, pay bills and drive them places, but he just gets angry, saying he can handle things. His doctor retired last year, and the new one barely knows him. Dad has known you for years, and he respects you, Reverend Dan. I didn't know where to go for help. I thought they might listen to you."

Vignette # 2: The nursing home visit
A young rabbi visited Ruth in the nursing home where she was recuperating after knee replacement surgery. Her five grown children were concerned about her being able to live alone anymore. This was also a time for testing an adjustment to a permanent residence in the assisted living section of the retirement community after she finished rehabilitation. When the rabbi entered her room, Ruth immediately piped up, "I don't like it here. It is not clean, and the nurses don't care about me. I want to go back to my own home. I can walk with a walker now after all." The rabbi acknowledged the comfort of her own home over any long-term care setting. Ruth continued, "And they insisted I come here after I left the hospital. I could have stayed home to recuperate. My family has not visited, and no one told me I would have to stay here more than a few days." Rabbi David

wondered if her complaints were fabricated, but he also heard of families who dump off family members in nursing homes and rarely visit afterward.

The rabbi became uncomfortable listening to her numerous complaints, so he changed the subject, asking about her life in the past. He knew her husband had died when her children were still at home. He commented how responsible her children were as adults, surely a legacy of her parenting ability. "Yes," she agreed, "but now they live their own lives, and do not care for me. I sacrificed so much for them and now they abandoned me."

That evening the rabbi called Ruth's daughter. She was not available, but the son-in-law talked about how his wife calls on her mother daily, doing everything she can. The caregiving needs had been increasing over the past six to nine months. The other siblings in the area also call regularly, and everyone helps out the best they can. Finally, after the decision was made about knee surgery, the siblings had a family meeting and agreed their mother had to live in a supervised environment. Ruth had totally resisted. She cries whenever anyone visits, and her children feel terrible. The rabbi wondered what he could do to be of help.

Vignette # 3: Grief turned to depression

Bill was a dedicated member of the church who headed up many committees over the years, as well as serving on the board in different capacities. He and his wife were true pillars of the community. His children lived out of state, and after his wife died suddenly Bill was not the same. It was over a year since her death, and Father John noticed that he began to attend Mass sporadically, a change from past behavior. Bill served on an important committee, and the chair complained that he did not show up for scheduled events. Father John noticed that Bill often looked unkempt, a definite change that was noted by others. His gait was slow and faltering, and he rarely talked to anyone after Mass. The priest wondered if Bill's grief had resulted in depression. He considered calling Bill's children, whom he had never met, to let them know of his concerns. He questioned how he might intervene.

Impact of demographics on religious organizations

Scenarios similar to those above are becoming commonplace in religious ministry largely due to the changing demographics of America and throughout the globe. In 2000 the U. S. census counted 35 million people over age 65, a 12% increase since 1990. The highest percentage increase of the older population are those 85 years and over (U.S. Census Bureau, 2000). With longevity also comes a greater likelihood of developing Alzheimer's disease and other dementias. Population estimates indicate that 25 to 50% of adults over age 85 suffer from dementia (Bachman et al., 1992; Evans et al., 1989), and approximately 370,000 new cases of Alzheimer's disease are diagnosed each year (Smith, Kenan, & Kunik, 2004). Prevalence estimates indicate that approximately 20 to 22% of seniors meet the criteria for some type of mental disorder (Gatz & Smyer, 2001).

It is highly likely that clergy of all denominations will have increasing contact with seniors and their adult children. According to a Gallup poll conducted in 2001, 80% of those aged 75 years or older are members of a church or synagogue. Seventy-two percent of the baby boomer generation, those born between 1946 and 1964, who are likely to have a role in caring for their elderly parents, are members of a church or synagogue (Gallup, 2002). In addition, although available data are not definitive, Gallup poll surveys support the notion that religiosity increases with age. The young in previous generations tend to be less religious than the old, and now that the former generation makes up the senior population, they too have become more likely to regularly attend religious services (Koenig & Brooks, 2002).

The role of religion in health care

Religious institutions have played a role in ministering to the sick and elderly for centuries. For example, the Christian church built the first hospitals in Western civilization around the 4th century. The nursing profession started with the Church, initially with the Sisters of Charity and later with the Deaconesses of the Protestant faith. By necessity physicians and ministers were one and the same in the early days of the American colonies (Koenig & Brooks, 2002). Religious organizations therefore gave rise to today's largely secularized health care system. Given its historical role in healthcare and its mandate to care for the sick, it seems reasonable then that institutionalized religion would continue to have a place in the health care of its members.

In roles analogous to those of primary care physicians, today's clergy are at the front line of influencing and guiding older adults toward using available resources and seeking appropriate medical and mental health intervention. Therefore it is highly beneficial to members of religious organizations when clergy strive to gain basic knowledge about cognitive changes in aging, psychopathology within the older population, as well as learn about available resources in their respective communities. This chapter presents a beginning set of guidelines for clergy to help them in their ministry to older adult members of their church or synagogue. We will review stereotypes of aging, describe common cognitive and emotional changes in the elderly, and suggest pragmatic strategies that clergy can use when intervening with late-life families.

Recognizing ageist stereotypes

Clergy need to recognize and strive to eliminate inaccurate stereotypes of aging that may impair effectiveness in working with this population. Examples of negative stereotypes include the notion that senility is inevitable with age, that most older adults are depressed, frail, ill, socially isolated, and stubborn; and that older adults have little to no interest in intimacy and sex (APA, 2003; Edelstein & Kalish, 1999). Positive stereotypes that suggest older adults are cute, childlike, or inherently wise are also to be avoided. Biases that are due to sympathy or the desire to overlook shortcomings can result in overly positive estimates of cognitive skills or mental health, resulting in failure to intervene when warranted (APA, 2003; Braithwaite, 1986).

Clergy are encouraged to develop realistic perceptions of both the strengths and vulnerabilities of older adults by examining their own attitudes and "blind spots" through consultation from colleagues or other professionals who are knowledgeable and experienced with older adults.

Recognizing signs of dementia

Scientific consensus is that most older adults experience decline in their cognitive capacity and/or efficiency, but the majority stay engaged in life-long interests, continue intellectual pursuits, engage in real-life problem solving, and are able to learn new things (APA, 2003). Recent research findings from the Nun Study (Snowdon, Otswald, Kane, & Keenan, 1989) and the New England Centenarian study (Perls, Silver, & Lauerman, 1999) have demonstrated that it is possible to live well into old age without significant decrement of mental functioning.

The changes in normal aging occurring most frequently are slowing of reaction time, speed of processing information, and reduction in visuo-spatial speed. Memory changes with age are common, as is the ability to attend to two things at one time, shift focus rapidly, and deal effectively with complex situations (Rogers & Fisk, 2001). The cognitive skills that usually remain intact in normal aging include language and vocabulary skills as well as common sense reasoning (APA, 2003).

Social skills also tend to remain intact in older adults, including those suffering from early to moderate stage Alzheimer's disease. As a result, many professionals do not recognize that the older person may be suffering from dementia. The older adult with significant memory impairment may exhibit the same personality attributes throughout their lives, smile appropriately in social settings, engage in pleasant verbal interchanges, and appear normal to casual inspection. They may cover their deficits quite well, and even make logical-sounding excuses for confusion about time or widely known facts. For example, "Oh, of course I don't know the date or the month. Now that I am retired I don't read the paper and pay attention to that any more. I'm not interested in politics so I don't care who the president is."

Despite the fact that many older adults manage their lives independently well into their 80s and 90s, an appreciable minority of older adults have significantly impaired functioning and quality of life as a result. The word dementia refers to a condition of decline from usual baseline cognitive abilities that include memory impairment as well as problems in at least one other area of every-day functioning. Dementia can be reversible due to acute illnesses, or it can be irreversible and progressive.

The most common causes for progressive dementia in older adults are

Alzheimer's disease and vascular disorders such as strokes, or a combination of the two. Patients with neurological disorders such as multiple sclerosis or Parkinson's disease also may experience mental declines. Other less common forms of dementia include Lewy Body dementia in which vivid visual hallucinations are frequently a primary symptom, and frontal-temporal dementia that presents with personality changes, apathy, lack of social awareness, and reduced impulse control (Smith et al., 2004). Cognitive impairment in old age exists in milder forms that are not inevitably progressive and for which the cause is not clearly known (APA, 2003). For example, sensory deficits in hearing and vision or depression or anxiety can trigger cognitive impairment. Chronic illnesses and many medications can also significantly impact thinking and memory.

In my work involving diagnosing of dementia the most common early symptoms that alert families that their older parent or spouse may be suffering from a progressive dementia include lack of recall of recently learned information and frequent repetitive questions. An example of a frustrated daughter talking to her mother who is staying with her for a week illustrates the point. "Mom, I told you this morning that I was coming home around 3:00 today and that if the contractor should come here a little early, tell him I will be there shortly. I can't believe you told him I never come home till 6:00, and you told him to leave!" Or a typically polite son snaps, "Mother, I have told you countless times I don't use cream and sugar in my coffee. Quit offering it to me and asking me the same question."

Family members also worry about Alzheimer disease when the parent or spouse starts having difficulty with tasks in everyday life that were once done easily. In a large scale study with French community dwellers, problems in 4 activities of everyday functioning were predictive of later dementia, including the ability to use the telephone, dependence on others for transportation, problems in medication management, and inability to handle finances (Barberger-Gateau, Fabrigoule, Helmer, Rouch, & Dartigues, 1999).

Evaluations done by specialists such as geriatricians and geropsychologists can be beneficial in differentiating signs of dementia and/or depression from normal age changes. Early detection and diagnosis of dementia are increasingly recognized as important because physicians can prescribe medications called cholinesterase inhibitors for patients in the early stage of dementia that help them maintain their independence longer (Mohs, et al. 2001). Clergy can be helpful in reassuring older adults who have mild cognitive impairment or early dementia that they also have many remaining competencies, are of value to their families and community, and should value their capacity to experience joy and pleasure despite declines in mental acuity and memory functioning.

Recognizing emotional problems of older adults

The prevalence of major depression in the older adults who live in the community is relatively low, but the numbers go up in primary care settings (10%)

and in acute care settings (15%) (Reynolds, Alexopoulos, Katz, & Lebowitz, 2001). Symptoms of depression include feelings of sadness, downcast moods, tearfulness, recurrent thoughts of suicide or death, diminished pleasure, preoccupation with physical illness, real or imagined, and lack of initiative. Untreated depression can lead to suicide (especially in white men over 75), alcohol use, excess disability from chronic illness, cognitive impairment, and overuse of health care services that impact the nation's economy and Medicare resources (Reynolds, Alexopoulos, & Katz, 2002). In a study of medical outcome, clinical depression was found to be as debilitating as advanced coronary artery disease (Wells & Burnam, 1991).

Other mental disorders include anxiety, adjustment disorders, substance abuse, personality disorders, psychotic disorders, or complicated grief. Older adults may experience recurrences of psychological problems they had in earlier years, have histories of chronic serious mental illness, or may develop new problems because of issues unique to old age, such as loneliness, retirement, loss of a spouse, physical disability, and feeling unwanted or no longer useful (Cummings, 1998). Depression and anxiety can be triggered by a spiritual crisis, be a response to the experience of a serious illness, or be caused directly by a medical condition (APA, 2003). Late life depression may co-exist with dementia, and it can be difficult to determine whether symptoms of apathy and withdrawal from others are due to depression or impairment in brain functioning (Lamberty & Bieliauskas, 1993). Determining the cause and appropriate treatment of symptoms of mental disorders in the older adult is a complex process, often needing a team of professionals.

Depression in late life is a treatable condition and should not be viewed as inevitable. There is increasing evidence demonstrating that a variety of forms of psychotherapy and psychological interventions are as effective in older adults as compared to the response of younger adults (Hartman-Stein & Potkanowicz, 2003; Pinquart & Soerensen, 2001; Zarit & Knight, 1996). Clergy can play an invaluable role in reinforcing the notion that seeking professional counsel for emotional problems is not a sign of moral weakness or "craziness."

Using religion as a coping strategy can be a powerful means for some adults of finding meaning in times of personal adversity and crisis that has long-term health benefits. Cognitively processing the consequences of personal tragedy in times of stress and crisis can be enhanced by the support found in a religious organization as well as through seeking understanding and internal peace from religious beliefs (Hartman-Stein & Potkanowicz, 2003). Clergy can be very helpful in providing guidance and comfort, but if emotional symptoms persist or their severity is great, clergy should not hesitate to seek consultation from a mental health professional and/or refer the individual for a medical and psychological evaluation.

What individual clergy can do: solving problems described in the vignettes.

An essential role for clergy is that of a supportive and active listener who has knowledge of community resources and agencies and is willing to refer to them. Clergy need to be familiar with organizations such as the Area Agency on Aging, volunteer senior companion programs, the Alzheimer Association, mobile meal programs, home health agencies, geriatric assessment centers in their area, as well as physicians, psychologists, and attorneys who specialize in working with older adults.

In the case described in the beginning of this paper, the following are potential strategies available to Reverend Dan:

1.   Initially listen to the adult daughter, empathize about how hard it must be for her and how helpless she must feel at times.

2.   Begin problem-solving sessions with her. For example, the clergy can suggest that the daughter talk to her father's family doctor about her observations of his memory problems and difficulties in managing his bills and medications. She could suggest to the physician that he refer her Dad for a consultation to a specialist or clinic that assesses memory loss. If the physician is not receptive (although most will be), she can make a referral herself for a second opinion or find a different primary care physician. Reverend Dan can reinforce the daughter's advocacy for her Dad.

3.   Regarding help in the home, encourage the daughter to proactively call the Area Agency on Aging to see what services are available for her parents, such as mobile meal programs, visiting nurse services, or private home health aides. These are best coordinated through the family doctor, but can be arranged independently as well.

4.   Encourage the daughter to engage the help of all of her siblings in coordinating care and obtaining consultations. Sometimes even in cases in which sibling rivalry has been fierce throughout the years, adult children can put aside past problems and rally around the cause of caring for Mom and Dad. Reinforce the idea that the daughter call a meeting with all siblings present or have a phone conference. It is best if she is not on a limb, providing all the care planning alone.

5.   If her parents are resistant to in-home services and consultations with the doctor and/or specialists, Reverend Dan may visit them at home. Using all of his powers of persuasion, showing empathy and genuine concern, he could try and convince her Dad into making a follow-up visit with the family doctor or medical consultation with a geriatrician as a first step. Reverend Dan should encourage the daughter to go along on this visit.

6.   If reason and persuasion do not prevail, and there is concern that the elderly parents are unsafe, Reverend Dan can refer the family to the adult protective service agency in their county. This is a local government-sponsored group that has the authority to investigate and monitor the home situation, thus providing an extra set of eyes and ears that watch out for the safety and well being of the frail older adult with diminished capacity.

7.   Reverend Dan can also advise the daughter to seek counsel of an elder law attorney to investigate legal options such as guardianship and durable

power of attorney, attend Alzheimer support meetings in the community, and refer to informative books such as *Alzheimer's for Dummies* (Smith et al, 2004).

8.   Caregivers often neglect their own health. The minister should gently inquire how the daughter is feeling. Does she have outlets and activities she enjoys? Is she caring for her own needs? Referring her for some brief counseling to ensure she is not becoming overburdened and depressed herself may be of great value to the entire family.

In the second vignette about Ruth who is miserable in the assisted living facility, examples of Rabbi David's options include:

1.   Learn more about what led to the family's decision to have their mother placed at the facility.
2.   Support the family if he discovers that Ruth exhibited some of the classic signs of early dementia and/or other mental health problems such as a personality disorder.
3.   Suggest a family meeting if he feels the family has inappropriately placed their mother without investigating in-home options. If the family refuses, and he is still uncomfortable with her placement, the clergy could counsel Ruth to contact her attorney or call the facility's ombudsman about her concerns. Such a strategy takes courage and risks alienating the family, but the clergy would be assured all options have been explored.
4.   If the placement does appear to be appropriate in light of health and/or mental health problems, continue to visit Ruth at the facility. During these sessions have several positive topics ready to discuss. Find out what activities the facility has available, encouraging her to pursue these activities rather than isolating herself in her room.

Examples of Father John's options for his grieving parishioner:

1.   Talk to Bill directly, voicing concerns about his behavior and changes noted, suggesting they have a few meetings together to talk about how he is coping as well as offering a referral to a bereavement counselor, mental health professional, or support group in the community.
2.   Given the severity of the behavioral changes, Father John should ask Bill directly if he considers suicide an option. Suicidal older adults often feel relieved if someone asks this question directly because it enables them to talk more openly. If Bill acknowledges frequent thoughts of suicide, but is unwilling to seek counsel with the priest or anyone about his situation, then Father John should address his deep concerns directly and openly, letting him know he must alert Bill's family that he needs medical/psychiatric intervention.

How religious organization can promote healthy aging

Besides having individual clergy provide one-on-one counsel and support to individuals, religious organizations can also take a proactive role in preventing mental health disorders or at least lessening their severity in the community at large. In the current Medicare system no preventive mental health services are reimbursed. In a study of over 300 newly-widowed older adults who were experiencing normal grief reactions, the intervention consisted of 14 small group sessions held over several months that focused on increasing a sense of self-efficacy, defeating learned helplessness, and restoring meaning to life (Cummings, 1998). The results of the study demonstrated that the psycho-educational program resulted in lower rates of using healthcare services and reduced or prevented symptoms of depression and complicated grief.

Churches and synagogues are in a unique position to offer bereavement programs that may be more easily accepted than those sponsored by funeral homes. The question then becomes who would run such programs and at what cost. Grants through community foundations are one source of funding. In larger churches one innovative direction is to employ a parish nurse as health educator, medical interpreter for patients being discharged from the hospital, or a trainer of volunteers in the congregation who would do most of the hands-on work (Koenig and Brooks, 2002). Geriatric social workers or geropsychologists could provide similar roles to a large church or several smaller churches that join together in the venture. With the drain expected on the Medicare system in future years, it is reasonable for religious institutions to begin to address health maintenance and disease prevention efforts in the community at large.

Religious organizations can take an active role in the positive psychology movement that emphasizes positive thoughts and feelings about the past, including gratitude and willingness to forgive (Seligman, 2002), as well as maximizing opportunities for joy, amusement, compassion, friendship, or serenity through support and discussion groups on the topic of positive psychology (Reuter, 2003).

Recent research findings are promising in regard to the possibility that modifying or forestalling cognitive declines. There is a growing body of research that supports the notion of neural plasticity across the lifespan, suggesting that cognitive and physical stimulation helps to maintain perceptual and other thinking skills (Hartman-Stein & Potkanowicz, 2003). In the Religious Orders Study of 801 Catholic nuns, priests, and brothers followed for over 4 years, frequent participation in common cognitive activities such as playing games such as cards, checkers, crosswords, and other puzzles or going to museums was associated with less risk of developing Alzheimer's disease (Wilson et al., 2002). The active processing of information was an essential feature of the activities, not merely engaging in physical exercise. Churches that offer regular activities such as book or movie discussion groups or visits to art galleries or traveling museum exhibits, for example, serve a function of enhancing cognitive skills of its members. Bringing in experts to talk about memory enhancement or sponsoring a series of workshops on the topic of healthy aging will likely prove to be popular for baby boomers and older adults alike.

Clergy and religious organizations can provide invaluable roles of supporting the needs of its late life families. Individual clergy are encouraged to include in their reading and study books information about the physical and behavioral health of older adults, as well as investigating continuing education programs about this burgeoning area of research. Also, institutional thinking that is "out of the box" can result in socially responsible programs by creating innovative services that will enhance the quality of life of members of the congregation and the community at large.

References:

American Psychological Association, Division 12-Section II, & Division 20 (2003). *Guidelines for psychological practice with older adults.* Washington, DC: Author.

Bachman, D.L., Wolf, P.A., Linn, R., Knoefel, J.E., Cobb, Belanger, A., et al. (1992), Prevalence of dementia and probable senile dementia of the Alzheimer type in the Framingham study. *Neurology, 42,* 115-119.

Barberger-Gateau, P., Fabrigoule, C., Helmer, C., Rouch, I., & Dartigues, J. F. (1999). Functional impairment in instrumental activities of daily living: An early clinical sign of dementia? *Journal of the American Geriatrics Society, 47,* 456-462.

Braithwaite, V. A. (1986). Old age stereotypes: Reconciling contradictions. *Journal of Gerontology, 41,* 353-360.

Cummings, N. A., (1998). Approaches to preventive care. In P. E. Hartman-Stein (Ed.), *Innovative behavioral healthcare for older adults: A guidebook for changing times* (pp. 1-17). San Francisco: Jossey-Bass Publishers.

Edelstein, B., & Kalish, K. (1999). Clinical assessment of older adults. In J. C. Cavanaugh and S. Whitbourne (Eds.), *Gerontology: An interdisciplinary perspective* (pp. 269-304). New York: Oxford University Press.

Evans, D.A., Evans, D. A., Funkenstein, H. H., Albert, M. S., Scherr, P.A., Cook, N. R., Chown, M. J., et al. (1989). Prevalence of Alzheimer's disease in a community population of older persons: Higher than previously reported. *JAMA: Journal of the American Medical Association, 262,* 2551-2556.

Gallup Poll. (2002, March 18-20). *Poll topics and trends: Religion.* Retrieved February 26, 2004, from http://www.gallup.com/poll/topics/religion2.asp

Gatz, M., & Smyer, M. A. (2001). Mental health and aging at the outset of the twenty-first century. In J. E. Birren & K. W. Schaie (Eds.), *Handbook of the psychology of aging* (5th ed., pp. 523-544). San Diego: Academic Press.

Hartman-Stein, P. E., & Potkanowicz, E. (May 31, 2003). Behavioral determinants of healthy aging: Good news for the baby boomer generation. *Online Journal of Issues in Nursing, 18, (2)*, Manuscript 5. Available:
www.nursingworld.org/ojin/topic21/tpc21_5.htm

Koenig, H., & Brooks, R. G. (2002). Religion, health, and aging: Implications for practice and public policy. *Public Policy and Aging Report, 12,* 13-19.

Lamberty, G. J., & Bieliauskas, L. A. (1993). Distinguishing between depression and dementia in the elderly: A review of neuropsychological findings. *Archives of Clinical Neuropsychology, 8,* 149-170.

Mohs, R.C., Doody, R. S., Morris, J. C., Ieni, J. R., Rogers, S. L., Perdomo, C. A., & Pratt, R. D. (2001). A one year, placebo-controlled preservation of function survival study of donepezil in AD patients. *Neurology, 57,* 481-488.

Perls, T.T., Silver, M.H. & Lauerman, J.F. (1999). *Living to 100: Lessons in living to your maximum potential at any age.* New York: Basic Books.

Pinquart, M., & Soerensen, S. (2001). How effective are psychotherapeutic and other psychosocial interventions with older adults? A meta analysis. *Journal of Mental Health and Aging, 7,* 207-243.

Reuter, J. M. (2003, October). *Positive Psychology.* Paper presented at meeting of the Health and Wellness Committee at Laurel Lake Retirement Community, Hudson, Ohio.

Reynolds, C.F., Alexopoulos, G.S., Katz, I.R. & Lebowitz, B.D. (2001). Chronic depression in the elderly. *Drugs and Aging, 18,* 507-514.

Reynolds, C. F., Alexopoulos, G. S., & Katz, I. R. (2002). Geriatric depression: Diagnosis and treatment. *Generations, 26,* 28-31.

Rogers, W. A., & Fisk, A. D. (2001). Understanding the role of attention in cognitiv aging research. In J. E. Birren & K. W. Schaie (Eds.), *Handbook of the psychology of aging* (5th ed., pp. 267-287). San Diego: Academic Press.

Seligman, M.E. (2002). *Authentic happiness.* New York: The Free Press.

Smith, P. B., Kenan, M., & Kunik, M. E. (2004). *Alzheimer's for dummies.* Indianapolis: Wiley Publishing.

Snowdon, D. A., Otswald, S. K., Kane, R. L., & Keenan, N. L. (1989). Years of life with good and poor mental and physical function in the elderly. *Journal of Clinical Epidemiology, 42,* 1055-1056.

U.S. Census Bureau. (2000). *The 65 years and over population: 2000.* Retrieved February 26, 2004, from www.census.gov/prod/2001pubs/c2kbr01-10.pdf

Wells, K. B., & Burnam, M. A. (1991). Caring for depression in America: Lessons learned from early findings of the Medical Outcomes Study. *Psychiatric Medicine, 9,* 503-519.

Wilson, R. S., Mendes de Leon, C. F. Barnes, L. L., Schneider, J. A., Bienias, J. L., Evans, D. A., et al. (2002). Participation in cognitively stimulating activities and risk of incident Alzheimer disease. *Journal of the American Medical Association, 28,* (6), 742-748.

Zarit, S. H., & Knight, B. G. (Eds.) (1996). *A guide to psychotherapy and aging: Effective clinical interventions in a life-stage context.* Washington DC: American Psychological Association.

About The Author

Paula E. Hartman-Stein, Ph.D. is founder of the Center for Healthy Aging in Kent, Ohio. A clinical geropsychologist and consultant, she is a senior fellow at the Institute for Life-Span Development and Gerontology at the University of Akron and adjunct faculty in the College of Nursing at Kent State University. Dr. Hartman-Stein regularly contributes columns on working with older adults for the newspaper, *The National Psychologist,* and has an edited book, *Innovative Behavioral Heath Care for Older Adults: A Guidebook for Changing Times.* Her address is:Center for Healthy Aging, 4030 State Rte. 43, Suite 202, Kent, OH. 44240-6554
e-mail: cha@en.com

She obtained her M.A. from West Virginia University and her Ph.D. degree in clinical psychology from Kent State University. She was awarded fellow status of the American Psychological Association, serves on the executive committee of the section of Clinical Geropsychology, and is a distinguished Practitioner in the National Academy of Practice in Psychology. She is active in national public policy initiatives that impact behavioral healthcare for older adults.

Chapter 10
Pastoral Interventions & Care for the Chronically Ill:
Building Bridges of Hope
by Martha Lansing, MD

'Hope is the elevating feeling we experience when we see – in the mind's eye – a path to a better future. Hope acknowledges the significant obstacles and deep pitfalls along that path. True hope has no room for delusion.Clear-eyed, hope gives us the courage to confront our circumstances and the capacity to surmount them."

Jerome Groopman, MD   (2004, p.xiv)

In 1948 the World Health Organization defined health as not only the absence of disease or illness, but also the presence of physical, mental, and social well-being. (World Health Organization, 1948) When one's health is changed through illness and one's physical, mental and social well-being is threatened, most individuals experience a degree of anxiety and fear: of vulnerability and hopelessness.

Some illnesses are short-lived, such as the measles or the flu. They last days to weeks, but eventually the individual regains full health and resumes full activity in all spheres of life. Other illnesses persist over months to years. These are considered chronic and include a wide variety of illnesses. The majority of adult chronic illnesses fall into three main categories – diabetes, cancer, and cardiovascular disease (especially hypertension and heart disease). Even though a person may regain a large degree of pre-illness function with appropriate treatment, the individual remains vulnerable. These persons must monitor their bodies for signs and symptoms of underlying disease. Perhaps they must take medications or make frequent visits to physicians or various types of therapists in order to sustain an optimal state. Today people remain alive with serious illness that used to be fatal, but the cost of being alive may include the need to take medication seven or eight times a day, as is the case with AIDS victims, for example.

When anxiety, fear, vulnerability and hopelessness arise in the context of chronic illness, pastoral interventions and care can help the individual work through a process of disorganization and despair to a place of reconsolidation and hope. This hope, as Groopman has noted, "… may help some to live longer, and it will help all to live better." (2004, p. 212).

This chapter will offer some guidelines to help pastors build these bridges of hope and comfort. First we will pose two sets of questions, or "templates", that can help both the pastor and the counselor understand the medical issues and the degree of disturbance or threat that a particular illness may cause in a person's life. Secondly, we will examine the process a chronically ill individual passes through from disbelief about the illness to adjustment to one's illness and limitations. We will see how an individual's characteristic style of coping with anxiety can affect this process.

Thirdly, we will give guidelines to help facilitate the individual's development of hopefulness and adjustment to life with the illness. We will note that it is vital to be sensitive to the patient's world.

The fourth segment will raise questions pastors and counselors must ask of themselves about personal and professional experience and anxiety about illness. Mindfulness of one's biases and emotional reactions when dealing with persons afflicted with illness is essential to helpful care.

We will touch briefly on some special issues related to caring for people with chronic illness. Children who are ill have developmental needs that are different from those of the adult. Families of chronically ill persons often experience significant stress in the face of illness. Family members are themselves subject to fear and hopelessness at the same time that they may be needed to provide support to the ill member. Lastly, people have existential tasks that vary according to developmental stage. Pastoral care is very helpful in dealing with all these issues.

In his book, *The Anatomy of Hope*, Jerome Groopman writes:
"Hope can only arise when you realize that there are real options and that you have genuine choices." (2004, p. 26) If they are to find the real options and the genuine choices, the patient and the pastor need to learn about the disease. Two templates, or sets of questions given by Goodheart and Lansing in their book, Treating People with Chronic Disease (1996), help one learn about one's illness.
The first set of questions, "The Medical Template", asks questions about the nature of the disease:
"What is the outcome of the disease?
What is the disease process?
What is the etiology of the disease?
What are the expected management needs?" (p.16)

Disease outcomes, processes and management needs are constantly changing. Illness is a dynamic process. Even the origins of a disease may change as medical science gains new information. Coronary heart disease used to be a rapidly fatal and severely limiting disease for most individuals. Individuals lived carefully controlled and highly medicated lives in order to preserve as much heart function as possible. New surgical procedures, the developments of stents and new medications have drastically changed the outcome one could expect only 25 years ago. Knowing the potential outcome of a disease may trigger fear, but knowing there are options and genuine choices may also bring about hope.

Disease processes vary and one needs to understand what to expect so one can make choices along the way. Diabetes type 2 is slowly progressive at first and there is much one can do to alter the process. Amyotropic lateral sclerosis is often rapidly and fatally progressive. Some diseases such as multiple sclerosis or systemic lupus may have a waxing and waning process with periods of painful debilitation alternating with periods of apparently normal healthy states. Other diseases like hypertension may have hidden processes that the patient cannot perceive. The disease progresses steadily causing damage to organs such as the brain, the kidney and heart. In such circumstances, individuals often stop taking their medications, or don't make needed life style changes until the effects of the disease become life threatening. Knowing the process a disease takes in the body can help one make choices about treatment and life priorities.

The etiology of a disease takes into account both the source of the disease and associated issues. Knowing the origin of a disease may create anxieties for both patients and their families, or may offer alternatives that can bring relief. Certain disease such as AIDS is associated with high risk behaviors. Individuals can feel guilty and not entitled to needed help. They may become hopeless because they feel responsible. People in our present society who smoke and develop heart disease often figure they have caused their problems and there is nothing to be done further. They continue to smoke. In fact these persons may have contributed to their problems, but the truth about their disease is that stopping smoking improves most forms of heart disease.

Other diseases are associated with elements in the environment such as asthma. People may become angry at the environment, or at their inadequate bodies or at those outsiders whom they in some way hold responsible for their problems; for example people who pollute the environment in various ways. Discovering the true associated issues and causes can often help people determine how to control the disease. Failing to discover can leave people bitter or hopeless.

Goodheart and Lansing assign what is needed to manage a disease into four categories: "auxiliary aids, mechanical and electrical; lifestyle changes; medical treatment; and adjunctive treatment including physical therapy and psychotherapy." (1996, p. 25)

Simple aids are eyeglasses and hearing aids. Canes, wheelchairs and walkers are other types. Many persons don't know what aids are available, because they don't ask for help. Others know but may feel embarrassed to be seen as dependent.

Life style changes are often demanding and may necessitate changes in identity, occupation and financial or social status. For example, the construction worker who develops lower extremity paralysis as a result of multiple sclerosis will need to change not only his job, but also his view of himself as a virile and physically strong individual. These changes can affect his family and social relationships as well. They may be seen in a very negative way by the mind which may become in Groopman's words, "frozen by fear, and fear overwhelms hope." (2004, p. 54) But there may be another alternative; one may find a way to develop other aspects of oneself that one had never planned if one can make needed life style changes.

Understanding the outcome, process, etiology and management needs of an illness starts the process of knowing about an illness. The second set of questions, "The Threat Template", (1996, p. 27) expands one's ability to deal with some of the psychological stresses an individual will be facing.

"Is the disease life threatening?

Is the disease understood, but progressively disabling, not amenable to management?

Is the disease not understood and unpredictable?

Is the disease understood and manageable?"

Each of the questions suggests some of the fears with which chronically ill persons may be struggling. Amyotrophic lateral sclerosis (ALS) is life threatening. The anxious question is, "how long will I live?" This disease is also progressively disabling. The anxious question is, "how rapidly will I become disabled?" There is some unpredictability as to how and when, but there are not disease-free or symptom-free periods as there are with lupus or multiple sclerosis. ALS is manageable for a period of time, sometimes for years using aids and assists, but eventually the disease becomes unmanageable and ends in death. Type 2 diabetes on the other hand is quite manageable for most people. While it demands often difficult life style changes, such as monitoring blood sugars, taking medication and maintaining diet and exercise control, it does not raise the anxiety of profound disability and agonizing death that ALS does.

Together the pastoral counselor along with the patient can explore the answers to the questions of both the medical and the threat templates. The more clearly one understands the illness, the better one will be able to manage the anxieties and fears triggered by the illness. As one discovers the limits and the possibilities attached to a particular illness, one becomes aware of real options and genuine choices that can be made as one deals with it. Seeking the answers to both sets of questions enables the patient and the pastoral counselor to develop a team with the healthcare providers, which can prove to be very helpful at critical points in the course of the illness.

What happens to a previously healthy individual who develops chronic illness? Consider the 60-year-old man, vigorous all his life, who suddenly experiences intense pain during exercise. He stops and the pain goes away. Over a period of days the pain recurs during exercise. He has smoked all his life, but has always been apparently healthy. Now he must admit that something is wrong. He tries to stop smoking and eat a little less butter, but the discomfort with exercise continues. He finally goes to see his physician because this discomfort is disturbing his usual sense of invincibility and well-being. After testing is completed, including a cardiac catherterization, he is told he has severe coronary artery disease. Unable to repair his problem with stents his physician tells him he needs surgery and he will need to take some medication for the rest of his life to keep his cholesterol low and his blood pressure controlled. For many persons who find themselves experiencing this common set of events, there now begins an intense wish to cure the problem. Whatever is wrong must be changed. Persons often seek the "best" surgeon, the "best" cardiologist, the most "up to date" procedures, and the "latest" medicines. The patient's family, friends and physicians can feel an intense pressure to help change what is wrong. Therapists, counselors, and pastors wishing to build hope at all costs can find themselves with family, friends and physicians drawn into a frenzy of activities that in the end is frustrating. The frantic searching is often based on false hopes of cure and ends far below the expectations of the searchers. All persons, including those who help, can find themselves overwhelmed with fatigue and hopelessness.

As acknowledgement of the presence of disease and one's helplessness to make it go away develops over time, there can occur great despair. Often it is during this phase that persons may begin to think, "what good does it do if I control my cholesterol now? The damage is done." Or, "These exercises only take valuable time from my now shortened life expectancy."

For many people, this is the time they begin to believe they are truly mortal. Perhaps this illness will not kill them, at least not right away, but sooner or later they will die. It is a time when many become clinically depressed. What is needed is the hope that life still has meaning and purpose and that the individual can adapt to the illness in a way that respects that meaning and purpose.

The last phase in a person's response to chronic illness comes from developing this hope. The individual begins to ask, "how can I live with this illness and how it is changing my life?" The individual has now passed through a process of disorganization, reorganization and consolidation. Goodheart and Lansing have identified this whole process of response to illness as the "Response Template". (1996, p. 32)

"Initial response: Something is wrong.
Awareness of chronicity: Something continues to be wrong.
Disorganization: Whatever is wrong is disturbing my life in significant ways.
Acknowledgement of helplessness: I cannot change what is wrong.
Adaptation to illness: How can I live with what is wrong and is changing my life?"

An individual's response to stress is affected by the level of threat, the nature of the illness and one's characteristic style of facing life problems. Another template identified as the "Psychological Template", (Goodheart & Lansing, p. 55) poses a third set of questions that can be used to understand how one characteristically approaches stress.

"How does the person manage reality?
How does the person manage anxiety?
How does the person manage relationships?
How does the person manage cognition?
What is the person's mastery-competence level? "

One usually knows when a patient is psychotic, living in fantasy and out of touch with reality. More commonly individuals have areas of reality distortion that may only become apparent under increased stress, such as at the onset of chronic disease. One middle-aged woman stopped taking the medicine to lower her blood pressure because she was sure the doctors were trying to make her sick. She had been functioning quite well as a court stenographer until her illness required taking several different medications. Her fear of her death and mortality that came when she was diagnosed with high blood pressure brought to light what her therapist called an schizotypal personality disorder. Focusing on the realities of her illness became an important way of helping her respond to illness and develop an adaptation that was positive and enabled her to live life again with purpose and meaning - and take her medication.

Understanding how a person defends against anxiety will help the pastoral counselor significantly. Some people begin to panic as soon as they feel pain. They may become so anxious that they seek emergency care over and over for even the slightest pain. Others are so highly defended that they do not seek treatment until the particular disease is well established and perhaps hard to treat effectively.

How does the person manage relationships? Can the chronically ill individual who is dependent on his significant other acknowledge the caretaker's need for time away, or is he demanding and unable to tolerate his caregiver's needs? Mr. Billings became very upset when he experienced a heart attack causing him to take early retirement. He could not tolerate his spouse continuing to work, despite the fact that they both needed her income and health insurance. Support for the spouse and supportive counseling for the patient eventually helped this couple stay together. In fact, from these challenges both were able to develop a more mature relationship with each other as well as with their children.

Managing cognition is another important factor in how an individual responds to illness. The thought process, one's alertness and attention, the judgment capacity and other aspects of cognition may be disrupted as a whole. Ellen was diagnosed with metastatic breast cancer. Her usual way of managing stress was to find out everything she could about what was bothering her and use a large number of various consultants to gather opinions. She tended to be overly obsessive, however, and it would usually take her a long time to make a decision because she was fearful about making a mistake. This delayed her treatment well past an optimal starting time. At each step along the way of treatment she spent agonizing hours going over and over each detail of the treatment, hoping it would be exactly right.

Contrast Ellen with Ann, who had a long history of working with others in a non-controlling fashion. She quickly gathered some information about her illness, and then selected three specialists. After she had interviewed each, she set about working right away with the one with whom she felt most comfortable. Together they formed a team about her health and Ann was able to give and take with this physician without the painful obsession that beset Ellen. Both persons had successful five year outcomes, but the experience of their treatments, though nearly identical in medical terms, was vastly different.

A person's mastery-competence level gives a sense of the overall functioning of the individual. There are numerous scales for assessing this aspect of function. The Global Assessment of Functioning (GAF) scale of the *Diagnostic and Statistical Manual of Mental Disorders,* 4th edition, (p. 32) is a widely used tool that can help the counselor develop an overall impression of an individual's mastery-competence level. This GAF scale can also be used to follow an individual over time and give clues as to how well a person may be coping with the illness.

Thus far we have looked at ways to obtain sufficient medical information to understand the issues a person is facing. We have outlined the process a person goes through in response to chronic illness and we have given some questions to ask to help assess a person's psychological functioning. This can affect the individual's response to illness. The goal of pastoral interventions is to partner with the chronically ill patient in a good enough manner to enable the individual to move from the disorganization and hopelessness that can be brought about by the illness to a place of reorganization and reconsolidation in which the person's life once again has creative purpose and meaning. Life becomes worth living even in the presence of devastating illness. Ideally, the illness may become an opportunity to grow spiritually and emotionally. As one takes up the helping role, first one should take the time to understand what the patient is dealing with. Often patients themselves are able to relate the facts about their illnesses. Sometimes they are too confused or overwhelmed. If the patient is unable to supply the answers to the questions posed by the templates, the counselor should find the answers in other ways. Today the internet provides a vast array of information that is rapidly accessed. Most diseases have national support or research groups that can readily provide needed information.

Once one has general information about a disease, one works with the patient or his significant others to get a clear understanding of the particular health issues for that patient. The outcome, process and management needs will be quite different for the person with diabetes and coronary artery diseases from the needs of the person with coronary artery disease alone. Likewise, the threats posed by coronary artery disease are different for a 40 year-old with a heart attack whose father died at age 50, than those for a 75 year old with a first heart attack whose father lived to be 90.

Secondly, one should assess where the person is in response to the illness. Is the person in the initial phases of illness moving towards disorganization, or is the person beginning to reorganize and reconsolidate? In the first case one needs to help the individual survive the disorganization that is occurring in response to the illness. Support for the individual is essential. This may include ways and means to help in both external and internal ways. Finding options that give genuine choices is a key. Help may be needed from the family or larger community as he or she copes with loss of health and well-being, perhaps also the loss of employment and income. Here is an opportunity to establish an enduring relationship that is the beginning of hope and the renewal of meaning and purpose that can develop in the reconsolidation phase.

During the reorganization phase patients will begin to reflect on the process. But with this reflection comes awareness of loss and corresponding mourning. Fears now arise about how the future will be. Many times well meaning helpers tell people that they should not worry. "Everything will be all right," they say. Individuals in this phase of illness know better. Patients tend to feel unheard and more isolated by such comments. Listening to and acknowledging loss, grief and fear is the way of building enduring relationships that eventually facilitate hope. Often this takes patience and courage, but a strong bond of trust can develop when the counselor can tolerate the fact that things may get worse, and may even end in suffering and death. Yet, even in this event there is solace and hope to be had. There are resources both external and internal that a person can draw upon to bring about reorganization and reconsolidation. Being with an ill person and accepting them without pressuring them to change what cannot be changed, yet finding means to facilitate what can be changed is the task of the helping person.

As reconsolidation occurs there is renewed meaning and purpose for the individual. There may still be anger and great sadness. The individual can now find renewed strength to manage priorities. If the disease is managed and minimally life-threatening, the person may now seem renewed like Phoenix rising from the ashes. Sometimes, and usually with considerable effort, one discovers a major shift in one's characteristic style of coping with life. More often there will be minor adjustments in coping strategies that make life work.

Helping persons, whether therapists, physicians, pastors, families or friends, will do well to be mindful of the patient's world. Are there adequate resources available for the patient to draw upon as he or she responds in various ways to illness? Simple issues like rides to and from physicians' and other health care providers' offices, or more complex issues of finances, career changes, etc. , all need attention. Other aspects of the patient's world to take into account include the person's past history of illness, the cultural background and diversity of life style, and the stage of life at which the disease develops.

Mr. Billings, mentioned above, had his heart attack five years before he planned to retire. He had been concerned about retirement prior to his illness. His fears were that his life would essentially be over once he retired. The heart attack and subsequent early retirement precipitated a crisis he might have dealt with better had life progressed more according to what he expected at that stage of life. He had not yet become the vice-president of his business, a position that he had hoped to achieve before retirement. With several years of therapy he was able to work through his anxieties and in the process develop new skills in managing relationships. Ten years after his heart attack, his wife finally retired and the couple now spends much of their time with their six grandchildren.

A person's past experience with illness, either his own or a family member's, can profoundly affect a person's response to illness. Mrs. Jones refused to go into a hospital for cancer treatment because she was certain she would die. Her grandmother and mother had both died the first and only time they went into a hospital. When this history was elicited by Mrs. Jones's friend and relayed to her physician, she was able to deal with her fears and finally get the treatment she needed. Five years following treatment she was still in remission. A friend made the connection with the physician and together the friend and the physician were able to open up the future for Mrs. Jones.

Society is diverse. Ethnicity, race, gender, sexual preference, age, education and socioeconomic status all affect an individual's response to illness. A young woman with a disfiguring arthritis may face ostracism from her peers. Health care options are limited for the poor. For example, an African American mother of two compared to the white male 45 year old CEO of a major pharmaceutical industry. Sensitivity to individual experience is fundamental to building relationships that can foster hope for the future.

Spiritual and religious practices are another important aspect of people's lives that must be allowed into treatment of chronically ill patients. In *Treating People with Chronic Disease,* (1996), the authors share the story of a young man with leukemia who belonged to a religious group which believed in anointing the sick. Family members prevailed upon the medical team to join with the pastor around the bedside for prayer and anointing. All who participated felt they were part of a healing team, which brought both hope and comfort to the patient and the family. There are many individual stories about healing and disease modification associated with hope and spiritual practices. There is some evidence that the emotions have a biological effect. People are working to explore these connections. For a detailed discussion of connections between the mind and the body, see Esther Sternberg, *The Balance Within: the Science Connecting Health and Emotions (2000).* This book begins to look at ways in which hope, positive beliefs and thoughts may biologically affect at least certain aspects of illness such as how a person feels pain and finds energy. There is much to be learned in this area. Until recently it has been very difficult to understand ways in which emotions may mediate body events.

To build bridges of hope and solace can be a rich experience for the pastor and spiritual counselor. Developing relationships with chronically ill people as they work through the process of disorganization, reorganization and reconsolidation will affect the helping person in many ways. Being with an ill person and accepting them without pressuring them to change that which cannot be changed, yet finding means to facilitate what can be changed requires that pastors be aware of the emotional reactions they experience around patients and illness.

Anxiety is perhaps the most universal experience felt around ill people. It is fueled by one's one beliefs about and experience with illness. People have many ways of dealing with anxiety. Some become frenetically active, seeking solutions in all kinds of ways. The helping person who tends to manage anxiety this way will be easily drawn into the patient's frantic search for a cure. Such a person can lose the nonjudgmental stance and find oneself pressuring the patient to try to change what cannot be changed.

Some helpers tend to flee, to get away when anxiety gets too great. During the early reorganization phase of a patient's response to illness, being with a patient while they are grieving can become so painful that the anxious helper leaves. Rather than building bridges of hope, they confirm a patient's fears that the situation is without hope.

People defend against anxiety in many other ways. Helpers may be angry at the disease, the medical establishment, or even at patients for not following treatment plans, or for simply not getting better when they should. There may be partial denial, "This disease is really not so bad." Such a position can lead again to pressuring a person to do more than he or she is able, again leading to a breakdown in relationship and the building of hope.

Whenever the helping person is preoccupied with the patient outside of the encounter, when intense feelings persist after leaving the patient, or when others comment on the helper's apparent over-involvement, one should think about what reactions he or she may be experiencing. These reactions to the patient and his illness are commonly called countertransferences. When examined and understood, countertransferences can be useful tools in understanding and working with the patient. For example, when you are listening to the patient's graphic description of his illness and you feel disgust, rather than expressing your disgust or leaving and abandoning the patient, explore the issue. First, explore silently in your mind. Then, if appropriate, explore with the patient what he is feeling about the changes in his body. Perhaps the patient is struggling with the fact that one now finds his body disgusting. How does one face this? Your own feeling, first identified, then explored with the patient, can help the person to move from disgust to solace, and even hope that one can live with the changes in the body that are so upsetting.

Other feelings when examined may arise more from the helping person's own unsettled conflicts. Take for example the strong wish to leave in the presence of helplessness. Such helpless overpowering anxiety could stem from a past personal encounter with a loved one who was ill and whom the helper felt unable to help. Now those feelings can come flooding back. In this situation, by understanding that one's wish to leave is related to one's wish not to be reminded of a painful past, one can perhaps find a way to bring oneself into the present and provide the support needed by the patient. The counselor may need to seek help or therapy to deal with the old painful feelings, but facing these old conflicts can bring new meaning and comfort to the helper who in turn can become a better helper to the patient.

Countertransference reactions are useful to the patient and the helping person. By dealing with them thoughtfully rather than trying to ignore them or acting-out the impulses they stimulate, both the patient and the therapist can find healing and hope.

Adults with chronic illness go through a process of disorganization, reorganization and reconsolidation. The task is to find renewed meaning and hope that will enable the individual to live the rest of life well despite the adjustment need and fears arising from illness. Chronically ill children are different. Developmentally they have not yet achieved a mature identity and sense of self. With children the task is, "to foster a sense of safety, security, regularity and predictability of life so that natural growth and healthy development of the self can occur." (Goodheart and Lansing, 1996, p. 117) Beyond surviving and managing day-to-day, children need help to have hope for the future and grow into adults whose lives have purpose and meaning.

As with adults, the pastoral counselor will seek information about the illness using the questions of the medical and threat templates given earlier. One will find a large diversity among children's diseases ranging from asthma, which may be mild or life threatening, to congenital heart disease; sickle cell anemia, Down's syndrome; leukemia and deafness. The course of these diseases varies widely. Asthma and juvenile arthritis may resolve as children reach adulthood. Leukemia may be cured. Some diseases such as cystic fibrosis and sickle cell anemia will shorten the life span. Some will demand lifelong adjustment such as blindness and deafness. Others can pose difficult management decisions in adulthood such as Down's syndrome and diabetes.

For very young children, parents carry the burden of knowing the medical information, and are responsible for managing the illness. As children mature, they will become more involved in knowing about and managing their illness. It is therefore essential that pastoral work with children includes the family as well as the child. Nicholas Hobbs, James Perrin and Henry Irey, in their book *Chronically Ill Children and Their Families* (1985, p. 80), describe the multiple challenges these families face:

> "Families with a chronically ill child confront challenges and bear burdens unknown to other families. The shock of the initial diagnosis and the urgent and compelling need for knowledge; the exhausting nature of constant care unpredictably punctuated by crises; the many and persistent financial concerns; the continued witnessing of a child's pain; tensions with one's spouse that can be aggravated by the fatiguing chronicity of care; the worries about the well being of other children; and the multitude of questions involving the fair distribution within the family of time, money, and concern - these are challenges that parents of chronically ill children must face."

Susan H McDaniel, Jeri Hepworth and William J. Doherty, present some questions that point to special issues that may need support in dealing with fami-

lies of chronically ill children: (1992, p. 221):
1. What beliefs and meanings do family members bring to the child's health problems?
2. Has the child's illness become part of dysfunctional triads in the family?
3. How are other relationships being attended to?
4. How are the siblings functioning?
5. What part of the problem is developmental and what part is illness-related?
6. How are the parents relating to health professionals?
7. How supportive is the family's social network?

Children and families will experience problems at different stages of a disease as well as at the child's different developmental stages. Therapy may need to be focused around coping and adaptation or around crisis management and trauma treatment. The key to getting it right is to understand the medical issues, the fears, the developmental stage of the child and the family issues. Helping families and children achieve balance in their lives is a major part of the task in building hope for the future and bringing comfort to overburdened families.

The family plays a role in dealing with the chronically ill adult as well as with the child. When a person has no supporting family and is socially isolated, he or she has a poorer prognosis for successful reorganization. The family includes all people who are kin or have "kinlike" relationships with the patient. These families should be considered from at least two points of view in the context of chronic illness. Most often it is the family that provides major support for the chronically ill person. The family may also be profoundly affected by a member's illness and must go through a similar process of disorganization and reorganization.

Julia Rowland (1989) has given five criteria for the assessment of social support: "the type of support being provided or needed, the source of support (providers), the quantity and availability of support, the quality and content of support given, and the perceived need by the recipient for support." (p. 59)

What is the best type of support depends on what is needed at a given time. For example, a cancer patient who has just completed treatment, whose hair has not yet grown back, may need encouragement to enable her to move back into and more fully resume her life. On the other hand, financial support may be most helpful to the individual who has just lost a job due to illness.

Who is the source of support? In one family siblings all lived together. A brother provided all transportation and much emotional support for the eldest sister who became bedridden with congestive heart failure. The younger 76-year-old sibling had to develop skills of managing the home and physically caring for the eldest. She needed help and support herself in order to take up this task, as she had debilitating arthritis in her knees.

Reviewing the marital/partner status of the patient, membership in social, professional and religious groups, involvement in social activities and the amount of social contacts assesses the quantity and availability of support. A family with many extended members nearby, that participates in school and church activities regularly, will have much more available support than a widowed man who lives several hours from his children and who rarely, if ever, participates in outside activities.

When assessing the quality of support whom you ask and when you ask may yield a variety of responses. In one family the couple described the support of the extended family as "wonderful" for a severely handicapped wife. On the other hand, the mother of the handicapped woman saw the support as "meager and inadequate". This mother felt guilty that she could not do more for her daughter because her Parkinson's disease limited her.

Finally, one needs to assess the perceived need for support. "Attempts to institute support interventions for patients who do not perceive or who deny their isolation is distressing or is doomed to failure." (Rowland, P.62) Listening for what is needed and then asking how best to help is the most effective way to offer support.

When assessing the family as a support system, examining each of these factors will help one know where support is most needed, what type of support is needed and if the family is able to give this type of support. If the family is unable, then finding ways to provide needed support is the best way to help.

There are many reasons why a family may be unable to help. Often the family itself is profoundly disorganized by a member's chronic illness. Some families like that of Mr. Billings become disorganized and must reorganize if they are to remain a family. Mr. Billings had to give up his role as primary provider to his wife. The latter had to assume that role, and give up some of her role as cook and housekeeper in order to assume a full-time job that provided health insurance. Such changes of roles are common, and each family member needs support and affirmation as they struggle to master their new roles and identities in the family.

An assessment of a family's needs should include an understanding of the ordeal the family is facing. What are the demands of the illness? What is the structure of the family? What roles does each assume? Will these need to be changed? What is the family belief illness? What is the point in the family life cycle? When children are young, the family focus will be on taking care them. When children are young adults the focus is on separating from one another and establishing independence. Illness can interfere with any of these tasks.

The life cycle has importance for the individual as well. There are existential issues about meaning and purpose that must be addressed at each age. Young adults are usually concerned with identity and their place in the future. More mature adults are concerned with purpose and accomplishment of meaningful achievement. Aging adults examine the life that has been lived and ask, "Has my living been worthwhile?"

Chronically ill people need pastoral care and intervention for the duration of their illness, throughout the life cycle. This is a demanding job. It is dynamic, as both the disease and its treatment change, and as the individual lives on.

We have explored ways to gain knowledge of the patient's illness and the patient's response to the illness. We have examined ways to understand a patient's characteristic style of dealing with anxieties and fears, and we have become aware of the needs to be sensitive to the patient's world. We understand that working with people with chronic illness means going with them through a process of disorganization through reorganization and reconsolidation. We have discovered that to do this work well, we must understand and monitor our own reactions to the anxieties stirred within us in response to the patient's illness. We have noted that children who are chronically ill have special developmental needs, and that families of ill persons need pastoral support and comfort as well as the ill persons themselves. Finally, we have seen that there are developmental issues about the meaning and purpose of life. Working through all these issues requires that we strive to find real options and genuine choices. In so doing we will build bridges of hope and solace.

BIBLIOGRAPHY

American Psychiatric Association. (1994). *Diagnostic and statistical manual of mental disorders* (4th ed.). Washington, DC: Author.

Goodheart, C.D., & Lansing, M.H. (1996) *Treating people with chronic disease: A psychological guide.* Washington, DC: American Psychological Association.

Groopman, J. (2004). *The anatomy of Hope: How people prevail in the face of illness.* New York: Random House.

McDaniel, S.H., Hepworth, J., & Doherty, W.J. (1992). *Medical family therapy.* New York: Basic Books.

Rowland, J.S. (1989). Interpersonal resources: Social support. In J.C. Holland & J.H. Rowland (Eds.) *Handbook of psycho oncology: Psychological care of the patient with cancer.* New York: Oxford University Press.

Sternberg E. (2000). *The balance within: The science connecting health and emotions.* New York: W.H. Freeman & Co.

World Health Organization. (1948). Constitution of the World Health Organization. *Geneva, Switzerland: WHO Basic Documents.*

About The Author

Dr. Lansing is the Program Director of the Capital Health System Family Medicine Residency Training Program of the University of Medicine and Dentistry of New Jersey Robert Wood Johnson Medical School (UMDNJRWJMS), where she is an Associate Professor in the Department of family medicine.

Since 1995 she has been the Medical Director of the Family Health Center, Plainsboro, NJ, where she teaches and practices family medicine and psychotherapy.

Her book, *Treating People with Chronic Disease, A Psychological Guide*, was co-authored with Carol Goodheart and published by the American Psychological Association in 1996. Today it is used frequently as a text in courses on treating people with chronic diseases.

Dr. Lansing is a member and fellow of the National Institute for Program Director Development and a Diplomate of the American Board of Family Practice. She is certified in Psychoanalytic Psychotherapy by the Institute for Psychotherapy and Psychoanalysis of New Jersey. Currently she holds active staff privileges at Capital Health System, Trenton, NJ, where she practices and serves on various committees.

Dr. Lansing is one of six Mercer county physicians in UMDNJRWJMS who has been named to *New York Magazine*'s Best Doctors. She is regularly listed in Castle Connolly's *How to Find The Best Doctors*, New York Metropolitan Area, and she is listed in the National Register's *Who's Who in Executives and Professionals*.

Chapter 11

Suggestions for Clergy in Ministering to Dying Persons & their Loved Ones: Conceptualizing Death & Developing a Framework of Life's Final Stage

by Kevin P. Kaut, Ph.D.,
James L. Werth, Jr., Ph.D.,
Andrea Sever, M.A., &
Nadia Hasan, B.S.

Department of Psychology
The University of Akron

Please address correspondence to the first author at:
Department of Psychology, The University of Akron, Akron, OH 44325-4301
Phone: 330-972-2196; Fax: 330-972-5174; E-mail: kpk@uakron.edu

The traditional role of clergy (i.e., ordained members of a specific faith tradition) is most often associated with a responsibility for the spiritual and theological needs of individuals. Regardless of denomination, the clerical representative to a particular religious body is generally viewed as possessing the formal education, experience, and preparation to support the spiritual health and welfare of its membership. Inherent in this role is the need to provide guidance and direction within the framework of a particular faith (i.e., doctrine or systematic theology) while promoting the growth and development of a specific congregational membership. Members of a particular faith tradition may look to a spiritual leader (e.g., pastor, priest, rabbi) for insight, assurance, and comfort in times of distress, particularly when experiencing challenging physical and emotional circumstances.

The role of the clergy in meeting the spiritual and emotional needs of a person in need may become of principal importance when an individual is facing a terminal condition. Confronted with the end of life, spiritual matters may be among the most prominent concerns expressed by dying persons (Ehman et al., 1999; Lo et al., 2002; Murata, 2003; Steinhauser, Clipp, et al., 2000; Stewart, Teno, Patrick, & Lynn, 1999; Strang, Strang, & Ternestedt, 2002). For some, it may be an expression of a deep faith developed through years of adherence to a particular religious tradition, whereas for others this may initiate a search for meaning, answers, and comfort through a religious framework long since abandoned. In either case, and for various positions between these two extremes, a representative of the faith may be one of the most highly valued persons for the dying person and family at this emotionally intense and exceptionally difficult time (see Koenig, 2002).

The readiness of clergy for dealing with dying and death is therefore of

considerable importance. The very nature of their training and work might suggest that clergy are well prepared to deal with the responsibilities and challenges involved in ministering to the dying. Indeed, if the role of a spiritual care provider near the end of life is to offer periodic visitation, prayer, scripture reading, and presentation of relevant sacraments or rites to a dying person, then clergy may easily satisfy criteria for ministerial success. However, research concerning spirituality near the end of life suggests that it may be more than theological formality (see Friedman, Mouch, & Racey, 2002; Mauritzen, 1988; Smith, 1993; Strang et al., 2002; Walter, 1996) and clergy should provide the dying person and family an opportunity to navigate the complex challenges of dying while promoting a life-affirming potential for personal growth and change (Larson & Tobin, 2000). This approach to spirituality should in no way diminish the importance of a particular theology, ritual, or practice associated with a specific faith tradition (Daaleman & VandeCreek, 2000; Kellehear, 2000). Indeed, these may be critical to many individuals facing the end of life. Yet, the inclusion of spirituality within a framework emphasizing an appropriate and supportive dying process (Chochinov, 2002; Patrick, Engelberg, & Curtis, 2001; Steinhauser, Clipp, et al., 2000) reflects the need to deliver spiritual care in the context of a more comprehensive plan for holistic intervention (Kearney & Mount, 2000).
Conceptualizing Dying and Death

Understanding the End-of-Life Scenario

Practicing clergy may benefit from a broader perspective—essentially an integrated and multidimensional framework—with which to approach the dying person. Inasmuch as medical personnel are encouraged to consider multiple facets of a patient's life when discussing treatment options and biomedical decisions (e.g., Anbar, 2001; Daaleman & VandeCreek, 2000; Kaufman, 2002; Lo et al., 2002; Steinhauser, Christakis, et al., 2000; Steinhauser, Clipp, et al., 2000), it is equally important that clergy recognize the multiple factors potentially impacting a person's openness to spiritual issues or ability to successfully consider issues of spiritual significance near the end of life (Kaut, 2002).

The physical dimension.

Persons living with a terminal condition are often dealing with much more than the prospect of death itself. Anticipating the end of life must be respected as an intensely intrapersonal experience, but one that also encroaches upon many different aspects of living. Clergy may be in a unique position to assess the multifaceted nature of a dying person's life experience and identify ways to integrate a sense of spirituality into her or his perspective of living while dying. This begins with an understanding of a person's life context and a consideration of the various issues potentially impacting the life of the dying person (see Figure 1; adapted from Kaut, in press). Although clergy may be viewed as singularly invested in providing spiritual support as part of an end-of-life treatment program (see Cherny et al., 1994, 1996; Chochinov, 2002; Lynn, 1997; Muir & Arnold, 2001; Quill, 2002), spiritual care is best viewed within a holistic framework—one that respects the multidimensional nature of spiritual expression (Kearney & Mount, 2000).

Recently, Kaut (2002) and Sulmasy (2002) underscored the importance of viewing spirituality within a broader framework, influenced by biomedical, psychological, social, and cultural circumstances (see also Block, 2001; Kagawa-Singer & Blackhall, 2001). Compartmentalizing spiritual needs as separate from other issues at the end of life may undermine an appreciation of the diverse factors influencing the expression of spirituality. Importantly, clergy should be familiar with the growing literature addressing the many concerns and expressed needs of dying persons and their families (Emanuel & Emanuel, 1998; Singer, Martin, & Kelner, 1999; Steinhauser, Christakis, et al., 2000; Steinhauser, Clipp, et al., 2000). Further review of Figure 1 suggests that spiritual intervention, albeit of principal importance to many near the end of life, is linked with numerous functional issues that must be considered as part of a well-integrated approach to spiritual care.

Successfully addressing spiritual issues with a dying patient may be influenced by various biomedical factors, including levels of pain; physical changes experienced throughout an illness; and visceral stressors such as nausea, vomiting, and breathing difficulties (for relevant discussions see Cherny et al., 1994, 1996; Rothschild, 1997; Singer et al., 1999). In addition, psychological issues such as fear, anxiety, depression, and concerns about the level of burden imposed on family may impact a patient's openness to spiritual matters as they approach the final stages of life (see Block, 2001; Cherny et al., 1994; Emanuel & Emanuel, 1998; Emanuel et al., 2000). Understanding the relationship between mind, body, and spirit is not merely interesting from an academic perspective, but provides relevant insight when entering into the spiritual dimension of a dying person (Kearney & Mount, 2000). The expression of spirituality at any one point in time may be viewed as an emergent property of cognitive, affective, and physiological status. Therefore, a spiritual care provider recognizes that discussions of spiritual questions, concerns, and aspirations (i.e., higher order human needs) may be predicated on the degree to which other psychological and biological needs are satisfied (see Marrone, 1999; see also Kaut, 2002).

The spiritual dimension.

The framework for clergy proposed here does not advocate a mere reductionistic view of human spirituality. Although such perspectives exist, spirituality is most commonly viewed as the embodiment of an individual's stated beliefs in— and relationship to—God or a higher power. For many, religion and spirituality are indistinguishable concepts given the close association between the notion of human spirit (and divine spiritual presence) and theological constructs associated with religious teachings (see Sulmasy, 2002). Members of the clergy will most likely approach the issues of dying, death, and existence beyond this life, through a religious framework shaped by theological training and preparation. A given doctrine with its system of faith and worship provides an important source of perspective, structure, and guidance when responding to the needs of the dying. However, there are likely to be circumstances where a dying person expresses an alternative spiritual belief (or no belief at all), with minimal relationship to traditional religious perspectives (e.g., Walter, 1993, 1996; see also Kearney & Mount, 2000). In these circumstances, clergy may be challenged to search for a person's core sense of spirituality, or at least to somehow reconcile possible differences between the tenets of "religion" and the broader application of "spirituality."

Further, what is spiritual for one person may not qualify as spiritual for another. For some, spirituality will not be defined according to a belief in God or an acceptance of specific religious teachings. Yet, they may ascribe to an intensely spiritual perspective guided by a unique understanding of their relationship to a higher power, others in their life, and a belief in existence (or the lack thereof) beyond this life (Walter, 1993, 1996). Spiritual identity may be a reflection of the meaning attributed to one's life and an expression of meaningfulness through a life of relationships, work, and accomplishment (Friedemann et al., 2002; Murata, 2003; Walter, 1996). Accordingly, clergy (e.g., hospital chaplains) may need to step outside of a given denominational framework and accept the perspective of a dying person as their starting point for exploring matters of spiritual importance (Mauritzen, 1988; Smith, 1993). Indeed, an individual's own spiritual construct (see Walter, 1996), or the search for a spiritual schema through which to understand illness and impending death (Marrone, 1999), are valuable expressions of the human spirit, and should be recognized as sacred elements supporting a person's own unique journey toward the end of life.

Clergy called to the service of a dying person without a shared belief in, or respect for, a specific religious tradition, may find the prospect of providing spiritual care a difficult or even impossible task. Nevertheless, the principal task here may be to understand the nature and needs of the dying person, while promoting his or her own search for spiritual identity and hope. Importantly, and regardless of denomination, clergy may be in a most unique position to model a life-affirming level of compassion, understanding, acceptance, and steadfast faith in the context of a terminal condition.

A Model of Spiritual Care Near the End Of Life

Entering into the life experience of a dying person requires sensitivity and awareness. A spiritual care provider must be sensitive to the needs, anxieties, and struggles inherent in an end of life scenario, but must also be aware of a dying person's functional limitations, capabilities, and resources. The multidimensional nature of dying and death (see Figure 1) reinforces the importance of identifying the relevant contextual factors potentially impacting the dying process.

Attending to biological and psychological issues.

Clergy must be prepared to consider the biomedical status of the dying person, while assessing the functional implications of disease, treatment, and disease progression (see Figure 2). Remembering that dying patients may be experiencing emotional difficulties (Block, 2001; Schuster, Breitbart, & Chochinov, 1999; Werth, Gordon, & Johnson, 2002) while also dealing with problematic physical symptoms (Emanuel & Emanuel, 1998; Rothschild, 1997) is essential. A spiritual care provider may observe only a fraction of a person's general functional status at any one moment in time. Stepping in and out of the life of a dying person to offer prayer, meditation, spiritual counsel, and ritual support are desired services of clergy; however, insight into the broader physical and emotional experience of the dying person, coupled with a recognition of their current (and historical) life context, may offer valuable perspectives for the effective delivery of spiritual care (see comments in Steinhasuer, Clipp, et al., 2000).

Essentially, when providing spiritual care clergy must understand the functional context in which the dying person lives, and anticipate how this status may influence the presentation and experience of spiritual or religious intervention. Modern perspectives of bio-psycho-social-spiritual integration near the end of life emphasize holistic (i.e., whole person) treatment, reflecting the need to understand the relationship between disease, body, mind, and spirit (Kaut, 2002; Sulmasy, 2002; see also Emanuel & Emanuel, 1998; Mauritzen, 1988; Steinhauser, Christakis, et al., 2000; Strang et al., 2002).

An awareness of how biological issues, cognitive status, and social disposition influence functional capacity will benefit the spiritual provider, promoting a more holistic view of the person's ability to engage in spiritual or religious discussions. Conceptually similar to Marrone's (1999) previous application of Maslow's human need hierarchy near the end-of-life, the framework proposed here (refer to Figure 2) reflects the importance of an informed spiritual care provider when ministering to the needs of the dying. Unmet physiological needs, distressing physical symptoms, and general fatigue or malaise may interfere with the ability to successfully engage in discussions of religious or spiritual importance. Moreover, functional losses in previously enjoyed life activities may contribute to a sense of futility or depression that can produce emotional distress and interfere with openness to spiritual issues (e.g., see Cherny et al., 1996; Lynn, 1997). Importantly, it is helpful to recognize that a deteriorating physical status may also influence a patient's emotional and spiritual condition. Clergy who focus solely on the delivery of spiritual care—although sincerely intent on meeting the spiritual needs of the dying person—may fail to recognize the spiritual distress that can result from physical and other functional declines.

Identifying functional capacity in various areas, including self-care, work, leisure activities, and communication skills may offer insight into a dying person's own resources and limitations (e.g., strength, motivation, endurance), while also providing an index of disease progression. Optimal levels of function may vacillate over time and gradually decline as treatments are modified and the biomedical condition worsens (see example, Figure 2). However, a decline in overall physical strength and reserve does not necessarily suggest comparable diminution of cognitive skills. Neurocognitive abilities (e.g., language comprehension, memory) may remain intact, even in the midst of physical decline and fatigue, thus preserving opportunities for continual spiritual care.

Ultimately, an awareness of a person's position along her or his unique end-of-life trajectory is of critical importance in preparing spiritual interventions. Failing to utilize time wisely, especially during periods of relatively good physical and cognitive health, may deprive a dying person of opportunities to deal with important social, emotional, and spiritual issues. Therefore, understanding the temporal nature of disease, and the potential impact on relevant functional skills, may promote better planning and the use of time devoted to spiritual care.

Blending spiritual elements within the biomedical context.

The process of dying and the eventual death of individuals in modern society are most frequently viewed within a biomedical perspective (for examples, see Faber-Langendoen & Lanken, 2000; Lynn, 1997; Rothschild, 1997). Investing in the spiritual care and welfare of a dying person naturally involves coming into contact with a world of medical issues, physical symptoms, and treatment options. The tendency to medicalize the dying process may minimize the essence of personhood, or "soul" in the dying person (see Kearney & Mount, 2000). In this regard, spiritual care is of paramount importance, particularly when this level of care embraces the whole person and promotes a sense of hope, understanding, and dignity (Chochinov, 2002) in the face of certain physical decline.

The search for meaning may be a central concern for dying persons (Block, 2001; Breitbart, 2002; Kearney & Mount, 2000; Lynn, 1997; Smith, 1993), especially as they struggle to understand the meaning of their illness while attempting to integrate a sense of personal life meaning in the context of dying. Clergy are not compelled to provide answers; however, they should offer to the dying person an opportunity for self-examination, reflection, and discussion of how living and dying fit within a spiritual perspective. Mauritzen (1988) has affirmed the essential nature of personal meaning as part of a spiritual framework, and has encouraged the incorporation of existential concepts when defining spirituality. Attempts to understand the meaning of one's existence may be part of the existential distress experienced by some (Cherny et al., 1994, 1996), and efforts to identify sources of past, present, or future distress (and meaning) may be an important task in the provision of spiritual care (see Cherny et al., 1996).

A dying person's search for meaning requires time, effort, and patience. As such, this search reflects an ongoing process that may have been formally initiated at the time of a diagnosis, but which continues—and may intensify—as the end of life approaches. Therefore, clergy may need to re-conceptualize their role near the end of life as more than a conveyor of religious ritual and practice, and embrace the potential to integrate the search for meaning within the structure inherent in a given theological or spiritual belief system. This does not suggest a limitation in the use of relevant theological constructs in the application of spiritual care (e.g., God, theological literature, sacraments, music), but argues for a broader recognition that such constructs must be judiciously blended within the life and dying of persons searching for meaning near the end of life.

Kearney and Mount (2000) emphasized the need to explore sources of meaning with dying patients, and included the ideas of Frankl (e.g., 1963) as fundamental to this search for meaning in the midst of dying. Clergy may facilitate this search by asking dying persons to recount sources of accomplishment or creativity, identify objects of love and affection (i.e., who or what has been loved?), articulate the nature of the perceived legacy left behind, and express their source of belief or hope for the future. If spirituality is a reflection of what gives meaning to life (Walter, 1996), then expressions of spirituality may be most evident as individuals come to terms with the meaningful events, people, and beliefs that have shaped their lives. More importantly, the existential issues framed by Frankl (i.e., accomplishments, love, legacy, and beliefs) further define spirituality as an emergent property of personhood dependent on the separate, albeit interrelated, elements found in life experiences, faith, and relationships.

The value of a personal relationship—be it with God, a higher power, or elements of the physical universe—is an important component in spiritual constructs, and reinforces the need for a belief in one's connection to something greater than oneself (i.e., transcendence; see Friedemann et al., 2002; Kearney & Mount, 2000; Kellehear, 2000; Strang et al., 2002; Walter, 1996). Affirmation of this relationship, or clarification of transcendent themes, may be an important task for clergy, and may be part of the process of integrating one's spiritual perspective with the physical realities of dying and death. A belief that the spiritual self transcends physical dimensions of time and space may be incompatible with current medical and scientific perspectives. Nevertheless, patients who are dying may eventually forgo attention to concerns of the physical body, and look beyond mortality for solace in a hope of life beyond the present. Clergy represent this source of spiritual perspective, but must be a hope-affirming presence in the midst of dying.

Ministering to Loved Ones and Family

Clergy must be prepared to enter into a relationship with the dying person and remain a presence in the life of this individual throughout the journey toward death (Kaut, 2002). In certain cases, a relationship may have been previously established, principally through church involvement or engagement in other religious activities. However, in the context of an end-of-life scenario the need to build on an existing foundation, or invest in the development of a new relationship, may require additional time and perspective. The life context of the dying person is likely to be altered, and issues of importance may also change. New stresses and demands are imposed on the cognitive and emotional resources of the dying individual and her or his loved ones, and "quality of life" may be viewed differently than ever before (see Singer et al., 1999; also, Steinhauser, Christakis, et al., 2000). Clergy need to be aware of a dying person's own desires for living and dying as death approaches, but must also recognize the influence of family members (broadly defined) and broader social-cultural influences on the process of dying (Kagawa-Singer & Blackhall, 2001).

The Family Context.

Lynn (1997) addressed the importance of understanding a dying person's own history and the role of family in the process of dying. The family is essentially the unit of care in an end-of-life scenario (Hallenbeck, 2000), requiring a consideration of family values, cultural factors, and personal-family history as potentially influencing the beliefs and practices near the end of life. Kagawa-Singer & Blackhall (2001) underscored the need for cultural sensitivity when dealing with families confronting the death of a loved one. Clergy dealing with the dying person may be familiar with the cultural heritage of the individual (this may not be the case for many hospital chaplains), and this knowledge of culturally or socially based attitudes, beliefs, and decision-making style (i.e., individual vs. family centered) may clarify certain behaviors, questions, or struggles within a family facing the prospect of death (for relevant reviews see Irish, Lundquist, & Nelsen, 1993).

Understanding family responsibilities.

Family members are often the caregivers near the end of life (Cherny et al., 1996; Emanuel et al., 1999; Emanuel, Fairclough, Slutsman, & Emanuel, 2000; Hallenbeck, 2000), and are likely to experience significant changes in their personal lives and levels of responsibility. Although present with the dying person, and witness to the difficult and challenging experience of their loved one, not all families will approach end-of-life care the same way. Nevertheless, clergy are likely to work with many family members struggling under new and diverse responsibilities inherent in an end-of-life context. The demands on family members can be extraordinary, and not always evident to those entering the life of a family on a brief and intermittent basis. Caregivers may be dealing with transportation needs, additional homemaking tasks, direct care of their loved one, medication monitoring, scheduling for medical visits, preparations for death (i.e., funeral and burial arrangements) and planning for their own lives after a loved one has died. In addition, financial burdens may weigh heavily on the minds of dying individuals and their families (Emanuel et al., 2000).

Changing responsibilities may also require changes in family roles. With this change may come the stress of adjustment, particularly as individuals confront difficult circumstances associated with a loved one's dying. Clergy are called upon to remain sensitive to the contextual factors impacting dying persons and their families, and should at least be aware of how these factors influence the quality of relationships present near the end of life. In the midst of the many details and tasks that must be managed throughout the process of dying, attention to matters of interpersonal significance should remain of utmost importance at this time.

The importance of relationships near the end of life.

Steinhauser, Christakis, and colleagues (2000) reported that "family presence" is among the most valued elements for individuals dealing with a terminal condition (see also Patrick et al., 2001). The search for meaning near the end of life may be facilitated by friends and family, and the involvement of important people should be encouraged throughout the dying process. Singer, Martin, and Kelner (1999) noted a number of important relationship issues to consider, suggesting that the dying person may need opportunities for intimacy, reconciliation, and closure as the end approaches. Clergy should be aware of these needs, and examine the relationships among members of the family to determine if certain issues should be addressed. However, sensitivity to family values, the history of relationship styles, and the influence of culture must also be considered when evaluating the relationship needs of a family (Stewart et al., 1999).

Ultimately, clergy should remain aware of a dying person's need for intimacy with others—even if this means the mere presence of another person (Patrick et al., 2001). Loneliness can intensify the anxiety, depression, and fear associated with dying; therefore, clergy may need to insure adequate support by family, friends, and others (e.g., church members, social workers, nurses and other medical personnel). The dying person may simply want the comfort of another in the midst of the journey toward death. Comfort can be provided in the form of physical contact, moments of sharing and conversation, the re-telling of life experiences and memories, or simple silence. In moments of silence, with the quiet assurance of the presence, attention, and mindfulness of another, a dying person may receive affirmation and sense of compassion from a loved one. Clergy may need to help family members understand that "presence in silence" can be meaningful in the life of the dying person. Filling moments of silence with conversation is not always of benefit. Sensitivity to the needs, desires, and physical status of the dying person (e.g., stamina, level of fatigue, symptoms) are important as clergy minister to the dying individual, but also as they prepare family members to provide support, comfort, and intimacy.

In fact, a dying person's need for intimacy and closeness with family may intensify as the end of life approaches. Closure near the end of life is important, and the dying person and family members need time to address unfinished business or resolve issues of value and relevance to the dying individual and those left behind (Steinhauser, Christakis, et al., 2000). This may be of particular importance where certain relationships have been strained or damaged in previous years (e.g., Singer et al., 1999). Clergy may be instrumental in promoting reconciliation, and should be prepared to encourage family members to resolve unfinished business prior to the time when a dying person is unable to interact with others. However, this requires an awareness of particular historical issues in the patient's life (see Lynn, 1997), and a timely intervention with relevant family members.

It should also be understood that clergy might be a principal source of intimacy and closure for many, particularly as they search for a connection to God or a source of hope and transcendence. The relationship with clergy may be important to many individuals near the end of life, and clergy must understand their central role in dealing with end-of-life struggles for a great many people. Clergy provide a source of comfort, strength, hope, and closure near the end of life. Indeed, their value is not only for the life of the dying, but also for the lives of family and friends who struggle with many challenges—physical, emotional, and spiritual—present as their loved one prepares to die (Emanuel et al., 1999, 2000).

Care for the fatigued family.

Although the family is the appropriate unit of care near the end of life (e.g., Hallenbeck, 2000), it is understandable that care providers entering an end-of-life scenario may focus primarily on the needs of the dying person. For clergy, this may mean providing religious support in the form of prayer, meditation, readings of religious literature, and the presentation of sacraments or ritual where desired (Kellehear, 2000). A review of Figures 1 and 2,[Pages 198,199] however, should reinforce the contention here that the family context is more than just a set of variables impacting the dying person. Family members might also be viewed as the "patient in need," (Cherny et al., 1996) presenting their own end-of-life trajectory accompanied by various contextual factors and constraints influencing their physical and mental health.

Given the many responsibilities facing the family dealing with a terminally ill loved one, the stresses experienced at this time might profoundly affect their functioning (Rosen, 1998). Clergy should be aware of signs suggesting that family members are suffering and in need of specialized attention. Cherny and colleagues (1994, 1996) have noted that persons providing care to a dying loved one may experience a range of difficulties, including depression, grief, and emotional distress (see also Schulz & Beach, 1999). Anticipatory grief (Rando, 2000) can be particularly troublesome, and the emotional drain of watching a loved one decline in health may be overwhelming. In addition, family members may suffer empathically as a loved one experiences pain, fatigue, or emotional distress associated with dying (Cherny et al., 1996). A family can become fatigued and distressed as well, thus adding another contextual factor to the many that can impact quality of life for persons who are preparing to die (Emanuel & Emanuel, 1998; Patrick et al., 2001; Singer et al., 1999; Smith & Maher, 1991).

Above all, it is important to remember that dying persons experience their own personal journey toward death, yet caregivers share this journey and experience it in unique and different ways. Moreover, caregivers must be prepared to continue beyond a loved one's death. Clergy must be sensitive to the fears and anxieties expressed by family members, and be ready to offer support and guidance where necessary.

Promoting family welfare.

Within the biomedical milieu that so often characterizes an end-of-life scenario (e.g., Brody, Campbell, Faber-Langendoen & Ogle, 1997; Faber-Langendoen et al., 2000; Lynn, 1997; Morrison, Meier & Cassel, 1996; Rothschild, 1997), there are many decisions to be made and critical issues in need of attention. The essence of the dying person's self, sense of meaning, and spiritual dimension can potentially be lost amid the reductionistic approach of modern medicine. Nevertheless, recent perspectives on quality care near the end-of-life refer to the need for collaborative intervention among physicians, nurses, psychologists. social workers, and clergy (Lynn, 1997; Muir & Arnold, 2001; Patrick et al., 2001; Quill, 2002; Werth et al., 2002). The incorporation of spiritual issues into treatment planning and service delivery serves to promote the well being of the dying person, but is also important to the family at this difficult time.

Clergy are important contributors on the end-of-life care team, and should view themselves as representing a significant source of support and comfort for the dying patient and family. They can promote family welfare in many different areas near the end of life, and should not restrict their role to traditional spiritual services alone. If spirituality is viewed as a gestalt principle, essentially the summation of diverse areas of human functioning and belief (Kaut, 2002; Mauritzen, 1988; Walter, 1996), then clergy should be prepared to address the multiple factors that contribute to a person's sense of spirituality. Clergy can be providers of information, or can offer guidance and emotional support when difficult information is presented. For those so inclined, this role necessitates an attention to matters of biomedical, social, psychological, and spiritual importance. Certainly, expertise is not expected in these different domains, but a familiarity with issues relevant to each domain might be helpful.

Promoting family welfare might best be accomplished through a set of behaviors that prepare the dying person and loved ones for the eventuality of death. However, this does not require a focus on dying; rather, an emphasis on living and pre-death consolidation of a dying person's life experience provides the foundation for this perspective on death preparation. As such, clergy should be a consistent and reliable presence in the life context of a dying person, available to the family unit as a whole. They might offer more than traditional religious services by embracing a notion of spirituality that incorporates the "whole person" into a spiritual framework. This does not devalue the absolute importance of religious teaching, materials, and prayer as an expression of the human spirit and spiritual hope. Yet, a holistic perspective affirms the life of the dying person, and permits the integration of life experiences, values, relationships, and beliefs (i.e., religious or otherwise) into a perspective of dying and death that is an extension of living.

Preparing the Dying Person and Loved Ones for Death

References to the process of dying as an "end-of-life journey" (Kaut, 2002; Smith, 1993) may seem to minimize or otherwise trivialize the gravity of the process. After all, there is no return from this particular journey, and few dying persons might describe their physical and emotional suffering in travel-like terms. Moreover, viewing death as a "good" or "healthy" process (e.g., Smith & Maher, 1991) may be a difficult concept for some dying individuals and family members to understand. Sachs (2000) suggests caution when using terms such as "good or healthy death" (see Emanuel & Emanuel, 1998; Smith & Maher, 1991; Steinhauser, Clipp, et al., 2000) and encourages care providers to avoid the establishment of inappropriate expectations at the end of life. Dying can be experienced within a supportive, life-affirming, and growth-promoting context—each reflecting a potentially good or healthy approach to dying; however, the process of dying remains an emotionally painful experience, and the prospect of death may continue to evoke feelings of anxiety, fear, and distress (Kearney & Mount, 2000). Clergy can support an optimal life context for the dying (i.e., contributing to what some might call a good death) by validating the grief and difficult emotions experienced at this time, while recognizing opportunities to help others embrace life (and death) through spiritual presence and valued relationships. The realities of the dying experience should never be minimized, yet clergy can facilitate a sense of peace, assurance, and hope in the face of life's certain end.

Dying as an extension of living.

Exley (1999) has previously described the importance of helping the dying person negotiate his or her own after-death identity. While living, yet dying, the focus for the dying individual might be to develop for family members a sense of who they were while alive. In a sense, the negotiation of a role for the dying person in the life of survivors may represent a philosophical perspective whereby dying is viewed as an extension of living. After death they live on in the memories of those left behind. Accordingly, preparing to die may involve mental and emotional investment in the process of life review as a means of identifying accomplishments or other positive aspects of life (see Cherny et al., 1994). Kearney and Mount (2000) referred to the development of a "clinical biography" (p. 367) as a means of promoting insight into the history of a person's individuality. A life retrospective (Kaut, 2002) is one way of connecting a dying person's past with his or her present circumstances, and can uncover sources of meaning and purpose that sustain him or her near the end of life.

Helping an individual understand the meaning of a terminal illness (see Block, 2001; Kearney & Mount, 2000) may foster a sense of peace while dying and an acceptance of death as part of living. An individual's approach to dying may be viewed as an expression of her or his life, and may establish part of her or his legacy beyond death. Clergy should look for opportunities to emphasize a person's individuality during the end-of-life progression and help him or her maintain a connection with the past (i.e., continuity of self) while supporting the beliefs and hopes that prepare him or her for death. Not every person will view the process of dying as "part of living." Caution should always be exercised when promoting a particular perspective with the dying person and his or her loved ones (Sachs, 2000; Stewart et al., 1999). Nevertheless, for those who can affirm such a perspective while dying, this might offer opportunities for a deeper examination of life and death.

Forgiveness near the end of life.
A deeper examination of life when confronted with death may reveal concerns or fear regarding certain relationships, behaviors, or transgressions in life. Being at peace with God or other higher power may be one of the most important experiences near the end of life (Steinhasuer, Christakis, et al., 2000), and the need for forgiveness may be of principal concern to many. Kellehear (2000) discusses the importance of considering a dying person's need "'to put things right' and forgive and be forgiven" (p. 151) as she or he deals with various spiritual needs near the end of life. Clergy represent a source of forgiveness and connection with God, yet must be careful to avoid judgment or proselytizing when dealing with the dying person (Mauritzen, 1988; Strang et al., 2002). Nevertheless, dying persons may be searching for meaning and forgiveness, and a belief in forgiveness may actually contribute to a sense of meaning near the end of life. Clergy must be sensitive to a dying person's need to explore issues of religious or spiritual significance, while recognizing potential sources of spiritual pain or distress (see Kearney & Mount, 2000). A relationship with God, or other higher power predicated on faith and forgiveness, may be a most important part of a person's preparation for the end of life.

Ultimately, closure before dying may depend upon a person's achieved sense of peace and reconciliation, connection with others (and God) in anticipation of death, and a hope in life beyond this existence. Achieving continuity across life dimensions (i.e., past, present, and future; see Kaut, 2002) is a worthy goal near the end of life, yet requires introspection, a spiritual framework, and the investment of resources—physical, intellectual, and emotional—toward a deeper appreciation of self and purpose within an end-of-life scenario.

Uniting Biological, Psychological, Social, and Spiritual Dimensions in Holistic Care

The modern hospice movement emphasizes care for the whole person, which requires attention to somatic, psychic, social, and spiritual needs (Mauritzen, 1988). A respect for the interdisciplinary nature of end-of-life interventions (Muir & Arnold, 2001) is the foundation upon which components of good and healthy dying are established (Smith & Maher, 1991; Steinhauser, Christakis, et al., 2000). Although caution is necessary when openly discussing such concepts with the dying person and her or his family members (Sachs, 2000), clergy can be instrumental in providing a good dying experience by attending to the various needs present near the end of life. Clergy must be aware of the relationship among biomedical, cognitive, affective, socio-cultural, and spiritual dimensions near the end of life because holistic care depends on careful consideration of each domain and recognition that one dimension (e.g., spiritual) can influence another (e.g., physical; see Kaut, 2002; Kearney & Mount, 2000).

Clergy are central to treating the whole person, and are essential for supporting the whole family. As a representative of religious or spiritual belief systems, they are uniquely poised to influence some of the most important elements near the end of life: purpose, meaning, and transcendence. The search for connectedness and closure near the end-of-life may be met through an affirmation of spiritual truths, but clergy must be present—physically and emotionally—to facilitate the process.

Presence must continue even after an individual has died. A bereaved family may benefit from sustained involvement of clergy, and clergy must attend to the continuity of care started even before the death of a family's loved one. The end of one journey may mark the beginning of another; clergy, having been present and supportive throughout the process of dying, may provide needed spiritual support and encouragement as survivors now confront the process of living beyond the death of a loved one.

References

Anbar, R. D. (2001). The closure and the rings: When a physician disregards a patient's wish. *Pediatric Pulmonology, 31,* 76-79.

Block, S. D. (2001). Psychological considerations, growth, and transcendence at the end of life: The art of the possible. *Journal of the American Medical Association, 285,* 2898-2905.

Breitbart, W. (2002). Spirituality and meaning in supportive care: Spirituality- and meaning-centered group psychotherapy interventions in advanced cancer. *Supportive Care and Cancer, 10,* 272-280

Brody, H., Campbell, M. L., Faber-Langendoen, K., & Ogle, K. S. (1997). Withdrawing intensive life-sustaining treatment—Recommendations for compassionate clinical management. *New England Journal of Medicine, 336,* 652-657.

Cherny, N. I., Coyle, N., & Foley, K. M. (1994). The treatment of suffering when patients request elective death. *Journal of Palliative Care, 10,* 71-79.

Cherny, N. I., Coyle, N., & Foley, K. M. (1996). Guidelines in the care of the dying cancer patient. *Pain and Palliative Care, 10,* 261-286.

Chochinov, H. M. (2002). Dignity-conserving care—A new model for palliative care (helping the patient feel valued). *Journal of the American Medical Association, 287,* 2253-2260.

Daaleman, T. P., & VandeCreek, L. (2000). Placing religion and spirituality in end-of-life care.*Journal of the American Medical Association, 284,* 2514-2517.

Ehman, J. W., Ott, B. B., Short, T. H., Ciampa, R. C., & Hansen-Flaschen, J. (1999). Do patients want physicians to inquire about their spiritual or religious beliefs if they become terminally ill? *Archives of Internal Medicine, 159,* 1803-1806.

Emanuel, E. J., & Emanuel, L. L. (1998). The promise of a good death. *Lancet, 351(Suppl II),*21-29.

Emanuel, E. J., Fairclough, D. L., Slutsman, J., Alpert, H., Baldwin, D., & Emanuel, L. L. (1999). Assistance from family members, friends, paid care givers, and volunteers in the care of terminally ill patients. New England Journal of Medicine, 341, 956-963.

Emanuel, E. J., Fairclough, D. L., Slutsman, J., & Emanuel, L. L. (2000). Understanding economic and other burdens of terminal illness: The experience of patients and their caregivers. Annals of Internal Medicine, 132, 451-459.

Exley, C. (1999). Testaments and memories: Negotiating after-death identities. *Morality, 4,*249-267.

Frankl, V. (1963). *Man's search for meaning.* New York: Pocket Books.

Faber-Langendoen, K., & Lanken, P. N. (2000). Dying patients in the intensive care unit: Forgoing treatment, maintaining care. *Annals of Internal Medicine, 133,* 886-893.

Friedman, M-L., Mouch, J., & Racey, T. (2002). Nursing the spirit: The framework of systemic organization. *Journal of Advanced Nursing, 39,* 325-332.

Hallenbeck, J. (2000). Best practices in the care of the dying. *Annals of Long-Term Care Online.* Retrieved January 23, 2004 from the World Wide Web: http://www.mmhc.com/engine.pl?station=mmhc&template=altcfull.html&id=1717

Irish, D. P., Lundquist, K. F., & Nelsen, V. K. (Eds.). (1993). *Ethnic variations in dying, death, and grief: Diversity in universality.* Washington, DC: Taylor & Francis.

Kagawa-Singer, M., & Blackhall, L. J. (2001). Negotiating cross-cultural issues at the end of life: "You got to go where he lives". *Journal of the American Medical Association, 286,*2993-3001.

Kaut, K. P. (2002). Religion, spirituality, and existentialism near the end of life. *American Behavioral Scientist, 46,* 220-234.

Kaut, K. P. (in press). End-of-life assessment: Emphasizing adaptive behavior within an eclectic bio-psycho-social-spiritual framework. In J. L. Werth, Jr., J. R. Anderson, &

Figure 1.

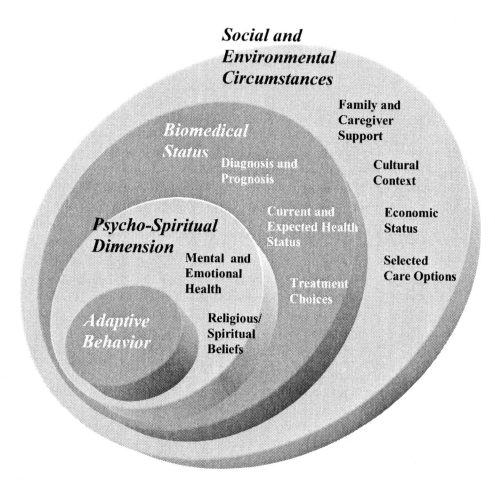

Figure 1. Multiple dimensions contributing to an end-of-life context.
An understanding of a dying person's ability to adapt and cope near the end of life
(i.e., adaptive behavior) requires an appreciation of various social-environment, biomedical, and psycho-spiritual dimensions. (Adapted from Kaut, in press)

Fig. 2:

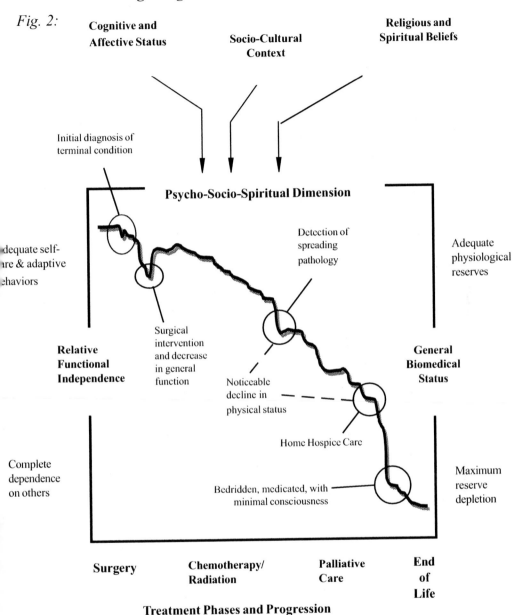

Figure 2. Intervention within an end-of-life trajectory.
Clergy benefit from a consideration of the dying person's relative functional capacity (i.e., independent engagement in life activities), and an awareness of the events occurring throughout an end-of-life trajectory. This hypothetical scenario illustrates a gradual decline in functional ability, and reflects various treatment phases associated with the progression of the disease. Awareness of the nature of disease and decline may facilitate an appreciation of the temporal parameters relevant to a person's ability to actively engage in mental and emotional work near the end of life. Moreover, it is important to recognize the socio-cultural, cognitive-affective, and spiritual resources (or needs) present near the end of life. (Adapted from Kaut, 2002)

About The Authors

Kevin P. Kaut, Ph.D. first obtained a Masters degree in School Psychology from the University of Akron (1990) and later earned his Ph.D. in biomedical science from Kent State University in collaboration with the Northeastern Ohio Universities College of Medicine (2000). He has practiced as a school psychologist (Mahoning County Public Schools, Ohio, 1990-1995), and is currently an Assistant Professor in the Department of Psychology, with a joint appointment in Biology, at the University of Akron. Present research interests include integrating biomedical and neuropsychological perspectives within a psychosocial-spiritual framework for assessment, intervention, and holistic care of patients and families dealing with end-of-life issues.

James L. Werth, Jr., Ph.D. earned his degree in Counseling Psychology from Auburn University in 1995 and his Masters of Legal Studies from the University of Nebraska - Lincoln in 1999. He was the 1999-2000 American Psychological Association William A. Bailey AIDS Policy Congressional Fellow where he worked on aging and end-of-life issues in the office of United States Senator Ron Wyden (D - OR). He has been employed as an Assistant Professor in the Department of Psychology at The University of Akron since August 2000. Also he works as a pro bono psychologist for the local HIV services organization where he provides counseling and supervises graduate students.

Chapter 12
Pastoral Care for Children & Adolescents Who Suffer With Grief: Special Bridges for Resolution & Peace

by Daniel H. Grossoehme, M.Div., BCC

A young mother whose youngest son has just died turns to you and asks, "Should we bring our five year-old son to the funeral?"

"It's been months since his grandmother died, and he still keeps asking the same question over and over: 'When are we going to see Nana again?' Every time I have to tell him she's dead it rips my heart out again."

"This is a little embarrassing to ask you, but, our son's hamster just died, and he wants to have a funeral for it. Can you give us any idea what we can do or say?"

When the editors told me that the guiding metaphor and title of this volume was bridges over troubled places, I recalled the yard where I lived as a young child. There was a fairly typical suburban backyard with a creek flowing through it, and then an unkempt hillside that went quite a ways beyond the creek, and which was much more exciting to play on than the yard. The creek itself varied in width and depth. There were places I could, even at seven years old, nimbly leap across; others where a convenient rock made crossing possible; one spot required a wooden bridge my father built, and one part was simply impossible.

There is also more than one way to bridge over the obstacle of grief and mourning for children and teenagers. Some grief experiences are easy for kids to cross; others require an aid partway through to help them; some require a grown-up to build them a way through, and some obstacles have to remain obstacles for a long time. This chapter presents a spectrum of ways through the obstacle of grief. Only the people who know the shape of the creek and the terrain beyond will be able to determine what will help a child or youth through, although this chapter will offer some guidance on which aids help in which situations. The "art" of pastoral care, however, still relies on the pastoral caregiver knowing what's required and offering their care.

There is no way to say, "Hello" to someone without there being an implied "Good-bye" to them at some point. The ending of relationships is as much of a part of living and loving as anything else. The sense of loss when someone in our family dies, or when we change places of residence, or move from one job to another, can affect all of us, including children and teenagers. Those who work in congregations will find themselves confronted by many opportunities to enter into these events of loss, and to help people deal with and make sense of their emotions. Caring for the youngest of God's children can present a special challenge, and also some unique opportunities. This chapter is meant to provide those persons with some basic information and resources to work with grieving children.

When bereavement comes to a child or youth who isn't able to handle the emotions that they are experiencing, it's easier for them to become "stuck" in being overwhelmed by the newness and/or the intensity of their emotions. That sense of being "stuck" becomes so persistent that a sense of hopelessness arises that may become severe enough to warrant a psychiatric diagnosis and treatment. Children grieve differently than adults, which means that sometimes adults don't recognize what a child is experiencing and are unable to help them. And sometimes, the adults themselves don't know what to do with their own feelings when there is a significant loss. Without effective adult guidance through the mourning process, the child again can become "stuck", overwhelmed, and hopeless.

Bereavement is a demonstrated risk fact for many psychiatric conditions, including depressive disorders, anxiety, onset of schizophrenia or schizophreniform psychoses or a psychotic relapse, and mania. A person of young age, poor social support and an underlying depressive disorder is at higher risk, at least for anxiety symptoms (Biondi and Picardi, 1996). Depression, self-injurious behavior and substance abuse were reported in a study of bereaved women who had been abused (Clark, Cole and Enzle, 1990). Death of a family member may trigger an underlying grief in someone who was abused for the loss of a nurturing relationship, protection, and self-worth, all of which were lost in the abusive relationship. For all of these reasons, grief deserves to be a focus of attention for a pastoral caregiver when a child or adolescent has been unable to resolve it on their own.

SOME DEFINITIONS

Moving through these experiences will be simplified by keeping distinct several terms that are frequently used as if they were synonyms. In this chapter, "grief" refers specifically to the person's *internal* response to a death or other loss. This is the feelings (or numbness) that a child or adolescent experiences. "Bereavement" is a somewhat archaic word (although still used in psychiatry instead of "grief") that connotes not only the pain one experiences in a loss, but a sense of having been "robbed" by the death. Bereavement's etymology means the sense of having had someone precious stolen from you through death, and suggests that there is a justice issue involved in how we understand death. One may hear comments such as, "He died too soon" or, "she was too young." Some theologies support such statements; others view death as always tragic but hear a judgmental tone is such statements that suggest that the deceased deserved more than they got. "Mourning" refers to some sort of *shared response* to a death or loss. Funerals, or other public rituals, crying with another person are all shared responses to a loss and are expressions of mourning. In general, pastoral caregivers have limited opportunities to alter a person's grief once it's started, but they can have a profound impact on mourning. It is possible to do some work with children and adolescents (and their parents) prior to a grief experience, through such educational efforts. It is possible to help a person deal with their grief in healthy ways that promote moving through the experience without becoming "stuck" in it.

Finally, a word about who this chapter is aimed at and one of the chapter's biases. I have used the phrase, "pastoral caregiver" throughout this chapter to refer to whoever is helping the child or family member move through their grief and mourning. Within the Christian tradition, this person will in many cases be an ordained clergy person because that is who families turn to. Unless I explicitly indicate otherwise, I use "pastoral caregiver" to mean anyone – ordained or lay. Little that is in this chapter *must* be done by a member of the clergy; virtually all of it is rooted in my understanding of the baptismal vow to, "…seek and serve Christ in all persons…" (*Book of Common Prayer*, 1979, p. 305) rather than in anyone's ordination vow. Helping people move through grief and mourning is something that we do because someone is in pain.

HOW CHILDREN GRIEVE

Pastoral caregivers may encounter the statement, "We need to do something for the children" or the question, "What do we do for the children?" after there has been a serious death in the family. Before stepping in with a problem-solving approach, pastoral caregivers do better to step back and recognize in this question the *adult's* feelings of helplessness. Children are awfully resilient, and many times grieve very well when the adults themselves are grieving well. It is much easier for the adults to focus on "how the children are doing" rather than move through some of their own emotions. Healing comes through helping the adults in many cases – and the children will heal as well.

One way to "help the children" and relieve the adults' sense of helplessness is an understanding of how children and teenagers grieve and mourn differently than adults do. When someone can normalize what the *adults* are experiencing, many adults report that the children are doing better! A child of any age will grieve; even an infant has the capacity to experience feelings. Smaller children won't be able to name their feeling, but this is different than viewing them as someone who doesn't feel. One of the basic differences between children and adults is language, and being able to name what is going on "inside." Not having a way to name what one is feeling makes it hard to get one's hands on it and deal with it – so is more likely to come out in behavior. This is partly why young children "act out" their feelings; what cannot be expressed in words comes out in actions. This gives rise to what is sometimes called, "the terrible twos." Any two-year old is full of emotions, but they do not yet have the words to express them, or the experience of seeing such feelings appropriately modeled, and so their feelings are expressed in behaviors. These actions can be playful or destructive.

Children express much of their lives through play or other creative outlets (such as drawing). After someone in the family has died, their feelings may come out through enacting a funeral, or having imaginary friends and playmates die, or through drawing pictures in which the deceased either figures prominently – or is conspicuously absent. Adults sometimes label such play as macabre or a sign that something is "wrong." Helping them understand that this is normal, and even encouraging them to join in the play, can go a long way towards helping them.

At times, the actions of children turn destructive, either towards themselves or others. Bereavement should not be used as an excuse to tolerate unacceptable behavior. Sometimes parents give children "a break" because they are grieving; however, part of what adults can teach about grieving is that behavioral expectations remain in force. If it wasn't acceptable behavior before, it shouldn't be after death. If the family's previous system of discipline isn't working, the pastoral caregiver may want to suggest one of the many books on the market designed to help parents with behavior modification.   If such behavioral modification continues to be ineffective, it may well be time to refer the family for family therapy. Sending only the child or teenager to a therapist creates the aura that that individual has a problem (their behavior) and that it is up to them to correct it. The family must live with the impact of the behavior, and ought to be involved in developing a new way of life.

The second significant difference between how children and adults grieve differently is the relative amount of time spent grieving acutely. Simply put, children grieve in "doses." That is, they grieve or mourn intensely for brief periods (minutes to and hour), and over a longer time span than adults (up to a year in some cases). Adults generally weep or move as if they are "in shock" for days or weeks after the death of a loved one, and the pain generally eases to a dull but constant ache after that. Children will seemingly "do fine," which adults sometimes mistakenly name a lack of love for the deceased, and then grieve briefly, and then appear fine, repeating this cycle over and over. Normalizing this for adults is one way to help surviving adults deal with their sense of helplessness. Teach them to let the kids grieve in their own way, and at their own speed, rather than expecting them to grieve like an adult.

As children mature, they begin to grieve and mourn more like adults. Most of this section has been written with school-age children in mind, and now it's time to recall that a middle adolescent will look less like a child and more like an adult – but not always. Figuring out "where they're at" is the challenge of working with children and adolescents. A major event in someone's life, such as a death, can also lead a person to regress developmentally for a period of time. If the emotions are strong enough, a fairly mature 17-year old may function like a 12-year old for a time. Rather than coming to help the child or teenager with a text-book solution to their grief problem, a more helpful approach is to assess how the child is functioning and what they need. It's also worth remembering that an immature adult won't necessarily function in an "age appropriate" way – not all adolescents are teenagers!

Grief in children and adults can mimic the signs of depression. Feelings like sadness, a lack of appetite, and similar feelings which the grieving person regards as typical given what they have just been through, are generally expressions of normal grieving and mourning. When such symptoms are still present in adults and older teens more than 2 months after an event, they generally warrant attention by a medical or mental health professional. Some feelings that are not typical of normal grief and mourning include the following: feeling guilty about something other than what one might have done or not done at the time of death; thoughts of death, other than being "better off" if they were dead, or that the should have died with the deceased; hallucinations, other than hearing or momentarily seeing, the deceased person; being unable to function with the normal routines of daily living; ongoing feelings of worthlessness (DSM-IV-TR, 2000, pp. 313, 314). When any of the foregoing items are present, it is definitely worth referring the person to a mental health professional.

One item worth noting is that it is not abnormal for a survivor to hear or transiently see someone who has died – such experiences can be normalized by pastoral caregivers with a comment like, "Oh, it happens all the time! Would you like to talk about it?" Some adolescents want to talk about such experiences, but are afraid of how adults might react if they do so. In one recent study, 37 % of adolescents hospitalized with mental health problems reported experiencing "communication with someone who has died"; among non-hospitalized adolescents, 17%-19% reported such experiences (Grossoehme, 2000). Such experiences can be door-openers to deeper conversations about what the adolescent believes about what happens when someone dies, and provides an opportunity for the pastoral caregiver to share what their tradition has to offer in such situations. One gift the pastoral caregiver can provide is the non-judgmental, emotionally safe place to explore what the child or adolescent is going through.

There may be times where the pastoral caregiver is aware that a child or teenager is having a difficult time after a death (or might reasonably be expected to have a difficult time) but may find it awkward to meet with the child for the first time. This may be the case with teenagers who are especially reserved and who may fear what might happen "meeting with the pastor." There are several excellent workbooks available (listed in the annotated bibliography at the end of this chapter) for children and adolescents. These workbooks may be given to the child with an acknowledgement that the pastoral caregiver is aware of their loss, and wonders if this might be helpful to them as they go through strong feelings. One of the advantages of these workbooks is that they are flexible – one can write, draw or paint one's way through them, and the pages don't have to be done in order. Adolescents' reluctance to use the book has frequently been overcome when they are told that they only need to do the pages that interest them at the time, and that they don't have to "finish" the book in a set time limit.

One of the best ways to use these books is to do them in "doses." With younger children, it might take the form of brief but regular visits to their house to play and draw with them, and work through the book a page or so at a time, with frequent "breaks" (days) between visits. With teenagers, one might contract to meet once every week or so, and have the teenager bring their workbook with them. They can be invited to share only what they feel comfortable sharing, and using this as a jumping-off point for further pastoral conversations about what they are going through and how their relationship with God and the other survivors is going.

A THEOLOGY OF DEATH

Pastoral caregivers are not likely to be asked about what they, personally, believe happens to us when we die – unless the answer is of great importance to the person asking, in which case, it is not the time to stutter and stammer or search for an answer, nor is it time to quote Biblical platitudes. However, the way in which each pastoral caregiver answers that question for her- or him- self underlies and determines much about how they will care for grieving children and adolescents. It is highly desirable to understand one's own beliefs and how they inform one's actions before there is a need to act. An excellent example of this is *The Hope of Heaven* (Helen Oppenheimer, 1988). Reading other theologian's responses to these issues can also be helpful; several are included in the bibliography of this chapter.

What follows is an example of how I have worked this issue out for myself at present; it is not necessarily "right" or "best", it's simply "mine." I offer it here as a structural example, and to encourage the reader to develop one of your own. There is no "soul" that is a separate but hidden part of us that is pre-existent and that "goes" to heaven (or hell). What lives in us is the spirit, and which at baptism was celebrated and recognized as God's own spirit; when it no longer enlivens our body, it returns to God's presence. God receives all events into God's own being, holding them, and out of them, offering new possibilities for each person so that they might more fully live as God intended them. This is certainly true in life; God takes what I am becoming and offers me new possibilities to grow out of what might politely be called, "my issues" and live a life more filled with agape love. In death, the spirit which returns to God continues to live; in God' being, how could it be otherwise? If the spirit lives, then it must also continue to grow and continue being made more nearly as God intended it to be. Christians have this promise that God is faithful; just as Jesus was resurrected to life, so shall each one of us be resurrected to life as well. If the spirit is alive, then it makes sense to pray for the person whose spirit has returned to God; it may even make sense to pray *to* that spirit, and ask for intercession on our behalf.

In this theology, God does not "will" or cause the death of anyone. God experiences not only the sadness and pain of the survivors, but experiences God's own sense of loss. God gathers these feelings, and out of them offers the world opportunities for healing.

RITUALS
Role of Children in funerals

Pastoral caregivers may be looked to by family members about the wisdom or the value of bringing children to a funeral. Their questions may arise out of a sense that a toddler may not "get" anything out of the experience; or from a sense of helplessness about responding to the child's questions or needs; fear that the younger child will act out; or other reasons. The person the child or adolescent lives with probably knows them best, but from a pastoral perspective, there is almost no reason not to include them. Ideally, they would attend at any age. If they are old enough to love, they are old enough to grieve – they just need to do it in their own way. However, if a child clearly says that they do not want to be present, this is something that needs to be listened to, and probably honored. If the parent or guardian does not feel comfortable enough, or energetic enough, to talk with them about what it is that they would be giving up, the pastoral caregiver may want to offer to have that conversation with the child, so that they are making a more informed decision.

The contents of this conversation will differ according to the faith traditions of each family. It is worth thinking about the reasons for participating in any ritual, and a matter of selecting one's words in a way that is appropriate to the child's age. At a simple level, participation in a ritual is an educational experience for a child. It's a way of "saying" that when something major happens (an older person we love dies), "This is how we show our sadness and how much we miss them." Any death, but especially the death of someone a child strongly loved or a death which is sudden, can create a sense of chaos in life. The flurry of activity near the end of a person's life may involve travel to be with them, multiple trips to a hospital or nursing home. School and or work schedules, and a child's time with peers are frequently disrupted. The funeral ritual, whatever form it takes, is one way to affirm that there is, despite seeming evidence to the contrary, order in the universe. Children, and even if they don't always admit it, adolescents, do like order and structure. Attending a funeral is one corrective to their feeling a lack of order and structure in life. One way to build some structure for them to hold on to is to invite them to participate in the service in a way that is reasonable for their abilities. Some adolescents may want to do a reading from the Scriptures, or poetry. Younger children may be given a concrete task to do at a certain time, such as standing at the graveside holding a bag of dirt that the minister will use to throw on the casket; or holding flowers for a parent. The important thing is to match the task with their developmental level, and to give them the opportunity to decline if they wish.

Rituals also are ways in which the faith community teaches its beliefs to the young. How closely will a four-year old listen to a sermon or eulogy? Probably not much, but they will absorb that the pastor in the Baptist church talked about people going to heaven to be with Jesus when they die. And experiencing the "tone" of the words spoken will communicate more to them about grief, love, and religious beliefs than the words themselves. Rituals are part of the mourning process because they are public expressions of feeling. Without using words, they are a way of saying to the child or adolescent, "You are not alone. We're sad too, and it's okay to feel what you're feeling. And this is what we believe about God in the face of death and sadness." Rituals provide a way to create community, so that the child doesn't think they are the only ones going through these feelings. Children learn appropriate ways to grieve through such means.

Funeral for a pet

This ritual may be adapted to suit the situation. To engage as many senses as possible in the experience, the rite includes a balloon launch. At some time prior to the service, the officiant provides a Mylar balloon (that is plain on at least on side) to the child, and invites them to write a letter or message on it. What they write is limited only by their imagination: it might be as simple as "I miss you" to a letter, or a drawing of the animal. This balloon is then launched by the child near the conclusion of the service. The rite itself is Christian and draws on the language of the Episcopal Church's *Book of Common Prayer* (1979, pp. 491-502). The officiant may be the parent, or an older sibling, or even the sibling closest to the animal. The pastoral caregiver may make this rite available to them as a guideline, suggesting how they might refine it to meet their needs. In some cases, the pastoral caregiver may be asked to be the officiant. This may be a sign of the family's desire for healing, and their need for someone whose energy is not so tied to grieving to step in and help them mourn.

In memory of N.
For thousands of years, dogs have been people's best and most loyal friends. The first drawings done by people show that the dog was the first domesticated pet. When the Earthly life of a dog is over, the grief and sadness are no less real than any other loss. God's promise to us is that all flesh shall rise to be with God. This includes all living things – dogs as well as people.

A Reading from the book of Isaiah (40: 1,2,5): "Comfort, comfort my people, says your God. Speak tenderly and say that your time of struggle and pain is ended, and the glory of LORD shall be revealed, and all flesh shall see it together, for the mouth of the LORD has spoken it."

Let us pray: As the mother of Moses laid him in the reeds at the river's edge, entrusting him wholly to your care because she could no longer keep him safe, so we entrust N. to your care. Keep him safe in your love until we come. We thank you for the good times we had with him, and for the special place he will always hold in M.'s heart. [all say firmly,] AMEN.

Everyone that God gives to me will come to me, says the LORD; I will never turn away anyone. He who raised Jesus Christ from the dead will also give life to our bodies, and those of all living creatures. My heart therefore is glad. In the sure and certain hope of resurrection to eternal life, we commit N. to your n3ever failing love and care. May the launching of this balloon carry our sadness, our love, and our trust that we will see him again with you.

[As the balloon is released by N's owner, the officiant says the following:] May *the LORD bless N. and keep him, the LORD make his face to shine upon him and be gracious to him, the LORD lift up his countenance upon him and give him peace. [all say firmly,]* AMEN.

Miscarriages, Stillbirths, and terminated pregnancies

These are difficult issues because they "aren't supposed to happen" (even though about one pregnancy in three ends in miscarriage) and aren't talked about openly in many circles. That silence is even stricter when it involves an adolescent, to whom this "wasn't supposed to happen in the first place." In many cases, the pastoral caregiver may be the last to know, largely because of shame that the adolescent or family might be feeling, and which especially might keep them from talking about it with anyone connected so overtly to God. The pastoral caregiver may need to help the adolescent and parent(s) disentangle the many different feelings that may be at play here – anger, shame, and grief. These events are deaths, and there is a need to ritualize the event in order to validate the possibilities that existed, and move into the future that is ahead. Until the grief is acknowledged and mourning can take place, it will be very difficult for the adolescent or family members to heal emotionally and perhaps relationally.

It is the adolescent whose grief is the focus; they should be the ones offered the option of having a ritual or funeral, though of course it may then be wise to obtain parental consent. Whether anyone else attends ought also to be the choice of the adolescent; it may or may not include parents. Outdoor settings are good because they allow for more creative rituals. Planning the ritual can be handled much the same as one would work with a family to plan a funeral for an elderly adult. Inquiring if they had picked out a name for the child, and using that name, is a way to make the child's brief life real. Exactly what is said or done in the ritual is largely determined by the beliefs of the adolescent's faith group, and the joint creativity of the teenager and pastoral caregiver. If an unborn child, however early in pregnancy, carries the same sense of personhood as an adult, then the ritual may look very much like a funeral common to that tradition. If not, then the ritual may be more one expressing sadness and healing for the teenager, and for the future.

Engaging as many senses as possible in the experience helps the rite "speak" on different levels. Writing a letter to the child (prior to the ritual) has been described as "the hardest thing I ever did –and one of the best" by several women who have done this. The letter may be read during the ritual, burned, or be written on a Mylar balloon that this launched at the ritual. Magician's "flash paper", obtainable from magic supply stores, burns dramatically, leaves no ash or residue, is safe to use indoors, and can be used to meaningfully in these situations without it becoming "hokey" for the teenager. In each of these, the pastoral caregiver can talk about releasing one's words to God (or the Higher Power) and to the child if that is consistent with one's beliefs, and of flame being symbolic of cleansing and purifying.

A simple ritual might consist of meeting outside in a garden (at the church or in the adolescent's backyard), and beginning with an opening prayer (for the unborn child if that is consistent with the tradition's theology, and certainly for the adolescent); including a reading from Scripture and some short comments appropriate to one's theology; followed by a closing prayer commending the child to God and concluding with the balloon launch or burning of the letter and burial of the ashes. If it's known, the child's name may be used (even using names for both genders – Kathryn-or-Peter –as if a single name may be meaningful). This basic structure can be adapted to suit the situation and the theology deemed appropriate.

Guided imagery

Guided imagery is something which may be offered to children and adolescents in special cases. If someone is having a particularly difficult time and was not ready or not able to attend the funeral, this may be used to help them prepare for visiting the gravesite for the first time. A teenager may not have been able to say something important to a peer who was killed in a car accident. It may also be used when an adolescent has experienced a miscarriage or stillbirth, or terminated a pregnancy. The possibilities that guided imagery may address are many. Some caution is in order when using this technique. Persons who are being guided are very relaxed and very suggestible during this; the power held by the Guide should never be taken lightly or abused. Guided imagery isn't a solution, but a means to one. It is necessary for the Guide to talk with the child or adolescent about their experience afterwards.

The example given below is a guided imagery developed to help a younger adolescent prepare to visit her father's grave for the first time since he was killed in a work accident. She was feeling guilty for not being able to attend the funeral (because she was so distraught), nor go to the grave; she wanted to go and yet was anxious about it. The following plan was developed: the guided imagery would be used one Friday; her mother and brother and she would follow the Sunday ritual they had prior to the Dad's death and attend church, eat at a particular restaurant, and then drive to the cemetery. They would discuss the experience with their pastoral caregiver the next day.

A quiet location with a comfortable chair was chosen for the Guided imagery. In the induction phase, the adolescent was instructed to relax her toes, and then her feet, followed by her legs up to the knees and then up to the waist. She was then instructed to relax her fingers, hands, arms, the elbow, and then to her shoulders. Progressive body relaxation was completed by telling her to relax the muscles in her lower back and moving up to her neck, forehead, cheeks, and jaw. After several deep breaths, she was told to picture herself standing at the top of the staircase with ten steps leading down; the guide would count them as they went down, and with each step down she would be more relaxed.

You're going to imagine making a trip to the cemetery to visit your father's grave for the first time. Who would you like to come with you on this trip? Would you be more comfortable with others or by yourself?...[periods indicate a silence of 5-10 seconds unless otherwise indicated] Gather anyone with you that you want to go with, and walk out of yourself and into the car...see yourself being driven to the cemetery...what conversation do you want to have in the car? Do you want silence?...Pay attention to your feeling as you drive along – are you feeling mad, glad, sad or scared?...Imagine yourself arriving at the cemetery...and driving in...and pulling up by the gravesite...when you're ready, open the car door and get out...Do you walk by yourself or do you hold hands with others?...Notice what the cemetery is like. Is it peaceful? Do you hear anything as you walk?...when you reach the grave, you can stand there, or sit down...What do you want to do with your time here?...Do you want to say anything to your father?...to God?...[a lengthy pause at this time is appropriate]...When you're ready to leave, see yourself standing up. Is there anything you want to say to those with you? When you are ready, walk back towards the car. Pay attention to how you feel – mad, glad, sad, scared...imagine you and the others getting into the car and driving towards home...as you arrive home, what do you wan to say or do when you first get there?...As you reach home and get out of the car, you are standing again at the bottom of a staircase with ten steps going up. We'll climb each one, counting as we go, and when you get to the top, you'll feel light and ready to open your eyes and come back to this room.

Silence should reign until the person opens their eyes and returns to the room. The Guide can help them talk about the experience – what were they feeling, and how are they feeling about visiting the gravesite for the first time now. Talking about what was the most difficult part of the imagery can be useful as well, to identify any problem areas that the pastoral caregiver might want to address. In this example, a follow-up visit with the pastoral caregiver was arranged for after the visit to the cemetery to talk about how this visit helped her begin to mourn for the first time.

Alterations may be made to fit the situation. The induction or relaxation phase is useable in most cases, with only what happens at the bottom of the staircase changing. In cases where there are unfinished words to say to someone, or in cases of miscarriage, the adolescent may be guided to a "special place" where they feel safe and comfortable – and where they can be joined by the person who has died, and interact with them. This allows the person to say what still needs to be said, and to reinforce the reality of the person's life, and their death. For reasons that should be obvious, guided imagery is not suitable for persons who are too easily suggestible, or who have difficulty differentiating reality from fantasy. In such cases, the pastoral caregiver can refer them to a mental health professional who can work together with the pastoral caregiver on these topics.

SUMMARY

Pastoral caregivers are in a prime position to interpret the unique ways in which children mourn and grieve to both the grieving child or adolescent, and to the adults in the family constellation. In particular, they can be of assistance in teaching what is developmentally appropriate at different ages, in helping normalize a child or teenager's feelings and experience, and in helping well-intentioned adults give the child or adolescent the freedom and space to grieve and mourn in their own unique ways. The younger the child, the fewer words they have to talk about their feelings, and the more likely they are to grieve and mourn through play, and to grieve in "doses" (short, intense bouts of strong feeling over a long time frame) rather than with high intensity for a brief period, tapering off over time as adults generally do. Related to this concept is the role of ritual, something that is particularly meaningful when working with children and adolescents. Rituals may be created to assist in mourning and grieving any type of loss, and may take place in a worship space, or at some other site that has meaning for the child. Rituals are particularly the province of the pastoral caregiver, as opposed to others who might be helping family members cope with a loss, as rituals are what mediate between experience and the numinous. Other helpful ways of assisting with a child or teenagers' feelings and beliefs around loss include workbooks, creative endeavors such as writing or artwork, and playfully being with them while allowing them to ask or respond to questions about the loss.

ANNNOTATED BIBLIOGRAPHY

Allan, J.T. (2002) *A Theology of God-Talk*. Binghamton, NY: Haworth Press. *Allan begins with the language commonly used about God around death ("God needed another angel") and views it from the perspective of mythic language – words that communicate a truth about God. He describes pastoral responses to the kind of beliefs and pain that such comments represent.*

Biondi M. & Picardi A. (1996). Clinical Biological Aspects of Bereavement and Loss-induced Depression: A Reappraisal. *Pschyother Psychosom, 65,* 229-245. *A technical article on the relationship between grief and psychiatric illness.*

Book of Common Prayer. (1979). New York: Seabury Press. *The liturgical prayer book of the Episcopal Church. Has outlines for funerals; the Commendation prayers may easily be adapted for use in situations such as miscarriage and stillbirth; has suggested Scriptural readings from both Hebrew and Greek Scriptues.*

Clark GT, Cole G & Enzle S. (1990) Complicated Grief Reactions in Women Who Were Sexually Abused in Childhood. *Journal of Psychosocial Oncology, 8,* 87-97. *A technical article on the relationship between grief and psychiatric illness.*

Emswiler, M. & Emswiler, J.P.(2000). *Guiding Your Children Through Grief.* New York:Bantam Books. *An excellent resource for anyone working with grieving children and adolescents. The chapter on creating "holding communities" – safe places for children to express and be themselves – is particularly important for pastoral caregivers. There is also a section on the particular needs of stepfamilies which is helpful. This book is intended for parents, and may be given to them by pastoral caregivers; it is also a "must read" for caregivers themselves.*

Grollman, E.A. (1987). *A Scrapbook of Memories.* Batesville, IN: Batesville Management Services. *A short workbook and coloring book for younger school age children to help them express their feelings after a death in the family.*

Grossoehme, D.H. (1999). *The Pastoral Care of Children.* Binghamton, NY: Haworth Press. *A text for clergy and lay pastoral caregivers who work infrequently with children; the chapters on theological reflection (dealing with the 'Why?' question), death and dying, and ritual may be especially helpful.*

Grossoehme, D.H. (2000). *Co-morbidity of bereavement and other mental illness among psychiatrically hospitalized adolescents.* Unpublished manuscript.

Oppenheimer, Helen. (1988). *The Hope of Heaven.* Cambridge, MA: Cowley Press. *A well-written account by a lay theologian about a scripturally sound, authentically Christian vision of eternal life, stripped away from the cultural accretions that color modern ideas. An excellent resource for thinking theological about death and eternal life.*

Shavatt, D. & Shavatt, E. (2001). *My Grieving Journey Book.* New York: Paulist Press. *Intended for older school-aged children (pre-teenagers), this workbook combines text which validates and normalizes children's feelings and allows for its expression through drawing and remembering.*

Traisman, E.S. (1992). *Fire in My Heart, Ice in My Veins.* Omaha, NE: Centering Corporation. *The title says it all. This is a book for adolescents who are troubled with strong and often conflicting feelings after the death of someone special. This book may be used following deaths of family, peers, and with miscarriages. There is a minimum of text; the words point to topics and feelings and invite their expression through stories, poetry or artwork, depending on the adolescent's interest and skills.*

Ward H. & Wild, J. (1995). *Human Rites.* London: Mowbray Press. *A book full of rituals for painful (and celebratory) experiences that are part of being human, and on which many religious traditions are silent. The rites may be used as written, or adapted for a specific situation.*

Wolterstorff, N. (1987). *Lament for a Son.* Grand Rapids, WI: Eerdman's Publishing. *One father's response to the death of his son; this text represents one way of making sense of tragic death and thinking through one's theology of death and the creation of meaning.*

About The Author

Daniel H. Grossoehme, M.Div., BCC, Staff Chaplain, Cincinnati Children's Hospital (College Hill Campus), Cincinnati, Ohio. Chaplain Grossoehme is the author of *The Pastoral Care of Children* (Haworth Press) and numerous journal articles on religious issues and pediatric healthcare, especially mental health and bereavement issues. He is an Episcopal priest and board-certified chaplain; Area Certification Chair, Association of Professional Chaplains; Immediate Past President, Assembly of Episcopal Healthcare Chaplains.

Chapter 13
Youth Aggression & Bullying:
Challenges for Pastoral Care Workers

by Conor McGuckin,
School of Psychology
Dublin Business School
Dublin 2
Republic of Ireland

&

Christopher Alan Lewis
School of Psychology
University of Ulster at Magee College
Londonderry
Northern Ireland
BT48 7JL

Address correspondence to: Conor Mc Guckin, School of Psychology, Dublin Business School, Balfe Street, Dublin 2, Republic of Ireland

Introduction
A study of over 15,000 6th-10th graders estimated that approximately 3.7 million youths engage in, and more than 3.2 million are victims of moderate or serious bullying each year in the US (Nansel, et al., 2001). While between 1994 and 1999 there were 253 violent deaths in school in the US, 51 casualties were the result of multiple death events. Bullying is often a factor in such schools-related deaths (Anderson, et al. 2001). These and other statistics clearly attest to the problem of bullying within US schools. However, bullying in schools and communities is an international problem and is present in most societies (Smith et al., 1999). For example, reported suicides of school children in Australia (Rigby, 1997), England (Marr & Field, 2001), Japan (Morita, Soeda, Soeda, & Taki, 1999), Ireland (O'Moore, 2000), Scotland (Henderson, 2002), Northern Ireland (Bell, 2001), and Norway (Olweus, 1993), have focused attention on the possible contribution of adverse peer relations.

Whilst the majority of research to date that has explored bully\victim problems has been European-based, there has been a recent upsurge in the level of community and academic attention directed towards this phenomenon in the US. Traditionally, the focus of community and academic concern in the US has been upon violence in schools, with the aim of reducing the number of violent incidents and deaths along with a reduction in the availability of provocatively aggressive instruments (e.g., guns, knives, catapults). Subsequent to recent violent events in some US schools (e.g., the Columbine High School shootings), attention has been directed towards exploring 'low-level' aggression (e.g., bullying) in the hope that tackling the roots of violent culture in schools may lead to a reduction in all types of violent acts.

Over the last twenty years, the challenge of understanding bully\victim problems has been taken up by an international field of researchers drawn from a wide range of cogent disciplines and has resulted in a burgeoning research literature. This work has largely focused on defining the subject matter (What is bullying?), describing the various social actors (Who is involved?), describing the effects of bullying (What are the effects?), and developing intervention programmes (What can we do about it?). A variety of different approaches aimed at tackling bullying behavior are described. Perhaps surprisingly, little specific attention has focused on the role of 'religion' in terms of either a research variable or as a community resource. Such omissions are particularly striking given that first, the 'religious variable' is well documented as a protective factor with regards to young people engaging in anti-social behavior (Francis, 2001), and second, the pastoral role, especially among young people, that is played by churches within most communities.

The aim of the present chapter is to provide answers to questions about bully\victim problems and thereby provide an accessible resource for parents, teachers, clergy, and those involved in pastoral work with children.

What is bullying?

Whilst there is no one standard operational definition of bullying, the writing of Olweus (1993) has been influential. Olweus originally defined bullying as: "A student is being bullied or victimized when he or she is exposed, repeatedly and over time, to negative actions on the part of one or more other students." (p. 9). Clarifying the meaning of the expression 'negative actions', Olweus asserts that a negative action is when someone intentionally inflict or attempts to inflict, injury or discomfort upon another, basically what is implied in the definition of aggressive behavior (Olweus, 1973). Such negative actions, according to Olweus (1993), may be carried out by direct (physical) means (e.g., hitting, pushing, kicking) and indirect (verbal) means (e.g., threats, taunts, name calling). Indeed, it is also possible to carry out such negative actions without the use of physical contact or words (e.g., social ostracism).

Olweus (1999a, 1999b) encapsulates the following three main criteria that capture the essence of bullying behavior: i) It is aggressive behavior or intentional 'harm doing'; ii). It is carried out 'repeatedly and over time'; iii). In an interpersonal relationship it is characterized by an 'imbalance of power'. Whilst the second of these criteria emphasises the repeated nature of bullying behaviors, Olweus (1999a) does concede that, in some circumstances, just *one* serious occurrence of a negative action could be regarded as bullying. However, he emphasises the point that: "The intent is to exclude occasional non-serious negative actions that are directed against one person at one time and against another on a different occasion." (Olweus, 1999a, p. 11). Indeed, Olweus asserts that it would also be possible to add a fourth criterion; that the bullying behavior often occurs without any apparent provocation. Furthermore, it has also been reported that when pupils are asked to define bullying, they too offer these three parameters (Arora & Thompson, 1987).

Who is involved?

Boys not girls?

There is a marked difference in reports of the bullying activities of the sexes: boys are involved in bullying behaviors more often than girls. For example, Olweus (1999b) reports that in his seminal large scale Norwegian study, boys conducted a large part of the bullying to which both girls and boys were subjected (60% and 80% respectively). Rigby and Slee (1999) report similar findings from their Australian studies (N = approximately 38,000). In a parsimonious summation of the research evidence in this area, Olweus (1994) concluded that:

> *"Many more boys than girls bully others ... a relatively large percentage of girls report that they are mainly bullied by boys ... there is a somewhat higher percentage of boys who are victims of bullying ... bullying with physical means is less common among girls ... girls typically use more subtle and indirect ways of harassment such as slandering, spreading rumours, intentional exclusion from the group and manipulation of friendship relations (e.g., depriving a girl of her best friends) ... It is the younger and weaker students that are most exposed to bullying." (p. 27).*

Boys and girls!

Historically, the study of female aggression and bullying behaviors has received little, if any, theoretical or empirical attention. It has only been in recent years that the concept of female aggression as a phenomenon in itself has been recognised as a vital component in the study of aggression and bullying. Two major factors have been reported as leading to this omission of females from the theoretical and empirical agenda of the aggression paradigm: i) that females were not aggressive, and that ii) early theoretical and empirical work in the area was driven from a 'male-centric' perspective.

As a first major factor in the exclusion of females from the theoretical and empirical study of aggression and bullying, females were not actually viewed as aggressive. For example, at the start of the 1960's, Buss (1961) held the view that aggression was a typically male phenomenon and that females were so seldom aggressive that female aggression was not worth the trouble to study. This view was reflected in Frodi, Macauley, and Thome's (1977) review of 314 studies on human aggression, in which it was found that whilst 54% of the studies concerned male only samples, only 8% were concerned with female only samples. With regards to bullying behaviors, Olweus (1978) was of a similar opinion to that of Buss (1961). Believing that bullying occurred so rarely among female adolescents, Olweus excluded girls as participants from his early research studies into bully\victim problems. Later, however, he changed his opinion and did include girls in his research studies (e.g., Olweus, 1986).

Such a view that females were not aggressive would appear to have been misguided. According to Björkqvist (1994), there is in fact no reason to believe that females should be less hostile and less prone to getting involved in conflicts than males. Björkqvist (1994) argues that whilst we can reject the notion of a direct hormonal (e.g., testosterone) link to sex differences in aggression, there is still the potential for the role of learning mechanisms in the development of sex differences in aggression. By being physically weaker, Björkqvist (1994) postulates that females simply have to develop means other than physical in order to obtain successful outcomes. Thus, we should not expect females to develop and use the same aggressive strategies for attaining their goals as males do.

The second factor regarding the absence of females from the early research in this area was that such research activities were conducted primarily by males and that aggression was conceptualised as 'male' and 'physical'. Björkqvist and Niemelä (1992), for example, point out that most studies on human aggression have been conducted by males, and even when females have been the object of study, aggression has been operationalised in typically male fashions - usually as direct physical aggression. Indeed, alerting us to the potential inadequacy of some research methodologies employed in the area, Björkqvist and Niemelä (1992) highlight that in the case of observational techniques to study childhood aggression in schoolyards, only direct physical aggression can clearly be distinguished by this methodology (however, it should also be noted that Tapper and Boulton [2002] have recently used electronic equipment to covertly record direct and indirect bullying behaviors among school pupils at play). Björkqvist and Niemelä (1992) concluded that there was little wonder that Maccoby and Jacklin's (1974) seminal review of research in the area considered it self-evident that males were more aggressive than females - the review was almost exclusively based on observational studies in kindergarten and school playgrounds, and rough-and-tumble play was regarded as aggression in many of the studies reviewed.

How do they bully?
Recent research has moved forward from the mistaken assumption that girls are not aggressive to the more realistic scenario that whilst there is a *quantitative similarity* between boys and girls in the amount of aggression displayed, there may be a *qualitative difference* in the methods employed by each sex. Regarding quantitative differences in aggression, Björkqvist (1994) points out that whilst there is room for potential misinterpretation in the conclusions drawn from Maccoby

and Jacklin's (1974) review, later reviews of sex differences in aggression (e.g., for example, Björkqvist & Niemelä, 1992) are much more cautious, and mention sex differences in terms of 'quality' rather than 'quantity'. Indeed, Björkqvist and Österman (1999) report that aggressive behavior (including bullying behavior) occurs more between opponents of the same sex than between opponents of different sexes. For example, Hyde's (1984) review of sex differences in aggression found that whilst only 5% of the variation in aggression scores could be explained by inter-sex differences, 95% could be explained by intra-sex variation, or coincidence.

This qualitative difference in aggressive strategies utilised by females reflects research findings suggesting that we should think more in terms of a 'direct-indirect' dichotomy of bullying behaviors. Such findings come from the revised view of the area from a less male-centric perspective. In conjunction with the discovery of a more pronounced qualitative difference between the sexes, age and developmental trends in aggressive strategy choice between the sexes have also been discovered. These key issues are now explored.

As has already been discussed, theoretical and empirical research in this area had traditionally been guided and conducted from a somewhat male-centric perspective. Such an approach has been shown to be somewhat lopsided by focussing almost exclusively on 'direct' (overt) bullying behaviors such as hitting and pushing, or verbal aggression, that are more typical and characteristic of boys and their peer interaction styles (Björkqvist, Lagerspetz, & Kaukianen, 1992; Lagerspetz, Björkqvist, & Peltonen, 1988). If we limit aggression to such physical strategies only, then it is certainly true that males are more aggressive than females, at least in Western societies (Björkqvist, 1994). Anthropological studies (For example Cook, 1992) have shown that this does not hold for all cultures. Whilst relatively few girls exhibit such overt aggressive behaviors (for example, Crick & Dodge, 1994), little has been known about the aggressive methods employed by girls. In attempting to rectify this situation, Björkqvist and Österman (1999) report that in the second half of the 1980's their research group became convinced that the traditional view of sex differences in aggressive behavior, suggesting that females display very little aggressiveness, was basically incorrect (see Björkqvist, 1994, for a review). Rather than a quantitative difference between the sexes, they felt it might be more of a question regarding quality, with girls perhaps displaying their aggressiveness in different ways from boys. In line with this thought, recent research has focussed on a more 'indirect' (covert), relationally-oriented form of aggression identified as more characteristic of girls. That differs markedly from the direct forms of aggression previously studied (for example, Lagerspetz, Björkqvist, & Peltonen, 1988). As opposed to direct forms of bullying with "… relatively open attacks on a victim …" (Olweus, 1993, p. 10) such indirect bullying has been defined by Richardson (1999) as "… behaviour intended to harm another living being without confronting the target, through other people or objects." (p. 30). Alternatively, it has been defined as "… harm delivered circuitously rather than face-to-face." (Archer & Parker, 1994, p. 109).

Aggressors who employ direct strategies are easily identifiable because noxious stimuli are delivered during direct confrontation with the victim. Examples of such direct strategies include hitting, pushing, or kicking the victim. On the other hand, indirect strategies involve the circuitous delivery of noxious stimuli, with the aggressor attempting to inflict harm while avoiding association with the aggressive act or engaging in direct confrontation with the victim (Richardson & Green, 1997a). Indirect aggressive strategies might involve denigrating the victim's character by spreading malicious rumours, destroying their property, or finding clandestine ways to make the victim 'look bad' (Crick, 1995).

Thus, whilst direct strategies are aimed at harming others through physical damage or the threat of such damage (e.g., hitting, kicking), indirect strategies are aimed at harming others through damage to their peer relationships or the threat of such damage (e.g., excluding a peer from their own play group).

Empirical studies have proffered support for this view of a qualitative difference in girls' bullying strategies. In a number of research reports from across the world, indirect\relational forms of bullying have been shown to be more typical of girls than boys (e.g., Ahmad & Smith, 1994). Whilst the notion of a 'direct-indirect' dichotomy is now widely recognized within the scientific community (Björkqvist, Lagerspetz, & Kaukianen, 1992; Lagerspetz, Björkqvist, & Peltonen, 1988).

The role of age?
According to Björkqvist, Lagerspetz, and Kaukiainen (1992) and Björkqvist, Österman, and Kaukiainen (1992), aggressive behaviors tend to appear in the following order, with gross aggressive strategies being gradually replaced by more refined strategies, over age: Stage 1 - Direct physical aggression, Stage 2 - Direct verbal aggression, Stage 3 - Indirect aggression

With regards to Stage 1, young children who lack, or have as yet to develop verbal skills, resort to direct physical aggression (e.g., hitting, kicking, biting). Verbal skills, when they develop, are quickly utilized not only for peaceful communication, but are also added to the child's repertoire of aggressive strategies (e.g., verbal threats, shouting) at Stage 2. At Stage 3, even more sophisticated strategies of aggression are made possible due to the development of social intelligence (e.g., scheming, backbiting). Thus, at this stage, there is the potential to adopt indirect strategies through which the target is attacked not directly, but circuitously through social manipulation, and whereby the aggressor attempts to remain unidentified and thus avoid counterattack (e.g., Archer & Parker, 1994; Lagerspetz, Björkqvist, & Peltonen, 1988; Richardson, 1999).

Goldstein (1999) reports that boys and girls differ little in bullying behaviors employed until about eight years of age. Starting around this age, girls become more indirect in bullying behaviors, a trend peaking around age 11 or 12 years of age. This trend is not reported to be apparent in boys until they are 15 years or older (Rivers & Smith, 1994). A number of studies have verified these trends. For example, in their study among 25 United Kingdom schools, Glover, Cartwright, Gough, and Johnson (1998) report that there was a shift from overt physical forms of bullying to more covert indirect forms. That is, bullying problems were continuing, but were changing in their nature and seriousness. Such findings support the model proposed by Björkqvist, Lagerspetz, and Kaukainen (1992) and Björkqvist, Österman, and Kaukiainen (1992) in that the use of indirect bullying strategies is dependent upon a certain degree of maturation that is required to manipulate the surrounding social environment. As girls have been found to develop language skills more quickly than boys (Maccoby & Jacklin, 1974), it is likely that they have the ability to employ such strategies at a much earlier age than boys. Examples of indirect bullying behaviors indicate that quite sophisticated social skills are required to manipulate social or friendship networks - for example; making friends jealous by being friendly with someone else, writing anonymous letters to the person they are upset with, criticising the person or revealing secrets about that person (Lagerspetz & Björkqvist, 1994).

Furthermore, although males and females experience hostile feelings to the same extent (Björkqvist, 1994), differences in genetic (e.g., physical strength) and environmental (e.g., cultural norms regarding female aggression) determinants may further lead females to a preference for indirect rather than direct forms of bullying. For both sexes, because physical forms of bullying are also dangerous to the perpetrator, they are likely to be replaced by verbal and indirect forms when the required skills have been developed. This supposition has been corroborated by empirical research (e.g., Björkqvist, Lagerspetz, & Kaukiainen, 1992).

In an attempt to further explain the age and sex differences presented in their model, Björkqvist, Österman, and Lagerspetz (1993) suggest that an effective way in which to view these is by the 'effect/danger ratio'. According to Björkqvist (1994):

"The *effect \ danger* ratio is an expression of the *subjective estimation of the likely consequences of an aggressive act*. The aggressor assesses the relation between a) *the effect of the intended strategy*, and b) *the danger involved, physical, psychological, or social*". The objective is to find a technique that will be effective (i.e., ensuring maximum effect on the victim), and, at the same time, incur to as little danger as possible." (p. 181).

Thus, the effect \ danger ratio implies that individuals will employ strategies that minimize personal danger while maximizing the effects of the aggressive response.

As noted earlier, whilst the use of physical aggression is effective, the aggressor, if unsuccessful, is also likely to get hurt (Björkqvist, 1994). By supplementing and\or eventually substituting physical means with verbal and\or indirect bullying strategies (i.e., movement from Stage 1 to Stage 3), the bully moves to a much more favourable effect\danger ratio. The more able the bully is at staying out of reach of the opponent, and at assessing the opponent's retaliation resources, the better he\she will be at avoiding counter-attack, thus minimizing risks to their safety. Therefore, a bully who is concerned about the risk of physical danger might find indirect strategies to be more appealing than direct strategies, because when executed successfully, indirect bullying strategies are highly effective and minimize risk to the bully.

To further explore the reasoning behind the differential use of direct and indirect strategies presented through the developmental model and effect/danger ratio, it is necessary to look at both the social structure of children's interaction networks and also their friendship patterns, as this provides the social structure in which direct and indirect aggression operate. Lagerspetz, Björkqvist, and Peltonen (1988) propose that networks in which the members are well-connected and know one another (i.e., dense social networks) inhibit the use of direct bullying strategies because the bully can be easily identified. Such networks may, conversely, facilitate indirect bullying behaviors (e.g., ostracizing group members, denigrating others' reputations) by providing the opportunity to efficiently (i.e., through the well-interconnected network) deliver harm circuitously to another member of the social network. The classroom, with it's dense social networks of highly interconnected children, could be viewed as a fertile ground for the development of indirect strategies. Whilst girls develop and favour dense social networks with well-defined social structures, the converse is true for boys' friendship patterns (Cairns, Perrin, & Cairns, 1985). Indeed, Besag (1989) suggests that, in their relationships, "… boys seek power and dominance, whereas girls need a sense of affirmation and affiliation, a feeling of belonging and shared intimacy expressed in exchanging confidences and gossip." (p. 40). From such differing emphases on the role of friendship patterns, and the fact that intra-sex aggression is more prevalent than inter-sex aggression (Björkqvist, 1994), boys typically bully in overt physical ways to effectively disrupt and damage the dominance hierarchies established and valued in their peer groups. Girls bully in social-relational ways (e.g., exclusion) that are specifically tailored to damage or destroy the social connections girls develop with their close peers (Owens, 1996). For the female bully, such methods would be more effective and suitable to the social structures and friendship patterns of girls' peer relationships at inflicting harm than would using physical aggression (Crick, 1995). Furthermore, these relationship-oriented strategies can also be accomplished with anonymity, thereby reducing the risk of harm to the aggressor - a highly economic effect\danger ratio (Björkqvist, Österman, & Lagerspetz, 1994). However, it has also been shown that when males are in a 'high density network', they are more interpersonally-oriented and may be more willing to express aggression indirectly than when in less dense networks (Green, Richardson, & Lago, 1996).

Thus, by using the notion of the effect\danger ratio to help explain sex differences and developmental trends in aggressive strategies, it becomes evident on a number of levels why boys and girls differ in their choices of bullying behaviors, and strategies to deliver these behaviors.

Who is involved?

When looking at the bullying phenomenon, common sense would indicate that not all of the actors in the phenomenon are partaking in the same role. Whilst quite obviously there is at least one bully and at least one victim in any bullying episode, recent research has diverted attention away from a 'dyadic' focus on the 'characteristics' of the bully and victim to the recognition of bullying as a 'whole-group process'. This is 'social' in nature, with all actors in the phenomenon playing some kind of role (e.g., Sutton & Smith, 1999).

Whilst all of these actors may not be present at an isolated bullying episode, the fact that bullying is 'repeated' in nature indicates that they are aware of what is going on (Salmivalli, Lagerspetz, Björkqvist, Österman, & Kaukiainen, 1996). Attention shall now turn to an analysis of this more fine-grained approach to the roles adopted by those involved in the bullying process.

Whilst the participant role approach of Salmivalli, Lagerspetz, Björkqvist, Österman, and Kaukiainen (1996) categorises pupil involvement under six distinct categories, the implicit taxonomy agreed upon by other researchers in the area categorises involvement under just four categories. However, it should be noted that whilst this taxonomy has just four distinct categories of involvement, provision is made for inclusion of *all* pupils in the social group (e.g., form class, year group) within one or other of these categories. The generally accepted category labels in this taxonomy are: bully, victim, bully\victim, and bystander (e.g., Kumpulainen, et al., 1998). The criteria for inclusion in each category are: Bullies (Pupils who bully other pupils but are not bullied themselves), Victims (Pupils who are victims but do not bully others), Bully\victims (Pupils who bully other pupils and are also bullied themselves), and Bystanders (Pupils who are neither bullied nor bully others).

Thus, as an alternative to the taxonomic system reflecting participant roles developed by Salmivalli, Lagerspetz, Björkqvist, Österman, and Kaukiainen (1996), it can be seen that this implicitly agreed upon taxonomy has great potential to categorise all pupils in a social group into one of four behavioral categories. Indeed, this taxonomic system has become the de facto standard for categorising the involvement of pupils in bully\victim problems.

What are the effects?

Bully\victim problems among school pupils may be viewed as transitory problems. However, some pupils choose a very permanent solution to such transitory problems - suicide (e.g., Macdonald, Bhavnani, Khan, & John, 1989). Whilst it is fortunately only a significant minority of victims that commit suicide, the links between involvement in bully\victim problems and the physical and psychological health of these pupils has been well researched and published. Such harm interferes with the social, academic, and emotional development of the pupil

(Olweus, 1978; Perry, Kusel, & Perry, 1988; Sharp & Thompson, 1992).

Why should we expect pupils involved in bully\victim problems to suffer poorer physical and psychological health? One answer can be derived from the stress and coping literature. For example, Rigby (1999) makes the point that being subjected to aversive stimuli (as in physical and verbal attacks), and the forced deprivation of social support (as when children are deliberately ostracised) can be extremely stressful. In addition, the repeated nature of bullying episodes may be difficult or impossible for a pupil to control or escape from. According to Perez and Reicherts (1992), these conditions are key determinants of individual stress reactions. Enduring the stress of being victimized may tax the immune system and lead to both psychological (Rigby, 1999) and physiological (Cox, 1995) alterations in an individual's functioning that may result in a range of health complaints (Vaernes, et al., 1991).

On physical health?

Two recent studies among English primary school pupils (Williams, Chambers, Logan, & Robinson, 1996; Wolke, Woods, Bloomfield, & Karstadt, 2001) have reported a relationship between bullying behaviors and poor physical health. Although Rigby (1999) found a relationship between bullying behaviors and poor physical health among primary school pupils, this association did not extend into the post-primary sample.

For example, Williams, Chambers, Logan, and Robinson (1996), reported symptoms of poor health, namely; 'not sleeping well' (4.2%), 'bed wetting' (7.7%), 'more than occasional headaches' (6.5%), and 'stomach ache' (7.8%), were more common among pupils who reported in the course of semi-structured interviews that they had recently been bullied at school (N = 2,962: age range = 8 to 9 years).

On mental health?

Whilst symptoms of poor physical health are generally overt and easily recognisable, the converse is true for psychological well-being. In conjunction with our need to be aware of the risk of involvement in bully\victim problems to impaired physical health, we need to be fully aware of the 'hidden' health costs of involvement in bullying behaviors; that is, the effects of involvement in bully\victim problems on the psychological well-being of pupils. For example, results from Kumpulainen, et al. (1998) four-year longitudinal research project confirmed clinical suspicion that pupils involved in bully\victim problems, especially as a bully\victim, were psychologically disturbed and were more likely than controls to be referred for psychiatric consultation. From a review of such psychiatric consultations, Salmon, James, Cassidy, and Javaloyes (2000) state that: "It is clear that bullying has a substantial effect on the mental health of adolescents." (p. 576). A more pessimistic warning has been sounded by Davies and Cunningham (1999). In concluding their review of the nature and extent of adolescent parasuicide in one health region of Northern Ireland, Davies and Cunningham (1999) asserted that: "This study suggests that bullying is one of the stressors most strongly associated with suicidal behavior in adolescents." (p. 11). Despite such findings, there is a relative scarcity of research concerning psychological well-being correlates of bullying and victimization (Dawkins, 1995; Kaltiala-Heino, Rimpelä, Rantanen, & Rimpelä, 2000).

Indices of psychological well-being that have been investigated in relation to involvement in bully\victim problems include: happiness, self-esteem, and depression. Attention now turns to a brief overview of the research evidence relating each of these well-being variables to involvement in bully\victim problems.

On happiness?
Research examining the relationship between involvement in bully\victim problems and happiness has reported that that both victims (Boulton & Underwood, 1992; O'Moore & Hillery, 1991; Rigby, 2002) and bullies (Forero, Mc Lellan, Rissel, & Bauman, 1999; Rigby & Slee, 1993) are unhappy.

For example, Boulton and Underwood (1992) found that among a sample of 296 (154 boys, 142 girls, mean age = 8.5 to 11.5 years) English school pupils 20.6% of the sample were bullied 'sometimes' (6.1%) or 'once or twice' (14.5%) as determined by The Bully Victim Questionnaire (Olweus, 1989). Regarding bullying others, 17.1% reported that they had bullied 'sometimes' (13.3%) or 'several times a week' (3.8%). Fewer pupils who reported being bullied ('sometimes' or 'several times a week') reported that they felt 'happy' or 'very happy' (67.2%) during playtimes compared to non-bullied pupils (91.4%).

On self-esteem?
Victims: Several studies from across the world have indicated that victimization is associated with lowered levels of self-esteem in school pupils of various ages (Andreou, 2000, 2001; Austin & Joseph, 1996; Boulton & Smith, 1994; Callaghan & Joseph, 1995; Collins & Bell, 1996; Lagerspetz, Björkqvist, Berts, & King, 1982; Mynard & Joseph, 1997; Neary & Joseph, 1994; Olweus, 1992, 1993; O'Moore & Hillery, 1991; O'Moore & Kirkham, 2001; Rigby & Slee, 1993). For example, based on the peer ratings of classmates to construct bully and victim categories, Lagerspetz, Björkqvist, Berts, and King (1982) report that victims in their study of 434 (212 boys, 222 girls, age range = 12 to 16 years) pupils from three Finnish schools had lower self-esteem than bullies and non-involved pupils as assessed with an adapted version of Olweus' (1978) Q-sort Questionnaire.

Indeed, in a meta-analysis of all cross-sectional research in this area between 1978 and 1997, Hawker and Boulton (2000) reported that victims of bullying were consistently found to have lower levels of self-esteem. Hawker and Boulton (2000) concluded that their meta-analysis established unequivocally the negative psychological outcomes of peer victimization.

Bullies:

In a recent review of this area, O'Moore and Kirkham (2001) reported that the literature relating to self-esteem and bullies is "… controversial …" (p. 270). For example, whilst some researchers report that being a bully is not associated with lower levels of self-esteem (Olweus, 1991; Pearce & Thompson, 1998; Rigby, 1996; Rigby & Slee, 1993), others have provided evidence to the contrary (Andreou, 2000; Austin & Joseph, 1996; Mynard & Joseph, 1997; O'Moore, 1997; O'Moore & Hillery, 1991; O'Moore & Kirkham, 2001; Rigby & Cox, 1996; Salmivalli, 1998). For example, using the Self Esteem Scale (Rosenberg, 1965), Rigby and Cox (1996) report on the link between being a bully and self-esteem. From their sample of 763 (352 boys, 411 girls, age range = 13 to 17 years, mean age = 14.69, SD = 1.16) post-primary pupils at a large co-educational school in Adelaide, Australia, they found that among girls, but not boys, low levels of self-esteem were associated with self-reported bullying behavior (as determined by The Bully Scale: Rigby & Slee, 1993).

Bully\Victims:

Bully\victims have been found to have even lower levels of self-esteem as compared to those pupils who are categorised as solely a bully or a victim (Andreou, 2000, 2001; Austin & Joseph, 1996; Mynard & Joseph, 1997; O'Moore, 1995, 1997; O'Moore & Hillery, 1991; O'Moore & Kirkham, 2001).

For example, Andreou (2001) reports that in a sample of Greek school children (N = 408: 197 boys, 211 girls, age range = 9 to 12 years, mean age = 10.7 years, SD = 1.9 years), bully\victims (10.3%) scored lower on the Social Acceptance and Global Self-Worth sub-scales of The Self-Perception Profile for Children (Harter, 1985) than did the bullies (17.4%), victims (18.6%), and not-involved pupils (53.7%).

On depression?

Victims: Several studies have indicated that victimization is concurrently associated with depression among both primary (Austin & Joseph, 1996; Callaghan & Joseph, 1995; Craig, 1998; Kumpulainen, et al., 1998; Neary & Joseph, 1994; Slee, 1995) and post-primary (Björkqvist, Ekman, & Lagerspetz, 1982; Salmon, James, Cassidy, & Javaloyes, 2000) pupils. Indeed, in Hawker and Boulton's (2000) meta-analysis, the strongest relationship found between victimization and indices of physical and psychological health was with depression.

For example, Neary and Joseph (1994) report that in their study of Irish convent schoolgirls (N = 60: age range = 10 to 12 years, mean age = 11 years), higher scores on their Peer Victimization Scale were associated with higher scores on The Depression Self-Rating Scale (Birleson, 1981) (r = 0.60, p < 0.001). Indeed, there was a statistically significant difference between the mean scores of self-identified victims (n = 12, mean = 14.00, SD = 5.86) and those pupils not self-identified as victims (n = 48, mean = 8.73, SD = 4.24) on The Depression Self-

Rating Scale (Birleson, 1981) (t = 3.56, p < 0.001 [1-tailed]). There was also a statistically significant difference between the mean scores of peer-identified victims (n = 30, mean = 11.03, SD = 4.50) and those pupils who were not identified as victims (n = 30, mean = 8.53, SD = 4.83) on The Depression Self-Rating Scale (Birleson, 1981) (t = 1.97, p < 0.05 [1-tailed]). Furthermore, compared to the mean scores of those pupils neither self- nor peer-identified as victims of bullying behaviors, both self- and peer-identified victims scored above the cut-off point of 11 (14.00 and 11.03 respectively) originally claimed to separate depressed from non-depressed children (Birleson, 1981).

Bullies: The evidence from a range of studies has highlighted that being a bully is concurrently associated with depression among both primary and post-primary pupils. (Austin & Joseph, 1996; Kumpulainen, et al., 1998; Rigby, 1997; Salmon, James, Cassidy, & Javaloyes, 2000; Salmon, James, & Smith, 1998; Slee, 1995; Zubrick, et al., 1997).

For example, in their study of 904 (age range = 12 to 17 years) post-primary English school pupils, Salmon, James, and Smith (1998) found that bullies (as determined by The Bully-Victim Questionnaire: Olweus, 1989) had significantly higher depression scores on The Short Mood and Feelings Questionnaire (Angold, at al., 1995).

Bully\Victims: the evidence from a range of studies has also highlighted that being a bully\victim is concurrently associated with depression among both primary and post-primary pupils. Indeed, it has been reported in some of these studies that the bully\victim category of actor suffers depression to a greater extent than any of the other categories of actor (Austin & Joseph, 1996; Craig, 1998; Swearer, Song, Cary, Eagle, & Mickelson, 2001).

Swearer, et al. (2001) report preliminary data (N = 133: 66 boys, 67 girls, age range = 11 to 13 years) from their longitudinal study into the psychosocial correlates of bullying and victimization that highlights that the bully\victim group (as determined by The Bully Survey: Swearer & Paulk, 1998) suffer from higher levels of depression (as assessed by The Children's Depression Inventory: Kovacs, 1992) than the other sub-groups of actor in bully\victim problems.

What about Religion?:
Whilst some individual difference variables have been studied in relation to bullying behaviors (e.g., personality), one salient individual difference variable that has only been tentatively explored has been that of religiosity.

The construct of religiosity has been demonstrated to be a protective mechanism against a range of anti-social behavior among young people. For example, among a sample of approximately 30,000 pupils from England and Wales, Francis (2001) reports on the power of self-assigned religious affiliation to predict adolescent values over a range of issues including; alcohol, sexual intercourse outside marriage, the law, pornography, and violence on television. Francis (2001) concluded that: "Even among young people, those most exposed to and shaped by the influences of modernity, religion shapes personal and social attitudes and behaviours." (p. 63). Thus, by extension, it may be possible that religiosity also shapes and influences attitudes to bullying behaviors. If this were the case, detailed information regarding this relationship between religiosity and involvement in bully\victim problems would have positive implications for those designing prevention and intervention strategies aimed at ameliorating the insidious nature of bully\victim problems.

Francis and Kay (1995) have explored the relationship between 'fear' of being bullied at school and religiosity among adolescents. As part of a major study designed to explore the place of religion and values in the lives of young people, Francis and Kay (1995) sampled approximately 13,000 year 9 and year 10 (age range = 13 to 15 years) pupils regarding a range of issues. Included in a module looking at school related issues was the item: 'I am worried about being bullied at school'. Whilst 52% of the sample disagreed with the statement, 25% said that they agreed with it, and a further 23% said that they were not certain. Thus, nearly half of all pupils *were* fearful of being bullied at school. Francis and Kay (1995) further report a sex difference in these data, with girls being more concerned than boys about being bullied. They report that as many as 28% of girls had a worry about being bullied, whereas the corresponding figure for boys was 22%; conversely 56% of boys were not scared of being bullied, as compared with 48% of girls. Also consistent with previous findings was the finding that there was a positive change across age, with 23% of year 10 pupils being worried about bullying compared to 27% of year 9 pupils.

Francis and Kay (1995) also report on the relationship between various single-item indices of religiosity (i.e., church attendance, belief in God) and fear of being bullied. Regarding 'church attendance', they report that churchgoers among the sample were more inclined to have a fear of being bullied. Twenty-nine per-cent of 'weekly' and 28% of 'occasional' churchgoers were worried about being bullied, compared with 22% of non-churchgoers; conversely, 46% of 'weekly' and 48% of 'occasional' churchgoers were not worried about being bullied, and this compared with 56% of non-churchgoers who were similarly free from this problem. As a further index of religiosity, Francis and Kay (1995) report on the link between fear of being bullied at school and 'belief in God'. Whilst theists ('I believe in God') and agnostics ('Uncertain that I believe in God') had a generally more favourable perspective of school, this was accompanied by a greater tendency to worry about being bullied at school. Whilst 27% of theists and 21% of agnostics reported being fearful of being bullied, the comparative figure for atheists ('I disagree that I believe in God') was 19%. Francis and Kay (1995) report that these worries were confirmed by the reverse perspective: 54% of theists and agnostics and 60% of atheists reported that they did not worry about being bullied at school.

According to the results of Francis and Kay's (1995) study, it would seem that religiosity maybe an important predictor of adolescent values over a wide range of areas, including bullying.

What can we do about it?

Involvement in bully\victim problems is not an inevitable part of growing up, but is a negative outcome of the necessity for children to be involved in social relationships in school, at home, from peer groups, and through the media. Through such interactions, bullying behaviors may be easily learned. As such, bullying behaviors can also be unlearned (i.e., intervention) or, better still, prevented. In the fight to reduce the incidence and impact of bully\victim problems, there are many prevention and intervention strategies that have been demonstrated to be effective for both teachers and parents. In the current section, attention is directed towards an overview of some anti-bullying programs and program components that have been demonstrated to be effective in this area.

Create a positive learning and growing environment

As a first step in ameliorating the insidious effects of bully\victim problems, it is imperative that adults create a supportive and inclusive environment in school and at home whereby bullying and low level aggression is not tolerated. In creating such a social context at school, school authorities may seek to develop appropriate training programs for all school staff that are in daily contact with children (e.g., see O'Moore, 2000 for discussion regarding teacher training). However, we have found that, all too often, training programs in this area are devised and delivered to teachers to the exclusion of all other staff in the school community (e.g., Mc Guckin, Hyndman, & Lewis, 2003). For example, the importance of training programs designed specifically for playground supervisors has been highlighted (e.g., Boulton, 1996; Sharp, 1994). By extension, it could be argued that specific training programs should also be developed for other adults who come into contact with children through their work (e.g., the clergy, lay ministers of the church). Mc Guckin and Lewis (2003) have reported upon the success of providing such training to various sections of the wider school community (e.g., teachers, parents, youth club officers).

The bridge between home and school is also an important, and often neglected, piece of the jigsaw. Here, the development of effective communication channels between teachers and parents would enable these adults to effectively consult with each other as to the development of anti-bullying policies and strategies. Quite often, the only structured meeting between teachers and parents is the annual parent-teacher meeting which is often viewed as an adversarial encounter. Indeed, within Northern Ireland, recent legislation has made it mandatory for every school to develop and implement an anti-bullying policy that has been developed through a process of consultation and input from everyone in the school community (i.e., teachers, parents, pupils; see also Ananiadou & Smith, 2002 for a review of legal requirements in European countries). Such work seeks to place the child at the centre of the research process and mirrors the creation of a Children's Ombudsman in Northern Ireland whose task it is to see that children 'have a voice' in every aspect of the social policy arena that directly affects them.

Whilst parents and teachers undoubtedly have a significant role to play in creating a positive learning and growing environment in which children learn that negative social interactions are not tolerated, those adults who interact with children in their wider ecological sphere (Bronfenbrenner, 1977) also have an important role in this area. That is, from a social and pastoral perspective, clergy and lay ministers can provide the necessary supportive environment in which children and their peers can consolidate the lessons learnt in school and at home regarding positive behavior.

Create a 'Telling School': Empower children to report what is happening

The creation of a 'telling' ethos in the school and playground has been consistently cited as being the single most important component in prevention and intervention programs (e.g., the 'Don't Suffer in Silence' program implemented by the UK government). That is, adults must work towards empowering children to feel able to report what is happening to them at the hands of their peers. Enabling the child to speak up and report what is happening without the fear of being called a 'snitch' will educate the child that it is wrong to 'Suffer In Silence'. The basic need to report bullying incidents should be regularly addressed within school at Assembly, during Registration, and in Pastoral Care classes. Henry (1999) has reported that such an approach has been efficacious in some schools in Northern Ireland. Thus, the intention should be to create a 'telling school' where pupils feel free to speak to those in authority without fear of the stigma of being called a 'rat' and safe in the knowledge that action will be taken to suppress the anti-social behaviors (Byrne, 1993). Indeed, 'telling' can be done silently by the provision of 'drop boxes' for pupils to place information in.

The importance of empowering children to report instances of bullying in this manner is evidenced in the fact that much bullying occurs without the knowledge of teachers and\or parents, and that many victims are reluctant to tell adults about their problems with bullies. Reluctance to tell adults of instances of bullying behaviors may stem from fear of reprisals, shame, or a concern that adults may not be able to help.

Indeed, before we can empower children to approach adults about bullying problems, adults themselves need to re-examine their own belief system regarding the taboo of 'telling' or 'snitching' on others who have acted in an anti-social manner. All too often, adults still operate within the notion of 'telling' as being indicative of a negative personality trait. In a 'spill-over' manner, it is still often the case that many teachers and parents advise children not to 'tell tales' or 'gossip', and to settle their problems themselves.

Empowering children to tell: Circle Time

One approach to helping children to develop the confidence and communication skills necessary to create a 'telling school' is 'Circle Time'. Circle Time has been utilised in organizations as a strategy for improving product quality by encouraging workers at different levels in the organization to share their views as to how best a job can be done. Within schools, Circle Time can be used with any age group of pupils and is just as valuable with senior pupils as with junior pupils. Circle Time enables both horizontal and vertical communication (i.e., pupil-pupil, teacher-pupil) between the teacher and the class about issues of concern in a non-threatening environment and can be utilised as a vehicle to promote self-esteem and positive behavior.

Circle Time meetings usually take place weekly and last between thirty and sixty minutes, according to the age and abilities of pupils. The teacher and the pupils sit in a circle and through a range of activities (e.g., drama strategies, talking and listening activities) and subsequent discussion, pupils are encouraged to think more about their own behavior and how it may effect others.

Having utilised Circle Time in an anti-bullying program that we have designed in Northern Ireland (Mc Guckin, et al., 2003), initial evaluation data has demonstrated that this approach serves to build confidence and self-esteem in all pupils involved. Through an understanding of mutual respect, children can learn that diversity between the members of their social group in various domains of self concept (e.g., social, academic, behavioral, physical appearance, health and well-being) can be accepted and understood, as opposed to being a source of 'ammunition' for bullying behaviors and gestures (e.g., racial bullying, teasing) (see for example Cash, 1995; Eslea & Mukhtar, 2000; Hugh-Jones, & Smith, 1999; Mooney, Creeser, & Blatchford, 1991; Mooney & Smith, 1995; Moran, Smith, Thompson, & Whitney, 1993). With the help of the clergy and lay ministry, the seeds of moral development that are sown in Circle Time activities can be fostered and developed through interactions with children in youth clubs and church societies. Indeed, considering that Circle Time activities are inexpensive and easy to facilitate, adults involved in church-related activities (e.g., youth clubs, societies) with children may wish to consider such activities when developing group activities with children.

Involve the voluntary sector

The voluntary sector is a rich source of help and assistance in the development of anti-bullying programs and policies. As previously highlighted, we have been involved over the last few years in the planning and delivery of community education classes. An integral part of these classes has been the involvement of a local community theatre group (Balor Community Development Group) who perform their short play on school bullying. This play has also been well received at The British Psychological Society (Northern Ireland Branch) Annual Conference (Lewis, 2000). After the play has finished (10 minutes duration), the audience is asked for strategies that 'Jim' or other actors in the play could have implemented to stop the bullying. When a strategy is offered, the person offering the strategy is encouraged to act it out with the actors ad-libbing around the new scenario. Perhaps the most rewarding aspect of these interactions is that those adults who offer strategies often see their futility when acted-out. Where practically possible, we would advocate the involvement of such community drama groups in anti-bullying programs. Indeed, drama and other curriculum developments (e.g., poetry, essay, art competitions) are often viewed as central to the development of successful anti-bullying programs.

Create an enriched play environment

As well as cultural changes to the children's social world, structural changes are also to be welcomed in the fight to reduce the incidence and impact of bullying behaviors. As a prime location for bullying incidents to happen, prevention and intervention programs have highlighted the central role that playground measures should take (e.g., Olweus, 1993). Smith and Sharp (1994) have noted that schools should develop a break\lunch-time policy with definite, high profile supervisory roles for non-teaching staff. Simple strategies that help reduce the potential for bullying situations include having pupils walk in single-file when in groups so as to reduce jostling and physical contact. As an example of the effectiveness of such work, Smith and Sharp (1994) report a decrease in bullying of between 40% and 50% where playground measures have been implemented.

Considering that much bullying takes place without the direct knowledge of adults, the playground, with its nooks and crannies (e.g., behind temporary classroom accommodation), is a fertile location for bullies to operate. Also, due to resource limitations, many schools often find that they cannot financially afford the cost of employing the required number of playground supervisors. Taking these two points into consideration, it is easy to see that the only people who can inform us as to the location of bullying behaviors are the children themselves. As part of creating a 'telling' culture, we have used Pupil Forums in our anti-bullying work within schools. Democratically elected representatives from each class group (usually elected during Circle Time activities) meet with a staff member or visiting member of the clergy who facilitates discussions regarding the issues of concern to the pupils. Through such discussions, rich information can be elicited from the children as to the locations of bullying behaviors. Importantly, as well as providing this level of information, the children often provide resourceful and imaginative suggestions for rectifying these issues through the Pupil Forums.

The 'No Blame Approach': An example of a standardised program

The 'No Blame Approach' (Maines & Robinson, 1998) is one intervention strategy that some schools have found helpful in tackling bully\victim problems. The 'No Blame Approach' is different from many approaches in that it is a participative and non-punitive approach that lets the bully know that his\her activities are known about. Without the need for costly materials, the approach can be implemented successfully by any teacher or relevant adult. The central components of the 'No Blame Approach' are that it:

       takes firm, clear, and cohesive action
       does not allow bullies 'off the hook'
       supports the victim
       makes it clear to bullies that all bullying behaviors have to
         cease immediately
       is a long-term approach
       involves the bully's peer group
       focuses on changing the behavior of the bully and those who
         support the bullying behaviour

Part of the success of this program is that it harnesses the support and co-operation of the wider social group in which the bullying occurs. Thus, everyone is viewed as having a role in the resolution of the problem. Indeed, the success of this simple program and its non-punitive approach has been mirrored in recent 'community restorative justice' programs developed by community groups and the police service in Northern Ireland.

Do prevention and intervention programs work?

As highlighted previously, the best prevention strategy that any school could implement is a 'bottom-up' evidence-based multi-component anti-bullying policy, drawing on experiences and lessons learned from other countries and with input from the whole school community (see also Rigby, 2002 for a meta-evaluation of anti-bullying programs). Indeed, research findings support the assertion that anti-bullying policies do make a difference (e.g., Glover, Cartwright, & Gleeson, 1998). However, it should also be remembered that good anti-bullying policies have two components: (i) that they are written, and (ii) that they are implemented. Olweus (1993) asserts that the chief features within such multi-component policies include:

General pre-requisites
    awareness and involvement

Measures at school level
    questionnaire survey
    school conference day on bully/victim problems
    better supervision during breaks and lunch time
    more attractive school playground
    parent circles

Measure at the class level
    class rules against bullying
    regular class meetings
    role-play, literature
    co-operative learning
    class meeting teacher - parents/children

Measures at the individual level
    serious talks with bullies and victims
    serious talks with parents of involved children
    teacher and parent use of imagination
    help from 'neutral' students
    help and support for parents

From implementation of the above components in his state-wide Norwegian research, Olweus (1991) reported a 50% reduction in the incidence of bully\victim problems. Indeed, these positive changes were reported to still be evident 20 months after program delivery, with no displacement from bullying at school to bullying on the way to and from school (Olweus, 1991). Similar (though not as high) results have been reported from other countries (e.g., Italy: Genta, Menesini, Fonzi, & Costabile, 1996; Australia: Rigby & Slee, 1998; England: Smith & Sharp, 1994; Canada: Pepler, Craig, Ziegler, & Charach, 1994) that have implemented the program. For example, in England, the program was implemented among approximately 6,000 pupils in attendance at 23 primary and secondary schools (age range = 8 to 16 years) in the northern industrial city of Sheffield (Smith & Sharp, 1994). Whilst a 17% reduction in the number of victims was evidenced in the primary school sector, there was a more modest reduction of 5% in the secondary school sector (bullying behaviour\reports generally decrease with age).

Conclusion:
Set against the background of the serious social problem of school bullying, the present chapter aimed to provide answers to questions about bully\victim problems in an accessible resource for parents, teachers, clergy, and those involved in pastoral work with children. At present most training initiatives are focused on teachers and laterally other school personnel (e.g., playground supervisors). However, it is imperative that there is a move towards a more holistic and whole community based approach to tackling youth aggression and bullying. Pastoral workers are well placed to drive such initiatives.

REFERENCES

Ahmad, Y. S., & Smith, P. K. (1994). Bullying in schools and the issue of sex differences. In J. Archer (Ed.), Male Violence (pp. 70-83). London: Routledge.

Ananiadou, K., & Smith, P. K. (2002). Legal requirements and nationally circulated materials against school bullying in European countries. Criminal Justice: The International Journal of Policy and Practice, 2, 471-491.

Anderson, M., Kaufman, J., Simon, T. R., Barrios, L., Paulozzi, L., Ryan, G., Hammond, R., Modzeleski, W., Feucht, T., Potter, L., & the School-Associated Violent Deaths Study Group. (2001). School-associated violent deaths in the United States, 1994-1999. Journal of the American Medical Association, 286, 2695-2702.

Andreou, E. (2000). Bully/victim problems and their association with psychological constructs in 8- to 11-year-old Greek schoolchildren. Aggressive Behavior, 26, 49-56.

Andreou, E. (2001). Bully/victim problems and their association with coping behaviour in conflictual peer interactions among school-age children. Educational Psychology, 21, 59-66.

Angold, A., Costello, E. J., Messer, S. C., Pickles, A., Windsor, F., & Silver, D. (1995). Development of a short questionnaire for use in epidemiological studies of depression in children and adolescents. International Journal of Methods in Psychiatric Research, 5, 237-249.

Archer, J., & Parker, S. (1994). Social representations of aggression in children. Aggressive Behavior, 20, 101-114.

Arora, C. M. J., & Thompson, D. A. (1987). Defining bullying for a secondary school. Education and Child Psychology, 4, 110-120.

Austin, S., & Joseph, S. (1996). Assessment of bully/victim problems in 8 to 11 year-olds. British Journal of Educational Psychology, 66, 447-456.

Bell, S. (2001, February 4). Bullied to death. Sunday Life Newspaper, p. 14.

Besag, V. E. (1989). Bullies and Victims in Schools: A Guide to Understanding and Management. Open University Press, Milton Keynes.

Birleson, P. (1981). The validity of depression disorder in childhood and the development of a self-rating scale: A research report. Journal of Child Psychology and Psychiatry, 22, 73-88.

Björkqvist, K. (1994). Sex differences in physical, verbal, and indirect aggression: A review of recent research. Sex Roles, 30, 177-188.

Björkqvist, K., Ekman, K., & Lagerspetz, K. (1982). Bullies and victims: Their ego picture, ideal ego picture and normative ego picture. Scandinavian Journal of Psychology, 23, 307-313.

Björkqvist, K., Lagerspetz, K. M. J., & Kaukainen, A. (1992). Do girls manipulate and boys fight? Developmental trends in regard to direct and indirect aggression. Aggressive Behavior, 18, 117-127.

Björkqvist, K., & Niemelä, P. (1992). New trends in the study of female aggression. In K. Björkqvist & P. Niemelä (Eds.), Of Mice and Women: Aspects of Female Aggression (pp. 3-16). San Diego, CA: Academic Press.

Björkqvist, K., & Österman, K. (1999). Finland. In P. K. Smith, Y. Morita, J. Junger-Tas, D. Olweus, R. Catalano, & P. Slee (Eds.), The Nature of School Bullying: A Cross-National Perspective (pp. 56-67). London and New York: Routledge.

Björkqvist, K., Österman, K., & Kaukiainen, A. (1992). The development of direct and indirect aggressive strategies in males and females. In K. Björkqvist & P. Niemelä

(Eds.), Of Mice and Women: Aspects of Female Aggression (pp. 51-63). San Diego, CA: Academic Press.

Björkqvist, K., Österman, K., & Lagerspetz, K. M. J. (1994). Sex differences in covert aggression among adults. Aggressive Behavior, 20, 27-33.

Boulton, M. J. (1996). Lunchtime supervisors' attitudes towards playful fighting, and ability to differentiate between playful and aggressive fighting: An intervention study. British Journal of Educational Psychology, 66, 367-381.

Boulton, M. J., & Smith, D. K. (1994). Bully/victim problems among middle school children: Stability, self perceived competence and peer acceptance. British Journal of Developmental Psychology, 12, 315-329.

Boulton, M. J., & Underwood, K. (1992). Bully/victim problems among middle school children. British Journal of Educational Psychology, 62, 73-87.

Bronfenbrenner, U. (1977). Towards an experimental ecology of human development. American Psychologist, 32, 513-531.

Buss, A. H. (1961). The Psychology of Aggression. New York: John Wiley and Sons.

Byrne, B. (1993). Coping With Bullying in Schools. Dublin: Columba Press.

Cairns, R. B., Perrin, J. E., & Cairns, B. D. (1985). Social structure and social cognition in early adolescence: Affiliative patterns. Journal of Early Adolescence, 5, 339-355.

Callaghan, S., & Joseph, S. (1995). Self-concept and peer victimization among schoolchildren. Personality and Individual Differences, 18, 161-163.

Cash, T. F. (1995). Developmental teasing about physical appearance: Retrospective descriptions and relationships with body image. Social Behaviour and Personality, 23, 123-130.

Collins, K., & Bell, R. (1996). Peer perceptions of aggression and bullying behaviour in primary schools in Northern Ireland. Annals of the New York Academy of Science, 794, 77-79.

Cook, H. B. J. (1992). Matrifocality and female aggression in Margeriteño society. In K. Björkqvist & P. Niemelä (Eds.), Of Mice and Women: Aspects of Female Aggression (pp. 149-162). San Diego, CA: Academic Press.

Cox, T. (1995). Stress, coping and physical health. In A. Broome & S. Llewelyn (Eds.), Health Psychology: Process and Applications (2nd Edn.) (pp. 21-25). London: Singular Publication Group.

Craig, W. M. (1998). The relationship among bullying, victimization, depression, anxiety, and aggression in elementary school children. Personality and Individual Differences, 24, 123-130.

Crick, N. R. (1995). Relational aggression: The role of intent attributions, feelings of distress, and provocation type. Development and Psychopathology, 7, 313-322.

Crick, N. R., & Dodge, K. A. (1994). A review and reformulation of social information-processing mechanisms in children's social adjustment. Psychological Bulletin, 115, 74-101.

Davies, M., & Cunningham, G. (1999). Adolescent parasuicide in the Foyle area. Irish Journal of Psychological Medicine, 16, 9-12.

Dawkins, J. (1995). Bullying in schools: Doctors' responsibilities. British Medical Journal, 310, 274-275.

Eslea, M., & Mukhtar, K. (2000). Bullying and racism among Asian schoolchildren in Britain. Educational Research, 42, 207-217.

Forero, R., Mc Lellan, L., Rissel, C., & Bauman, A. (1999). Bullying behaviour and psychosocial health among school students in New South Wales, Australia: Cross sectional survey. British Medical Journal, 19, 344-348.

Francis, L. J. (2001). Religion and values: A quantitative perspective. In L. J. Francis, J. Astley, & M. Robbins (Eds.) The Fourth R for the Third Millennium: Education in Religion and Values for the Global Future (pp. 47-78). Herndon, VA.: Lindisfarne Books.

Francis, L. J., & Kay, W. K. (1995). Teenage Religion and Values. Leominster: Gracewing.

Frodi, A., Macaulay, J., & Thome, P. R. (1977). Are women always less aggressive than men? A review of the experimental literature. Psychological Bulletin, 84, 634-660.

Genta, M. L, Menesini, E., Fonzi, A., & Costabile, A. (1996). Le prepotenze tra bambini a scuola: Risultati di una ricerca condotta in due città italiane [Psychological bullying among children in school: Research conducted in two Italian cities]. Età Evolutiva, 53, 73-80.

Glover, D., Cartwright, N., Gough, G., & Johnson, M. (1998). The introduction of anti-bullying policies: Do policies help in the management of change? School Leadership and Management, 18, 89-105.

Goldstein, A. P. (1999). Low-Level Aggression: First Steps on the Ladder to Violence. Champaign, Ill.: Research Press.

Green, L. R., Richardson, D. R., & Lago, T. (1996). How do friendships, indirect, and direct aggression relate? Aggressive Behavior, 22, 81-86.

Hawker, D. S. J., & Boulton, M. J. (2000). Twenty years' research on peer victimization and psychosocial maladjustment: A meta-analytic review of cross-sectional studies. Journal of Child Psychiatry and Psychiatry and Allied Disciplines, 41, 441-455.

Henderson, D. (2002, September 13). Girl, 12, found hanged after bullying campaign. The Scotsman.

Henry, S. (1999). An Investigation into the Effectiveness of the Anti-Bullying Policy in a Co-Educational Secondary School. Unpublished master's thesis, University of Ulster at Jordanstown, Northern Ireland.

Hugh-Jones, S., & Smith, P. K. (1999). Self-reports of short- and long-term effects of bullying on children who stammer. British Journal of Educational Psychology, 69, 141-158.

Hyde, J. S. (1984). How large are gender differences in aggression? A developmental meta-analysis. Developmental Psychology, 20, 722-736.

Kaltiala-Heino, R., Rimpelä, M., Martunnen, M., Rimpelä, A., & Rantanen, P. (1999). Bullying, depression and suicidal ideation in Finnish adolescents: School survey. British Medical Journal, 319, 348-351.

Kovacs, M. (1992). Children's Depression Inventory. New York: MHS.

Kumpulainen, K., Räsänen, E., Henttonen, I., Almqvist, F., Kresanov, K., Linna, S. L., Moilanen, I., Piha, J., Purra, K., & Tamminen, T. (1998). Bullying and psychiatric symptoms among elementary school-age children. Child Abuse Neglect, 22, 705-717.

Lagerspetz, K. M. J., & Björkqvist, K., (1994). Indirect aggression in boys and girls. In L. Rowell Huesmann (Ed.), Aggressive Behavior: Current Perspectives (pp. 131-150). New York: Plenum Press.

Lagerspetz, K. M. J., Björkqvist, K., Berts, M., & King, E. (1982). Group aggression among school children in three schools. Scandinavian Journal of Psychology, 23, 45-52.

Lagerspetz, K. M. J., Björkqvist, K., & Peltonen, T. (1988). Is indirect aggression typical of females? Gender differences in aggressiveness in 11- to 12-year old children. Aggressive Behavior, 14, 403-414.

Lewis, C.A. (2000). Conference abstracts - Annual Conference of the British Psychological Society (Northern Ireland Branch). Carrigart Hotel, Carrigart, Co. Donegal, Republic of Ireland, 5-8th May 2000. Belfast: Northern Ireland Branch, British Psychological Society.

Maccoby, E. E., & Jacklin, C. N. (1974). The Psychology of Sex Differences. Stanford, CA: Stanford University Press.

Macdonald, I., Bhavnani, R., Khan, L., & John, G. (1989). Murder in the Playground: The Burnage Report. London: Longsight Press.

Maines, B., & Robinson, G. (1992). Michael's Story: The No-Blame Approach. Bristol: Lame Duck Books.

Marr, N., & Field, T. (2001). Bullycide: Death at Playtime. Didcot, Oxfordshire: Success Unlimited.

Mc Guckin, C., & Lewis, C. A. (2003). A cross-national perspective on school bullying in Northern Ireland: A supplement to Smith, et al. (1999). Psychological Reports, 93, 279-287.

Mc Guckin, C., Hyndman, M., & Lewis, C. A. (2003). The Glenview Anti-Bullying Project. The Psychological Society of Ireland Annual Conference. Bunratty, Ireland. November 20-23. The Irish Psychologist, 30, 49.

Mooney, A., Creeser, R., & Blatchford, P. (1991). Children's views on teasing and fighting in junior schools. Educational Research, 33, 103-112.

Mooney, S., & Smith, P. K. (1995). Bullying and the child who stammers. British Journal of Special Education, 22, 24-27.

Moran, S., Smith, P. K., Thompson, D., & Whitney, I. (1993). Ethnic differences in experiences of bullying: Asian and white children. British Journal of Educational Psychology, 63, 431-440.

Morita, Y., Soeda, H., Soeda, K., & Taki, M. (1999). Japan. In P. K. Smith, Y. Morita, J. Junger-Tas, D. Olweus, R. Catalano, & P. Slee (Eds.), The Nature of School Bullying: A Cross-National Perspective (pp. 309-323). London and New York: Routledge.

Mynard, H., & Joseph, S. (2000). Development of the multidimensional peer-victimization scale. Aggressive Behavior, 26, 169-178.

Nansel, T. R., Overpeck, M., Pilla, R. S., Ruan, W. J., Simons-Morton, B., & Scheidt, B. (2001). Bullying behaviors among US youth: Prevalence and association with psychosocial adjustment. Journal of the American Medical Association, 285, 2094-2100.

Neary, A., & Joseph, S. (1994). Peer victimisation and its relationship to self-concept and depression among schoolgirls. Personality and Individual Differences, 16, 183-186.

Olweus, D. (1973). Personality and aggression. In J. K. Cole & D. D. Jensen (Eds.), Nebraska Symposium on Motivation 1972 (pp. 261-321). Lincoln: University of Nebraska Press.

Olweus, D. (1978). Aggression in the Schools: Bullies and Whipping Boys. Washington, DC: Hemisphere.

Olweus, D. (1986). Aggression and hormones: behavioural relationship with testosterone and adrenaline. In D. Olweus, J. Block, & M. Radke-Yarrow (Eds.), Development of Antisocial and Prosocial Behaviour (pp. 51-72). New York: Academic Press.

Olweus, D. (1989). Bully/Victim Questionnaire For Students. Department of Psychology, University of Bergen.

Olweus, D. (1991). Bully/victim problems among schoolchildren: Basic facts and effects of a school-based intervention program. In D. J. Pepler & K. H. Rubin (Eds.), The Development and Treatment of Childhood Aggression (pp. 411-448). Hillsdale, NJ:

Lawrence Erlbaum.

Olweus, D. (1992). Victimisation by peers: Antecedents and long-term outcomes. In K. H. Rubin & J. B. Asendorf (Eds.), Social Withdrawal, Inhibition and Shyness in Children (pp. 315-341). Hillsdale, NJ: Erlbaum.

Olweus, D. (1993). Bullying at School: What We Know and What We Can Do. Oxford, and Cambridge, MA: Blackwell Publishers.

Olweus, D. (1994). Annotation: Bullying at school: Basic facts and effects of a school based intervention program. Journal of Child Psychology and Psychiatry, 35, 1171-1190.

Olweus, D. (1999a). Sweden. In P. K. Smith, Y. Morita, J. Junger-Tas, D. Olweus, R. Catalano, & P. Slee (Eds.), The Nature of School Bullying: A Cross-National Perspective (pp. 7-27). London and New York: Routledge.

Olweus, D. (1999b). Norway. In P. K. Smith, Y. Morita, J. Junger-Tas, D. Olweus, R. Catalano, & P. Slee (Eds.), The Nature of School Bullying: A Cross-National Perspective (pp. 28-48). London and New York: Routledge.

Owens, L. D. (1996). Sticks and stones and sugar and spice: Girls' and boys' aggression in schools. Australian Journal of Guidance and Counselling, 6, 45-57.

O'Moore, A. M. (1995). Bullying behaviour in children and adolescents in Ireland. Children and Society, 9, 54-72.

O'Moore A. M. (1997). What do teachers need to know? In M. Elliott (Ed.), Bullying: A Practical Guide to Coping for Schools (pp. 151-166). London: Pitman in Association with KIDSCAPE.

O'Moore, A. M. (2000). Critical issues for teacher training to counter bullying and victimisation in Ireland. Aggressive Behavior, 26, 99-111.

O'Moore, A. M., & Hillery, B. (1991). What do teachers need to know? In M. Elliott (Ed.) Bullying: A Practical Guide to Coping In Schools (pp. 59-69). Harlow, UK: David Fulton.

O'Moore, A. M., & Hillery, B. (1991). What do teachers need to know? In M. Elliott (Ed.) Bullying: A Practical Guide to Coping In Schools (pp. 59-69). Harlow, UK: David Fulton.

O'Moore, A. M., & Kirkham, C. (2001). Self-esteem and its relationship to bullying behaviour. Aggressive Behavior, 27, 269-283.

Pearce, J. B., & Thompson, A. E. (1998). Practical approaches to reduce the impact of bullying. Archives of Disease in Childhood, 79, 528-531.

Perez, M., & Reicherts, M. (1992). Stress, Coping and Health: A Situation-Behaviour Approach: Theory, Methods, Applications. Seattle: Hogrefe and Huber.

Pepler, Craig, Ziegler, & Charach, 1994

Perry, D. G., Kusel, S. J., & Perry, L. C. (1988). Victims of peer aggression. Developmental Psychology, 24, 807-814.

Pepler, D., Craig, W., Ziegler, S. & Charach, A. (1994). An evaluation of the anti-bullying intervention in Toronto schools. Canadian Journal of Community Mental Health, 13, 95-110.

Richardson, D. R. (1999). What is indirect aggression? Discriminating between direct and indirect aggression. Aggressive Behavior, 25, 30-31.

Richardson, D. R., & Green, L. R. (1997). Circuitous harm: Determinants and consequences of nondirect aggression. In R. Kowlaski (Ed.), Aversive Interpersonal Behaviours (pp. 172-188). New York: Plenum Press.

Rigby, K. (1996). Bullying In The Schools And What To Do About It. Melbourne: The

Australian Council For Educational Research Ltd (ACER).

Rigby, K. (1997). What children tell us about bullying in schools. Children Australia, 22, 28-34.

Rigby, K. (1998a). Suicidal ideation and bullying among Australian secondary school students. The Australian Educational and Developmental Psychologist, 15, 45-61.

Rigby, K. (1999). Peer victimisation at school and the health of secondary school students. British Journal of Educational Psychology, 69, 95-104.

Rigby, K. (2002). New Perspectives on Bullying. London: Jessica Kingsley Publishers Ltd.

Rigby, K., & Cox, I. (1996). The contribution of bullying at school and low self-esteem to acts of delinquency among Australian teenagers. Personality and Individual Differences, 21, 609-612.

Rigby, K., & Slee, P. T. (1993). Dimensions of interpersonal relation among Australian children and implications for psychological well-being. The Journal of Social Psychology, 133, 33-42.

Rigby, K., & Slee, P. T. (1998). Bullying in Australian Schools. The XVth Biennial Meeting of the International Society for the Study of Behavioural Development. Berne, Switzerland.

Rigby, K., & Slee, P. T. (1999). Suicidal ideation among adolescent school children, involvement in bully-victim problems, and perceived low social support. Suicide and Life-Threatening Behavior, 29, 119-130.

Rivers, I., & Smith, P. K. (1994). Types of bullying and their correlates. Aggressive Behavior, 20, 359-368.

Rosenberg, M. (1965). Society and the Adolescent Self-Image. Princeton, NJ: Princeton University Press.

Salmon, G., James, A. C., Cassidy, E. L., & Javaloyes, M. A. (2000). Bullying a Review: Presentations to an Adolescent Psychiatric Service and within a school for emotionally and behaviourally disturbed children. Clinical Child Psychology and Psychiatry, 5, 563-579.

Salmon, G., James, A., & Smith, D. M. (1998). Bullying in schools: Self-reported anxiety, depression and self-esteem in secondary school children. British Medical Journal, 317, 924-925.

Salmivalli, C. (1998). Not Only Bullies and Victims. Participation in Harassment in School Classes: Some Social and Personality Factors. Unpublished doctoral dissertation, Turku, Finland: Annales Universitatis Turkuensis, ser. B-225.

Salmivalli, C., Lagerspetz, K., Björkqvist, K., Österman, K., & Kaukiainen, A. (1996). Bullying as a group process: Participant roles and their relations to social status within the group. Aggressive Behavior, 22, 1-15.

Sharp, S. (1994). Training schemes for lunchtime supervisors in the United Kingdom. In P. Blatchford & S. Sharp (Eds.), Breaktime and the School: Understanding and Changing Playground Behaviour (pp. 118-133). London: Routledge.

Sharp, S., & Thompson, D. (1992). Sources of stress: A contrast between pupil perspective and pastoral teachers' perspectives. School Psychology International, 13, 229-242.

Slee, P. T. (1995). Peer victimisation and its relationship to depression among Australian primary school students. Personality and Individual Differences, 18, 57-62.

Smith, P. K., Morita, Y., Junger-Tas, J., Olweus, D., Catalano, R., & Slee, P. (Eds.) (1999). The Nature of School Bullying: A Cross National Perspective. London and New

York: Routledge.

Smith, P. K., & Sharp, S. (Eds.) (1994). School Bullying: Insights and Perspectives. London and New York: Routledge.

Sutton, J., & Smith, P. K. (1999). Bullying as a group process: An adaptation of the participant role approach. Aggressive Behavior, 25, 97-111.

Swearer, S. M., & Paulk, D. L. (1998). The Bully Survey. Unpublished manuscript. University of Nebraska-Lincoln.

Swearer, S. M., Song, S. Y., Cary, P. T., Eagle, J. W., & Mickelson, W. T. (2001). Psychosocial correlates in bullying and victimization: The relationship between depression, anxiety, and bully/victim status. Co-published simultaneously in Journal of Emotional Abuse, 2, 95-121; and in R. A. Geffner, M. Loring, & C. Young (Eds.), Bullying Behaviour: Current Issues, Research, and Interventions (pp. 95-121). New York: The Haworth Maltreatment & Trauma Press.

Tapper, K., & Boulton, M. (2002). Studying aggression in school children: The use of a wireless microphone and micro-video camera. Aggressive Behavior, 28, 356-365.

Vaernes, R. J., Myhre, G., Asch, H., Hommes, T., Hansen, I., & Tonder, O. (1991). Relationships between stress, psychological factors, health and immune levels among military aviators. Work and Stress, 5, 5-16.

Williams, K., Chambers, M., Logan, S., & Robinson, D. (1996). Association of common health symptoms with bullying in primary school children. British Medical Journal, 313, 17-19.

Wolke, D., Woods, S., Bloomfield, L., & Karstadt, L. (2001). Bullying involvement in primary school and common health problems. Archives of Disease in Childhood, 85, 197-201.

Zubrick, S. R., Silburn, S. R., Gurrin, L., Teoh, H., Shepherd, C., Carlton, J., & Lawrence, D. (1997). Western Australian Child Health Survey: Education, Health and Competence. Perth: Australian Bureau of Statistics and Institute for Child Health Research.

About the Authors

Conor Mc Guckin is a lecturer in psychology at Dublin Business School. He holds degrees from the Open University and the University of Ulster. His research interests are bullying, and the psychology of religion. He has recently completed a major project on bullying in Northern Ireland.

Christopher Alan Lewis is a lecturer in psychology at the University of Ulster at Magee College in Northern Ireland. He holds degrees from the University of Ulster. He is a Chartered Health Psychologist, an Associate Fellow of the British Psychological Society, and a Fellow of the Psychological Society of Ireland. He has published extensively in the psychology of peace, conflict and aggression, and the psychology of religion. He is Co-editor of the international journal *Mental Health, Religion and Culture*.

Chapter 14
Pastoral Care & Counseling of Couples & Families

by Jennifer S. Ripley, Ph.D.;
Stephanie D. Kemper, M.A.;
School of Psychology and Counseling
Regent University

Note: The authors would like to thank the Marriage Research Team of the Spring of 2003 at Regent University for the many ideas communicated here that were germinated in research team meetings: Raquel Hatcher, Robin Seymore, Rachel Lile, April Cunion, Jonathan Denman and Mary Beth Covert.

You're not surprised to hear the father in this family on the phone with you. The family has struggled with conflict, children that are in trouble at school, and a marriage that lacks love and caring. He asks you to meet and talk about what he should do now. The problems not only affect the individuals in the family, and the family as a whole, but your congregation. You feel they aren't maturing in their faith due to their family problems, and their ability to take leadership in the congregation is stunted. While you care deeply for this family, you feel tired. Perhaps you have thought "there must be a better way of helping couples and families in trouble, and prevent other couples from facing the troubles this family is facing." We hope this chapter will help you to rejuvenate your approach to couples and family ministry by using the congregation as your resource.

Clergy report that the single most common problem faced in pastoral care is helping couples and families (Cwik, 1997; Jones & Stahmann, 1994). The help provided stretches from educating premarital couples to addressing violence in the family. Despite this, a study of 230 Christian clergy (76 Lutheran, 49 Methodist, 60 United Church of Christ; 46 Presbyterian; Jones & Stahmann, 1994) found that only half of clergy surveyed had received specific training or supervision in pastoral care of couples and families. Many clergy have had to learn on the job how to help the couples and families in their congregation and community survive and thrive. The purpose of this chapter is to provide some practical, down to earth help to those on the front lines of supporting the American family, one of the most beleaguered social institutions of this day.

Research has indicated that while couples therapy is more effective than no treatment, couples therapy still has a low success rate (Gottman, 1999), particularly when looking at long-lasting effects. Couples and family counseling faces a unique obstacle of not only trying to change how one person sees the world and behaves in it, but helping two or more people who are daily interacting with each other change their on-going patterns of interaction . It is a challenging task for the most experienced of helpers. Not to lose heart, however, because the rewards are equally powerful. Even a small positive change in a couple or family has far-reaching effects into the community, workplace, extended family and children born to the couple. It is a goal worth pursuing.

This chapter will take a community-based approach to pastoral care, rather than a counseling approach. There are many good books on pastoral counseling for couples and families that we would recommend (Anderson, 1984; Friedman, 1985; Worthington, 1999; Wright, 1995). However, our approach is to utilize the faith community itself as the point of intervention and care for couples and families rather than rely solely on an individual pastoral counselor. For our purposes, the term "faith community" will mean the group of people that pastor is overseeing, whether that is a church, synagogue, a set of home-groups or a parish. The advantages of this approach are numerous for clergy including the use of expertise within the congregation, stretching time and energy resources for clergy, and encouraging the development of lay leadership. We expect most pastors will use a combination of pastoral counseling and leading a community-based approach.

What are the Needs of Couples and Families in Your Care?

It is important to have a clear and accurate understanding of what the state of marriages and families is in your community, what the perceived needs are, and what resources your community has to meet those needs. This may not be obvious to pastors. Families who come for pastoral counseling are often in very difficult circumstances and other couples can be adept at hiding their circumstances. A recent questionnaire completed as a dissertation project by Vanessa Martiny under Dr. Ripley's supervision at a Christian university found that among graduate students about 15% were struggling in their marriage. Another intervention at the same Christian university that screened out couples who had experienced relationship violence in the previous year had to screen out 5 couples out of 26 who had shown interest in a marital enrichment intervention. A study by Cwik (1997) also found that rabbis saw an extensive amount of couples with violence when offering care to their congregation.

Although good data is not available, we suspect these numbers are optimistic for religious groups. Even considering the many affirmative effects of practicing a faith and being part of a religious community (Butler, Gardner & Bird, 1998; Fiese & Tomcho, 2001; Horowitz, 1999; Mahoney et al, 1999), many couples struggle in their marriage and family life. Since pastors provide care across the family life span, the chances of families needing care at some point in their life is relatively high. To complicate the estimates, some communities that face a lack of social or economic privileges may find even higher rates of family strains and violence (Yanowitz, 2003).

How will you assess the needs of the families in your care?

We would encourage clergy to make an assessment of the status of the families in their care. Some well-crafted questions, perhaps created in conjunction with a researcher, can give pastors a good understanding of the strengths and weaknesses of the parish couples and families. Interviews and focus groups of randomly selected members in the religious community can also be a way of obtaining information about the perceived needs of those in the community. Pastors could give well validated and reliable questionnaires that measure marital satisfaction such as the brief, three question Kansas Marital Satisfaction Questionnaire (Crane, Middleton, & Bean, 2000). A comparative analysis of some of the leading measures of relationship satisfaction can be found in an article by Heyman, Sayers & Bellak (1994). Marital conflict (including violence) can be assessed using the Revised Conflict Tactics Scale (Straus, Hamby, Boney-McCoy, & Sugarman, 1996). Leaders can "float" ideas to congregation members to ascertain interest in programs being considered for implementation. Open-ended questions can also obtain information on the ideas and feelings of congregration members.

Should you go it alone or create a leadership team?

An early decision when beginning or renewing marriage and family life ministries is whether there are opportunities to partner with others in providing care for those in the congregation. We propose that an ideal situation would partner the clergy member in charge of pastoral care with a mental healthcare provider who has extensive experience with couples and families (such as a licensed marriage and family therapist or psychologist that specializes in marriage and family therapy) and lay members of the congregation who have a calling or gift in helping others and are natural leaders. This group of people can then tackle the questions asked in this chapter, make decisions on what types of interventions to implement in their community, implement the interventions, and assist the clergy in managing problems that arise with couples and families.

Creating a Vision

Proverbs 29:18 states that "Without a vision, the people perish." Creating a vision for the marriage and family ministry, based on knowledge of the needs of the community, can be an invigorating challenge. There are a plethora of books and materials on developing a vision for a congregation, however,that is not the purpose of this chapter. For our purposes, a vision for marriage and family ministry is an ideal that members can aspire to of what marriage and family life should and can be. A good vision should not depress couples and families that struggle with an ideal that is too lofty for most, yet it should provide hope for members of the community that a better marriage and family life is possible. It should communicate that the congregation and clergy will provide support for a strong family life, and that the obtaining of this strong and growing family life is a worthwhile endeavor. When creating a vision for couples and families in pastoral care, the following should inform the choices.

1. What is the overall vision of the religious community? Is there a focus on evangelism? Scripture teaching? Discipleship? Sacraments? Social needs? No single religious group can focus on everything, but instead tend to do a couple of things well. The couple and family vision should connect well with the overall vision of the community.

2. What is the family-life-stage of the community? Most religious groups tend to have a large number of members in the same family-life-stage. There are specific points of intervention that have typically been fruitful in helping families, especially during pre-engagement and engagement, the first year of marriage, at the birth of a first child, during particular stresses such as job losses or the declining health of a parent, and at the death of a family member. Interventions at each of these times in the family life cycle can produce long-lasting positive effects on the family

3. What community resources are available? Often religious congregations can work together or with secular agencies and groups to provide marital enrichment workshops or events, parenting classes or other supportive environments that individual congregations do not have the resources to provide.

4. What specific goals will help us achieve this vision? We would challenge clergy and leadership teams to consider three different areas to set goals—community-wide, family-focused and individuals. At the *community level* the goals would be to develop community norms for marriage and family issues in the parish or congregation. These can be goals that permeate the overall vision of the congregation and specific type of programs being implemented to create the expectation of positive change and support. At the *family level* there are numerous programs and opportunities to support couples and families as they seek to create a good and healthy family life. We will offer an evaluation of some of these programs later in this chapter. At the *individual level,* each person in the community can be encouraged to uphold marriage and the family as a good institution, support pro-family values and causes, and receive religious teachings on marriage and family regardless of their personal family status.

Making Decisions

Once an assessment of the needs of the couples and families in the clergy's care is completed (either formally or informally), and a vision of a good and healthy marriage and family life is defined for the leadership, then the pastor and team is going to need to make some decisions. We offer two resources for these decisions. One is a general list of choices of programs for implementing marriage and family initiatives in a congregation. The next is a critique and evaluation of some of the most common religious marriage programs with an emphasis on programs that have been empirically evaluated.

Choices for Implementation

Leaders or a leadership team can be creative in considering opportunities that best fit their unique congregation. We will list some of our ideas:

- Teaching from church leaders on marriage and family. Ministers can not only directly teach on marriage and family issues but use marriage and family illustrations in teachings in general.
- Creating or reviewing policies to ensure that the institution of the family is being supported. This can include requirements for marriage in the congregation or ceremonies for the baptism or dedication of an infant. Many families will interact with clergy at these important points in their family's life. Policies that encourage a spiritually meaningful experience should be encouraged, not just completing a perfunctory obligation. In many areas of the country clergy have come together to create community-wide policies for marrying in religious institutions to encourage pre-marital counseling or other family-supportive policies. The Smartmarriages initiative and Marriage Savers organization have some recommendations for community policies (Smartmarriages.com, marriagesavers.com).
- Creating or maximizing existing periodic "marriage and family" holidays or events. Some religions have holidays that already are practiced in the home or center around family life. The importance of practicing the faith in the family home has been demonstrated as important in supporting the marriage relationship (Fiese & Tomcho, 2001; Mahoney et al., 1999) and in passing on the faith to children. A congregation might celebrate marriage and the family on certain dates of the year such as Valentine's Day, Mother's Day and Father's Day.
- Forming classes, small groups or cell groups on a variety of marriage and family related topics. There are a wide variety of curriculum that can be used for these kinds of groups. We review some of the most popular versions in the next section of this chapter.
- Providing library readings, brochures, on-line resources for education and information. Leaders can review the library holdings of the religious community, brochures available to congregants and the organization's website for the inclusion of pro-family materials to be made available to congregants.
- Conducting retreats or seminars which create stronger community ties and an opportunity for education and experiential activities. This has become an increasingly popular activity among many religious groups to create stronger ties between married couples or families (regardless of traditional or non-traditional family status) through retreats.
- Implementing lay-person counseling or mentoring programs. The Saving Your Marriage Before It Starts books and program (Parrott & Parrott, 1997) and McManus' program (www.marriagesavers.org) are

reviewed later in this chapter. These offer a curriuculum for a marriage mentoring program. Lay-counseling has also become an important arm of pastoral care. The training and supervision of lay counselors should include lay-counseling for problems with couples and families.

- Offering financial support for families that are in economic need in their congregation or community. Religious groups can also consider including family-supportive services such as providing babysitting for couples to have a date-night, financial support for attending professional counseling or assisting some in covering the costs relevant to programs implemented within the parish or community. There may be other opportunities for groups to provide practical support for families in need.

Review of Specific Ministries for Couples and Families: A Critical Analysis

This section of the chapter will review seven researched programs for couples with an emphasis on an analysis of the research of each program. Premarital and marital enrichment programs are often used in religious communities as a way to strengthen marriages within the congregation or to reach out to couples and families in their community. While the goal of most programs is to strengthen marriages and ultimately decrease the chances of divorce, they tend to be quite diverse in the way they seek to do so. Our goal is to specifically review marital programs. While there are many family or parenting focused programs as well, we chose to focus on marriage as our area of primary expertise. Of particular emphasis are the religious elements and research outcomes of marital, including premarital, programs found in psychological journals and books.

Marriage programs vary in aims, techniques, leadership, time, and format. While a few programs that intertwine religious principles and research have originated and been implemented in religious settings, many have been developed in a university or community setting and adapted for use in religious congregations. Programs vary in the religious components they possess, as well as the extent to which they have been researched and shown to be effective.

Great Start

Founders: University of Chicago Divinity School directed by Don Browning
Focus: Premarital and Newly- married couples
Format: 4-5 weekly group sessions, 2 ½ hours each

The Great Start program (http://divinity.uchicago.edu/family/) was developed in partnership with the Religion, Culture and Family Project at the University of Chicago Divinity School. While this program is officially retiring in 2004, many components of the program can still be replicated. The program is aimed at helping couples prepare realistically for marriage and prevent divorce by building a skilled, happy, and growing relationship. Great Start curriculum combines two published programs, Couple Communication Program (CCP; Miller, Wackman, & Nunnally, 1983) and Prevention and Relationship Enhancement Program (PREP; Markman, Floyd, Stanley, & Lewis, 1986; Markman, Stanley, & Blumberg, 1994), with mainline Christian theological principles for marriage. Elements derived from CCP include the teaching of effective speaking, listening, and conflict resolving skills, while PREP elements include couple assessments and feedback to assist couples in further developing their relationship skills. Each couple works with an instructor certified by both CCP and PREP who facilitates their participation, PREP inventories, conducts the program, and offers follow-up skill reinforcement. Great Start instructors generally work in the context of a church congregation as part of a pre-marriage or early-marriage ministry.

While the Great Start program is comprised of PREP and CCP, two programs that have been highly evaluated and found to be effective in improving couple communication, no empirical evaluation of Great Start was located. An assessment of the program's impact on couple's marriages is needed to determine its effectiveness.

Marriage Encounter

Founders: Catholic Church
Focus: Married Couples
Format: Intensive weekend program, total of 44 hrs.

Marriage Encounter (www.wwme.org) is one of the pioneer marriage enrichment interventions conducted. Created by the Catholic church, this religiously-based intervention utilizes discussion groups and an experiential approach. Couples attend Marriage Encounter weekends held in a variety of geographical locations. Following each lecture session, couples are provided open-ended questions to discuss with an emphasis on expressing feelings. The aim of such exercises is increasing marital unity through eliciting feelings within the couples that are similar to those the couple experienced when they first married. The culmination of the intensive weekend experience is a group renewal of marriage vows.

Religious elements of Marriage Encounter stem its' origins in the Catholic Church, then eventually developed into a separate entity and expanded to serve Jewish and Protestant couples (Doherty, McCabe, & Ryder, 1978). Leaders include clergy and couples who had previously attended Marriage Encounter. The overarching goal of the program is unity, which is viewed as God's plan for marriage. Presentations are designed to promote unity through lecture and exercises.

As with many pioneer programs, it has experienced conflicting reports of effectiveness. Though the program has been reportedly beneficial to many couples, it appears to have been harmful to others (Lester & Doherty, 1983), especially couples entering the program who were already in some degree of unhappiness or conflict. Well-designed experimental clinical trials have not been published and interest in investigating the approach appeared to wane after the 1980's. A more recent investigation of the program is warranted to understand Marriage Encounter's continued and current impact on marriages.

Prevention and Relationship Enhancement Program
Founders: Markman, Floyd, Stanley, & Lewis, 1986
Focus: Premarital and Marital Couples
Format: Weekly classes or intensive weekend session, total of 12-15 hours

Prevention and Relationship Enhancement Program (PREP; Markman et al, 1986; Markman et al., 1994; www.prepinc.com) is a marital intervention aimed at building couple communication skills and preventing the development of maladaptive patterns of communication. Program elements designed to reach this aim include the presentation of structured models of communication that present clear rules concerning the communication process (Stanley, Markman, St. Peters, & Leber, 1995). The learning of such models are thought to increase the chance that a couple can successfully resolve a problem through communication. Additionally, PREP addresses each partner's relationship expectations, and encourages the sharing of expectations with one's spouse through couple exercises (Stanley et al, 1995). PREP seminars are led by instructors trained at a 2 or 3 day workshop. Given that there are no specific credentials required, clergy and lay-leaders can attend the training and lead the seminar for their congregation. A directory of previously trained PREP instructors is also available.

The original PREP curriculum includes two optional presentations that address the impact of spiritual values on the marriage relationship. Exercises center around the identification of each spouse's spiritual beliefs and values, and a dialogue regarding how each individual's beliefs can culminate in a shared world view for the couple. "Christian PREP" has also been developed based on the original PREP theory integrating Judeo-Christian principles for marriage (Stanley & Trathen, 1994). Skill-building interventions are employed as with the original PREP, while scripture is used to deepen the meaning of the material. There is a germinating "Jewish PREP" that is also developing, and has produced a self-help book but not a different program or training.

Overall, the PREP program is one of the most extensively researched programs reviewed. It has found to be effective in decreasing negative communication, increasing positive communication, and increasing levels of marital satisfaction in PREP participants when compared to control group at 4- and 5- year follow-up (Freedman, Low, Markman, & Stanley, 2002; Halford, Sanders, & Behrens, 2001; Markman et al., 1993). There are some questions as to whether the German weekend version of the program would be equally effective with American couples. However, PREP has shown itself to be beneficial in improving marriages, and has been revised based on conducted research. It is also among the first of empirically-based programs that has been adapted to be used in community settings and led by community leaders.

Saving Your Marriage Before It Starts
Founders: Parrott & Parrott, 1995
Focus: Premarital and Newly-married couples
Format: Weekend-intensive program, 6 hours of curriculum

SYMBIS is a psychoeducational marital enrichment intervention that targets the improvement of relationships in effort to decrease chances of divorce (Parrott & Parrott, 1997). Elements designed to reach such aims include exercises that address the strong influence of each partner's family of origin. Individuals are viewed as a part of a transgenerational family system that influences the individual's marital expectations, perceptions of family roles, and "unconscious rules" that govern his or her behavior and interaction with his or her partner (Parrott & Parrott, 1997). A unique feature of SYMBIS is its use of a "marriage mentoring program" in which a newlywed couple is paired with a more "seasoned" couple for one year following the program in an effort to continue supporting the new marriage. SYMBIS curriculum and materials (including books, workbooks, and video) is disseminated in bookstores, intended for use as a couple or group. SYMBIS weekends are also available for couples to attend.

The SYMBIS program incorporates a discussion on building spiritual intimacy in its final module. Based on Christian principles, this module exposes couples to spiritual disciplines that can help strengthen their relationship. Exercises center around individual reflection on one's spiritual journey, as well as how one's religious principles can help the individual value his or her mate.

An initial evaluation of the SYMBIS program assessed the effects of the program on 402 participants (Ripley et al., 2000). The main analysis indicated that individuals with low marital adjustment before the program showed significant improvement compared to those with high levels of adjustment. However, individuals with high beginning scores reported a decline in measures of marital satisfaction. There is no research on the long-term impact of programs like this.

Strategic Hope-Focused
Founders: Worthington, 1999
Focus: Married couples
Format: Weekend-intensive program, 6 hours of curriculum

Strategic Hope-Focused marriage enrichment stems from Worthington's (1999) model of brief marriage counseling. The 6-hour program seeks to promote hope in the marriage as well as build couple skills in order to strengthen relationships and decrease divorce. Program content targets couple communication and problem-solving skills, increasing couple intimacy, and an emphasis on couple commitment. *Hope-Focused Marriage Counseling* (Worthington, 1999) is available in bookstores.

Hope-Focused marriage enrichment has at its heart the model of "faith working through love" as seen in Galatians 5:5-6. This model utilizes scripture and Biblical principles surrounding commitment, valuing one's spouse, as well as forgiveness in marriage. While the model has successfully faced empirical scrutiny (Ripley & Worthington, 2002; Worthington et al., 1997), only the assessment and feedback portion of the approach has been tested for specifically Christian participants in a pilot project (Ripley et al., 2002). This finding is consistent with other research showing that assessment and feedback alone is an effective intervention (Worthington et al., 1995). The implications for churches are that relatively simple assessment and feedback tools, or hiring professionals to provide this service, can be a cost and time-effective intervention tool. This type of service can be appealing to community members who might not otherwise access a religious community as a family resource. It is also easy to protect the privacy of participants, who might be in community leadership roles.

TIME for a Better Marriage
Founders: Don Dinkmeyer and Jon Carlson, 1984
Focus: Marital Couples
Format: 10 weekly sessions

TIME (Training in Marriage Enrichment) for a Better Marriage (Dinkmeyer & Carlson, 1984) is designed to help couples learn the skills needed to build loving and supportive relationships. The founders seek to teach couples how to encourage each other, communicate effectively, and maintain equality. A healthy marriage is viewed as a safe environment in which partners are equal or congruent — free to be themselves, express their feelings, build their self-esteem, and, in turn, nourish their relationship. The basic principles of TIME for a Better Marriage include a recognition that marriages require time commitments and that small changes are important in bringing about large changes. It is recommended that group leaders be married couples who can effectively model appropriate marital interactions. *Time for a Better Marriage: Training in Marriage Enrichment* is available in bookstores.

Dinkmeyer and Carlson (1984) suggest that psychologists work in close alignment with clergy, designating spiritual matters to clergy while assessing personality/psychological issues in the TIME counseling format. The program has been suggested for use in church study groups, and a component of the program focuses on the compatibility of couples' priorities and values. Though TIME curriculum has been published and discussed (Carlson, 2003; Huber, 1986), no empirical evaluations of TIME were found.

Traits of a Happy Couple
Founders: Larry Halter, Ph.D., 1988
Focus: Marital Couples
Format: Five weekly 2-hour sessions, total of 10 hours

Traits of a Happy Couple (THC; Halter, 1988) is a psychoeducational program that seeks to build couple communication and problem solving skills, and overall enhance the marital relationship. Sessions consist of lecture and time to practice skills in areas such as common causes of conflict and ways to resolve it and practice in giving support to one's spouse. Couples are encouraged to practice learned skills and methods between each session. THC books are available through some book distributors, though the book is currently out of print.

THC curriculum combines skill-building material with explicit scripture and theological principles. Groups that are religiously-affiliated also discuss how material is consistent with their religious values.

An initial study evaluated the effects of THC on 290 churched and non-churched individuals. It was reported that both populations experienced an increase in marital adjustment in couples after attending the workshop (Noval, Combs, Wiinamaki, Bufford, & Halter, 1996). A later study (Combs, Bufford, Campbell, & Halter, 2000) found increases among the THC participants (13 couples) on measures of marital adjustment when compared to those who received no treatment. At six month follow-up, gains were held by the overall group scores, men, but not for women.

Researched Non-Religious Programs

Additional programs that are worthy of mention are those marital enrichment programs that are well-researched, but do not have religious elements. For example, Couples Communication Program (CCP; Miller, Wackman, & Nunnally, 1983) is a well-established program designed to strengthen communication skills. It is one of the most extensively researched communication skills programs with over 70 published studies. Overall findings report a very positive impact on communication following the program as well as increases in relationship satisfaction (Wampler, 1990; Knights, Schneider, & Denardo, 1985). Relationship Enhancement (RE; Guerney, 1977) is also a program designed to build communication skills, and targets not only married couples, but parents and children as well. Evaluations of the program have indicated that participants experienced gains in listening and self-disclosure skills (Ridley, Avery, Harrell, Haynes-Clements, & McCunney, 1981; Avery, Ridley, Leslie, & Miholland, 1980), relationship satisfaction, (Ross, Baker, & Guerney, 1985), as well as over-all communication skills (Ridley & Sladezeck, 1992; Ridley, Jorgensen, Morgan, & Avery, 1982). While these programs do not have religious principles integrated in the curriculum, their strong research backing demonstrates utility as marriage enrichment programs. The integration of religious principles may be an option that instructors consider.

Additional Marriage and Family Ministries

There is also a variety of well-known marriage and family ministries that are strong resources to Christian church congregations, but do not actively disseminate research. Other religions have ministries that are less well known. Gary Smalley's ministry (http://smalley.gospelcom.net) provides monthly marriage simulcast conferences, as well as a variety of books and videos on marriage and family issues. Family Life Today with Dennis Rainey (www.familylife.com) is a ministry that focuses on different aspects of family relationships through its radio broadcasts, conferences, books, and videos. Another well-known ministry is Focus on the Family with James Dobson (www.family.org) that focuses on a variety of issues within the family through a daily radio show, books, Sunday School curriculum, and other resources. Finally, Marriage Savers headed by Mike McManus (www.marriagesavers.org) is an organization that seeks to equip local congregations through marriage enrichment seminars and the development of marriage mentor ministries. Many of these can be adapted to groups of other faiths.

Some Concluding Thoughts

Sometimes clergy are concerned that there will be an impression of a lack of support for single non-married people, or non-traditional families, in the community if there is a supportive program for couples and families. The American family has certainly changed in the last 50 years, and the non-traditional family should be considered at every stage of pastoral care for couples and families. However, we would join others (Hunt, 2002) who encourage clergy and religious leaders not to shrink from strong support for intact families as a religious and socially healthy institution. Support for single people, divorced, and single parents is also very much needed in a community. Talk with single people in the congregation about the plans to implement or renew a couples and family initiative. Ask for their participation on a leadership team to offer their important perspective.

In conclusion, we hope that these pragmatic concepts have offered clergy ideas and guidelines for implementing or renewing a marriage and family life ministry in their community. Our approach encourages clergy to not only directly intervene with families themselves but use the religious community and local community as a resource for supporting the marriages and family in their care. The local faith community can make all the difference in the lives of families.

References

Anderson, H. (1984). *The Family in Pastoral Care.* Philadelphia: Fortress.

Avery, A. W., Ridley, C. A., Leslie, L. A., & Milholland, T. (1980). Relationship enhancement with premarital dyads: A six-month follow-up. *American Journal of Family Therapy, 8,* 23-30.

Butler, M.H., Gardner, B.C., & Bird, M.H. (1998). Not just a time-out: Change dynamics of prayer for religious couples in conflict situations. *Family Process, 37,* 451-478.

Carlson, J. (2003). *Time for a better marriage.* Atascadero, CA: Impact Publishers, Inc.

Combs, C. W., Bufford, R. K., Campbell, C. D., & Halter, L. L. (2000). Effects of cognitive-behavioral marriage enrichment: A controlled study. *Marriage & Family: A Christian Journal, 3,* 99-111.

Crane, D. R., Middleton, K. C, & Bean, R. A. (2000). Establishing criterion scores for the Kansas Marital Satisfaction Scale and the Revised Dyadic Adjustment Scale. *American Journal of Family Therapy, 28,* 53-60.

Crohn, J., Markman, H., Blumberg, S., & Levine, J.R. (2000). Fighting for your Jewish marriage. Jossey-Bass. New York.

Cwik, M. S. (1997). Peace in the home? The response of rabbis to wife abuse within American Jewish congregations part 2. *Journal of Psychology and Judaism, 21,* 5-30.

Dinkmeyer, D., & Carlson, J. (1984). *TIME for a better marriage.* Circle Pines, MN: American Guidance Services.

Doherty, W. J., McCabe, P., & Ryder, R. G. (1978). Marriage encounter: A critical appraisal. Journal of Marriage and Family Counseling, 4, 99-107.

Foley, G. (1995). *Family-centered church: A new parish model.* Kansas City: Sheed and Ward.

Fiese, B. H., & Tomcho, T. J. (2001). Finding meaning in religious practices: The relation between religious holiday rituals and marital satisfaction. *Journal of Family Psychology, 15,* 597-609.

Freedman, C. M., Low, S. M., Markman, H. J., & Stanley, S. M. (2002). Equipping couples with the tools to cope with predictable and unpredictable crisis events: The PREP program. *International Journal of Emergency Mental Health, 4,* 49-56.

Friedman, E. (1985). *Generation to generation: Family process in church and synagogue.* New York: Guilford Press.

Gottman, J.M. (1999). The marriage clinic. W. W. Norton & Co: New York.

Guerney, B., Jr. (1977). *Relationship enhancement: Skill training programs for therapy, problem prevention, and enrichment.* San Francisco: Jossey-Bass.

Halford, K. W., Sanders, M. R., & Behrens, B. C. (2001). Can skills training prevent relationship problems in at-risk couples? Four-year effects of a behavioral relationship education program. *Journal of Family Psychology, 15,* 750-768.

Halter, L. L. (1988). *Traits of a happy couple.* Waco, TX: Word books.

Heyman, R. E., Sayers, S. A., & Bellak, A. S. (1994). Global marital satisfaction versus marital adjustment: An empirical comparison of three measures. *Journal of Family Psychology, 8,* 432-446.

Horowitz, J.A. (1999). Negotiating couplehood: The process of resolving the December dilemma among interfaith couples. *Family Process, 38,* 303-323.

Huber, C. H. (1987). Premarital counseling using "TIME for a Better Marriage." *Individual Psychology, 43,* 77-88.

Hunt, R.A. (2002). Health, marriage, and the practice of ministry. In J. Wall, D. Browning, W. J. Doherty & S. Post (Eds), Marriage, health and the professions (pp.167-185). Grand Rapids, Michigan: W.B. Eerdmans.

Jones, E. F., & Stahmann, R. F. (1994). Clergy beliefs, preparation, and practice in premarital counseling. *The Journal of Pastoral Care, 48*, 181-186.

Knights, W. A., Schneider, L., Denardo, R. (1985). The Minnesota Couples Communication Program and clinical pastoral education. *Journal of Pastoral Care, 39*, 43-48.

Lester, M. E., & Doherty, W. J. (1983). Couples' long-term evaluations of their Marriage Encounter experience. *Journal of Marital and Family Therapy, 9*, 183-188.

Mahoney, A., Pargament, K. I., Jewell, T., Swank, A. B., Scott, E., Emery, E., & Rye, M. (1999). Marriage and the spiritual realm: The role of proximal and distal religious constructs in marital functioning. *Journal of Family Psychology, 13*, 321-338.

Markman, H. J., Floyd, F., Stanley, S., & Lewis, H. (1986). Prevention. In N. S. Jacobson & A. Gurman (Eds.), *Clinical handbook of marital therapy* (pp. 173-198). New York: Guilford Press.

Markman, H. J., Renick, M. J., Floyd, F., Stanley, S., & Clements, M. (1993). Preventing marital distress through communication and conflict management training: A four and five year follow-up. *Journal of Consulting and Clinical Psychology, 62*, 1-8.

Markman, H., Stanley, S., & Blumberg, S. L. (1994). *Fighting for your marriage: Positive steps for preventing divorce and preserving a lasting love.* San Francisco, CA: Jossey-Bass.

Miller, S., Wackman, D. B., & Nunnally, E. W. (1983). Couple communication: Equipping couples to be their own best problem solvers. *The Counseling Psychologist, 11*, 73-77.

Noval, L. S., Combs, C. W., Wiinamaki, M., Bufford, R. K., & Halter, L. L. (1996). Effects of cognitive-behavioral marriage enrichment on marital adjustment of church couples. *Journal of Psychology and Theology, 24*, 47-53.

Parrott, L., III, & Parrott, L. (1997). Preparing couples for marriage: The SYMBIS model. *Marriage & Family: A Christian Journal, 1*, 49-53.

Ridley, C. A., Avery, A. W., Harrell, J. E., Haynes-Clements, L. A., & McCunney, N. (1981). Mutual problem-solving skills training for premarital couples: A six month follow-up. *Journal of Applied Developmental Psychology, 2*, 179-188.

Ridley, C. A., Jorgensen, S. R., Morgan, A. C., & Avery, A. W. (1982). Relationship enhancement with premarital couples: An assessment of effects on relationship quality. *American Journal of Family Therapy, 10*, 41-48.

Ridley, C. A., & Sladeczek, I. E. (1992). Premarital Relationship Enhancement: Its effects on needs to relate to others. *Family Relations, 41*, 148-153.

Ripley, J. S., Parrott, L., III., Worthington, E. L., Jr., & Parrott, L. (2000). An initial evaluation of the Parrotts' Saving Your Marriage Before it Starts (SYMBIS) seminar: Who benefits? *Marriage & Family: A Christian Journal, 1*, 83-97.

Ripley, J. S., Borden, C. R., Albach, K., Barlow, L. L., Kemper, S. D., Valdez, S., Babcock, J., Smith, C. & Page, M. (2002). Providing personalized feedback for marriage enrichment through distance formats: A pilot project. *Marriage and Family: A Christian Journal, 5*, 215-228.

Ripley, J. S., & Worthington, E. L., Jr. (2002). Hope focused forgiveness group interventions to promote marital enrichment. *Journal of Counseling and Development, 80*,

453-465.

Ross, E. R., Baker, S. B., Guerney, B. G. (1985). Effectiveness of Relationship Enhancement therapy versus therapist's preferred therapy. *American Journal of Family Therapy, 13,* 1-21.

Stanley, S., Markman, H. J., St. Peters, M. & Leber, B. D. (1995) Strengthening marriages and preventing divorce: New directions in prevention research. Family Relations, 44, 392-401.

Stanley, S. M., & Trathen, D. W. (1994). Christian PREP: An empirically based model for marital and premarital intervention. Journal of Psychology and Christianity, 13, 158-165.

Straus, M. A, Hamby, S. L., Boney-McCoy, S., & Sugarman, D. B. (1996). The revised Conflict Tactics Scale (CTS2). The Journal of Family Issues, 17, 283-317.Wampler, K. S. (1990). An update on research on the Couple Communication Program. Family Science, 3, 21-40.

Worthington, E. L., Jr. (1999) *Hope-focused marriage counseling: A brief guide to therapy.* Downers Grove: Intervarsity Press.

Worthington, E. L., Jr., Hight, T. L., Ripley, J. S., Perrone, K. M., Kurusu, T. A., & Jones, D. R. (1997). Strategic hope-focused relationship-enrichment counseling: Investigations of outcome and process. *Journal of Counseling Psychology, 44,* 381-389.

Worthington, E. L. Jr., McCullough, M.E., Shortz, J.L., Mindes, E.J., Sandage, S.J., & Chartrand, J. M. (1995). Can Couples Assessment and Feedback Improve Relationships?: Assessment as a Brief Relationship Enrichment Procedure. *Journal of Counseling Psychology, 42,* 466-475.

Wright, H.N. (1995). Marriage counseling: A practical guide for pastors and counselors. Ventura, CA: Regal Books.

Yanowitz, K.L. (2003). Diversity in families. *Sex Roles, 49,* 299-300.

About The Authors

Jennifer S. Ripley, PhD, is associate professor of psychology at Regent University. A graduate of Virginia Commonwealth University, she studies marriage dynamics and interventions with a special emphasis on application in church settings. Correspondence regarding this chapter can be sent to jennrip@regent.edu

Stephanie D. Kemper, M.A., is a doctoral candidate in psychology at Regent University. She holds a master's degree in Christian Education and has developed and studied marital interventions in church settings.

Chapter 15
The Value of Forgiveness in Pastoral Care

by Julie Juola Exline PhD., Case Western Reserve University
and
Christine Smith M.Div., Laura's Home: A Ministry of The City Mission

In daily life, human beings inevitably hurt and offend one another. We behave selfishly, focusing on our own interests while neglecting those of others. We sometimes lash out at one another out of sheer spite. In other cases we offend others without knowing it, as we simply fail to consider their preferences or feelings. The damage from these transgressions pervades human relationships, playing out in the form of petty feuds, bitter divorces, murder, and war. When people have been deeply offended, they often find it natural to focus on the injustice, nurse a grudge, and perhaps seek vengeance. Those less comfortable with aggressive feelings might try to overlook the offense or to downplay its severity. In this chapter we will focus on another potential response: Offended parties can try to forgive.

We have structured this chapter as follows. After considering what forgiveness means, we will discuss some of its potential benefits. We will then raise some of the difficulties, risks, and controversies that often surround forgiveness, and we will suggest some ideas about how to address these difficulties in pastoral or clinical settings. Due to space constraints, we will focus primarily on forgiveness between individuals. However, we will also offer brief discussions of repentance and self-forgiveness along with the spiritual dilemma of anger toward God. Note that we do not attempt to present a complete process model of how forgiveness unfolds, as many different models exist in the literature (e.g., Enright & Fitzgibbons, 2000; Worthington, 1998b, 2003). Rather, our goal is simply to introduce some of the clinically important issues that surround forgiveness.

What Does Forgiveness Mean?

What does it mean to forgive? Scholars continue to debate about the precise definition of forgiveness (for discussions of definitional issues, see Enright & Fitzgibbons, 2000; Enright, Freedman, & Rique, 1998; Exline, Worthington, Hill, & McCullough, 2003). Because of the confusion surrounding the definition, we would like to start with a careful description of what forgiveness is *not*. Generally, social scientists agree that forgiveness does not mean condoning, excusing, or forgetting offenses, downplaying them or pretending that they never occurred. Forgiveness also does not imply trust; a person might forgive someone while still choosing not to remain in a close relationship with the offender. People might also forgive others while allowing them to suffer the consequences of their actions—which might include legal punishment.

Most formal definitions of forgiveness focus on its emotional side: To forgive means to make a decision, while acknowledging the seriousness of a wrong, to release or forego bitterness and vengefulness. Forgiveness might also involve an increase in positive feelings toward the offender, though there is some debate about whether this is a necessary ingredient (e.g., Enright et al., 1998). Some writers have described forgiveness as an altruistic gift or a gift of grace, one that is freely given in spite of not being deserved by the offender (e.g., Enright et al., 1998; Smedes, 1984, 1996; Worthington, 1998b, 2003; Yancey, 1997).

It is often helpful to make a distinction between the decision to forgive and the actual emotional work of forgiving (Worthington, 2003). As we discuss later, people often decide to forgive but find that their emotions are slow to follow. As such, it is often helpful to frame forgiveness as a process rather than a one-time event. Also, although most definitions focus on the private, emotional side of forgiveness, forgivers also have to decide whether and how to communicate forgiveness to the person who hurt them (for discussions, see Baumeister, Exline, & Sommer, 1998; Exline & Baumeister, 2000). We will address these issues in more detail later in the chapter.

Assessing Forgiveness and Unforgiveness

How can we tell if someone is struggling with unforgiveness? Some people will directly admit, if asked, that they do not want to forgive or have been unable to do so. But given the confusion that often surrounds the definition of forgiveness, it might be useful to ask more specific questions. Solid empirical measures do exist and are constantly being refined (for recent reviews, see McCullough, Hoyt, & Rachal, 2000; Thompson & Snyder, 2003). Such measures can be helpful in identifying unforgiveness at a trait level and in response to specific situations. They can also be useful in looking at changes in forgiveness over time. However, these self-report measures require that people have some insight into their emotional responses and are willing to honestly acknowledge them.

Even when it is not practical to administer formal measures, it is often possible to recognize signs of bitterness or coldness. For example, unforgiving people often want to dwell on old hurts, seeking sympathy and support for their positions without seeming to gain any resolution. They may be preoccupied with assigning blame. Some will cut off contact with those who hurt them, imposing a stony wall of silence. In conversation, those who have not forgiven often make cutting remarks about their offenders, and they may have trouble acknowledging anything positive about them. Some may completely refuse to speak of their offenders or will speak of them as though they do not exist (e.g., "My father is dead to me"). Their nonverbal behavior might also suggest anger when the person or the offense is mentioned (e.g., increased muscular tension and agitation; reddening or sweating; change in voice tones, such as speech becoming more loud or rapid). Although these means of assessing unforgiveness are by no means foolproof, they can all be useful indicators.

Why Forgive? Religious Teachings and the Paradoxical Power of Forgiveness

Pastoral counselors may already be convinced—at least at an intellectual level—of the value of forgiveness. Major world religions such as Christianity, Judaism, Islam, Hinduism, and Buddhism all promote the value of forgiveness (Rye et al., 2000). However, in this chapter we will take most of our examples from the Christian faith. As Christians, we thought it prudent to focus on our own tradition rather than to take the risk of misrepresenting other faiths with which we are less familiar. Unless we indicate otherwise, Biblical quotes are from the Revised Standard Version (RSV).

The theme of forgiveness lies at the very core of Christianity. According to Christian thinking, the foundation of salvation centers on receiving God's free gift of forgiveness through the atoning death of Jesus Christ (John 3:16). Christ directly commands people to forgive those who have hurt them, as in the parable of the unmerciful servant (Matt. 18: 23-35) and in his admonition to Peter to forgive not merely seven times but "seventy times seven" (Luke 17: 3-4). Jesus even declares that if people do not forgive others, they will not receive forgiveness from God for their sins (Matt. 6: 14-15).

For some devout Christians, Christ's words and actions provide ample justification for trying to forgive. However, it seems unlikely that this logic would persuade those of other faiths. Jews, for example, are more likely than Christians to believe that forgiveness should be contingent on repentance by the offender (Dorff, 1998). Mixed feelings about forgiveness also arise among Christians. The Bible heavily emphasizes not only God's mercy and forgiveness but also God's justice (e.g., Job 8:3; Psalm 9:8; see Worthington, 2003, for a review). People vary considerably in the extent to which they value justice (and other conscientiousness-related virtues) over mercy (and other warmth-oriented virtues), with most people tending to favor one type over the other (Worthington, Berry, & Parrott, 2001). The idea of forgiveness might appeal readily to those who favor mercy, while those who favor justice might balk at it. Given these differences in the value assigned to forgiveness, it seems prudent for professionals—even those working within religious counseling settings—to have information about other potential reasons to forgive, along with the arguments against forgiveness.

We now turn to some of the potential benefits of forgiveness. At least in the short term, people may resist forgiving if they are not convinced that it will directly benefit the self. (Worthington, 2003, pp. 25-27). Accordingly, we begin by highlighting these potential benefits for self-interest.

Self-related benefits for the forgiver. The emotion of anger clearly has adaptive value. People get angry when they witness unfairness, and they also get angry when they are blocked from achieving their goals. Anger is a powerful signal of injustice and unfulfilled desires. In the short term, feelings of anger can help people to feel powerful and motivated to correct unfair situations. When used constructively, anger can be a potent force in the service of justice and positive change.

But what happens when feelings of anger stay around long after an offense has passed? We contend that chronic feelings of bitterness and vengefulness are like emotional poisons, poisons that can even pass from generation to generation through cycles of hatred. (A literal example of this self-poisoning can be seen in alcohol abusers, who sometimes remark that they are "getting drunk at" their offenders.) Removal of these damaging emotions can feel like a tremendous burden being lifted from the self, as supported by research suggesting that forgiveness leads to reduced depression levels (e.g., Freedman & Enright, 1996). Forgiveness provides freedom from the negative cycle of angry rumination that is a core part of unforgiveness (e.g., McCullough et al., 1998). Because the process of having to regulate negative emotions requires considerable mental energy and self-control (Tice & Bratslavsky, 2000), anything that reduces those negative emotions should free energy to focus on other goals. When viewed in this context, it becomes clear how forgiveness is different from simply suppressing or "swallowing" anger. Attempting to suppress negative emotions such as anger taxes our mental and emotional resources, while resolving or releasing negative emotions should do the opposite—freeing up energy instead of consuming it.

To the extent that forgiveness provides relief from negative emotion, it may also be good for physical health. A growing body of empirical research suggests that chronic anger and hostility can promote both cardiovascular problems and impaired immune system functioning (see Williams, 1993). Although the literature focusing specifically on forgiveness and health is still in its infancy, some studies do suggest that forgiveness is an effective way of decreasing the physiological arousal associated with anger (e.g., Witvliet, 2001; Witvliet, Ludwig, & van der Laan, 2001).

Forgiveness can also provide a sense of personal strength. When offended parties can stop being preoccupied with their mistreatment, they set themselves free in a sense. Their minds are no longer enslaved by rumination about the offense. Some forgivers speak of relief that their offenders are no longer "taking up space" in their heads. To the extent that forgiveness is a conscious decision, people may also feel a sense of empowerment in having moved past the hurt and the helplessness associated with feeling like a victim. (Note, however, that some may cling to the benefits of the victim role; for further discussion, see Baumeister et al., 1998; Exline & Baumeister, 2000). Also, to the extent that forgiveness entails replacing negative emotion with positive emotion (Worthington, 2003), these positive emotions (e.g., love, happiness, pride) may provide energy and a sense of well-being. These positive emotions may also motivate people to build their personal and social resources so that they can cope with future challenges (Fredrickson, 2001).

Clearly, then, forgiveness has the potential to directly benefit the forgiver. However, the emotional changes described here may be difficult to make, especially in cases of deep hurt. As such, many sufferers will have to go through a lengthy process of forgiveness before they see these psychological payoffs. Also, these self-related benefits may not be specific to forgiveness per se. Forgiveness is not the only way to resolve feelings of anger and hurt (Worthington, 2003). People might also find relief in many other ways: They might pursue justice, reframe the situation in some way so that it seems less harmful or more beneficial, or simply distract themselves from their angry thoughts. Any of these could bring some relief from a sense of anger and victimization. What seems more specific to forgiveness, when compared to these other anger-reduction techniques, are the relational and spiritual benefits that forgiveness can foster. We turn to some of these next.

Relational benefits. At its core, forgiveness is not simply about resolving anger; it is about healing wounds within relationships. By dampening the impulse toward revenge, forgiveness will help to prevent further escalation of conflicts. And although forgiveness does not always lead to reconciliation, it often does. When people cease to feel resentful toward others, they often begin to see their offenders in a more positive light and may be willing to take the risk of restoring the relationship. Many models of forgiveness focus on the idea of forgiveness as an altruistic gift, a gift that is given out of love and not because the offender deserves it. And when people receive genuine acts of love and kindness, they will often (though not always) be spurred to behave kindly in return. Once the defenses of pride are down and people begin to empathize with their offenders, offended parties may also begin to realize that they were not truly innocent victims. Perhaps they had some part in triggering or escalating the offense. This is not always the case, obviously, but it is often the case—particularly in ongoing relationships in which people's lives are deeply intertwined. Having seen their own role in the transgression, individuals may then be willing to take the step of apologizing or making amends to the other person. These relationship-restoring steps may, in turn, prompt positive responses from the other person. We acknowledge that many things can go wrong in this cycle, and we will address some of those in a later section. But we contend that most of the time, a willingness to forgive will be a healing force within relationships.

Spiritual benefits. Although the potential spiritual benefits of forgiveness have received little empirical attention to date, there is certainly reason to suggest the potential for significant gains in this area. Within theistic traditions, forgiveness can be viewed as a means of drawing closer to God. In theological systems in which people are encouraged or commanded to forgive, an unforgiving attitude might be viewed as sin that will create a rift in one's relationship with God. As such, devout believers may attempt to forgive, in part, out of a desire to obey God—and, to some extent, from fear of the consequences of disobedience. On the brighter flipside of this equation, a decision to forgive could bring a sense of closeness to God, particularly to the extent that it reflects obedience to God's commands or identification with a redeemed or God-inspired part of the forgiver's nature.

The actual process of forgiving could also steer people toward God. For example, some studies suggest that in order to forgive others, people may benefit by acknowledging their own capability for wrongdoing (e.g., Exline, Baumeister, Witvliet, Bushman, & Kok, 2003; Worthington, 2003). Focusing on one's own sins will reduce self-righteousness, which should in turn make people less harsh in their judgments of others (Matthew 7: 3-5). Awareness of one's sins should also prompt people to approach God for forgiveness—though perhaps only if they have an image of God as being forgiving rather than cruel (see, e.g., Benson & Spilka, 1973).

Believers may also turn to God to ask for help in finding the strength to forgive, especially when the process seems exceptionally difficult. Within Christianity, for example, wounded people may identify with the suffering, humility, and forgiving attitude of Christ. Consider the last words of Christ on the cross: "Father, forgive them; for they know not what they do" (Luke 23:34). The New Testament also provides powerful examples of other Christians who engaged in extraordinary acts of forgiveness, such as Stephen in response to his stoning (Acts 7:59-60). In addition to looking toward such examples of forgiveness, Christians may seek the transforming power of the Holy Spirit in giving them the strength to forgive and to love unconditionally. Some will ask God directly to heal their emotional wounds (e.g., hurt, fear, anger). Others will take comfort primarily by entrusting the situation into God's hands—including their desires to see justice done. This is most evident throughout the book of Psalms. For example, many of the Lament Psalms reflect the outpouring of hearts wounded by enemies and cries to God for justice (e.g., Psalm 22; Psalm 35).

When People Won't (or Can't) Forgive:
Risks and Barriers Associated with Forgiving

Based on prior research in psychology, it is clear that certain types of situations help to set an ideal stage for forgiveness (see Exline, Worthington, et al., 2003, for a review). To make forgiveness easy, the offense would be a minor, unintentional one without serious negative consequences (e.g., Boon & Sulsky, 1997). The offense would take place within a close relationship in which both parties are committed to each other (e.g., Finkel, Rusbult, Kumashiro, & Hannon, 2002). As soon as the harm was recognized, the offending party would offer a sincere apology along with other attempts at amends (e.g., Ohbuchi, Kameda, & Agarie, 1989; Witvliet, Worthington, & Wade, 2002). In this ideal climate for fostering forgiveness, the offended party would be an agreeable, emotionally stable person who would get over negative emotions easily and would not ruminate about problems or hurts (McCullough & Hoyt, 2001). The offended person would also have a values system—religious or otherwise—that favors forgiveness, creating a predisposition to view forgiveness as a wise choice (e.g., Berry, Worthington,

Parrott, O'Connor, & Wade, 2001). The presence of any of these factors will make forgiveness easier.

But in real life, offenses often do not conform to this pattern. People have the potential to wound each other deeply, and pain and anger can become chronic as people ruminate over injustices. Relationships are often strained and unsteady even before serious offenses occur. The parties might even be strangers to one another, as in street crimes. Often, both parties view themselves as innocent victims and remain blind to their own roles in the conflict. In fact, perpetrators of the most devastating crimes—rapes, murders, and the like—often do not seem to see their own actions as wrong. Instead, they see their actions as justified based on a global sense of being victimized (Baumeister, 1997). Even when offenders do recognize their wrongdoing, fear, pride, or distance may block them from apologizing (Exline & Baumeister, 2000).

In everyday life, then, forgiveness will often be a tall order. As with other processes in which people are not ready to change (see Prochaska, 2000), extensive time and discussion may be required before a person will even consider the prospect of forgiving. And not all will decide to forgive. Some individuals may not be willing to consider forgiveness at all, and others will decide against forgiveness after a process of deliberation. As such, regardless of what an individual believes about the appropriateness of forgiveness, it can be risky to pressure others to forgive. Doing so can create a sort of "double victimization" in which someone who has been deeply hurt is now being shamed for not forgiving (Lamb & Murphy, 2002). In response to internal or external pressure, wounded people may try to forgive before they are emotionally prepared to grapple with the painful issues at hand. Attempted shortcuts to forgiveness may be costly, promoting denied or suppressed emotions rather than true forgiveness. Again, we reiterate the importance of helping individuals see forgiveness as a process, not a one-time event. The exploration of forgiveness-related themes is clearly a delicate clinical issue, one that demands awareness of the many reservations and difficulties surrounding forgiveness. We outline some of these below.

Different understandings of forgiveness. As discussed above, scholars have worked to develop careful definitions of forgiveness. In everyday life, however, people's definitions do not always align with these scholarly definitions. A recent large-scale survey (Jeffress, 2000) demonstrated that in the minds of many Americans, forgiveness *does* imply reconciliation, forgetting offenses, and releasing offenders from consequences —even though scholarly definitions indicate that none of these elements should be part of forgiveness. In daily life, then, people may balk at the notion of forgiving because they believe that forgiving will require them to do things that seem weak or unwise. For example, a battered woman might not want to forgive her husband because in her mind, forgiveness implies the need to reconcile and to forget about past abuse. Such examples highlight the need to be clear about what forgiveness is and what it is not, particularly in clinical settings in which forgiveness is being discussed as an option. To the extent that discussions of forgiveness focus on transcending lesser goals (e.g., petty revenge; the energizing effects of anger) in favor of higher goals (e.g., good health; healed relationships; allegiance to personal ethical codes), such discussions might help to frame forgiveness as a strength.

Waiting for repayment. When people hurt one another, the resulting injustice creates what Worthington terms an *injustice gap* (Worthington, 2003; see also Exline, Worthington, et al., 2003): In the eyes of the offended party, a gap exists between the way things are and the way that they should be. Theoretically, anything that helps to reduce the degree of injustice makes this injustice gap smaller. For example, the injustice gap will shrink if the offender suffers punishment or offers an apology, or if goods that were taken are restored to the offended party. The reduced sense of injustice, in turn, makes forgiveness easier and more likely.

Some people insist that injustice be remedied—fully or at least partly— before they will consider forgiveness as an option. This insistence on repayment appears to be greater in individuals who have a high sense of personal entitlement (Exline, Baumeister, Bushman, & Campbell, 2004). Entitled individuals are those who see themselves as especially deserving of respect and special treatment, and they are highly invested on collecting on debts owed to them. From their perspective, to not insist on repayment would imply a lack of self-respect. People might also insist on repayment if they have a strong tendency to insist on justice (Worthington et al., 2001). Or they might be following religious teachings or personal principles that favor conditional rather than unconditional forgiveness (see Weisenthal, 1998). In the eyes of someone who is preoccupied with repayment, the notion of forgiveness as an unearned gift might seem distasteful or even wrong. And even when forgiving does not seem wrong, pride often gets in the way and makes people reluctant to do anything that might be construed as backing down or giving up ground. It may be very threatening to surrender one's identity as a tough, justice-dealing vigilante who others dare not offend.

But what if someone insists on repayment before forgiving and is unlikely to ever receive such payment? Some offenders simply have no remorse or insight about their transgressions. Others die or move away, and still others are unknown to their victims. In any of these cases, offended parties are unlikely to get direct repayment from the offenders. In such cases, it is useful to consider other ways to reduce the injustice gap. There are many possibilities (Worthington, 2003), and we list just a few here. One approach is to try to see the situation from the offender's perspective and to try to think of valid reasons why he or she committed the offense. This sort of empathic approach often facilitates forgiveness (e.g., McCullough et al., 1998). To reduce the sense of themselves as innocent victims, offended parties might try to find some benefit in the situation. They might also reflect on times in which they have hurt others (Exline, Baumeister, et al., 2003)—especially if they have been forgiven and have received forgiveness for those offenses

(Worthington, 2003). For people who believe that God has forgiven their sins, being reminded of this fact could promote gratitude and motivation to pass on the unearned gift of forgiveness to other people—especially if they believe that they did nothing to earn God's forgiveness (see Yancey, 1997). The New Testament encourages followers of Christ to forgive others as they have been forgiven (Luke 6:37; Ephesians 4:32, Colossians 3:13). Of course, none of these approaches are likely to be easy, especially when offended parties are furious at their offenders and want the satisfaction of seeing them lowered in some way.

Fear of being hurt again. Sometimes people are reluctant to forgive because they fear that forgiving will open them up to being hurt again. In such cases, the fear might center not on forgiveness per se but on how it is expressed to the other person. People might fear communicating forgiveness in a way that seems to minimize the offense or release the offender from consequences. Because of this risk, some people might try to make a firm boundary between private forgiveness and communicated forgiveness. For example, in a situation in which the perpetrator is known to be exploitative or abusive, an offended party might choose to "silently" forgive without choosing to communicate this to the offender (see Baumeister et al., 1998).

But it is often not so simple to draw a line between private forgiveness, communicated forgiveness, and reconciliation. For example, these three concepts often seem to merge together in Scripture, as in the parable of the prodigal son (Luke 15: 11-24) and passages about God's reconciliation of the world unto Himself (II Corinthians 5:19). Another issue is that in daily life, forgiveness is often driven by feelings of love. When rooted in love, the private act of forgiving could easily "warm up" one's feelings toward the offender. These warm feelings may press a forgiver to reconcile, trust, or at least treat the offender in a kind way. We believe that most of the time, these attempts to reach out to the offender will be more helpful than harmful. For example, one laboratory-based study revealed that offenders behaved better after being forgiven than after not being forgiven (Kelln & Ellard, 1999). However, if the offender is someone bent on exploitation, he or she might be especially prone to take advantage of people who seem kind, trusting, and unassertive. This risk highlights the importance of communicating forgiveness in an assertive way—especially when offenders are prone to exploitation or do not seem to be taking responsibility for their actions. With such offenders, it seems important to communicate that harm was indeed done, to take steps to protect the self, and to set clear limits about what will happen if further mistreatment occurs.

Protective anger on behalf of another person. One issue that has only begun to receive empirical attention is the notion that people can become intensely angry even when they were not the direct targets of an offense. If they care about the person who was directly harmed, they might take offense themselves, holding on to angry feelings out of a sense of loyalty or protectiveness toward the person who was directly hurt (e.g., Exline, 2002). They might believe that if they reduce their angry feelings, they will be failing to support their loved one. One might even imagine a situation in which the person who was directly hurt forgives quickly (or perhaps condones or forgets the offense). This person's parent or spouse might remain angry on principle, reasoning that someone needs to remain angry to ensure that the injustice is not forgotten. This righteous anger on behalf of others has been discussed in anecdotal accounts of crimes such as Holocaust atrocities (Weisenthal, 1998).

In cases in which people stay angry out of loyalty, it might be useful to focus on how they can directly support their loved one without having to burden themselves (or, perhaps, the person who was hurt) with longstanding bitterness and resentment. For example, they might be able to encourage their loved ones to stand up for themselves, or they might be able to provide comfort or other help in times of need. In some cases, it might be helpful to consider the possibility that the protective person's expressions of continued anger and bitterness might actually be more harm than help to the loved one. Their repeated expressions of hostility might make it more difficult for the directly offended person to forgive, and they might suggest a lack of support for one who is earnestly trying to forgive or reconcile.

Ongoing anger and hurt in spite of decisional forgiveness. Often people find that in spite of a conscious decision to forgive, their emotions are slow to change. They may continue to feel deep hurt and flashes of rage even after a sincere decision to forgive, and they may berate themselves for continuing to have these negative feelings. In such cases it might be helpful to point out that although humans have some control over their emotions, they do not have perfect control. Anger and fear are "hot emotions" that demand attention. They cannot always be whisked away through an effort of will.

It is also important to note that forgiveness is not a cure-all in the wake of transgression (Lamb & Murphy, 2002). Offenses do not only cause anger; they can also cause deep hurt, grief, mistrust, fear, and nagging questions about why the offense occurred (Worthington, 2003). Wounded people might find that they can forgive—that is, they can resolve their feelings of anger and bitterness—but they cannot rid themselves of the other negative feelings and thoughts left in the wake of the offense. In traumatic situations, intrusive thoughts or flashbacks may further complicate the picture. Any of these sources of distress might require focused therapeutic attention.

Healing these emotional wounds may take time, regardless of whether the wounded person has forgiven or is trying to forgive. What techniques might help to heal these wounded emotions? We mention a few here, although readers may also wish to turn to clinically-oriented texts for more detailed discussions and models of the forgiveness process (e.g., Enright, 2001; Enright & Fitzgibbons,

2000; Worthington, 1998a, 2003). Simply being able to talk through the issues with a counselor or another supportive person is likely to be helpful for many. In addition to offering support, it will often be helpful to look for repeated patterns of hurt. If it is possible to uncover a core issue underlying many different hurts, this understanding can aid in healing and also reduce the risk of future hurts.

Also, a growing body of research suggests that when people do emotionally expressive writing about painful events, they experience emotional and physical health benefits—particularly to the extent that the writing helps them to fit the events into a meaningful story (e.g., Pennebaker & Seagal, 1999). This is actually an ancient technique. Again, many Psalms are expressions of hurt, anger, fear and turmoil lifted up to God in written, musical form. Some of our research suggests that writing "imaginary letters" (i.e., not to be mailed) to the offender can be helpful, assuming that they are not limited to name-calling and other expressions of hostility (Exline & Molnar, 2001). Although less studied empirically, it seems reasonable to propose that those not inclined toward writing might try other forms of creative expression such as poetry, music, or art.

Within some Christian circles, forgiveness interventions include techniques that emphasize God's supernatural power at work in people's everyday lives. For example, some interventions include requests for God's supernatural healing for wounded emotions (e.g., "with his stripes, we are healed", Isaiah 53:5). Christians may pray for the strength to forgive, and they may seek God's protection against the formation of "seeds" or "roots" of bitterness (Hebrews 12: 14-15). They may also request insights from God about core problems that have caused or further inflamed the wound. In some Christian circles, individuals will also seek deliverance or protection from evil forces that are seen as causing or perpetuating unforgiveness (e.g., MacNutt, 1995).

What if God Is the Target of Anger?

As discussed above, people often turn to God for help when they are trying to forgive. But what if God is the target of anger? Regardless of whether a person believes that God can transgress or make mistakes, people often feel offended by God (e.g., Exline & Martin, 2004; Novotni & Petersen, 2001; Yancey, 1988). Most often, these feelings arise when people hold God responsible for some form of suffering that seems undeserved. These can include serious illness, natural disasters, or freak accidents, but they can also include everyday events such as a bad breakup or failing to receive a coveted job promotion. Anger toward God can lead to serious crises of faith, particularly if people respond to their anger by turning away from God (Exline, Fisher, Rose, & Kampani, 2004).

People are often afraid to admit feelings of anger toward God on the grounds that such feelings are morally wrong (Exline & Martin, 2004; Novotni & Petersen, 2001). As such, an important first step is simply to be able to acknowledge these feelings. This does not mean that these feelings need to be expressed in a hostile way, only that their presence is acknowledged. For example, a recent intervention by Zornow (2001) focuses on use of the Psalms as part of "crying out" to God.

Anger toward God may subside if people can put a positive spin on the situation. For example, they may uncover some deeper meaning or benefit in the situation, or they may decide that God was not really to blame. For those who have distanced themselves from God out of fear or mistrust, another crucial step is to simply open up these lines of communication. This might take the form of spoken or written prayer or perhaps the use of imagery. To the extent that people believe that God desires close relationships with people, any technique that reaffirms God's love for the self is likely to be helpful.

The Other Side of the Coin:
Problems with Repentance, Receiving Forgiveness, and Self-Forgiveness

Not only are people harmed by the transgressions of others; they also commit their own transgressions and must face decisions about repentance and seeking forgiveness. As with forgiveness, repentance holds out tremendous promise for helping to heal relationships. Recall that apology and acknowledgment of wrongdoing are major predictors of forgiveness; therefore, those who humble themselves to make these sorts of peace offerings greatly increase their odds of being forgiven. The Psalms of David suggest that confessing sins to God can be good for the soul, bringing a profound sense of peace upon receiving God's forgiveness (Psalm 32:1-5). Judeo-Christian traditions place a heavy emphasis on the spiritual requirement of repenting to God (e.g., Isaiah 30:15; Ezekiel 18:30; Matthew 3:2; I John 1:9). The requirement of repenting to others is also central within New Testament teachings (e.g., James 5:16) and within Judaism, where it is often framed within the practice of *Teshuvah* or return (Dorff, 1988; Schimmel, 2002).

In spite of these potential benefits, many barriers can block people from engaging in genuine acts of repentance: lack of insight, pride, shame, and fear of negative consequences, to name just a few (Exline & Baumeister, 2000). Smith (2004) outlines some ways in which people can fall short of true repentance. For example, offenders may make superficial apologies or amends in order to keep the situation smooth, then quickly return to behaviors that harm the other person. Others will do just the opposite, correcting their behavior but leaving the offended party yearning for a direct apology. Some offenders will not accept responsibility and will attempt to shift the blame to other sources, including the offended party. Others cannot repent because they remain totally blind to their wrongdoing—a situation that can easily arise when offended parties are reluctant to confront their offenders. The literature on Twelve Step programs provides an excellent place to learn more about the barriers and issues surrounding repentance, particularly those related to pride (Kurtz & Ketcham, 1992). Writings on reconciliation also offer helpful insights about repentance and the need to rebuild trust in these delicate situations (e.g., Holeman, 2003; Schimmel, 2002; Worthington, 2003).

In other cases the problem is not a lack of repentance but difficulty letting go of chronic feelings of anger, guilt, and condemnation toward the self.

Granted, a certain degree of guilt may be essential to foster repentance (Baumeister, Stillwell, & Heatherton, 1994; Holmgren, 1992; Tangney & Dearing, 2003). But what if repentance has already been made or has been blocked somehow—perhaps by the death of the offended party or by belief that confession would only cause further harm? When offenders continue to berate themselves for their misdeeds, they create a heavy burden for themselves. Granted, some people may believe that this burden is deserved, and they will see virtue in continuing to carry it. However, carrying this high level of negative emotion is likely to take a toll on the person's emotional, spiritual, and perhaps even physical well-being.

As interpersonal forgiveness relieves anger toward others, self-forgiveness relieves anger toward the self (Flanigan, 1996; Holmgren, 2002). Self-forgiveness also parallels interpersonal forgiveness in that it does not imply minimizing or abdicating responsibility for one's offense (Holmgren, 1992). Although self-forgiveness has not been studied as much as interpersonal forgiveness, it conceptually shares many of the same basic elements: After taking responsibility and making amends where possible, a person makes a conscious decision to release harsh, condemning feelings and attitudes toward the self.

For many people, an important precursor of self-forgiveness is seeking and receiving forgiveness from God. Formalized processes of confession and penance are likely to be helpful for some, whereas others may turn to more private processes of prayer and reflection. Regardless of what means people use to seek God's forgiveness, the process may be daunting for those who have an image of God as punitive, unforgiving, or disapproving of the self. A poor self-image might also make it hard for a person to forgive the self or to accept God's forgiveness, but pride may also play a role: Even if they believe that God has forgiven them, some people will continue to punish themselves because they take pride in holding themselves to perfectionistic standards of behavior. In any of these cases, a central goal may be to help people acknowledge their limitations and wrongs while maintaining a compassionate stance toward themselves (see Neff, 2003).

Summary and Conclusions

There is no question that forgiveness can be difficult, especially in cases of deep hurt. Wounded individuals may equate forgiveness with condoning or reconciliation—options that may seem weak or even dangerous. They may hold onto their anger for principled reasons, out of a desire to protect themselves or someone they love. Even when people sincerely want to forgive, they may find that their anger is slow to fade and their wounds are slow to heal. In some cases, anger may be directed toward God, the self, a faceless group, or someone who has died. Each of these cases present unique challenges in facing the problem of forgiveness.

Still, we believe that there is sufficient evidence to suggest that forgiveness is worth the effort. Granted, people can learn many important things from their anger, an emotion that gives important messages about injustice and unfulfilled desires. Anger can be a signal that a person needs to protect or assert the self, perhaps trying to change a situation so that damage can be repaired and not repeated. But we contend that once people have learned from their anger and acted constructively in response to its signals, they will not benefit from holding on to this emotion over long periods of time. When anger turns to bitterness, it becomes a heavy burden. Similarly, feelings of shame, guilt, and fear can become heavy burdens for those who have offended others. We believe that when people learn how to release these burdens, they actually give themselves a gift: a powerful tool for personal, spiritual, and relational growth.

References

Baumeister, R. F. (1997). *Evil: Inside human violence and cruelty.* New York: W H. Freeman.

Baumeister, R. F., Exline, J. J., & Sommer, K. L. (1998). The victim role, grudge theory, and two dimensions of forgiveness. In E. L. Worthington, Jr. (Ed.), *Dimensions of forgiveness* (pp. 79-104). Philadelphia: Templeton.

Baumeister, R. F., Stillwell, A. M., & Heatherton, T. F. (1994). Guilt: An interpersonal approach. *Psychological Bulletin, 115,* 243-267.

Benson, P. L., & Spilka, B. (1973). God image as a function of self-esteem and locus of control. *Journal for the Scientific Study of Religion, 13,* 297-310.

Berry, J. W., Worthington, E. L., Jr., Parrott, L. III, O'Connor, L., & Wade, N. G. (2001). Dispositional forgivingness: Development and construct validity of the Transgression Narrative Test of Forgiveness (TNTF). *Personality and Social Psychology Bulletin, 27,* 1277-1290.

Boon, S. D., & Sulsky, L. M. (1997). Attributions of blame and forgiveness in romantic relationships: A policy-capturing study. *Journal of Social Behavior and Personality, 12,* 19-44.

Dorff, E. N. (1998). The elements of forgiveness: A Jewish approach. In E. L. Worthington, Jr. (Ed.), *Dimensions of forgiveness* (pp. 29-55). Philadelphia: Templeton.

Enright, R. D. (2001). *Forgiveness is a choice: A step-by-step process for resolving anger and restoring hope.* Washington, DC: American Psychological Association.

Enright, R. D., & Fitzgibbons, R. P. (2000). *Helping clients forgive: An empirical guide for resolving anger and restoring hope.* Washington, DC: American Psychological Association Books.

Enright, R. D., Freedman, S., & Rique, J. (1998). The psychology of interpersonal forgiveness. In R. D. Enright & J. North (Eds.), *Exploring forgiveness* (pp. 46-63). Madison: University of Wisconsin Press.

Exline, J. J. (2002, February). *When loved ones suffer harm: Protectiveness, loyalty, and other's forgiveness as predictors of one's own anger.* Poster presented at a meeting of the Society for Personality and Social Psychology, Savannah.

Exline, J. J., & Baumeister, R. F. (2000). Expressing forgiveness and repentance: Benefits and barriers. In M. E. McCullough, K. Pargament, & C. Thoresen (Eds.), *Forgiveness: Theory, research, and practice* (pp. 133-155). New York: Guilford.

Exline, J. J., Baumeister, R. F., Bushman, B. J., & Campbell, W. K. (2004). *Perceptions of entitlement: A barrier to forgiveness?* Manuscript submitted for publication.

Exline, J. J., Baumeister, R. F., Witvliet, C. V. O., Bushman, B. J., & Kok, C. (2003, March). Moral humility as a facilitator of forgiveness. Symposium presentation in J. Exline (Chair), *New frontiers for forgiveness: Religious differences and links with humility.*

Presented at the first annual Mid-Winter Research Conference on Religion and Spirituality, Timonium, MD.

Exline, J. J., Fisher, M., Rose, E., & Kampani, S. (2004). *The emotional side of atheism: Anger toward God as a predictor of unbelief.* Manuscript in preparation.

Exline, J. J., & Martin, A. (2004). Wrestling with God. Chapter to appear in E. L. Worthington, Jr. (Ed.), *Handbook of forgiveness research.* New York: Guilford.

Exline, J. J., & Molnar, N. P. (2001, August). Letters, logic, and a lack of self-righteousness: Facilitators of forgiveness. In P. Hill (Chair), *Forgiveness as positive science: Theory, research, and clinical applications.* Symposium at the annual meeting of the American Psychological Association, San Francisco, CA.

Exline, J. J., Worthington, E. L., Jr., Hill, P., & McCullough, M. E. (2003). Forgiveness and justice: A research agenda for social and personality psychology. *Personality and Social Psychology Review, 7,* 337-348.

Finkel, E. J., Rusbult, C. E., Kumashiro, M., & Hannon, P. (2002). Dealing with betrayal in close relationships: Does commitment promote forgiveness? *2002-02942-007Journal of Personality & Social Psychology,* 82, 956-974.

Flanigan, B. (1996). *Forgiving yourself.* New York: Macmillan.

Fredrickson, B. L. (2001). The role of positive emotions in positive psychology: The broaden-and-build theory of positive emotions. *American Psychologist, 56,* 218-226.

Freedman, S. R., & Enright, R. D. (1996). Forgiveness as an intervention goal with incest survivors. *Journal of Consulting and Clinical Psychology, 64,* 983-992.

Holeman, V. T. (2003). Marital reconciliation: A long and winding road. *Journal of Psychology & Christianity, 22,* 30-42.

Holmgren, M. R. (2002). Forgiveness and self-forgiveness in psychotherapy. In S. Lamb & J. G. Murphy (Eds.), *Before forgiving: Cautionary views of forgiveness in psychotherapy* (pp. 112-135). New York: Oxford.

Jeffress, R. (2000). *When forgiveness doesn't make sense.* Colorado Springs: Waterbrook.

Kelln, B. R. C., & Ellard, J. H. (1999). An equity theory analysis of the impact of forgiveness and retribution on transgressor compliance. *Personality and Social Psychology Bulletin, 25,* 864-872.

Kurtz, E., & Ketcham, K. (1992). *The spirituality of imperfection: Storytelling and the search for meaning.* New York: Bantam.

Lamb, S., & Murphy, J. G. (Eds.). (2002). *Before forgiving: Cautionary views of forgiveness in psychotherapy.* New York: Oxford.

MacNutt, F. (1995). *Deliverance from evil spirits: A practical manual.* Grand Rapids, MI: Chosen Books.

McCullough, M. E., & Hoyt, W. T. (2002). Transgression-related interpersonal motivations: Personality substrates of forgiveness and their links to the Big Five. *Personality and Social Psychology Bulletin, 28,* 1556-1573.

McCullough, M. E., Hoyt, W. T., & Rachal, K. C. (2000). What we know (and need to know) about assessing forgiveness constructs. In M. E. McCullough, K. Pargament, & C. Thoresen (Eds.), *Forgiveness: Theory, research, and practice* (pp. 65-88). New York: Guilford.

McCullough, M. E., Rachal, K. C., Sandage, S. J., Worthington, E. L., Jr., Brown, S. W., & Hight, T. L. (1998). Interpersonal forgiving in close relationships II: Theoretical elaboration and measurement. *Journal of Personality and Social Psychology, 75,* 1586-1603.

Neff, K. D. (2003). The development and validation of a scale to measure self-compassion.

Self & Identity, 2, 223-250.

Novotni, M., & Petersen, R. (2001). *Angry with God.* Colorado Springs, CO: Piñon.

Ohbuchi, K., Kameda, M., & Agarie, N. (1989). Apology as aggression control: Its role in mediating appraisal of and response to harm. *Journal of Personality and Social Psychology, 56,* 219-227.

Pennebaker, J. W., & Seagal, J. D. (1999). Forming a story: The health benefits of narrative. *Journal of Clinical Psychology, 55,* 1243-1254.

Prochaska, J. O. (2000). Change at differing stages. In C. R. Snyder & R. E. Ingram (Eds.), *Handbook of psychological change* (pp. 109-127). NY: Wiley.

Rye, M. S., Pargament, K. I., Ali, M. A., Beck, G. L., Dorff, E. N., Hallisey, C., Narayanan, V., & Williams, J. G. (2000). Religious perspectives on forgiveness. In M. E. McCullough, K. I. Pargament, & C. E. Thoresen (Eds.), *Forgiveness: Theory, research, and practice* (pp. 17-40). New York: Guilford.

Schimmel, S. (2002). *Wounds not healed by time: The power of repentance and forgiveness.* New York: Oxford.

Smedes, L. B. (1984). *Forgive and forget: Healing the hurts we don't deserve.* New York: Harper & Row.

Smedes, L. B. (1996). *The art of forgiving.* Nashville: Moorings.

Smith, C. (2004). *Let the healing begin!* Manuscript in preparation.

Tangney, J. P., & Dearing, R. L. (2003). *Shame and guilt.* New York: Guilford.

Tice, D. M., & Bratslavsky, E. (2000). Giving in to feel good: The place of emotion regulation in the context of general self-control. *Psychological Inquiry, 11,* 149-159.

Thompson, L. Y. & Snyder, C.R. (2003). Measuring forgiveness. In S. J. Lopez, & C.R. Snyder, (Eds.), *Positive psychological assessment: A handbook of models and measures* (p. 301-312). Washington, DC: American Psychological Association.

Wiesenthal, S. (1998). *The sunflower: On the possibilities and limits of forgiveness* (Revised and expanded edition). New York: Schocken.

Williams, R. D. (1993). *Anger kills.* New York: Crown.

Witvliet, C. V. O. (2001). Forgiveness and health: Reflections on a matter of faith, health, and physiology. *Journal of Psychology & Christianity, 29,* 212-224.

Witvliet, C. V. O., Ludwig, T. E., & van der Laan, K. L. (2001). Granting forgiveness or harboring grudges: Implications for emotion, physiology, and health. *Psychological Science, 121,* 117-123.

Witvliet, C.V.O., Worthington, E.L., Jr., & Wade, N.G. (2002). Victims' heart rate and facial EMG responses to receiving an apology and restitution. Psychophysiology, 39, S88.

Worthington, E. L., Jr. (Ed.) (1998a). *Dimensions of forgiveness: Psychological research and theological perspectives.* Philadelphia: Templeton.

Worthington, E. L., Jr. (1998b). The pyramid model of forgiveness: Some interdisciplinary speculations about unforgiveness and the promotion of forgiveness. In E. L. Worthington, Jr. (Ed.), *Dimensions of forgiveness* (pp. 107-137). Philadelphia: Templeton.

Worthington, E. L., Jr. (2003). *Forgiving and reconciling.* Downers Grove, IL: Intervarsity Press.

Worthington, E.L., Jr., Berry, J.W., & Parrott, L. III. (2001). Unforgiveness, forgiveness, religion, and health. In T. G. Plante & A. Sherman (Eds.), *Faith and health* (pp. 107-138). New York: Guilford.

Yancey, P. (1988). *Disappointment with God: Three questions no one asks aloud.* New York: Harper Collins.

Yancey, P. (1997). *What's so amazing about grace?* Grand Rapids: Zondervan.

Zornow, G. B. (2001). *Crying out to God: Prayer in the midst of suffering.* Unpublished manuscript.

About The Authors

Julie Juola Exline, Ph.D., received her Ph.D. in clinical psychology from Stony Brook University in 1997 and completed her postdoctoral research in the field of social psychology. She currently serves as an Assistant Professor of Psychology at Case Western Reserve University. Dr. Exline conducts research on moral and religious issues using the perspectives of clinical and social psychology. She has published extensively in these areas and recently received the Margaret Gorman Early Career Award in the Psychology of Religion.

The **Reverend Christine A. Smith** currently serves as a pastoral counselor at Laura's Home - A Christian based, residential recovery program for homeless women and their children in the greater Cleveland area. Rev. Smith provides individual pastoral counseling to clients, develops and implements educational curriculum and acts as a liaison to community agencies

Correspondence should be addressed to Julie Juola Exline, Department of Psychology, 11220 Bellflower, Case Western Reserve University, Cleveland, Ohio 44106-7123. Phone: (216) 368-8573. FAX: (216) 368-4891. E-mail: julie.exline@case.edu.

Chapter 16
Spiritual Meditation as a Resource for Troubled Parishioners

by Amy B. Wachholtz & Kenneth I. Pargament
Bowling Green State University

Utilizing Spiritual Meditation with Troubled Parishioners
Brief History of Meditation

It has been said about Irish history that it can either be covered in a single paragraph or in 15 volumes. The same is true of the history of meditation. Meditation has been used for millennia, across many different cultural traditions, and for many different purposes. Meditation has a long history of association with spiritual and religious practices. Though it is nearly impossible to date the entry of meditation into spiritual practice, it can be traced back at least 3000 years (Walsh, 1995), with codified instructions of how to perform certain techniques dating back to 200 B.C.E. (Johnson, 1986).

While the well-known stereotyped image of meditation (an old man wearing loose robes sitting in the lotus position) is a hybrid product of Asian-based techniques, Western religious traditions also have a rich history of meditation practices (Schopen & Freeman, 1992). The early Christians, known as the Desert Fathers, used a meditation practice based on repetition of "kyrie eleison" to reach a "nowhereness and nomindness" state (Merton, 1960). Later, in the 5th century AD, Hesychius taught his parishioners to repeat the phrases that became known as "The Jesus Prayer" in order to know God (Kadloubovsky & Palmer, 1951). However, despite their early popularity, spiritual meditation practices largely fell out of use during the mid-1800's among European and North American Christians. This phenomenon has been attributed to two influences: the rise of religious emotionalism and the scientific revolution that occurred in these parts of the world (Schopen & Freeman, 1992). However, the decline in interest was short-lived, for meditation reemerged from Eastern/Asian traditions into popular Western/Euro-American culture approximately 100 years later.

Functions of Meditation in Pastoral Counseling

Meditation has the unique ability to affect individuals across physiological, emotional, and spiritual dimensions. Physically, spiritual meditation can lower heart rate and blood pressure (O'Halloran, et al., 1985; Wennenberg, et al., 1997), reduce negative physical reactions to stressful situations (Alexander, Rainforth, & Gelderloos, 1991), reduce muscle tension (Carlson, Bacaseta, & Simanton, 1988), and increase pain tolerance (Wachholtz & Pargament, 2002). Most individuals who use spiritual techniques report improved health and greater relaxation (Elkins, Anchor, & Sandler, 1979; McKinney & McKinney, 1999).

Spiritual meditation may also soothe individuals struggling with emotional turmoil. It can provide a means through which people center themselves on their priorities and reduce their level of agitation over the small daily hassles of life that are of little importance from a larger perspective. Spiritual meditation "shift[s] awareness to deeper levels of the mind" (Alexander, et al., 1991, p. 209), such that individuals become aware that surface level tensions are not really that important and should not interfere with higher priority relationships and goals.

For pastoral counselors, meditation can be a valued resource since it provides the client with insight into misplaced priorities and unnecessary stresses. By emphasizing critical priorities and de-emphasizing other stressors, meditation may help clients struggling with depression and anxiety in their every day lives (Wachholtz & Pargament, 2002). Even those facing major problems, such as health crises, may find that the practice of meditation leads to better psychological health, more general happiness, and greater life satisfaction (Alexander, et al., 1991; Carlson, et al., 1988; Ferguson, 1980; Yates, Chalmer, St. James, Follansbe, & McKegney, 1981).

Not only does spiritual meditation help individuals center themselves, it also helps them go beyond themselves and focus on their spiritual relationship with God. Meditative techniques may increase feelings of spiritual support from, and spiritual connection to, God (Astin, 1997; McKinney & McKinney, 1999). Parishioners in the midst of a crisis may feel very alone, perhaps even alienated from God (Pargament, 1997). It may seem as though God has disappeared from their lives. Pastoral counselors can use spiritual meditation to encourage people to rekindle their relationship with God and derive spiritual support from that relationship. Spiritual support stems from a positive approach to God and a feeling that God is a benevolent higher power; this connection can be facilitated by spiritual meditation.

Forms of Meditation "Different Bridges for Different Waters"

From various cultural perspectives on meditation, we have come to understand that there is no one "right way" to meditate. Similar to the Japanese saying "there are many paths up the mountain," there are many ways to use spiritual meditation to enhance personal and spiritual health. In this limited space, we cannot describe spiritual meditation in all of its forms. We can, however, review a few categories of spiritual meditation. It is important to keep in mind, though, that meditation is a fluid practice, and one form of meditation may meld into another. As individuals develop in their skills, they may feel drawn to a particular type of meditation, or may choose to blend one form of meditation with another, in which case these admittedly artificial categorical boundaries are less useful. The following forms of meditation will be discussed along with general directions of how to perform them and possible target populations that may benefit from the use of each type. These forms of meditation can be categorized according to whether they involve movement or stillness, and whether they are directive or non-directive.

	Moving	Still
Directive Meditation	Singing Dancing	Devotional Sacred
Non DirectiveMeditation	Walking	Meditative Prayer

First, we can distinguish between *moving* and *still* forms of spiritual meditation. Still forms of meditation again bring to mind the stereotypical view of an individual sitting in the lotus position without moving for long periods of time. In this type of meditation, the self moves beyond the cares of the body to a spiritual focus. Focusing the mind beyond the physical level can open individuals to new understandings of God and strengthen that relationship.

In contrast, moving meditations integrate physical sensations into the meditation. Here, the body is used to gather information about the environment or to express the experience of meditation (e.g. sacred dance meditations, walking a labyrinth). Meditation can also be distinguished according to how the mind and body are used. Directive (or contemplative) forms of meditation use the body and the mind to focus very narrowly on a particular task or topic (e.g. childbirth, the works of a prophet). This minute focus facilitates an increased awareness and comprehension of a specific aspect of the individual and his/her spirituality. In contrast, rather than holding a tight focus on a particular idea, Non-Directive meditation encourages people to reach a state in which they are focused on nothing. These forms encourage practitioners to let go of their stress, their preconceived ideas, and other potential impediments to their spiritual growth. By doing so, practitioners may seek to broaden their minds, open themselves to new connections and understandings, and find themselves more refreshed and ready to return to their daily tasks.

As individuals progress through the practice of meditation, they often blend one or more style of meditation, a practice which we encourage in advanced practitioners. Novice practitioners may find it more helpful to maintain the simplicity of one type of meditation until they become familiar with that practice before increasing the complexity of their meditation time by adding other forms

Meditative Prayer

Meditative prayer is one form of still, non-directive spiritual meditation. Also called centering prayer, meditative prayer encourages individuals to center themselves mentally on the focus of their spirituality (God, Allah, Mother Earth, etc.) and then simply remain open to thoughts, images or ideas that arise during that time. Among Christians, meditative/centering prayer can be traced back in the literature to Evagrius Ponticus (A.D. 399). Centering prayer has been described as "a method of refining intuitive faculties and opening awareness to the spiritual level of one's being" (Mauk, 1998, p. 50). It is designed to help practitioners shift their attention from daily life problems to finding a greater understanding of their spiritual selves in communion with the Higher Being. While the technique is labeled a form of prayer, it is also a form of meditation since it is not "goal oriented," in the sense that the practitioner is not instrumental in the course or outcome of the meditation. During this meditation practice, the meditator does not ask for forgiveness, put forward petitions, or specifically praise or worship the higher being (Carrington, 1998). Instead, the meditator is encouraged to adopt the attitude of cognitive and spiritual openness in communication with God.

Pastoral counselors may encourage clients to begin a prayer session with this form of prayerful meditation in which the usual cares of the day drop away and are replaced with an exclusive focus on communicating with God. This form of meditation is particularly useful for the overly busy client. The modern lifestyle often progresses with such momentum that it does not allow quiet time with God. This form of spiritual meditation creates time to slow down the pace of life by sitting in silent openness with God. Thus, when there is no shortage of desire to communicate with God, but a shortage of time to simply be with God and listen to the "still, soft voice" of God's response, this form of meditation can create that sacred space.

Sacred Meditation

In sacred meditation, quiet time serves as a resource for spiritual growth. Unlike meditative prayer, this form of meditation is more directive and thus requires a more active role from the participant. In sacred meditation, individuals bring specific issues to God by choosing a focus topic for their meditation, and then remaining open to a collaborative understanding of the problem and the development of clarity on the issue. Like prayer, the individual brings a specific issue to God; however, unlike prayer, the individual maintains a focus on the issue throughout the meditation time, a focus that is often supported by verbal phrases. Over time the individual finds it easier to extricate him/herself from the daily stressors that can cloud the mind. This focused time in communication with God can bring the issue into sharper focus for the collaborative development of a solution.

Sacred meditation is often focused around a meaningful meditative phrase. These phrases take the form of words or short prayers that are repeated in order to contemplate sacred ideals, such as the ancient " Jesus Prayer," mentioned earlier, which is familiar to many Roman and Orthodox Catholics (Kadloubovsky & Palmer, 1951). Such focusing phrases or prayers can be found across many traditions and can be used to enter, focus, or sustain meditative states (Carrington, 1998). Thus, sacred meditation may be useful to novice meditators who often find it difficult to maintain a singular focus on an issue for the duration of the meditation time without some help.

However, since the meditative phrase focuses the meditation time, it is important to choose the meditative focus phrase carefully, with the needs of each individual in mind. For example, the individual seeking counseling for emotional distress may wish to focus on "peace," whereas an individual seeking spiritual discernment may choose "understanding". Either the individual or a spiritual director/counselor may choose the phrase, but if chosen by the counselor it must be a phrase that the individual is comfortable with and finds applicable. Practitioners use this meditative phrase to focus themselves, and quiet their minds. Once they feel centered, they may stop repeating the meditative phrase and sit silently. However, when they find themselves drifting away, (e.g. thinking about work, errands, daily stressors), they use the meditative phrase to recenter themselves.

Sacred meditation may be most helpful with clients who have specific questions they are seeking to answer (ex. discerning a life path, deciding between choices). This form of meditation can also assist those struggling with problematic areas of their lives (ex. addiction, anger), or feel that their spirituality requires strengthening (e.g., empathy for others, trust in God). Since this form of meditation calls for a focusing meditative phrase to direct and encourage spiritual growth, it allows the pastoral counselor to adapt the meditation to the individual needs of clients.

Devotional Meditation

Another form of directed, still meditation is Devotional Meditation. In Devotional Meditation, individuals integrate passages from religious texts (Bible, Quran, Torah, writings of religious saints or scholars, prayers or songs) or religious images (prophets, saints, slave escaping from Egypt, Jesus on the Cross, etc.) into their meditation time to gain a deeper understanding of the passage, and through that understanding, strengthen their spiritual lives.

This form of meditation may already be familiar to a number of readers since it is not uncommon for clerics to use a form of devotional meditation when writing their weekly sermons or homilies based on religious scriptures (occasionally attempting frantic meditation in hopes of Saturday night inspiration). Troubled clients might find this form of meditation particularly useful when studying sacred literature, when attempting to integrate the message of a particular passage into their lives (e.g., "Do unto others…"), or when trying to identify with religious characters (e.g., a troubled client may identify with Job).

In the first step of devotional meditation, participants reflect silently on the passage, sandwiched between reading the material. Reading the passage first, acquaints people with the passage for the first time or refreshes the memory of those who are familiar with it. The second step, quiet meditative reflection on the passage, opens individuals to new ideas about or feelings elicited from the text. Participants may find that they struggle with the text/image, or find that they are uplifted in a new way. In the final step, re-reading the passage, people integrate those new ideas and feelings about the text into the reading, and come away from the experience with a new comprehension of the sacred text. Obviously every meditation time will not elicit an epiphany, however in the struggle to understand the complex mysteries of faith, individuals may find that they come to greater understandings of themselves in relation to these texts.

Musical Meditations

St. Augustine said that, "to sing is to pray twice." For some clients, music may be their primary means of connecting to God. Through music they can pray (twice!), experience God, and refresh their spirits. Pastoral counselors may recommend a singing meditation for those who consider music and singing as major aspects of their lives. Musical meditations are often considered directive meditations because they require focus on the topic of the meditation, however, some non-structured forms of musical meditations can also be developed (ex. tuneless humming during meditation).

The singing meditation technique is similar in some ways to the ancient tradition of liturgical chanting still found in the Christian tradition among monks, and within Jewish and Islamic prayer traditions. However, since the second World War, the Taize Community in France has, largely single-handedly, refreshed the traditional meditative singing by integrating simple melodies with prayerful statements, such as *Sing to God* and *My Soul Longs for You*, derived from languages and cultures from around the world (Taize, 1998). The simple songs in meditative singing are repeated over and over, both during specific meditation times, and throughout the day. Through the repetition of these simple melodic phrases, the individual is able to integrate the positive experience of meditation more fully into everyday life.

Another form of musical meditation is dancing meditation or sacred dance. Both clients who commonly express themselves through music and those who have difficulty being still for periods of time may benefit from this form of meditation. Sacred dance as a group activity is increasing in popularity, perhaps because it may have the added benefits of promoting feelings of group cohesion and spiritual social support. Sacred dance can also be a solitary activity that allows the dancer to focus on a specific idea throughout the course of his/her meditation time. By combining physical expressiveness with a mental focus, some practitioners feel that they are able to develop a deeper unity with God that is unobtainable through mental focus alone.

Meditative dance is a common spiritual activity among groups other than Christians as well. One example of a well-known form of sacred dance is "Whirling Dervish." Alone, or in groups, Sufi Muslims dance while chanting or singing a phrase to help them focus on a specific quality of God. For example, if Sufi practitioners wished to focus on the strength of God, they would dance and chant *Mallik Almolook*, the Arabic translation of "O King of kings" (Abu Raiya, 2004; Dr. Joseph F. Smith Medical Library, 1999).

In musical meditations, performance is not the goal. Unlike most other forms of meditation, singing and dancing are popular forms of entertainment, and for some who are deeply connected to using music in performances, it may be difficult to separate the performance from the activity of meditation. However, it is critical for people to release themselves from rigidity of performance and simply use the music as a means to find inner unity with God.

Walking Meditation

Walking meditation can be traced back at least 5000 years, and is currently used in Eastern and Western religious traditions (Kern, 2002). Within the Christian tradition, the walking meditation of the labyrinth is a practice that goes back at least a millennia, and has waxed and waned in popularity depending on social, political, and religious influences. During medieval times, walking the labyrinth often substituted for holy pilgrimages when bandits, road, weather, and/or financial conditions made travel too difficult and dangerous (Kern, 2002). Even with the conveniences of modern travel, the labyrinth continues to be an important tradition. One of the most famous, found inside Chartres Cathedral in Chartres, France, still sees hundreds of pilgrims a day, though one is required to move the chairs and pews out of the way to complete the full circuit as it is laid out on the main transept of the cathedral.

Labyrinths are circular walking patterns that are traditionally designed in 7, 11, and 12 circuits. The individual begins at the entrance and follows a pathway that weaves itself back and forth inside the circumference of the circle. Unlike a maze, there is only one pathway to follow. There are no dead ends and the path does not cross over itself.

The labyrinth encourages practitioners to conceive of the meditation as a journey deeper into their spirituality. It can also be used as a symbol of repentance since the Hebrew basis for the modern word "repent" means to "turn again" and, as meditators travel, they repeatedly turn back and forth. Through their turning, they move ever closer to the center and (symbolically) to God.

Despite the strong historical and symbolic significance of the labyrinth, a labyrinth is not mandatory for a walking meditation. If one is not available, walking around church aisles on a quiet day, on a familiar nature track, or on a design drawn on a garage floor garage can be substituted. The repetitive rhythm of walking a familiar track can leave the mind free to focus on the spiritual meditation (Curry, 2000).

Walking meditation is often considered a non-directive meditation, though specific spiritual questions or topics can be used as a focus if a more directive approach is desired (Curry, 2000). While walking in the sacred space of the labyrinth, or through other walking meditations, practitioners simply open themselves to communication with God. Walking meditators report that they occasionally find themselves spontaneously praying, or repeating favorite Bible verses, but often they walk silently and openly in the spiritual presence of God and feel at peace.

Practical Information for Pastoral Counselors Using Meditation

It is important to note that time, environment, posture, and props each play a part in setting the tone for meditation. For a meditation novice, a daily ten-minute session is a good start. While this may not seem very long, many people are often surprised at how difficult it can be to maintain a concentrative focus for that long. Theresa of Avila put it aptly when she described the mind as "an unbroken horse that would go anywhere except where you want it to." Starting off by meditating for too long a time may cause the individual to become discouraged and give up too quickly. As the process becomes more familiar, the practitioner should be able to increase the amount of time to approximately 20 minutes a day.

The practitioner should attempt to meditate at the same time everyday. Controlling the timing makes it easier for meditation to become a habit and less easily pushed back by changes in scheduling. Most meditators come to feel that this time is a special part of their day, and vigorously protect it from the incursion of other distractions. Some physical characteristics should also be noted when timing meditation practice. Practitioners should avoid meditating directly before a meal (when they may be distracted by a growling stomach) or directly after a meal (when they may feel more inclined to sleep than meditate). Similarly, do not meditate during a time of the day when sleep might be more of a focus than meditation. Otherwise, practitioners are more likely to find themselves distracted and may quickly become bored rather than having a positive meditation experience.

The environment of a meditation session can influence the efficacy of meditation (Shapiro & Walsh, 1984). A meditator should choose an environment that is quiet, without distractions. Interruptions from television, telephones, doorbells, street noises, pets, and other people should be kept at an absolute minimum. Repeated distractions that intrude on meditation time can increase stress levels and remind practitioners of all of the other tasks that they "should" be doing instead of meditating. This could create anxiety and shift the focus away from meditation.

A meditator's position may also contribute to their perceptions of meditation. Meditation can occur standing up, lying down, sitting, kneeling, or in an intricate yoga position. While some schools of meditation would disagree, generally, as long as the individual is comfortable, the exact position of the body is not critical. What is critical is that the person is positioned such that he/she 1) is comfortable and in a position where he/she can ignore minor discomforts without falling asleep, and 2) has a straight spine (as medical conditions allow) that allows for full, deep breaths. The importance of deep, cleansing breaths is stressed across many school of meditation. It can have a relaxing effect and signal to the self that it is entering a time of meditation. If an individual is in a position where he/she is slouched over, the physical attitude often translates into his/her attitude toward the meditation exercises, which may lead to more frustration than spiritual growth.

Props are also important to some of the forms of spiritual meditation presented here, such as music or spiritual readings. Some schools of meditation place critical importance on the presence and location of certain items. Meditative props are similar to those used during one's prayer time: a religious text, religiously themed music, candles, rosary/prayer beads, or a new object, such as a prayer mat. We prefer to leave it to the discretion of the meditator and his/her counselor as to what places them in an attitude of spiritual contemplation.

The practice of meditation is often an experience in contrasts: between flexibility and stringency, focused concentration and open awareness, and physical comfort and mental vigilance. Despite stereotypes to the contrary, meditation is not a simple task. While a novice might react with, "you just sit and think? How easy," the initiated meditator soon discovers that appearances are deceiving.

Prior to recommending it to clients, pastoral counselors should gain their own experiences in meditation. Novice meditators find it quite difficult to maintain a constant focus for 10 minutes. However, the key is to avoid becoming discouraged and upset. It is quite common to find oneself drifting away into other thoughts (errands, to-do lists, etc), before the 5 minute mark is up. Clients should be encouraged to avoid becoming angry, upset, or discouraged, and instead gently return to the attitude of spiritual meditation.

The choice of environment, posture of the meditator and use of props, are all window dressing for meditation. Meditators should not become so involved in perfecting their window dressing that they miss the point of the spiritual meditation exercise. The external items should support rather than interfere with the journey of spiritual exploration.

Example Scripts and Scenarios for Spiritual Meditation
Parishioners in Physical Pain

Spiritual meditation can be ideal for clients who are in physical pain that limits their mobility and autonomy. Spiritual meditation can encourage them to continue to develop in their relationship with God while potentially easing some of the pain that they are experiencing. We have included a brief script for a pastor-led meditation that might be used with clients experiencing pain. Feel free to use it as a starting point which can be further developed and personalized for the particular needs, desires, and theological beliefs of the individual client. One of the authors (A.W.) uses variations of this form of meditation in response to migraine headaches and has found it quite helpful. It takes some intense concentration, but it can offer release from the pain for periods of time. When using this method with clients', read the script out loud at a slow, relaxed pace.

"First take a few deep breaths. Feel how you are wonderfully made. The air flows in your nose as you inhale and out your mouth as you exhale. Concentrate on your breathing, breath by breath. With each breath, feel yourself opening to God's healing touch. Don't rush your breathing, let it just go at your natural rhythm as you inhale deeply and slowly exhale. After a while when you feel that your breathing has become deep and regular, begin to focus your mental attention away from your breath and focus inward. Observe your pain. Where is it located? What is its source? What part of your body is free of pain? Does the pain move? Notice how the pain changes a little bit over the time that you observe it. Imagine yourself like Moses standing in front of the Red Sea. Watch how, like the sea, the pain occurs in waves. At times there is more pain, as the waves roll in high crests, while at other times, in the spaces between the waves, the pain seems to be less.

At times the waves feel like they might overwhelm you, call on your faith and the strength of God to assist you.

"Wait for the space between the waves when there is less pain. When you experience the space of less pain, feel where the boundaries of the pain are, and force the waves to stay within those boundaries even when the waves of pain increase. The waves of pain can only come up to the boundaries that you create, and then they roll out again. Each time the waves of pain roll out, claim that space as pain free. Feel God working with you to keep pushing back the waves of pain each time the waves roll until you can see the "bare rock" of your body uncovered from the waves of pain. Each time the waves come further apart in time, claim that time way from the pain. Each time the waves of pain recede from a part of your body claim that part of your body from the pain. As the pain attempts to push past the boundaries, ride the wave of pain and then push it further back as you and God claim more and more of your body from the pain. Keep pushing the pain into a smaller and smaller space until you have reclaimed you body. As you push the pain into a smaller space, you will be able see the clear path across the pain to the other side. Walk the road through the pain until you put the pain behind you. Feel God's strength on either side of you, holding back the barriers of pain as you feel you body is pain free. Even if you lose your concentration and the pain overwhelms you, don't become upset with yourself. You know that God is there to support you and that together, you have the tools to reclaim the path to your pain free body. Simply use the imagery to work through the meditation again until you push the pain back into its boundaries."

Parishioners Seeking Discernment

Spiritual meditation can be a valuable part of a spiritual exploration, or when clients are seeking to create a closer relationship to God. The script presented below is a combination of sacred meditation and walking meditation. The individual begins by entering a labyrinth or other very familiar path and a topic they wish to gain deeper insight into.

"Begin to move slowly around the pathway. As you walk the pathway become aware of the sensations around you. Feel how the air flows in through your nose and out through you mouth. Is it warm? Is it cold? Dry or moist? Just feel how you are wonderfully made as your breath enters your body and leaves. Now, become aware of how the ground feels when you place your foot upon it. Feel how your body feels and the changes it makes as it takes each step. Feel how your body has been knit together. As you continue to walk slowly take a moment to thank God for the wonderful gift of life and movement. Listen for the sounds you make as you move and for the sounds that occur that are outside of your movement. Open all your senses to God's creation."

"Now consider the topic that you wish to explore with God. This could be an issue of faith, an area of greater discernment, or simply a desire to draw closer to God. Consider a brief word or phrase that encompasses this journey.

Begin repeating your phrase softly to yourself as you continue to walk your path. Increase your focus on that phrase as you continue to repeat it. After a time, when you feel focused, you can slowly stop repeating the phrase as your external voice gently quiets, let the phrase settle into your soul and open yourself up to God. Continue in silent contemplation as you slowly continue your walking path. If you find yourself drifting away from your topic, softly repeat your phrase until you gently return your thoughts to your topic."

Parishioners with Depression or Anxiety

A form of devotional meditation can be very helpful for participants with depression and anxiety, a variation of this meditation may also work for clients who are feeling ill. The script below is based on the 23rd Psalm since it is a well-known verse across religious traditions. However, any religious text or image can be used in devotional meditation.

"Concentrate on your breathing. Draw in your breath deeply through your nose, and release it slowly through your mouth. With each incoming breath, feel God's healing presence enter your body. With each outgoing breath, release your cares and worries. When you have released your cares and worries, read Psalm 23. Close your eyes. Draw an image of your mind of the green valley that is described in the passage. It is a place of peace, of wholeness, of gentleness and comfort. Now place yourself in that image. How does it feel to be in such a place? Feel yourself surrounded by the love of God. As you look up, you can see your cares and worries off in the distance, but they cannot touch you here because this is a place of restoration and healing. As you look at those dark clouds of your concerns off on the horizons, you hear a whisper in your ear, "do not fear, my child, I will be with you." You realize that you are not alone. God is with you, both here in this place of comfort and refreshment, and out in the world when you may be attacked with cares and worries. Feel God's presence inside and sur-rounding you as you prepare to leave this place of comfort, knowing that you can always return when your soul needs to rest. You begin walking toward the dark clouds in the distance, but for some reason they do not look as frightening as they did before. You walk with God's love, and you know you are not alone. Open your eyes and read Psalm 23 again. Perhaps you will discover it as a new source of strength, something to remind you in your everyday life that you always walk in the presence of God's love."

Case Study

Carol[1] is a middle-aged woman experiencing a severe depressive epi-sode. After taking prescribed anti-depressants for approximately 6 months with only minor improvements in her mood, her physician referred Carol for psycho-therapy. In her initial interview, Carol indicated that her faith was a source of strength for her and that in the past, she often used her faith to "get through tough times." Carol said, historically, if she was under a lot of stress, "I just had to make it through 'til Sunday" when she could attend her small, hometown church of which she had been a member her entire life.

Carol reported that during the early onset of her depression she stopped feeling "moved" at church. This feeling of spiritual numbness increased as her depression worsened. She said that while church and her faith used to be very important to her, now she "just go[es] through the motions" on Sunday and feels lonely during her church experience. She was able to state that she *knew* from church that God loved her but she could no longer really *feel* that love. This difference between knowing and feeling led her to wonder whether God abandoned her or had stopped reciprocating her love for some reason.

In conjunction with other therapeutic techniques, Carol and her therapist used the Sacred Meditation technique to bring her head and her heart in line with one another. Carol and her therapist worked together to devise a meditation phrase that would address her feelings of being separated from God. Carol felt that the phrase, "God loves me" best identified her desired focus of meditation.

Initially, Carol had difficulty concentrating on this phrase for long periods of time. However, she responded well to 5 minutes of meditation a day and increasing the time by 3 minutes a week until she reached 20 minutes of daily meditation. Even after only a few weeks of practice, Carol began reporting that she felt more enthusiasm about attending weekly church services. After approximately 6 weeks of meditation, Carol's weekly mood scores began improving and she identified fewer thoughts about being abandoned by God. At that time she stated there were times when she was again able to feel God's love rather than the spiritual numbness that had been characteristic of her depression.

After 5 months of consistent practice of spiritual meditation, Carol continues to struggle with the symptoms of depression. However, compared to her initial interview, Carol consistently reports better mood and fewer crying episodes. She has adopted a healthier lifestyle, taken a more active role in her treatment, and reconnected with some of her social circle. Carol attributes some of her success in therapy to her renewed relationship with God, "I feel less alone. I know God is with me and will get me through this. Even when I'm crying and can't seem to stop, sometimes, I'll feel God beside me and I know I'm going to be OK." Carol receives comfort and strength from her relationship with God which has helped her in her fight against depression.

Spiritual versus Secular Meditation Techniques

Meditation continues to gain recognition within the medical and psychological fields, though conflict remains regarding the role of spirituality in what are generally considered secularly-based disciplines. Some leaders in the field, such as Herbert Benson, author of the Relaxation Response, seem to suggest that meditation does not require a spiritual component to be effective (Benson, & Proctor, 1984). Indeed, this may be true for some individuals, since it is unlikely that spiritually-based forms of meditation would be effective with individuals who are not interested in developing their spirituality. But there remain a number of unanswered questions that are critical to a pastoral counselor in choosing a meditation technique to share with their clients. Does spirituality add anything to meditation? Is it even possible to completely extricate spirituality from meditation given meditation's deep historical and cultural roots in religion and spirituality?

Harris and colleagues (1999) ask many of the same questions that researchers continue to struggle with today. "Are the spiritual or religious components of various meditative practices in essence 'delivery systems' for the actual mechanism of change, that is the relaxation response? Or do the spiritual or religious components, when present, contribute to observed effects of meditative practice in a more integral or facilitative way, allowing the relaxation response to work in a way that otherwise could not or would not happen? Or do the spiritual and religious components act as an additional and separate 'active ingredient'?" (Harris, et al., 1999, p. 419). Or, as we propose, is there a separate, spiritual mechanism that is unique and valid in and of itself?

We believe there is a unique spiritual mechanism. Furthermore, it may be difficult to separate out this spiritual component from practices that are deeply rooted in spiritual traditions, such as meditation. Rye and Pargament (2002) illustrate this point in their research in which they compared spiritual and secular forgiveness. They evaluated the effects of two psycho-educational forgiveness interventions, one that explicitly included spiritual tools for forgiving another individual (e.g. prayer), and one intervention that taught solely secular methods of forgiveness. Both spiritual forgiveness and secular forgiveness groups proved to be more effective than a no treatment comparison condition in facilitating forgiveness. Although participants in the spiritual forgiveness group did not show any more forgiveness or better mood than those in the secular forgiveness group, many individuals in the secular forgiveness group reportedly used their spirituality to help them forgive, even though these techniques were not explicitly taught (Rye & Pargament). It appears that, at least for many people, certain tasks (e.g., forgiveness) have an inherently spiritual component that is interwoven in what is presumed to be a "secular" task.

Like forgiveness, we believe that meditation is not a wholly secular process. For example, there is some evidence that spiritual meditation may have added benefits over secular meditation. In 2002, we conducted a test of the comparative benefits of spiritual and secular meditation (Wachholtz, & Pargament). We taught meditation naïve individuals identical meditation techniques, only changing the focus of the technique between a spiritual focus and a secular focus. Participants practiced their meditation 20 minutes daily for two weeks. After two weeks, participants returned to the lab and practiced their meditation while researchers recorded physiological measures (e.g. heart rate, blood pressure) and pain tolerance. Individuals in the spiritual meditation group reported significantly greater increases in spiritual health, and mood, and displayed greater pain tolerance than the secular meditation group.

It is also important to note that, even when individuals are asked to perform secular meditation, they often report a spiritual benefit (Astin, 1997; Wachholtz & Pargament, 2002). In our study noted above, we were particularly intrigued with the finding that the secular group also showed a significant increase in their reported spiritual well being from their pre-meditation levels, albeit less so than the spiritual meditation group. These findings suggest that there may be a spiritual component that is inextricably linked to even ostensible "secular" meditation practices

These findings also suggest that spiritual methods of meditation may contain a unique and valuable spiritual ingredient that is relatively lacking in secular forms of meditation. We propose that there is a value in the spiritual journey that is not necessarily a part of the context of secular meditation. What are the critical spiritual ingredients of meditation? Two are of particular note, each of which grows out of a relationship with a "divine other." First, meditation may provide the practitioner with spiritual support, strength, and satisfaction that cannot be easily replicated by human social support. Feelings of spiritual support have been connected with reduced general anxiety (Kaczorowski, 1989) and, specifically, death anxiety (Alvarado, Templer, Bresler, & Thomas-Dobson, 1995) in a medically ill population, above and beyond the beneficial effects of other forms of social support. Second, through spiritual meditation, practitioners can begin to identify their ultimate priorities; that is, those aspects of their lives that hold greatest *spiritual* significance. Over time, they can then integrate their spirituality into their daily lives through greater focus on and attention to these priorities.

In sum, spiritual meditation may take many different forms and offer "many paths up the mountain." Spiritual meditation can be a powerful source of strength, and comfort to assist pastoral therapy clients in achieving their goals. Through the continued, regular use of spiritual meditation, clients may show spiritual growth and find they are better able to access their spiritual resources through a closer ongoing relationship with God. While this may not solve all of their problems, clients will know that they are not alone in their struggles. Spiritual meditation gives clients another means of connecting with God and becoming aware of the love, comfort, and strength God offers to them. They may come to understand that despite the troubles and difficulties that assail them, God is with them.

Bibliography

Abu Raiya, H. (trans.) (January 28, 2004). Personal Communication. Bowling Green State University, Bowling Green, OH

Alexander, C.N., Rainforth, M.V., & Gelderloos, P. (1991). Transcendental meditation, self-actualization, and psychological health: A conceptual overview and statistical meta-analysis. *Journal of Social Behavior and Personality, 6,* 189-248.

Alvarado, K.A., Templer, D.I., Bresler, C., & Thomas-Dobson, S. (1995). The relationship of religious variables to death depression and death anxiety. *Journal of Clinical Psychology, 51,* 202-204.

Astin, J., (1997). Stress reduction through mindfulness meditation: Effects on psychological symptomatology, sense of control, and spiritual experiences. *Psychotherapy and Psychosomatics, 66,* 97-106.

Benson, H., & Proctor, W. (1984). *Beyond the Relaxation Response.* Times Books, NY.

Carrington, P. (1998). *The Book of Meditation.* Boston: Element.

Carlson, C.A., Bacaseta, P.E., & Simanton, D.A. (1988). A controlled evaluation of devotional meditation and progressive relaxation. *Journal of Psychology and Theology, 16,* 362-368.

Curry, H. (2000). *Way of the Labyrinth: A Powerful Meditation for Everyday Life.* Penguin Compass: New York.

Dr. Joseph F. Smith Medical Library. (1999). *Meditation.* Retrieved January 21, 2004, from www.chclibrary.org/micromed/00056320.html

Elkins, D., Anchor, K.N., & Sandler, H.M. (1979). Relaxation training and prayer behavior as tension reduction techniques. *Behavioral Engineering, 5,* 81-87.

Ferguson, P.C. (1980). An integrative meta-analysis of psychological studies investigating the treatment outcomes of meditation techniques. Unpublished doctoral dissertation, University of Colorado, Boulder,CO.

Harris, A.H.S., Thorensen, C.E., McCullough, M.E., & Larson, D.B. (1999). Spiritually and religiously oriented health interventions. *Journal of Health Psychology, 4,* 413-433.

Johnson, W. (1986). *Riding the Ox Home: A History of Meditation from Shamanism to Science.* Beacon Press: Boston.

Kaczorowski, J.M. (1989). Spiritual well-being and anxiety in adults diagnosed with cancer. *Hospice Journal, 5,* 105-116.

Kadloubovsky, E., & Palmer, G.E. (Eds.), (1951). *Writings from the Philakalia on prayer of the heart.* London: Faber and Faber.

Kern, H. (2002). *Through the Labyrinth: Design and Meanings over 5000 Years.* Presel: New York.

Mauk, J. (1998). Spirituality through centering prayer in school nursing. *Journal of School Nursing, 14,* 49-51.

McKinney, J.P., & McKinney, K.G. (1999). Prayer in the lives of late adolescents. *Journal of Adolescence, 22,* 279-290.

Merton, T. (1960). *The wisdom of the desert.* New York: New Directions.

O'Halloran, J.P., Jevning, R., Wilson, A.F., Skowsky, R., Walsh, R.N., & Alexander, C. (1985). Hormonal control in a state of decreased activation: Potentiation of arginine vasopressing secretion. *Physiology and Behavior, 35,* 591-595.

Pargament, K.I. (1997). *The Psychology of Religion and Coping.* New York: Gilford Press.

Rye, M. S., & Pargament, K.I. (2002). Forgiveness and romantic relationships in college:

Can it heal the wounded heart? *Journal of Clinical Psychology, 58,* 419-441.

Schopen, A. & Freeman, B. (1992). Meditation: The forgotten western tradition. *Counseling and Values, 36,* 123-135.

Shapiro, D.H., & Walsh, R.N. (1984). *Meditation: Classic and Contemporary Perspectives.* New York: Aldine.

Taize. (1998) Meditative Singing. Retrieved January 15, 2004, from www.taize.fr/en/enmusmed.htm

Wachholtz, A.B. & Pargament, K.I. (2002). Is Spirituality a Critical Ingredient of Meditation? Comparing the Effects of Spiritual Meditation, Secular Meditation, and Relaxation on Spiritual, Psychological, Cardiac, and Pain Outcomes. Unpublished Master's Thesis, Bowling Green State University.

Walsh, R., (1995) Asian Psychotherapies. In R. Corsini & D.Wedding (eds.) *Current Psychotherapies, 5ᵗʰ Ed.* Itasca, IL: Peacock.

Wenneberg, S., Schneider, R., Walton, K., Maclean, C., Levitsky, D., Salerno, J., et al. (1997). A controlled study of the effects of the Transcendental Meditation program on cardiovascular reactivity and ambulatory blood pressure. *International Journal of Neuroscience, 89,* 15-28. Yates, J.W., Chalmer, B.J., St. James, P., Follansbee, M., & McKegney, F.P. (1981).

Religion in patients with advanced cancer. *Medical and Pediatric Oncology, 9,* 121-128.

About The Authors

Amy Wachholtz is a doctoral student in the clinical psychology program at Bowling Green State University where she is studying behavioral medicine and psychology of religion. She received her Masters of Psychology from this program in 2002, and her Masters of Divinity from Boston University School of Theology in 2000. She also completed a Certificate in Bioethics from the Boston Theological Institute in 2000. Her research interests focus on how spiritual and religious beliefs affect mental and physical health. For this work, she has won a number of research excellence awards from annual conferences and universities.

Kenneth Pargament is professor of clinical psychology at Bowling Green State University and adjunct professor of psychology in the counseling psychology and religion Ph.D. program at Boston University. He received his Ph.D. in clinical psychology from the University of Maryland in 1977. Dr. Pargament has been a leading figure in the effort to bring a more balanced view of religious life to the attention of social scientists and health professionals. A prolific researcher, Dr. Pargament has published extensively on the vital role of religion and coping with stress and trauma. He is author of *The Psychology of Religion and Coping: Theory, Research, Practice.* His awards include the William James Award for excellence in research in the psychology of religion from Division 36 of APA, the Virginia Staudt Sexton Mentoring Award from APA for guiding and encouraging others in the field, and two exemplary paper awards from the John Templeton Foundation. He has consulted with NIH, several foundations, and the World Health Organization.

Note:
[1] Identifying information has been altered.

SECTION THREE:

ISSUES FOR CLERGY WELLNESS:
MAINTAINING BRIDGES FOR STRENGTH & MINIMIZING MORBIDITY

Chapter 17
The Role of Clergy as Universal Donors

by Mark L. Berman, Ph.D.

Teacher. Helper. Supporter. Leader. Stimulator. Encourager. Role Model. These are a few of the terms which may appropriately be used to determine what clergy actually do on the job.

Clergy clearly are members of a helping profession. Their job descriptions may not explicitly state this, yet they are often relied upon for more than presenting sermons, marrying congregants, or presiding at burial services. Their powerful interest in people means that thy are commonly seen as go-to persons who provide meaningful advice concerning a wide range of issues, problems, and challenges, not all of them strictly religious in nature. The desire and willingness to be of service to others can be a tremendous strength. However, there is a downside potential as well. Consider John, a prototypical clergy. John is a legend. Beloved by church members due to his constant accessibility, willingness to lend an ear, and his helpful advice. John gives freely of his time, and never seems to want or expect much in return. Quite literally, John is there for anyone and everyone. You likely know someone who as a priest, minister, or rabbi operates the way John does, who never turns down someone in need, and whom you can count on for support as long as he is still breathing.

Regardless of how heavy John's current workload is at the moment, and no matter how many weddings he is to officiate at, John will take a time out to attend to others' needs. He will dutifully ignore his own needs, adjust his schedule, or put off something until later in order to be of service. Due to his reputation for unstinting helpfulness, when the going gets tough, the beleaguered and just plain needy come to John for assistance.

I refer to persons such as John as Universal Donors. Many congregations have one or more of them working there. To those on the receiving end of their large largesse, donors may be indispensable to its operation. To some they may be viewed as saviors.

Caution: There definitely is an alternative way to look at John. Over the long haul he and other Universal Donors may be prime candidates for feeling of dissatisfaction and resentment, as well as frequent outages of personal energy. Why is this the case? Quite unintentionally, they may have positioned themselves to experience frequent high level depletion of their energies, particularly emotional and physical energy. No matter how vast their supply of these energies may have been earlier, it is simply outstripped by ceaseless demands and, most important, always giving in to those demands.

A key part of the problem for clergy who operate as Universal Donors is that people tend to expect that they will always be there for them. In fact, some may even become highly dependent on them.

Clergy such as John may eventually find themselves on a kind of endangered species list. Here are some reasons for this:

1. Universal Donors (UD) devote very considerable time and energy to assisting others, and tend to devote far less time to attending to their own needs.

2. UD clergy may receive positive feedback because of   how much they help others. While pleasant, rewarding, and comforting, this tends to strengthen behaviors involved in donating, and therefore increases the likelihood that they will be displayed in the future. For some UD types, the more thanks and satisfaction they receive for their efforts, the more difficult it may be to shift their focus to dealing with challenges in their own lives.

3. Recipients of donors' assistance may erroneously come to believe that donors' needs are minimal, and that they are met through the process of donating. Or they may operate as if donors have no needs. They may believe or act as if Universal Donor types are essentially need-free. Otherwise, how could they have the energy to help so many persons? This state of affairs can be highly frustrating and disappointing to the clergy involved. Sometimes seen as very strong individuals who have few if any substantive challenges in their lives, they may find themselves all alone when it comes to dealing with their own problems/issues.

4. Universal Donors sometimes get themselves in the   position of co-dependents. This is the case if their input makes it difficult for or prevents the recipient from learning to deal with situations on their own, or with minimal outside assistance. In such instances the Donor may become part of the problem.

How do you personally stack up in these issues?
Consider the following questions:

a. I often provide a lot of assistance to others even if it means that I do not pay much if any attention to important needs of my own. True/False (circle one).

b. Whenever someone asks me for help I drop whatever I am doing and focus my attention solely on them. True/False.

c. People commonly see me as a Reverend (or Father or Rabbi) who mainly if not entirely is oriented toward being as helpful to them as is possible. True/False.

d. A number of people seem to be quite dependent upon me to help them with a myriad of challenges/challenges/issues. True/ False.

e. I feel more and more that what I do for others is not sufficiently appreciated. True/ False.

f. I often wish that I could just do my job and not be utilized so often by others who want my assistance.
   True/False.

g. Few if any people support me on the job in other than a superficial manner. True/ False.

h. Most of my parishioners don't seem to be aware that I have needs too. True/ False.

i. Too often I assist people who are perfectly able to solve their own problems or meet their own challenges without my help. True/False.

j. I often feel overburdened by others' problems.
   True/False.

If you answered "True" on three or more items you may be a
Universal Donor. If you suspect that this might be the case, you may find the following pointers helpful:

I. Determine what your most important needs are emotionally, physically and intellectually.

II. Consider which of these needs are not being substantially met on a regular basis.

III. Devise a plan for dealing with your unmet needs.

IV. Determine which individuals come to you most often for your advice, support, and the like.

V. Of those persons who frequently come to you, which ones do you know or suspect may be leaning on you excessively, and could or should be doing more things on their own?

VI. Develop an informal needs test to help determine whom to help and how much to help them. Are they using you as a crutch?

VII. Reward yourself verbally and otherwise for attending to your own needs. If you don't attend sufficiently to your own needs eventually it may be impossible for you to help others to meet their needs.

VIII. Work on asserting yourself and selectively saying "no" to congregants.

VIII. Keep your highest priorities uppermost in your thoughts. Deal first with your most pressing issues, devoting the bulk of your energies to them. Only when you these are met should you consider functioning as a Donor, and only if doing so will not substantially deplete the energy you need to meet your own needs.

Helping Congregants Is Not a Vice

Providing support or assistance to congregants and others is not, in itself, a vice or even a cause for concern. Nor do such actions have to be counterproductive in any way, or energy-depleting. In fact, under the right conditions quite the opposite may be the case.

Clergy need, however, to be selective and prudent in regard to how much to give of their time and energy, and under what conditions to do so. To aid in this determination consider the following key questions:

Is my help really needed? Is my help likely to benefit the recipients? Am I and the church/synagogue/mosque deriving benefits from my assistance to this person which are roughly equal to the amount of time and energy I am devoting to him or her? How much energy depletion am I experiencing as a result of helping this person, and do I have a plan or system for avoiding personal energy outages?

If the answers to several or more of the preceding questions (particularly the first two) were in the negative, how should I deal with future requests for help from specific individuals?

The solution is not to stop being helpful to, concerned about, or interested in people and their welfare. The goal is to create a balance between attending to one's personal needs, and the needs of others.

To assist or not to assist? How much help is enough? How much is too much, but for you and the recipient's benefit? The bottom line is that you can avoid operating as a Universal Donor and still function as a clergy whom others enjoy, respect and appreciate.

Chapter 18
Energy & Stress Management for Clergy Self Care

by Mark L. Berman, Ph.D.

How would you judge the following statement: "Members of the clergy face only positive, energy-enhancing and stress reducing situations in their professional lives". Does this mirror reality? How nice if that were the case. The fact is that essentially all clergy must deal with a wide variety of experiences which can be highly stressful, as well as very energy-depleting. Here are a few examples:

Being overloaded for extended periods of time by weddings, funerals. baptisms, bar and bat mitzvahs, and other key events.

Inability to spend significant amounts of time with one's family, due to the needs and demands of congregants.

Lack of explicit praise from at least some of those served by the clergy.

Feeling inadequately trained to deal with the number of rapidly-developing changes in task assignments, job executives.

Facing work challenges almost totally on their own, as opposed to having a support network involving colleagues.

Insufficient or even non-participation in relaxing and/or stress-reducing activities.

Ongoing major conflicts with one or more congregants.

Excessive negative self-talk.

Serving a community as a minister, priest, rabbi, or related professional can be and often is highly rewarding, both to clergy and to the recipients of their services. The value of what is provided sometimes approaches the astronomical. Yet one thing is certain. The complexity of clergy's jobs has increased significantly over the years, in some instances dramatically. So have the demands placed on them. It was commonplace in the not so distant past for clergy to lead fairly if not highly relaxed lives. Today that tends to be challenging if not almost impossible to achieve. To be a minister, et al at the present time typically involves substantial stress as well as depletion of personal energy.

What can be done about energy loss? Start with some basic questions: How do you know when you are fatigued? How do you go about pinpointing the causes of your tiredness? Is it physical at base? Is it the result of emotional strain? Might it be due to your using your brain too long and/or too hard? Or is it a combination of all three factors?

Determining which kind of energy is in short supply is not a mere academic exercise. It is crucial that you ascertain this with precision and care. Lacking proper knowledge, you may operate at a reduced energy level year after year.

To effectively manage your energy supply you need to think on terms of three kinds of energy. The first, physical energy, is strongly influenced by physical exertion. But other things affect it a well. The second, emotional energy, is heavily influenced by emotionally-charged situations, while the third, intellectual energy, is highly affected by prolonged and/or intense intellectual activity.

Physical Energy and Fatigue

Reverend Carl is far from a sedentary kind of guy. In fact, if left to his own devices he would participate daily in golf as well as tennis. But the demands on him from congregants and others are more than sufficient to preclude this possibility. It is not surprising that Carl has a very substantial supply of physical energy, but there are times when he feels pooped. How can he tell if his fatigue is physically-based? One way he knows this is when he lacks sufficient steam to take on a task that is primarily physical in nature, and which he normally could participate in without strain. At such times his thoughts may center upon resting his body, lying down, or simply avoiding activity which involves physical exertion.

How did Carl develop the ability to be aware of physically-based fatigue? This kind of self-awareness usually begins to develop at an early age, as parents and other caretakers advise children that "it's naptime" or admonish them to "be careful not to get too tired". Through scores of such experiences, most people become aware that there are indeed limits to their physical energy and, hopefully, that these limits should not be exceeded for very long.

The effects of injunctions such as the preceding tend to be so powerful that it is common for individuals to assume that their fatigue is physically-based, when it is actually emotional or intellectual tiredness that they are experiencing. By operating from this misassumption, actions designed to restore energy may fail to relieve tiredness, and may even make matters worse.

Emotional Energy and Fatigue

Father Jim determines that a congregant who is involved in a vicious child custody battle requires his assistance. The gentleman's life has been adversely impacted for many months. Jim, who has counseled numerous other individuals with similar problems, invests a considerable amount of time and energy into this project. Such work can be exhausting. Like many of his colleagues, Jim doesn't really have a shoulder to cry on. There are few people he can share his personal stresses and pains with. And helping someone in a very tough situation often is taxing in a variety of ways. Plus, those who know Jim tend to see him as incredibly strong, and therefore as not needing their support. The bottom line? He is basically on his own.

Jim is aware of his tiredness. Fortunately he has the requisite knowledge to determine the basis of his fatigue. He has not recently engaged in pronounced physical exertion. He has no major health problems. He hasn't just finished taking part in extended intellectually-demanding activities. Therefore, emotional energy depletion appears to be the main causal factor.

Emotionally-based tiredness tends to be more challenging to assess than physically-based fatigue, in part because few people have had the training necessary to develop an awareness of it. In addition, there would be a stigma attached even to merely acknowledging that their emotional energy has been substantially drawn-down.

Intellectual Energy and Fatigue

Rabbi Samuel knows he is intellectually fatigued when he experiences unusual difficulty with tasks that he normally completes with relatively little effort. For example, processing ideas, understanding relationships, remembering details, and analyzing statistics. When he feels tired, and he has been very involved in intellectually-demanding activities over the past few weeks, it is likely that it is intellectual energy that is depleted. This is especially the case if he is able to rule-out illness, lack of sleep, physical exertion, conflictual relationships, or other possible causes of his tiredness.

Measuring Energy Levels

Assume that at this very moment you feel blasted, shot, totally wasted. How do you go about determining the nature of your energy depletion? What options are available to you?

Most of the people I have worked with over the years initially had minimal or no knowledge that it was possible to measure their energy levels. It was fairly common for them to have rarely even thought about their personal energy supply, let alone measured it. This was the case even though every single one of them had experienced profound fatigue on one or more occasions.

Few people question a physician's routine request to check their blood pressure, take their pulse, or open their mouths and say "ah". This is standard when you go in for a checkup r you seek treatment for a specific ailment. In almost all cases it would be unthinkable to go to a physician and not have them or their nurse carry-out these procedures. Why? Because they generally yield a considerable amount of useful information, they may be completed quickly, and the cost is relatively low.

The same logic applies to the determination of personal energy levels. There are innumerable tangible benefits to be gained from this. Among these are:
- Alerting you to the need for corrective action to
- minimize or terminate involvement in energy-depleting activities. And prompting you to take
- energy-enhancing actions as soon as possible.

Determining which energy is being impacted the most.
Allowing for interventions to be tailored precisely to the need at hand.

Reducing the chances of burnout, or of energy depletion of sufficient magnitude to adversely affect performance.

The skills needed to accurately assess energy level include the ability to observe oneself objectively, free of wishful thinking and bias. Other skills include clearly and accurately recording observations, and effectively analyzing the information gathered.

After you have uncovered the bases for your fatigue, determined the kinds of actions needed to remedy the situation, and implemented procedures to accomplish your goals, the next step is to ascertain the effectiveness of your efforts. How successful were you in dealing with your depleted energy level(s)? Does it appear that you targeted the appropriate type(s) of energy? Did you reduce your energy expenditures? Did you increase your supply?

If you do not succeed initially in your attempt to reverse energy depletion, what do you believe contributed to your lack of success? What new tack might you take to deal with this problem? Stay tuned for answers to these questions.

Your Current Energy Levels

The following exercise will enable you to determine how energized you are at any given moment, a well as assist you in pinpointing which energy type is most depleted. Use a five-point rating scale:

"1" : Your energy level is at its peak in one or more areas, referring here to physical, emotional, or intellectual energy.

"2" : Your energy level in a particular area is fairly high, but not at its peak.

"3" : Your energy level in a particular area is mid-range; i.e., neither high nor low.

"4" : Your energy level in a particular area is fairly low, but not very low.

"5" : Your energy level in a particular area is very low.

Current Physical Energy

Which of these statements best applies to you at this moment:

I feel very vigorous. Like I could climb Mount Everest. **Rating: 1.**

I feel fairly energetic. I could take on something that is somewhat physically taxing. **Rating: 2.**

I'd prefer not to do anything that requires much physical effort. **Rating: 3.**

I'm kind of spent, and I'd rather rest than exert myself. **Rating: 4.**

I'm exhausted, and I have absolutely no physical energy to expend. **Rating: 5.**

      If you selected the first statement, you appear to have almost unlimited physical energy at this time. If you selected the second statement, you appear to have considerable physical energy, though perhaps you currently are not operating at your peak. If you selected the third statement, your energy supply appears to be somewhat diminished. If you selected the fourth statement, your supply appears to be quite low, but enough to carry-out tasks which place minimal demands on it. If you selected the fifth statement, you appear to essentially have no physical energy whatsoever at this time.

Current Emotional Energy

Which of these statements best applies to you at this moment:

I feel that I can very easily handle any and all situations, no matter how emotionally-draining they may be. **Rating: 1**.

I can deal with all but the most emotionally-draining situations at this time. **Rating: 2.**

I'd prefer not to engage in anything emotionally-draining right now, but I will if I have to. **Rating :3**.

I'd really like not to participate in anything that could be emotionally-draining right now. **Rating: 4.**

I am totally unable to take on anything that is the least bit emotionally-draining at this time. **Rating: 5.**

      If you selected the first statement, you appear to have almost unlimited emotional energy at present. If you selected the second statement, you appear to have considerable emotional energy, though you may not be at your peak. If you selected the third statement, you appear to have a somewhat diminished supply of emotional energy. If you selected the fourth statement, your supply of emotional energy appears to be quite low. If you selected the fifth statement, you appear to have essentially no emotional energy at present.

Current Intellectual Energy

Which of these statements best applies to you at this moment:

I feel that I can process or deal with an almost unlimited amount of information and ideas, that I can very readily comprehend things, and that I am thinking very clearly. **Rating: 1.**

I feel that I can handle all but the most intellectually-demanding tasks right now. **Rating: 2.**

I'd prefer at the moment not to have to do a lot of "hard thinking" or concentrating at this time. **Rating: 3.**

I'd strongly like not to engage in any task that requires me to use my brain right now. **Rating: 4.**

I am totally unable to take on anything which requires me to think or concentrate at this moment. **Rating: 5.**

If you selected the first statement, you appear to have almost unlimited intellectual energy at this time. If you selected the second statement, you seem to have considerable intellectual energy at this point in time, but perhaps you are not operating at your maximum. If you selected the third statement, your current supply may be somewhat diminished. If you selected the fourth statement, you currently appear to possess a fairly low supply of intellectual energy. If you selected the fifth statement, your intellectual energy appears to be essentially non-existent at this time.

What did you learn about yourself as a result of the preceding evaluation? How did you rate yourself in terms of which energy was highest and which was lowest? Do you feel that these current findings reflect your typical energy levels?

I recommend that you take a few minutes at the start and finish of each day to look at your energy levels from the following perspective:
• Does there appear to be a fairly consistent pattern in terms of those times of the day when your physical energy id likely to be especially high or low? Make the same determination concerning both emotional and intellectual energy.

Which tasks or activities seem to have the most positive impact on your physical energy level? Your emotional energy level? Your intellectual energy level?

Based on the preceding information, what actions might you take at the start of each day, during the day, and at the end of each day to restore or increase your energy supply.

What changes, if any, might you make in such things as the sequence of work-related tasks you engage in, so you can better manage your energy and be more productive.

Precise measurement is where it is "at". Without it you are likely to engage in guesswork due to invalid or inadequate data. The impact on you at the least will be negative and, at the the worst, catastrophic. Remember: you do not have to slavishly devote your life to gathering this information. A little effort expenditure early on will almost certainly pay substantial dividends in the future.

Postscript

The following questionnaire is designed to increase your awareness of how to keep your stress level as low as possible, and your energy and mood levels as high as you can.

1. What is the average number of hours you work per day and per week?
2. How many breaks, including lunch, do you take in a typical weekday?
3. What are the most positive, pleasant, and/or enjoyable aspects or features of your job?
4. Approximately how much time do you spend per day in these positive, pleasant, and/or enjoyable work activities?
5. What are the most negative, unpleasant, and/or least enjoyable aspects or features of your job?
6. Approximately how much time do you spend per day in these negative, unpleasant, and/or least enjoyable work activities?
7. Which work activities are most draining of your energy?
8. Which work activities have the most negative effect on your mood.
9. Which work activities are most relaxing for you?
10. Which work activities are usually most effective at increasing your energy level?
11. Which work activities are usually most effective at improving your mood?
12. When is your stress level usually highest (either at particular times of day, or before/during/after certain events, situations, or experiences)?
13. When is your stress level usually lowest?
14. When is your energy level usually highest?
15. When is your energy level usually lowest?
16. When is your mood level usually highest?
17. When is your mood level usually lowest?
18. Rate your current degree of job satisfaction: very low, fairly low, moderate, fairly high, very high.
19. What specific goals/objectives did you have regarding your job when you first entered it?

20. What percentage of these original goals/objectives do you believe you have reached/accomplished/achieved? Less than 10%; between 10 and 25%; between 26 and 50%; between 51 and 75%; between 75 and 90%; 91% or more.

21. Aside from work-related stresses, which relationships stress you the most? Your spouse; your children; other relatives; friends; co-workers.

22. Rate how much of the total stress you experience comes from work: none; a little; a fair amount; a lot; a great deal.

23. Same as #22 regarding energy loss (how much is due to work).

24. Same as #22 regarding lowered mood (how much is due to work).

25. During a typical workday, do you ever engage in stress-reducing exercises/activities? Yes. No. If yes, what are they?

26. Same as #25 regarding energy-increasing exercises/activities.

27. Same as #25 regarding mood-improving exercises/activities.

28. What are the most typical, common negative self-statements you have concerning any aspect of your work?

29. How often do you reward yourself for "good work" on the job? Never; rarely; once in a while; fairly often; very often.

30. What are the main obstacles to your progress at work?

THANK YOU VERY MUCH FOR RESPONDING TO THIS QUESTIONNAIRE. THE INFORMATION YOU HAVE GATHERED SHOULD IMPROVE YOUR ABILITY TO ASSESS AND MANAGE YOUR STRESSS, MOOD, AND ENERGY LEVELS.

Chapter 19
Recognising & Understanding Burnout Among the Clergy: A Perspective from Empirical Theology

by Leslie J Francis
Director of the Welsh National Centre for Religious Education and
Professor of Practical Theology,
University of Wales, Bangor, UK

and

Douglas W Turton
Research Associate,
Centre for Ministry Studies,
University of Wales, Bangor, UK

address for correspondence:

The Revd Professor Leslie J Francis
Welsh National Centre for Religious Education
University of Wales, Bangor
Normal Site
Bangor
Gwynedd LL57 2PX
UK

Telephone: 01248 382566
Fax: 01248 383954
E-Mail: L.J.Francis@Bangor.ac.uk
*Web site:*www.bangor.ac.uk/rs/pt

SUMMARY

Building on previous research, the present study distinguishes between two key components of burnout among the clergy. According to this model, burnout is diagnosed by the conjunction of the presence of negative affect and the absence of positive affect. Data from 1,278 stipendiary parochial clergymen in the Church of England are then employed to model the power of five sets of variables on predicting susceptibility to burnout. The findings demonstrate that personality factors provide better prediction of burnout than personal factors, contextual factors, family factors, and ministry factors. On the basis of this key conclusion, recommendations are offered regarding the ways in which routine personality profiling can be employed to reduce the incidence of burnout among the clergy, with consequent benefits for clergy well-being, for clergy families, and for parish sustainability and growth.

INTRODUCTION

Balanced affect

Bradburn's (1969) model of psychological well-being provides a helpful way for interpreting the experiences of the work-related health of many clergy in the contemporary world. Bradburn's key point concerns the orthogonality of positive affect and of negative affect. In other words, positive affect and negative affect are not opposite ends of a single continuum, but two independent continua. Translated into work-related health, Bradburn's model recognises that it is possible for high level of job satisfaction (positive affect) to live side-by-side in the same individual with high levels of job-related stress (negative affect). According to this model, the highest level of psychological well-being is experienced when high levels of positive affect (job satisfaction) combine with low levels of negative affect (work-related stress). The lowest level of psychological well-being is experienced when low levels of positive affect (job satisfaction) combine with high levels of negative affect (work-related stress). For many, however, a satisfactory level of psychological well-being occurs when high levels of negative affect (work-related stress) are off set by high levels of positive affect (job satisfaction). Such an account of psychological well-being makes sense of the following kinds of observations reported among the clergy.

On the one hand, one set of studies draws attention to the high level of job satisfaction experienced by the clergy. For example, several studies have compared the levels of job satisfaction reported by members of different professional groups. Sales and House (1971) found that clergymen, along with scientists and university teachers, reported the highest levels of job satisfaction. More recently, Goetz (1997) reviewed the results of several American surveys and concluded that the clergy demonstrated 'a remarkably high degree of work satisfaction'. In the United Kingdom Rose (1999), using data from the British Household Panel Survey which identified 143 occupational groups, found that clergy were showing the second highest level of satisfaction with their job, with only medical secretaries scoring higher.

In his questionnaire survey completed by 372 Church of England clergymen, Fletcher (1990) assessed job satisfaction by a simple multi-choice item. In response to this item: 53% of the clergy reported that 'I feel it is a worthwhile job and would not dream of doing anything else'; 20% reported that 'I feel it is a worthwhile job, but I wouldn't mind doing something else for a living'; 8% reported that 'I feel it is a worthwhile job, but I can think of lots of other jobs I would like to do'; 14% reported that 'I feel it is a worthwhile job, but the Church should look seriously at alternatives to full-time ministry'; 1% reported that 'I feel it is a worthwhile job, but it's not for me and I would get out if I could'; and 2% reported that 'I think it is a worthwhile job, but I dislike it very much and would clearly love to do something else'. Reflecting on these responses, Fletcher (1990:28) concluded that 'if this item is scored on a 1-6 scale (where 6 = very dissatisfied) the mean score for the clergy is 1.95 and constitutes very high satisfaction levels'

On the other hand, a second set of studies draws attention to high levels of stress experienced by the clergy. For example, in his book *Ministry Burnout*, Sanford (1982) identified eight characteristics of the clerical profession likely to generate stress and exhaustion. The job of ministry is never finished. Ministers cannot easily tell if their work is having any results. The work of ministry can be repetitive. Ministers are dealing constantly with people's expectations. Ministers must work with the same people year in and year out. Because ministers work with people in need there is a particularly great drain on their energy. Ministers deal with many people who come to their church not for solid spiritual food but for egocentric temporary palliatives. Ministers must function a great deal of the time through a persona, while the effort of maintaining an effective persona can place a considerable drain on energy. Ministers may become exhausted by failure.

In her book *Clergy Stress*, Mary Anne Coates (1989) identified the roots of clergy stress within four main areas, as the strain of caring, the strain of relating to God, the strain of proclaiming, and the strain of being. She argued that clergy often experience difficulty in dealing with the stress caused by such factors because they find it especially difficult to admit to the pressures of their work, feeling perhaps that they should somehow be 'better' than their secular counterparts.

In his book *Burnout: stress in the ministry*, John Davey (1995) argued that ministry is a particularly stressful occupation and identified four main sources of stress for the clergy. The first area concerns the ministerial role, balancing role expectations with role performance, and confronting role conflict, role ambiguity and role overload. The second area concerns career development. The third area concerns appropriate support and recognition. Clergy perceive themselves to be overworked, under-appreciated, and lack confidence that their particular skills and aptitudes will be recognised and utilized by those in authority. The fourth area concerns the interface between home and work and the problems of balancing the use of the parsonage as the centre for domestic and professional life.

In a study concerned specifically with clergy marriages, Kirk and Leary (1994) devote a chapter to identifying the sources of clergy stress in contemporary society. In particular they draw attention to five factors. First, they point to the problems of marginality. Contemporary clergy, they argue, 'will inevitably at some point experience their ministry, and, because role and person are intimately linked, themselves as marginal to the society of the late-twentieth century'. Second, they point to the problem of alienation. A sense of alienation, they argue, 'may be induced by the fact that a parish priest must to a certain extent consider himself rootless, free to go where he is sent in God's name, but at the same time tied by the nesting instincts of a wife and family'. Third, they point to social isolation. Clergy, they argue, 'have the same social and emotional needs for friendship, enjoyment, fun and support as most other people, but it can be difficult for these to be met within the parish'. Fourth, they point to a lack of leisure time and financial constraints. Isolation will be increased, they argue, by 'a constant shortage of money and the leisure to visit friends and family'. Fifth they point to the problem of illness. They argue that a huge toll is taken on the health of the clergy by the following factors: a job which is often seven days a week, lack of leisure time and holidays, constant nagging worries about money, frequent moves, the inescapability of living 'over the shop', the pressures of bearing so many expectations, so much pain, the new skills to be learned, the new role to be discerned, the upheaval and change in the church, the feeling of being at worst a failure, at best an irrelevance.

In his book *Education for Reflective Ministry*, van der Ven (1998) claims that 'all pastors suffer from chronic stress of some sort'. His view is that chronic stress is caused by the following factors:
> the superficiality of many contacts, the dependency of core members of the

parish, the impossibility of satisfying everybody's wishes and needs, the difficulty of coping adequately with criticism from parishioners, and the inadequacy of their preparation for pastoral work. Time pressure is also experienced as a source of stress, and is often considered the most pressing problem, both professionally and privately. Financial problems are another stressing factor. Finally, all of this has repercussions on the pastor's family life: there is not enough time for one's partner and children, and the boundaries of the family are not seldom porous (van der Ven, 1998:1).

In her book *The Cracked Pot*, Warren (2002) found that many clergy were depressed, many experienced a sever loss of confidence, and some had grievances of being neglected by their bishop. One priest she interviewed had ten weeks off work because of stress in his family and in the parish. During that time he felt suicidal, but did not feel that he could go to the archdeacon or bishop as he felt so ashamed and wanted to give up. Another priest she interviewed indicated that he had moved parishes because he did not feel like a priest anymore. He got completely exhausted and left to escape. He indicated that he was close to tears most of the time and was experiencing a loss of faith. Although he was talking about this crisis with friends and his wife, he felt that he could not just go off and have a crisis of faith. Being a priest was his work, life, home and everything.

Warren found that burnout and breakdown were also the experience of clergy families. One priest indicated that his wife had experienced a breakdown which was triggered by stress in work, and by concern for the children and for her husband. Moving from a previous parish had been difficult but he had to get her away from the parish they were now in. This priest had experienced good written support from his bishop, had received visits from fellow clergy, and been given money to go on holiday. What upset him was that neither the archdeacon nor the bishop had visited.

Yvonne Warren interviewed two clergy who had experienced breakdown because their wives had left them. One indicated that he had spent very little time with the family when the children were small. Because his wife's work had involved commuting to other parts of the country, they had spent very little time together. He felt that she had left as she could not cope with carrying his burdens as well as her own. The other indicated that, since the marriage breakdown, he had ceased to manage the business of living. He had not smoked for years, but since his wife left he chain-smoked.

In another questionnaire survey of 1278 Church of England parochial clergy, reported by Turton (2003), 43% indicated that they worked too hard in their parochial ministry, 39% indicated that they were exhausted at the end of the day, 25% indicated that they were emotionally drained because of parish ministry, 34% indicated that they experienced feelings of paranoia, and 32% indicated that they had no energy for their parochial ministry.

Defining professional burnout
Bradburn's (1969) model of balanced affect is not greatly dissimilar from the definition of professional burnout advanced by Christina Maslach and Susan Jackson and operationalised through the Maslach Burnout Inventory. Maslach and Jackson (1986:1) conceptualise professional burnout in the following way:

Burnout is a syndrome of emotional exhaustion, depersonalisation, and reduced personal accomplishment that can occur among individuals who do 'people work' of some kind.

This definition combines two indicators of negative affect (emotional exhaustion, and depersonalisation) with one indicator of positive affect (personal accomplishment). According to this definition burnout is recognised by high levels of negative affect (emotional exhaustion and depersonalisation), and by low levels of positive affect (personal accomplishment).

The first aspect of the burnout syndrome is increased feeling of *emotional exhaustion*, where workers, through their own emotional giving, find that they can no longer continue to give at an emotional level. Emotional exhaustion will often be associated with such expressions as, 'I don't care any more', and, 'I don't have any feelings left' (Maslach, 1978). As emotional resources are depleted, members of the caring professions feel that they are no longer able to give of themselves at a psychological level.

The second aspect of the burnout syndrome is the development of *depersonalisation*. As their work begins to take its psychological toll, members of the caring professions can begin to adopt negative, cynical and dehumanised attitudes towards, and feelings about, their clients, which will include certain types of language, compartmentalism, intellectualism and other withdrawal techniques (Maslach and Pines, 1977). Clients are often viewed as somehow deserving of their problems, and are often blamed for their own victimisation (Ryan, 1971).

The third aspect of the burnout syndrome is the experience of *reduced personal accomplishment*. Alongside emotional exhaustion and depersonalisation, members of the caring professions can begin to lose the sense of personal accomplishment and achievement in their work. They cease to feel that their work is worthwhile to themselves or beneficial to others. The positive affect derived from work-related satisfaction has been eroded.

In a more recent conceptualisation of this three component model of burnout, Maslach, Schaufeli, and Leiter (2001) employ the following descriptions.
The three key dimensions of this response are an overwhelming exhaustion, feelings of cynicism and detachment from the job, and a sense of ineffectiveness and lack of accomplishment. The exhaustion component represents the basic individual stress dimension of burnout. It refers to feelings of being overextended and depleted of one's emotional and physical resources. The cynicism (or depersonalisation) component represents the interpersonal context dimension of burnout. It refers to a negative, callous, or excessively detached response to various aspects of the job. The component of reduced efficacy or accomplishment represents the self-evaluation dimension of burnout. It refers to feelings of incompetence, and to a lack of achievement and productivity at work.

Assessing professional burnout
The Maslach Burnout Inventory was developed and refined by Maslach and Jackson (1986) in order to provide a psychometric assessment of their three dimensional model of burnout. In the original form of their instrument emotional exhaustion is assessed by a nine-item subscale. The items describe feelings of being emotionally overextended and exhausted by one's work. An example item on this dimension is one referring directly to

burnout, 'I feel burned out from my work.' Depersonalisation is assessed by a five-item subscale. The items describe an unfeeling and impersonal response towards the individuals in one's care. An example item on this dimension is 'I feel I treat some recipients as if they were impersonal objects.' Personal accomplishment is assessed by an eight-item subscale. The items describe feelings of competence and successful achievement in one's work with people. An example item on this dimension is 'I feel I'm positively influencing other people's lives through my work.' In contrast to the other two subscales, lower mean scores on the subscale of personal accomplishment correspond to higher degrees of experienced burnout. Maslach and Jackson (1986) score the Maslach Burnout Inventory by inviting respondents to evaluate each of the 22 items on a seven point scale of frequency, from *never*, through *a few times a year or less, once a month or less, a few times a month, once a week*, and *a few times a week* to *every day*.

Since its initial publication the Maslach Burnout Inventory has been used widely across different professional groups and across cultures. Professional groups include studies among air force personnel (Harrington, Bean, Pintello, and Mathews, 2001), child welfare workers (Daley, 1979), clinical social workers (Adams, Matto, and Harrington, 2001), community service workers (Mitchell and Hastings, 2001), day care workers (Maslach and Pines, 1977), drug and alcohol service employees (Price and Spence, 1994), family practice physicians (van Dierendonck, Schaufeli, and Sixma, 1994), hospice nurses (Payne, 2001), hotel workers (Zapf, Seifert, Schmutte, Mertini, and Holz, 2001), nurses (Garrett and McDaniel, 2001), pharmacists (Gupchup, Lively, Holliday-Goodman, Siganga, and Black, 1994), police officers (Burke, 1994), public welfare workers (Lee and Ashforth, 1990), rehabilitation workers (Riggar, Godley and Hafer, 1984), school psychologists (Huebner, 1993), sociotherapists (Buunk, Ybema, Gibbons, and Ipenburg, 2001), sports coaches (Price and Weiss, 2000), student affairs administrators (Berwick, 1992), students in teacher training (Chan, 2001), and teachers (Bakker and Schaufeli, 2000).

In the course of this international research across professional groups, careful and proper attention has been given to scrutinising the psychometric properties of the Maslach Burnout Inventory. Reliability and validity have been supported by studies like Abu-Hilal and Salameh (1992), Corcoran (1985), Iwancki and Schwab (1981), Pierce and Molloy (1989), Powers and Gose (1986) and Schaufeli and van Dierendonck (1993). The factor structure has been tested and generally supported by studies like Belcastro, Gold and Hays (1983), Byrne (1991, 1993), Gold (1984), Gold, Bachelor and Michael (1989), Gold, Roth, Wright, Michael and Chen (1992), Green and Walkey (1988), Green, Walkey and Taylor (1991), and Walkey and Green (1992).

Assessing clergy burnout
Although widely used among professionals engaged in other caring occupations, comparatively few studies have used the Maslach Burnout Inventory among clergy and religious professionals. Examples of such studies are provided by Warner and Carter (1984), Strümpfer and Bands (1996), Rogerson and Piedmont (1998), and Stanton-Rich and Iso-Ahola (1998).

Warner and Carter (1984) administered the Maslach Burnout Inventory to 33 pastors, to 28 pastors' wives, to 64 non-pastoral males, and 64 non-pastoral females. They found that it was the pastors' wives who scored highest on the emotional exhaustion subscale, whereas the pastors themselves did not score significantly higher than the non-pastors. They argued that this finding was related to the age of the pastors in their sample on the following grounds:

Pastors who have been in ministry longer will have developed coping techniques to prevent or reduce emotional exhaustion. Those who have not developed adequate coping techniques would be expected to have left the ministry many years prior (p 130).

Strümpfer and Bands (1996) administered the Maslach Burnout Inventory to 110 South African Anglican priests. They found that burnout correlated significantly with person-role conflict and with quantitative workload. Comparing the emotional exhaustion scores of these clergy with the test manual Strümpfer and Bands (1996:71) state that 'it cannot be concluded that the present sample suffered from unusual levels of burnout.

Stanton-Rich and Iso-Ahola (1998) administered the Maslach Burnout Inventory to 241 active clergy in the Western North Carolina Conference of the United Methodist Church. They found that leisure behaviour and leisure satisfaction were inversely related to burnout.

Rodgerson and Piedmont (1998) administered the Maslach Burnout Inventory to 252 full-time pastors serving congregations in the American Baptist Churches of the United States of America, together with measures of personality, religious problem solving and work-related perceptions. They found that the model of religious problem solving proposed by Pargament, Kennell, Hathaway, Grevengoed, Newman and Jones (1988) added a small but significant prediction regarding clergy scores on two of three subscales of burnout: depersonalisation and personal accomplishment.

Rutledge and Francis (2004) suggested that a major problem preventing the more extensive use of the Maslach Burnout Inventory among clergy concerned the way in which the wording of some of the individual items failed to engage with the experience and vocabulary of religious professionals. With permission from the Consulting Psychologists Press, Rutledge and Francis (2004) proposed a revision of the Maslach Burnout Inventory involving four steps. The American original was Anglicised. The items were shaped to reflect the experience and language of parochial ministry. Additional items were developed to bring the three subscales to the same length of ten items each. The response scale was changed from a seven-point measure of frequency to a five-point measure of attitudinal intensity.

This modified form of the Maslach Burnout Inventory designed specifically for use among clergy has now been used in two major studies reported by Rutledge and Francis (2004) and by Francis, Louden and Rutledge (2004). In the first study, Rutledge and Francis (2004) mailed a questionnaire to a 15% random sample of all male clergy identified on the Church Commissioners' pay roll as being engaged in stipendiary parochial ministry in England (see Rutledge, 1999). A total of 1,476 questionnaires were mailed resulting in 1,071 usable responses, representing an overall positive response rate of 72.6%. Just 3% of the respondents were under the age of 30, 19% were in their thirties, 31% were in their forties, 31% were in their fifties, 15% were in their sixties, and 1% were in their seventies.

In the second study, Francis, Louden and Rutledge (2004) mailed a questionnaire to all regular and secular priests in England and Wales involved in parochial ministry, identified by a composite list generated from the Catholic Fund for Overseas Development (CAFOD) and the Catholic Directory of England and Wales (see Louden and Francis, 2003). A total of 3,581 questionnaires were successfully mailed and 1,468 were returned useful for analysis, giving a response rate of 41%. Just 2% of the respondents were under the age of 30, 13% were in their thirties, 20% were in their forties, 25% were in their fifties, 26% were in their sixties, 12% were in their seventies, and 2% were in their eighties.

Three main conclusions can be drawn from these two studies. First, both studies support the good psychometric properties of the modified form the Maslach Burnout Inventory designed for use among clergy. The following alpha coefficients were achieved among Anglican clergy: emotional exhaustion, 0.89; depersonalisation, 0.81; and personal accomplishment, 0.78. Similar results were found among Roman Catholic clergy: emotional exhaustion, 0.88; depersonalisation, 0.82; and personal accomplishment, 0.79.

Second, among both groups of clergy the data demonstrate how emotional exhaustion and depersonalisation are both related to age, but how personal accomplishment is unrelated to age. The significant negative correlation between age and scores both on the emotional exhaustion subscale and on the depersonalisation subscale, but not on the personal accomplishment subscale is consistent with findings among other professional groups as reported by Bartz and Maloney (1986), Lee and Ashforth (1991), Jackson, Barnett, Stajich, and Murphy (1993), and Price and Spence (1994). Thus, older clergy are less likely than younger clergy to suffer from either emotional exhaustion or depersonalisation. Two theories may account for these differences between younger and older clergy. Clergy who suffered from emotional exhaustion or depersonalisation at a younger age may already have left parochial ministry, either on grounds of ill health or to seek alternative employment. Older clergy may have learnt how better to pace their work so as to avoid such signs of burnout.

Third, comparison between the findings from the two surveys enables the overall level of burnout experienced by Roman Catholic priests in England and Wales to be compared with the level of burnout experienced by Anglican priests in England. It is clear from these data that, according to the two subscales of the Maslach Burnout Inventory, Roman Catholic priests experience a higher level of emotional exhaustion and depersonalisation than is the case among Anglican priests in England. At the same time, Roman Catholic priests experience a higher level of personal accomplishment than is the case among Anglican priests in England. These differences between Roman Catholic priests and Anglican priests are worthy of comment for two reasons. First, the differences draw attention to the way in which the separate assessment of positive affect (personal accomplishment) and negative affect (emotional exhaustion and depersonalisation) provide a more nuanced account of burnout. As is consistent with Bradburn's (1969) pioneering analysis, positive affect and negative affect are not opposite poles of one continuum. At one and the same time Roman Catholic priests can be *both* more emotionally exhausted *and* more personally satisfied with their ministry than is the case among Anglican priests. Second, the differences draw attention to the way in which the experiences of parochial ministry may differ between Roman Catholic priests and Anglican priests in England and Wales. The higher levels of emotional exhaustion and depersonalisation among Roman Catholic priests is consistent with the view that the sharp drop in the numbers of Roman Catholic priests is now putting more serious strain on the ministry-related demands placed on the remaining and diminished workforce, in comparison with the Anglican Church which has suffered less radical reduction in clergy numbers. The higher levels of personal accomplishment among Roman Catholic priests is consistent with the view that Roman Catholic ministry in England and Wales remains better delineated than Anglican ministry, in the senses of relating to a more clearly defined faith community, of being supported by distinctive social networks as exampled by the Catholic school system, and of leading worship among larger congregations (see, for example, Francis, 1996).

Personality and burnout

Theoretically based models of burnout point to the importance both of situational or contextual factors and of personality variables in predicting individual differences in susceptibility to experienced burnout. The two pioneering studies reported by Rutledge and Francis (2004) and by Francis, Louden and Rutledge (2004) set out to test the extent to which personality functions as a predictor of clergy burnout. In operationalising this research question they employed the three dimensional model of personality proposed by Eysenck and Eysenck (1975), which measures three orthogonal higher order personality factors: extraversion, which moves from introversion at the low scoring end, through ambiversion, to extraversion at the high scoring end of the theoretical continuum; neuroticism, which moves from emotional stability at the low scoring end, through emotional instability, to neurotic disorder at the high scoring end of the theoretical continuum; and psychoticism, which moves from tendermindedness at the low scoring end, through toughmindedness, to psychotic disorder at the high scoring end of the theoretical continuum.

The way in which terms like extraversion, neuroticism, psychoticism, tendermindedness and toughmindedness are employed within Eysenck's dimensional model of personality is best illuminated by the operationalisation of these constructs in the successive editions proposed by the Eysenck Personality Inventory (Eysenck and Eysenck, 1964), the Eysenck Personality Questionnaire (Eysenck and Eysenck, 1975), the Revised Eysenck Personality Questionnaire (Eysenck, Eysenck and Barrett, 1985), and the Eysenck Personality Scales (Eysenck and Eysenck, 1991). In the test manual to the most recent edition, Eysenck and Eysenck (1991) offer the following definitions for the operationalised forms of these constructs. The person who records high scores on the extraversion scale is described as someone who is:

> sociable, likes parties, has many friends, needs to have people to talk to, and does not like reading or studying by himself. He craves excitement, takes chances, often sticks his neck out, acts on the spur of the moment, and is generally an impulsive individual. He is fond of practical jokes, always has a ready answer, and generally likes change (p 4).

The person who records high scores on the neuroticism scale is described as:

> an anxious worrying individual, moody and frequently depressed. He is likely to sleep badly, and to suffer from various psychosomatic disorders. He is overly emotional, reacting too strongly to all sorts of stimuli, and finds it difficult to get back on an even keel after each emotionally arousing experience (p 4).

The person who records high scores on the psychoticism scale is described as someone who:

> may be cruel and inhumane, lacking in feeling and empathy, and altogether

insensitive. He is hostile to others, even his own kith and kin, and aggressive, even to loved ones. He has a liking for odd and unusual things, and a disregard for danger; he likes to make fools of other people, and to upset them (p 6).

Alongside the three scales designed to measure the three major dimensions of personality, Eysenck's instruments also include a fourth scale. The fourth scale was originally intended to detect 'faking good' and is known as a lie scale. The notion of the lie scale has not, however, remained as simple as that original intention. The continued use of lie scales has resulted in them being interpreted as a personality measure in their own right (McCrae and Costa, 1983; Furnham, 1986).

A similar pattern of relationships between the three components of burnout proposed by Maslach and Jackson (1986) and the four measures proposed by Eysenck and Eysenck (1975) were found among both the Anglican clergy and the Roman Catholic priests. Among the Anglican clergy extraversion correlated -.22 with emotional exhaustion, -.16 with depersonalisation, and +.45 with personal accomplishment; neuroticism correlated +.50 with emotional exhaustion, +.39 with depersonalisation, and -.31 with personal accomplishment; psychoticism correlated +.15 with emotional exhaustion, +.28 with depersonalisation, and -.05 with personal accomplishment; the lie scale correlated -.06 with emotional exhaustion, -.18 with depersonalisation, and +.09 with personal accomplishment. Among Roman Catholic priests extraversion correlated -.13 with emotional exhaustion, -.17 with depersonalisation, and +.38 with personal accomplishment; neuroticism correlated +.52 with emotional exhaustion, +.46 with depersonalisation, and -.34 with personal accomplishment; psychoticism correlated +.10 with emotional exhaustion, +.13 with depersonalisation, and -.03 with personal accomplishment; the lie scale correlated -.15 with emotional exhaustion, -.24 with depersonalisation, and +.11 with personal accomplishment. These correlations lead to three main observations.

First, neuroticism scores emerged as the strongest and most consistent predictor of individual differences over the three dimensions of burnout. Clergy who scored higher on the neuroticism scale were more likely to suffer from emotional exhaustion, to display signs of depersonalisation, and to enjoy fewer feelings of personal accomplishment. This finding is consistent with the finding of Francis and Rodger (1994) that clergy who score high on Eysenck's neuroticism scale are likely to be more dissatisfied with their ministry. It is also consistent with the finding of Manlove (1993) that scores on Eysenck's neuroticism scale are positively associated with burnout among child care workers, and with the finding of Rodgerson and Piedmont (1998) that neuroticism is the strongest predictor of burnout among clergy in terms of the five factor model of personality proposed by Costa and McCrae (1992).

Second, psychoticism scores emerged as significant predictors of emotional exhaustion and depersonalisation, but not of personal accomplishment. Clergy who scored higher on the psychoticism scale were more likely to suffer from emotional exhaustion and to display signs of depersonalisation. This is consistent with the wider theory that toughminded individuals are less likely to show empathy to others, less likely to be properly in tune with their own feelings, and less likely to be at ease with themselves or with other people (Eysenck and Eysenck, 1976).

Third, extraversion scores emerged as significant predictors of emotional exhaustion, depersonalisation, and personal accomplishment. Introverted clergy were particularly likely to enjoy fewer feelings of personal accomplishment. Introverted clergy were also more likely to suffer from emotional exhaustion and to display signs of depersonalisation. This finding is also consistent with the finding of Rodgerson and Piedmont (1998) who employed the Costa and McCrae (1992) index of extraversion among Baptist clergy in the United States of America. The relationship between introversion and burnout lends weight to the view that many aspects of the clerical profession presuppose a predisposition toward extraversion. At the same time, it has to be recognised that ministry candidates tend to be more introverted than the general population (Francis, 1991). On the other hand, no relationship was found between burnout and Eysenck's measure of extraversion among child care workers by Manlove (1993) or among teachers by Capel (1992).

Contextual factors
The growing body of research in England and Wales employing the modified form of the Maslach Burnout Inventory has also begun to examine the possible influence of contextual factors on predicting individual differences in clergy burnout. An initial study in this area is reported by Francis and Rutledge (2000) who employed the instrument to test the thesis that rural clergy are under greater stress than their colleagues working in other kinds of environments. Their data indicated that, after controlling for individual differences in age and personality, rural clergy have a (small but significant) lower sense of personal accomplishment than comparable clergy working in other types of parishes, but that they suffer neither from higher levels of emotional exhaustion nor from higher levels of depersonalisation.

A second study in this area is reported by Francis and Turton (2004) who employed the instrument to test the thesis that the practice of reflective ministry may lead to lower levels of stress and burnout among clergy. The data demonstrated that clergy who expect to engage a supervisor and expect to reflect on their practice of ministry with the support of a professional supervisor or spiritual director also benefit from a (small but significant) higher level of personal accomplishment.

These two studies both suggest that personality is a much more powerful predictor of individual differences in burnout among the clergy than either of the two contextual factors isolated for examination. Further research is clearly needed to test and to extend this important conclusion.

Research questions
Against this background, the aim of the present study was to replicate and to extend the research reported by Rutledge and Francis (2004) and by Francis, Louden and Rutledge (2004). A new survey of Anglican clergy in England was established using the modified form of the Maslach Burnout Inventory and the Eysenkian dimensional model of personality alongside a wide range of contextual factors, family factors, and ministry factors which might function as predictors of individual differences in professional burnout among the clergy.

METHOD
Sample
The questionnaire was mailed as part of a larger battery of texts to a random sample, generated by the Church Commissioner's database, of 2,000 male stipendiary parochial clergy working in the Church of England with at least five years experience since ordination to the diaconate. Just 33 of the questionnaires were not successfully delivered, and completed questionnaires were received from 1,278 of the recipients, making an overall response rate of 64.9%.

The respondents comprised one priest in his late twenties, 133 in their thirties, 451 in their forties, 441 in their fifties, 247 in their sixties, and three in their seventies; 87% were married, 10% single, 1% widowed, and 2% separated or divorced and not remarried.

Measures
Burnout. Burnout was assessed by a modified form of the Maslach Burnout Inventory (Rutledge and Francis, 2003) in which each of the three subscales comprised ten items arranged for scoring on a five point Likert scale: *agree strongly, agree, not certain, disagree,* and *disagree strongly.* The Emotional Exhaustion subscale included the following items: 'I feel burned out from my parish ministry', and 'I feel fatigued in the morning when I get up and have to face another day in the parish.' The Depersonalisation subscale included the following items: 'I don't really care what happens to some of my parishioners', and 'I find it really difficult to listen to what some parishioners are really saying to me'. The Personal Accomplishment subscale included the following items: 'I have accomplished many worthwhile things in my parish ministry', and 'I feel exhilarated after working closely with my parishioners'.

Personality. Personality was assessed by the short form of the Revised Eysenck Personality Questionnaire (Eysenck, Eysenck and Barrett, 1985) which proposes a 12-item measure of extraversion, a 12-item measure of neuroticism, and a 12-item measure of psychoticism. It also contains a 12-item lie scale. Each item is assessed on a dichotomous scale: *yes* and *no.* Extraversion is assessed by items like: 'Do you like mixing with people?' and 'Are you a talkative person?' Neuroticism is assessed by items like: 'Are your feelings easily hurt?' and 'Does your mood often go up and down?' Psychoticism is assessed by items like 'Do you prefer to go your own way rather than act by the rules?' and 'Would you take drugs which may have strange or dangerous effects?' The lie scale comprises items like 'Are all your habits good and desirable ones?' and 'Have you ever cheated at a game?'

Contextual factor. Length of time in the present parish was assessed on a six-point scale: *under 3 years, 3-4 years, 5-6 years, 7-8 years, 9-10 years,* and *11 or more years.* Number of churches was assessed on a six-point scale, from *one* to *six or more.* Presence of a full-time curate and presence of a ministry team were each assessed on a two-point scale: *yes* and *no.* Church orientation was assessed by three seven-point semantic grids anchored by *evangelical* (1) and *catholic* (7), by *liberal* (1) and *conservative* (7), and by *charismatic* (1) and *non-charismatic* (7). Ministry position was assessed on a four-point scale: *incumbent, priest in charge, team rector,* and *team vicar.*

Personal factors. Marital status distinguished between seven categories: *single, married, widowed, divorced, widowed but remarried, divorced but remarried,* and *separated.* Age was assessed in decades.

Family factors. Nine key family factors were included in the survey to assess potentially formative influences before the age of 18 years: are you an only child; do you have brothers; do you have sisters; were you adopted as a child; did either or both your parents die; was there a death in your immediately family; did you more house more than twice; did your parents separate; did your parents divorce? Each question was assessed on a two-point scale: *yes* and *no*.

Ministry factors. Sixteen key ministry factors were included in the survey: I take a day off each week; I go on retreat at least once a year; I participate in an annual peer review process about my ministry; I see a spiritual director; I go to confession; I see a personal counsellor; I consult a work supervisor; I say the daily office; I go to a support group weekly; I attend most chapter meetings; I attend most archdeacon's visitations; I attend most deanery synods; I undertake in-service training each year; I go to a weekly prayer group in the parish; I take weekends off when I have no services to take; I take my full annual leave. Each question was answered on a two-point scale: *yes* and *no*.

Data analysis

The data were analysed by means of the SPSS Statistical Package (SPSS Inc, 1988) employing the frequencies, reliability, Pearson correlates, and regression routines.

RESULTS

Table 1 presents the scale properties for the three measures of the modified form of the Maslach

Table 1:   Scale properties for indices of burnout and personality

	alpha	mean	sd
Burnout			
Depersonalisation	0.80	23.2	5.2
Emotional exhaustion	0.88	25.0	6.8
Lack of personal accomplishment	0.75	23.2	4.0
Personality			
Extraversion	0.85	7.0	3.5
Neuroticism	0.82	4.8	3.2

Burnout Inventory and for the four measure of the short-form Revised Eysenck Personality Questionnaire. The scales of depersonalisation, emotional exhaustion, lack of personal accomplishment, extraversion, neuroticism, and lie scale all achieve satisfactory levels of internal reliability. The less satisfactory performance of the psychoticism scale is consistent with the known weaknesses of this instrument (Francis, Brown and Philipchalk, 1992).

In view of the sample size and number of relationships being examined in the following analyses, the probability level has been set at the one percent level.

Personality Factor

Table 2 presents the correlation coefficients between the four scales of the short-form Revised Eysenck Personality Questionnaire and the three scales of the modified Maslach

Table 2   Correlations between personality and burnout

	Depersonalisation	Emotional exhaustion	Personal accomplishment
Extraversion	-.0723 **	-.1624 ***	-.3901 ***
Neuroticism	.3649 ***	.5458 ***	.3737 ***
Psychoticism	.0107	-.1314 ***	-.0807 ***
Lie Scale	-.1718 ***	-.0255	-.1083 ***

Note: ** P<.01; *** P<.001
The scale of personal accomplishment is coded in that a high score indicates lack of personal accomplishment.

Burnout Inventory. These correlation coefficients demonstrate that high extraversion scores are associated with lower depersonalisation, lower emotional exhaustion, and higher personal accomplishment; that higher neuroticism scores are associated with higher depersonalisation, higher emotional exhaustion, and lower personal accomplishment; and that higher psychoticism scores are associated with lower emotional exhaustion and higher personal accomplishment. Eysenck's fourth construct, the lie scale, is generally interpreted as an index of social conformity. The data demonstrate that high scores on the lie scale are associated with lower depersonalisation and higher personal accomplishment. The strong association between burnout and the two personality dimensions of extraversion and neuroticism is consistent with the earlier findings of Rutledge and Francis (2004) among Anglican clergy and of Francis, Louden and Rutledge (2004) among Roman Catholic priests. Here is further evidence that personality factors provide significant prediction of individual differences in burnout.

Personal Factors:

Table 3 presents the mean scores on the three scales of depersonalisation, emotional

Table 3   Mean burnout scores by age

	Depersonalisation		Emotional exhaustion		Personal accomplishment	
	mean	sd	mean	sd	mean	sd
30 - 39 years	24.0	5.0	24.9	6.5	22.8	3.3
40 - 49 years	23.4	5.2	25.8	7.0	23.3	3.9
50 - 59 years	23.1	5.5	25.0	6.7	23.2	4.3
60 - 69 years	22.5	4.8	23.8	6.8	23.2	3.9

exhaustion and lack of personal accomplishment by age. The data demonstrate that there are significant differences between the four age groups in terms of emotional exhaustion (F = 4.9. P<.01), but not in terms of depersonalisation (F = 3.0, NS) or lack of personal accomplishment (F = 0.6, NS). The older clergy record lower levels of depersonalisation and emotional exhaustion. These findings are consistent with the earlier findings of Rutledge and Francis (2004) among Anglican clergy and of Francis, Louden and Rutledge (2004) among Roman Catholic priests.

The second personal factor included in the analysis concerned marital status. In view of the small number of clergy in some of the cells, the data were recoded into two categories: those who were currently married and those who were not currently married. Married clergy recorded significantly lower scores on the scale of depersonalisation (r = -.0962, P< .001), but marital status was significantly related to neither emotional exhaustion (r = -.0435, NS) nor lack of personal accomplishment (r = -.0395, NS).

Compared with personality factors, the personal factors of age and marital status are only weak predictors of individual differences in burnout.

Contextual Factors:
Table 4 presents the mean scores on the three scales of depersonalisation, emotional exhaustion,and lack of personal accomplishment by current ministry position.

Table 4   Mean burnout scores by current ministry position

	Depersonalisation		Emotional exhaustion		Personal accomplishment	
	mean	sd	mean	sd	mean	sd
Incumbent	23.2	5.3	25.1	6.8	23.3	4.1
Priest in charge	23.4	5.2	25.5	6.5	23.7	3.5
Team rector	22.1	4.9	23.1	6.7	21.5	3.9
Team vicar	23.0	5.2	25.0	7.2	23.5	4.0

The data demonstrate that there are no significant differences according to ministry position in terms of depersonalisation (F = 1.4, NS) or of emotional exhaustion (F = 2.8, NS). There are, however, significant differences in terms of personal accomplishment (F = 7.1, P<.001). Clergy serving in the role of team rector are less likely to experience lack of personal accomplishment than clergy serving in the roles of incumbent, priest in charge, or team vicar.

Table 5 presents the correlation coefficients between the three scales of depersonalisation, emotional exhaustion, and lack of personal accomplishment and seven other contextual factors. None of these seven contextual factors is significantly correlated with either depersonalisation or emotional exhaustion. Three of these factors are, however, significantly correlated with lack of personal accomplishment. The data demonstrate that all three indices of burnout are unrelated to length of time in present appointment, to the number of churches in the pastoral unit, and to church orientation in terms of location on the evangelical-catholic continuum and on the liberal-conservative continuum. The sense of personal accomplishment is however related to three contextual factors. Clergy who have a full-time assistant curate are more likely to enjoy a sense of personal accomplishment. Clergy who have a ministry team are more likely to enjoy a sense of personal accomplishment. Clergy who have been influenced by the charismatic movement are less likely to enjoy a sense of personal accomplishment.

Table 5   Correlations between contextual factors and burnout

	Depersonalisation	Emotional exhaustion	Personal accomplishment
How long in your present church	-.0562	-.0550	-.0052
How many churches are you responsible for	.0075	-.0026	.0084
Do you have a full-time assistant curate	-.0223	-.0519	-.1197 ***
Do you have a ministry team	-.0119	-.0295	-.1332 ***
Are you evangelical or catholic	.0194	-.0217	.0207
Are you liberal or conservative	-.0119	-.0226	-.0719
Are you charismatic or non-charismatic	-.0348	.0080	-.1224 ***

Note: **P<.01; *** P<.001

The scale of personal accomplishment is coded in that a high score indicates lack of personal accomplishment.

Compared with personality factors, the contextual factors shaped by the nature and style of current ministry are much less useful predictors of individual differences in burnout.

Family factors

Table 6 presents the correlation coefficients between the three scales of depersonalisation,

Table 6   Correlations between family factors and burnout

	Depersonalisation	Emotional exhaustion	Personal accomplishment
Are you an only Child	.0205	-.0501	.0124
Do you have brothers	.0412	.0547	-.0235
Do you have sisters	-.0296	.0042	-.0144
Were you adopted as a child	-.0206	-.0227	-.0374
Did either/or both parents die	-.0082	.0225	.0090
Was there a death in your immediate family	.0173	.0582	.0245
Did you move house more than twice	.0422	.0090	-.0253
Did your parents separate	-.0442	-.0300	-.0602
Did your parents divorce	-.0484	-.0305	-.0653

Note: **P<.01; *** P<.001
The scale of personal accomplishment is coded in that a high score indicates lack of personal accomplishment.

emotional exhaustion, and lack of personal accomplishment and nine family factors. None of these nine family factors is significantly correlated with depersonalisation, emotional exhaustion, or lack of personal accomplishment.

Compared with personality factors, family factors like being an only child, experiencing separation, divorce or death of a parent, being adopted, or moving house more often than usual are of no real use in predicting individual differences in burnout.

Ministry factors

Table 7 presents the correlation coefficients between the three scales of depersonalisation,

Table 7   Correlations between ministry factors and burnout

	Depersonalisation	Emotional exhaustion	Personal accomplishment
I take a day off each week	.0238	-.0364	-.0091
I go on a retreat at least once a year	-.0386	-.0309	-.1573 ***
I participate in an annual peer review process	-.0690	-.0575	-.1096 ***
I see a spiritual director	-.0024	.0233	-.0727 **
I go to confession	-.0087	-.0191	-.0080
I see a personal counsellor	.0611	.1025 ***	.0083
I consult a work supervisor	.0243	-.0228	-.0784 **
I say the daily office	-.0308	-.0688	-.0837 **
I go to a support group weekly	-.0096	-.0297	-.0615
I attend most chapter meetings	-.0774 **	-.0150	-.0113
I attend most archdeacon visitations	.0029	.0322	.0173
I attend most deanery synods	-.1052 ***	-.0889 **	-.0571
I undertake in-service training each year	-.0313	-.0242	-.0768 **
I go to a weekly prayer group in the parish	-.0896 ***	-.0849 **	-.1294 ***
I take weekends off when I have no services to take	-.0017	-.0257	-.0138
I take my full annual leave entitlement	-.0294	-.0712	-.0579

Note: ** $P<.01$; *** $P<.001$

The scale of personal accomplishment is coded in that a high score indicates lack of personal accomplishment.

emotional exhaustion, and lack of personal accomplishment and 16 ministry factors. The data demonstrate that six of these ministry factors are unrelated to all three aspects of burnout. There is no relationship between burnout and taking a day off each week, going to confession, going to a weekly support group, attending archdeacon visitations, taking weekends off, and taking the full annual leave entitlement. Three ministry factors are significantly correlated with depersonalisation. Lower depersonalisation scores are associated with attending most chapter meetings, attending most deanery synods, and going to a weekly prayer group in the parish. Three ministry factors are significantly correlated with emotional exhaustion. Lower emotional exhaustion scores are associated with attending most deanery synods, and going to a weekly prayer group in the parish. Higher emotional exhaustion scores are associated with seeing a counsellor. Seven ministry factors are significantly correlated with personal accomplishment. Higher sense of personal accomplishment is associated with going on a retreat at least once a year, participating in an annual peer review process, seeing a spiritual director, consulting a work supervisor, saying the daily office, undertaking in-service training each year, and going to a weekly prayer group in the parish.

Compared with personality factors, ministry factors (like going to a weekly prayer group in the parish), explain much less variance in the experience of depersonalisation, emotional exhaustion, and lack of personal accomplishment.

CONCLUSION
Building on previous research, the present study has distinguished between two key components of burnout among the clergy. According to this model burnout is diagnosed by the conjunction of the presence of negative affect (operationalised in terms of depersonalisation and emotional exhaustion) and the absence of positive affect (operationalised in terms of personal accomplishment). A new empirical study has then examined the relative power of five sets of factors to predict individual differences in susceptibility to burnout across the two measures of negative affect and the one measure of positive affect. The conclusion has been drawn that personality factors provide a much stronger prediction of burnout than the other four sets of factors included in the study, namely personal factors (like age and marital status), contextual factors (like number of years in present appointment and number of churches in the parish), family factors (like childhood experiences of parental death or divorce), and ministry factors (like taking a day off each week, or attending prayer groups).

In particular, using Eysenck's three dimensional model of personality, the present study, together with the two earlier studies reported by Rutledge and Francis (2004) among Anglican clergy and by Francis, Louden and Rutledge (2004) among Roman Catholic priests, has drawn attention to the centrality of extraversion and of neuroticism in predicting clergy susceptibility to burnout. Clergy who score low on neuroticism and high on extraversion are significantly less likely to suffer from emotional exhaustion, depersonalisation, and lack of personal accomplishment.

The findings from this analysis has important implications for the management of clergy burnout. If personality factors are more predictive of susceptibility to burnout than contextual factors, then church leaders and church managers are in quite a strong position to begin to predict the individual clergy most vulnerable to suffering from burnout on the basis of routine personality measurement. Put crudely, neurotic introverts are much more likely to become victims of burnout than stable extraverts, and this holds true across a range of different ministry contexts.

Personality profiling is something which can be undertaken at the stage of candidating for ministry. At this initial stage it can be predicted that candidates scoring high on neuroticism and low on extraversion stand a higher chance of suffering from burnout later in ministry. The Church which identifies and validates the divine call to ordained ministry in such candidates may also have a proper responsibility to equip such candidates for exercising a fulfilling and worthwhile ministry. While it may be totally inappropriate to use personality profiling of this nature to guide the selection procedure, it may be totally appropriate to use such profiling to care for candidates after selection. Proper care may be expressed in two ways.

First, personality profiling may be used to enhance the candidate's self-insight and awareness of potential psychological weaknesses, and to alert the candidate to consequent pitfalls in ministry. Enhanced self-awareness may prove to be the most powerful antidote to falling into the traps that lead to professional burnout in ministry.

Second, personality profiling may be used to sensitise those who hold pastoral care responsibility for the clergy to individual needs and vulnerabilities. Some clergy may need and benefit from pastoral care much more than other clergy. If, for example, in the Anglican context bishops could have access to the appropriate psychological profiling of clergy within their care, it might be irresponsible for them to refuse to take cognisance of such data. Properly used, such data could reduce the level of burnout experienced by individual clergy, reduce the harm caused to clergy families by burnout, and reduce the damage done to individual churches by malfunctioning leaders.

Properly used in the service of the church, personality psychology might be seen as a God-given tool designed to improve clergy well-being and to promote church growth.

ACKNOWLEDGEMENT

The modified form of the Maslach Burnout Inventory for use among parochial clergy has been modified and reproduced by special permission of the publisher, Consulting Psychologists Press, Palo Alto, CA 94303 from MBI - Human Services Survey by Christina Maslach and Susan E Jackson. Copyright 1986 by Consulting Psychologists Press, Inc. All rights reserved. Further reproduction is prohibited without the publisher's written consent. The publishers refused permission to publish the actual items from the modified Maslach Burnout Inventory in papers reporting the research.